Shojo Beat

Meteor Prince

Vol. 1

Story & Art by Meca Tanaka

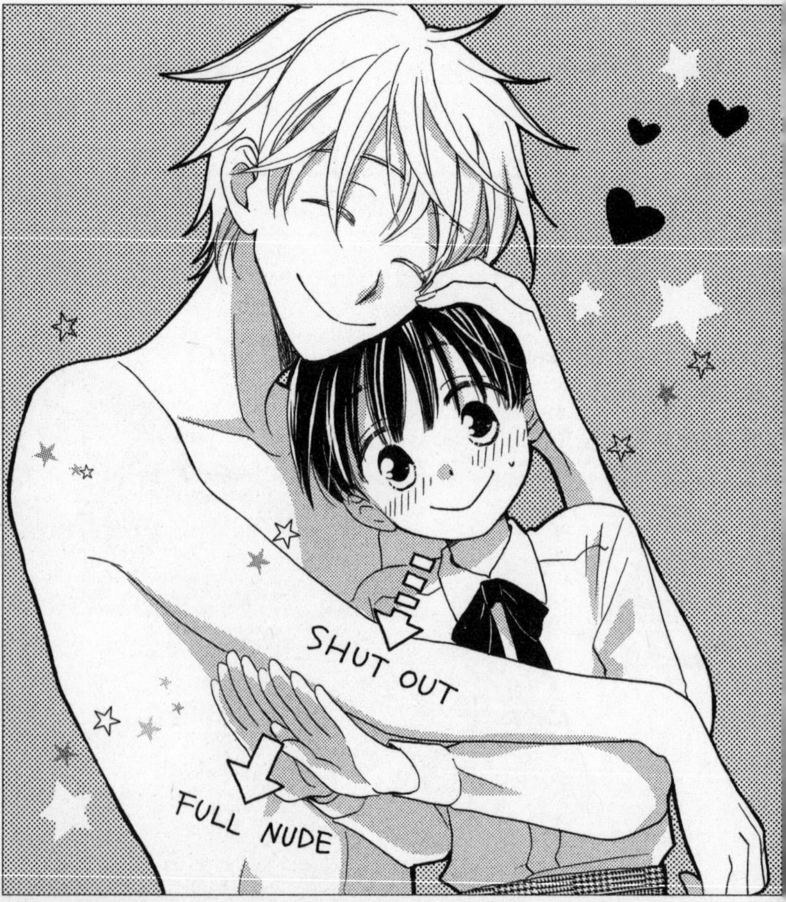
SHUT OUT
FULL NUDE

Meteor Prince

Contents

Creating the Color Illustration for the Chapter Title Page

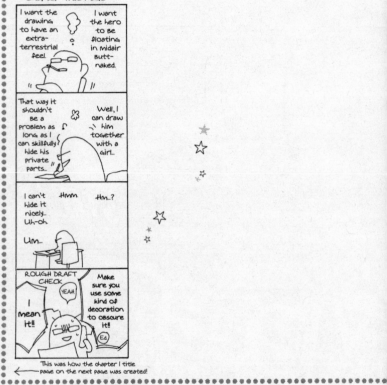

I want the hero to be floating in midair butt-naked.
I want the drawing to have an extra-terrestrial feel.
Well, I can draw him together with a girl...
That way it shouldn't be a problem as long as I can skillfully hide his private parts...
Hm...?
Hmm.
I can't hide it nicely... Uh-oh.
Um...
ROUGH DRAFT CHECK
Make sure you use some kind of decoration to obscure it!!
Ed.
YEAH!
I mean it!!

This was how the chapter 1 title page on the next page was created!

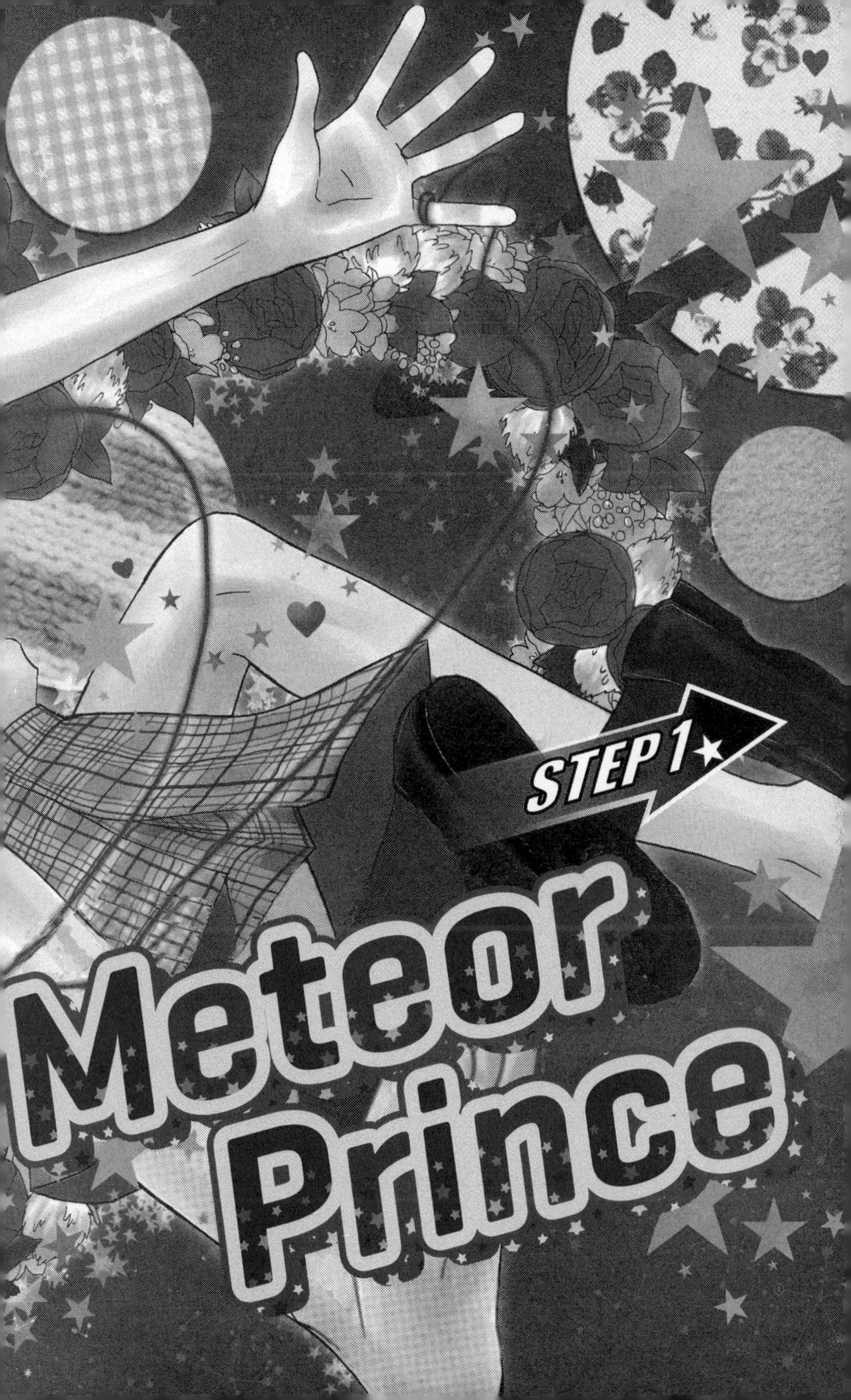
STEP 1
Meteor Prince

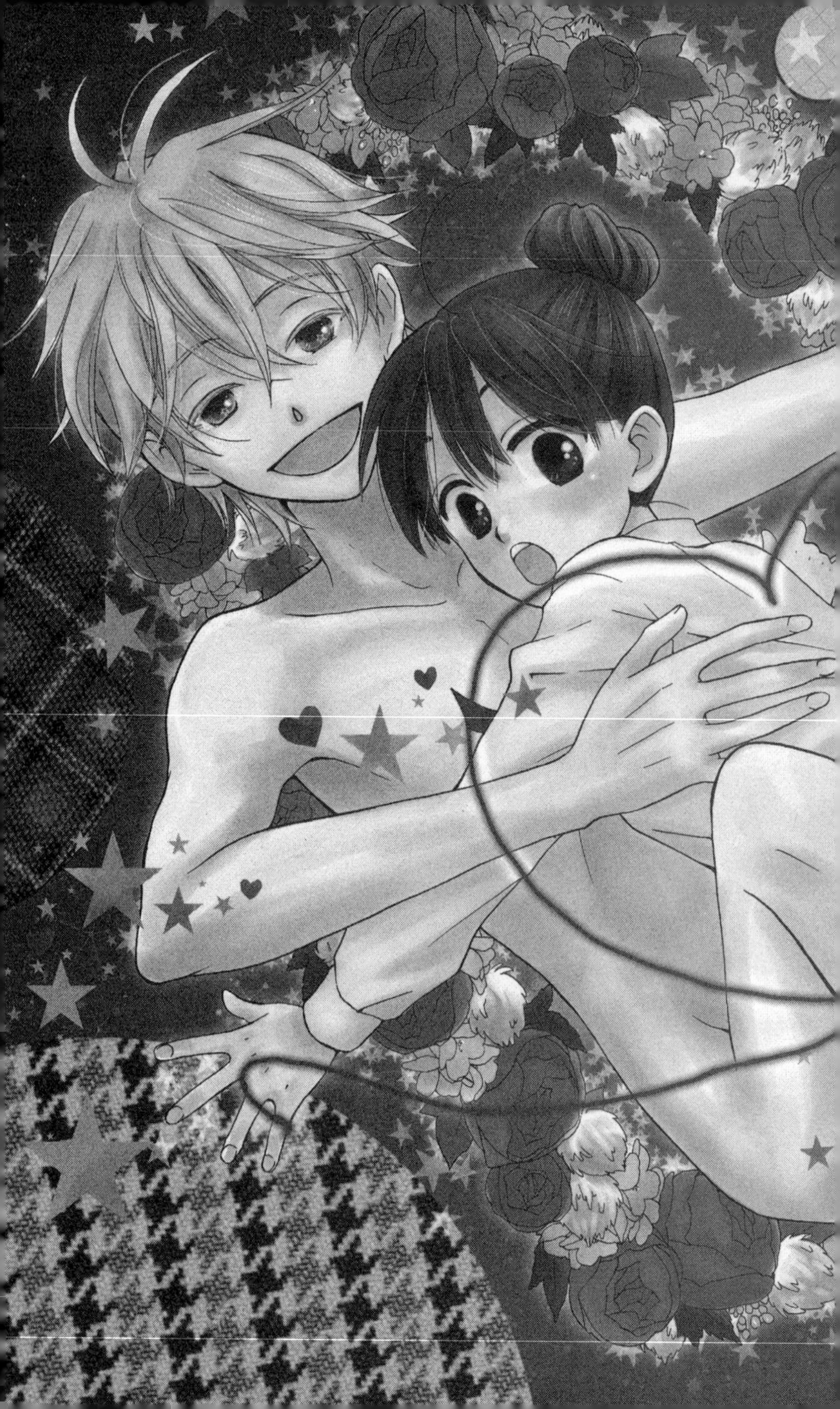

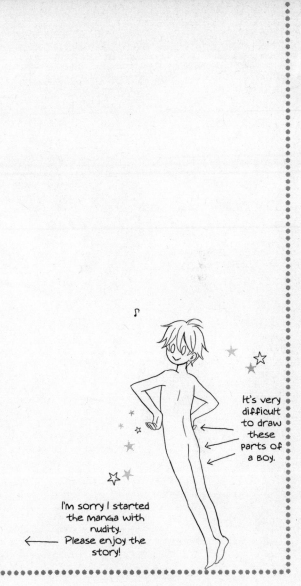

It's very
difficult
to draw
these
parts of
a boy.

I'm sorry I started
the manga with
nudity.
Please enjoy the
story!

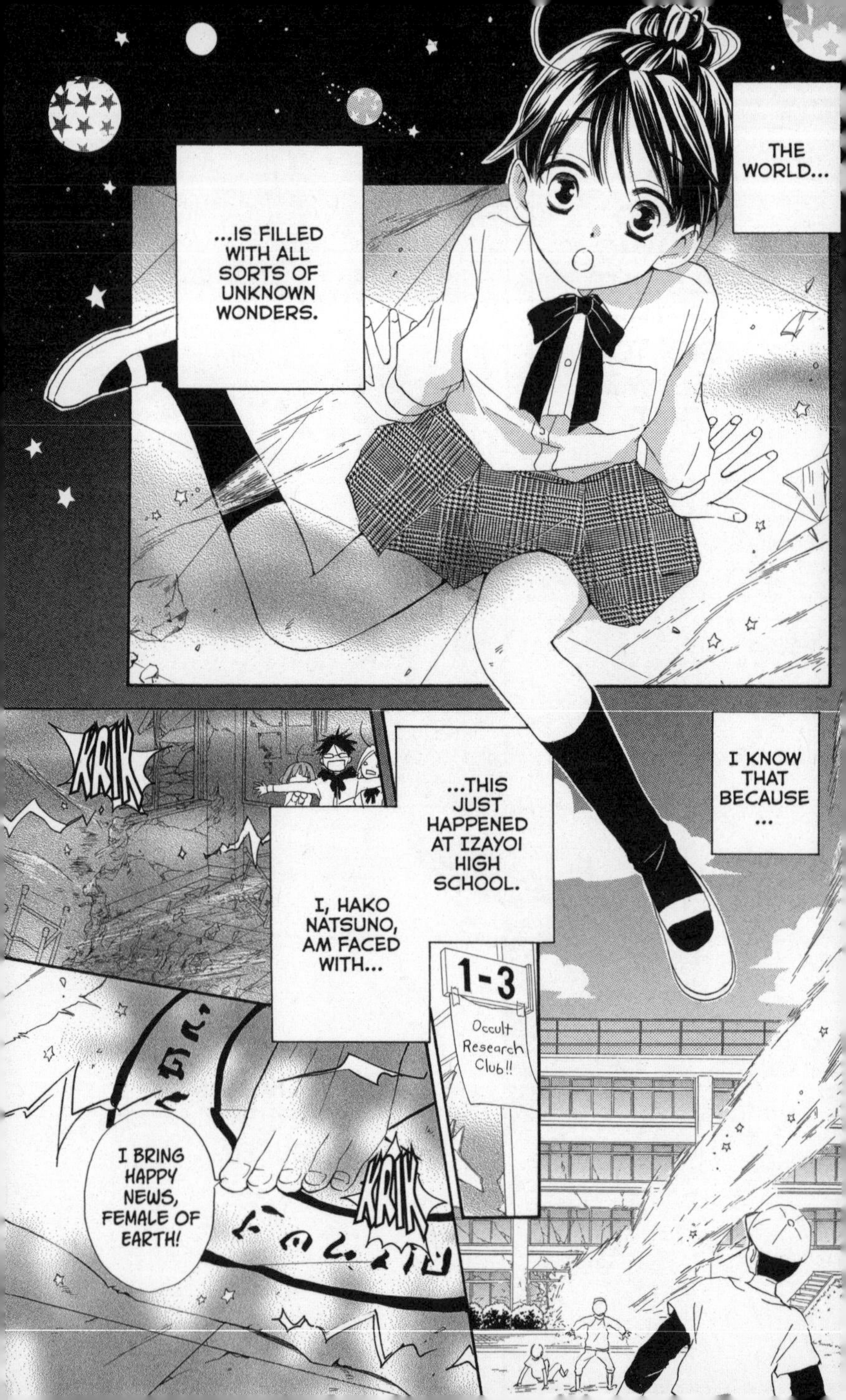
THE WORLD...
...IS FILLED WITH ALL SORTS OF UNKNOWN WONDERS.
I KNOW THAT BECAUSE ...
...THIS JUST HAPPENED AT IZAYOI HIGH SCHOOL.
I, HAKO NATSUNO, AM FACED WITH...
KRIK
1-3
Occult Research Club!!
KRIK
I BRING HAPPY NEWS, FEMALE OF EARTH!

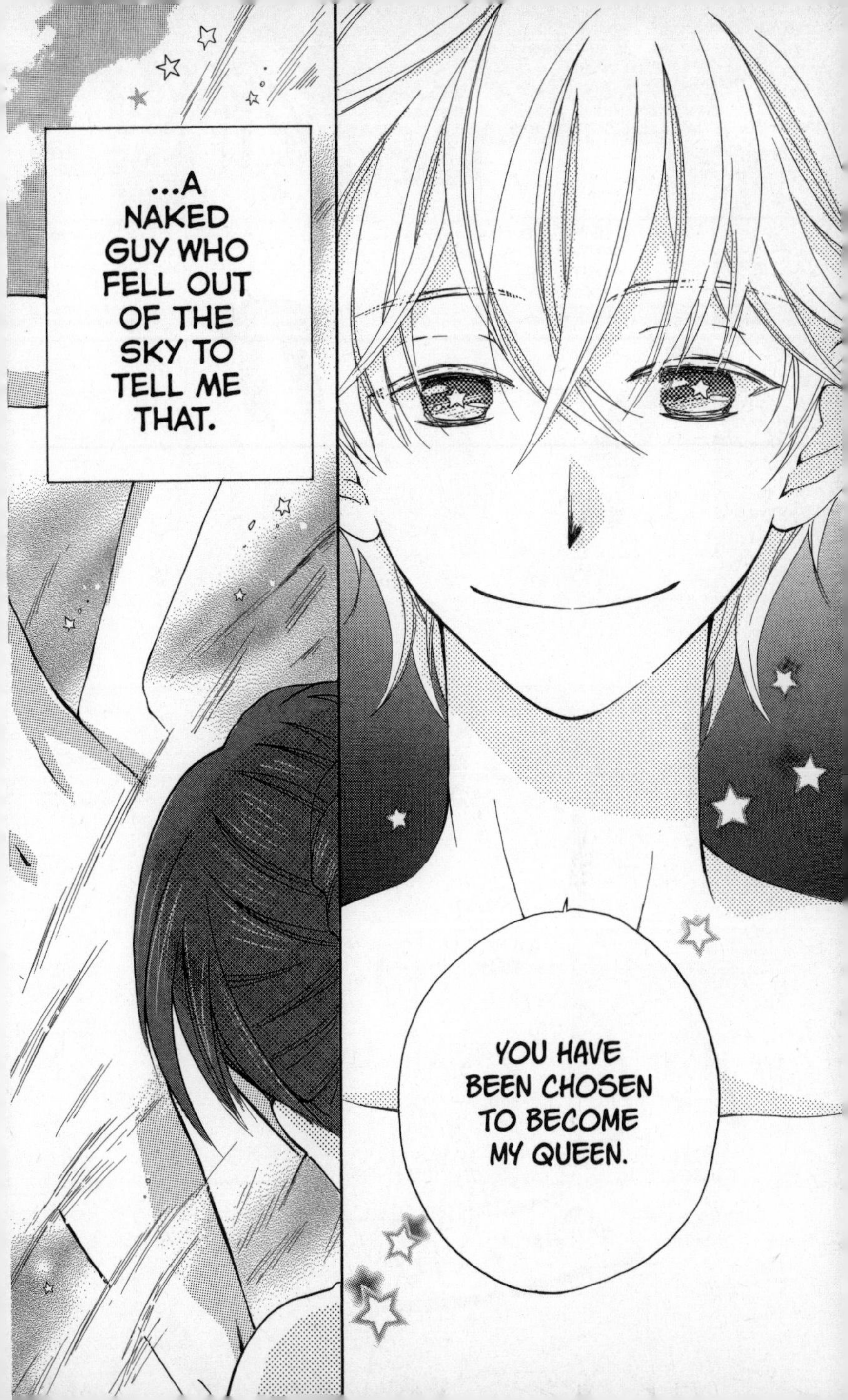
YOU HAVE BEEN CHOSEN TO BECOME MY QUEEN.
...A NAKED GUY WHO FELL OUT OF THE SKY TO TELL ME THAT.

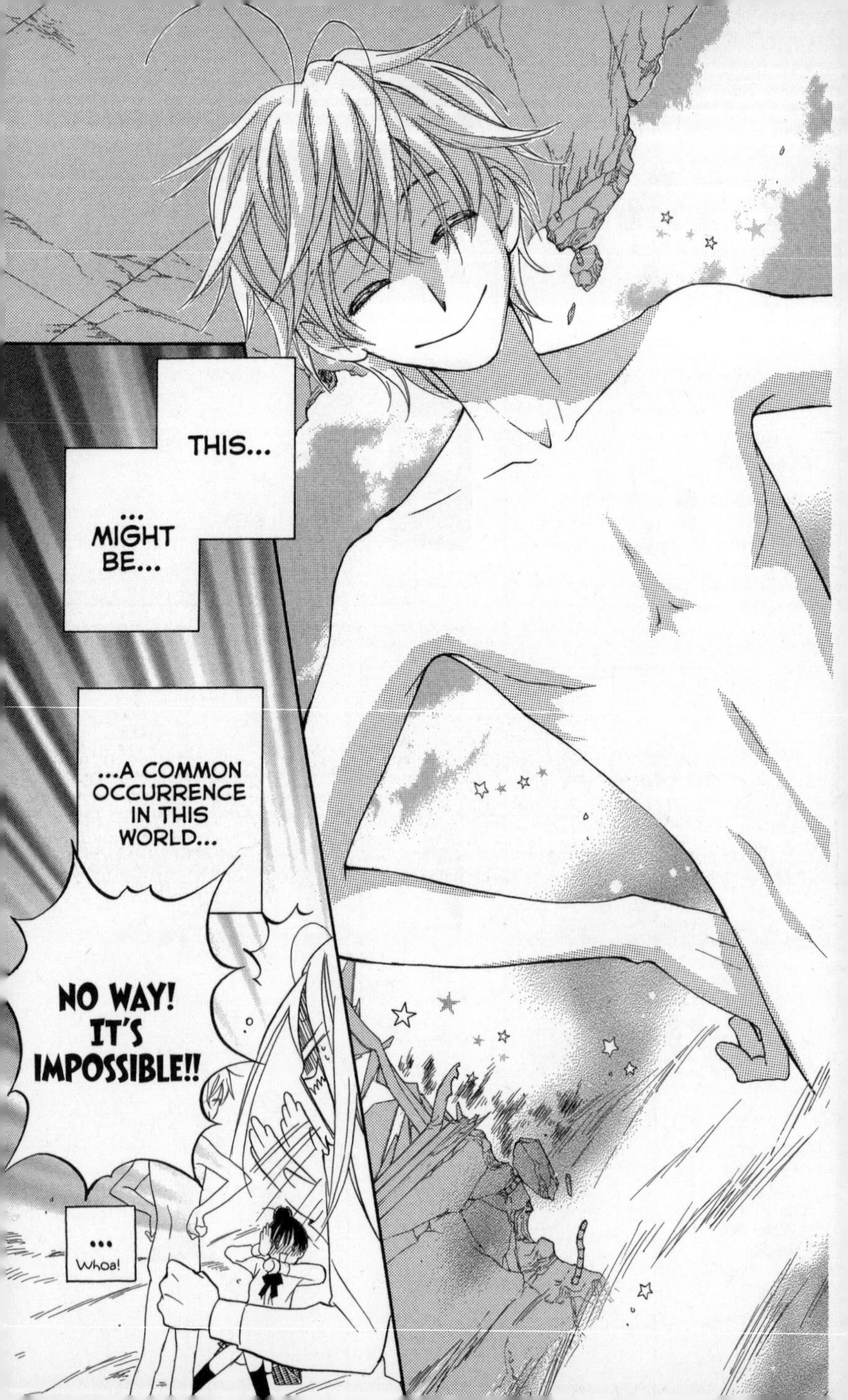
THIS...
...MIGHT BE...
...A COMMON OCCURRENCE IN THIS WORLD...
NO WAY! IT'S IMPOSSIBLE!!
...
Whoa!

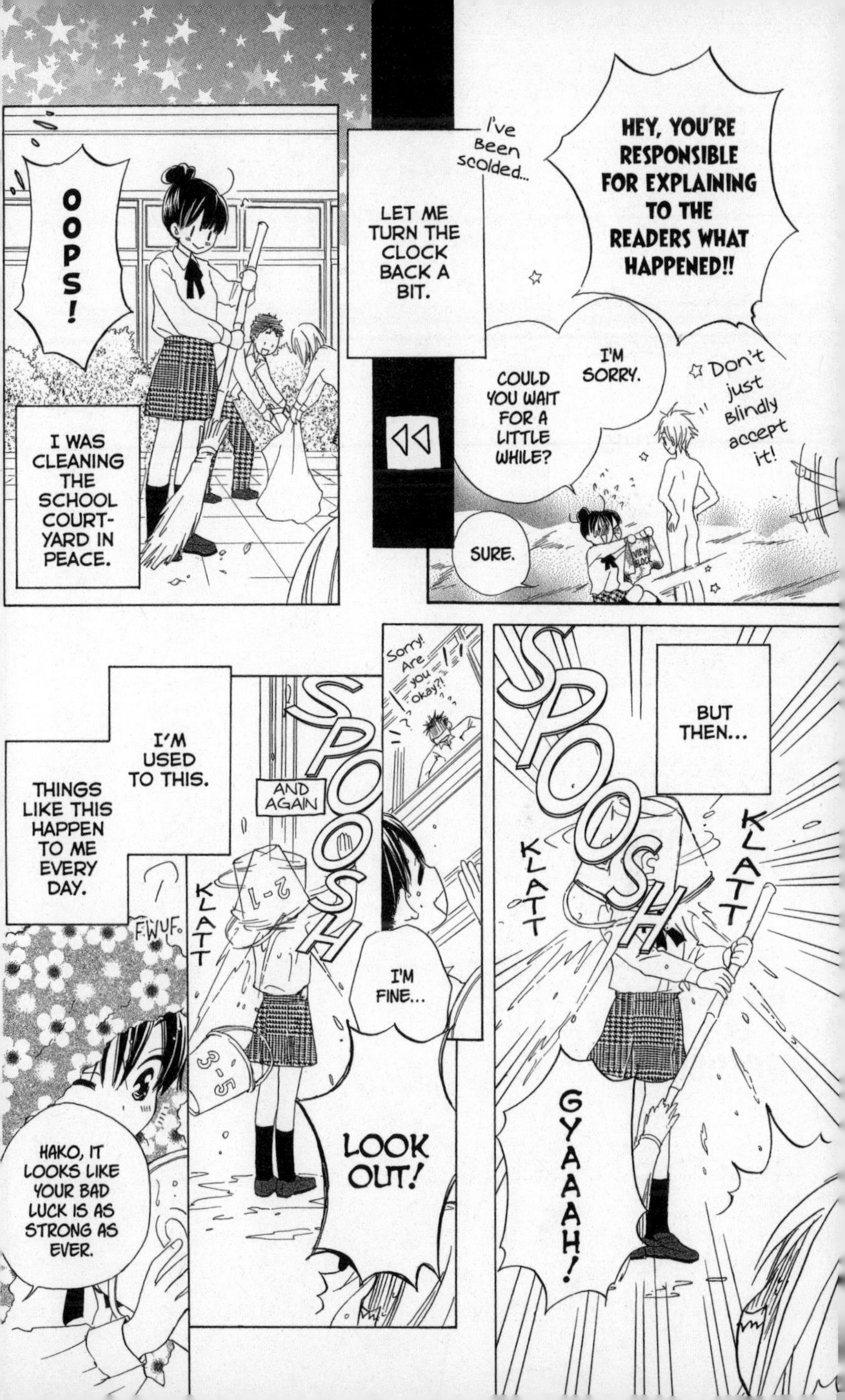
HEY, YOU'RE RESPONSIBLE FOR EXPLAINING TO THE READERS WHAT HAPPENED!!
Don't just Blindly accept it!
I'M SORRY.
COULD YOU WAIT FOR A LITTLE WHILE?
SURE.
I've Been scolded...
LET ME TURN THE CLOCK BACK A BIT.
OOPS!
I WAS CLEANING THE SCHOOL COURT-YARD IN PEACE.
BUT THEN...
SPOOOSH
KLATT
KLATT
GYAAAH!
Sorry! Are you okay?!
SPOOOSH
AND AGAIN
KLATT
I'M FINE...
LOOK OUT!
I'M USED TO THIS.
THINGS LIKE THIS HAPPEN TO ME EVERY DAY.
FWUF
HAKO, IT LOOKS LIKE YOUR BAD LUCK IS AS STRONG AS EVER.

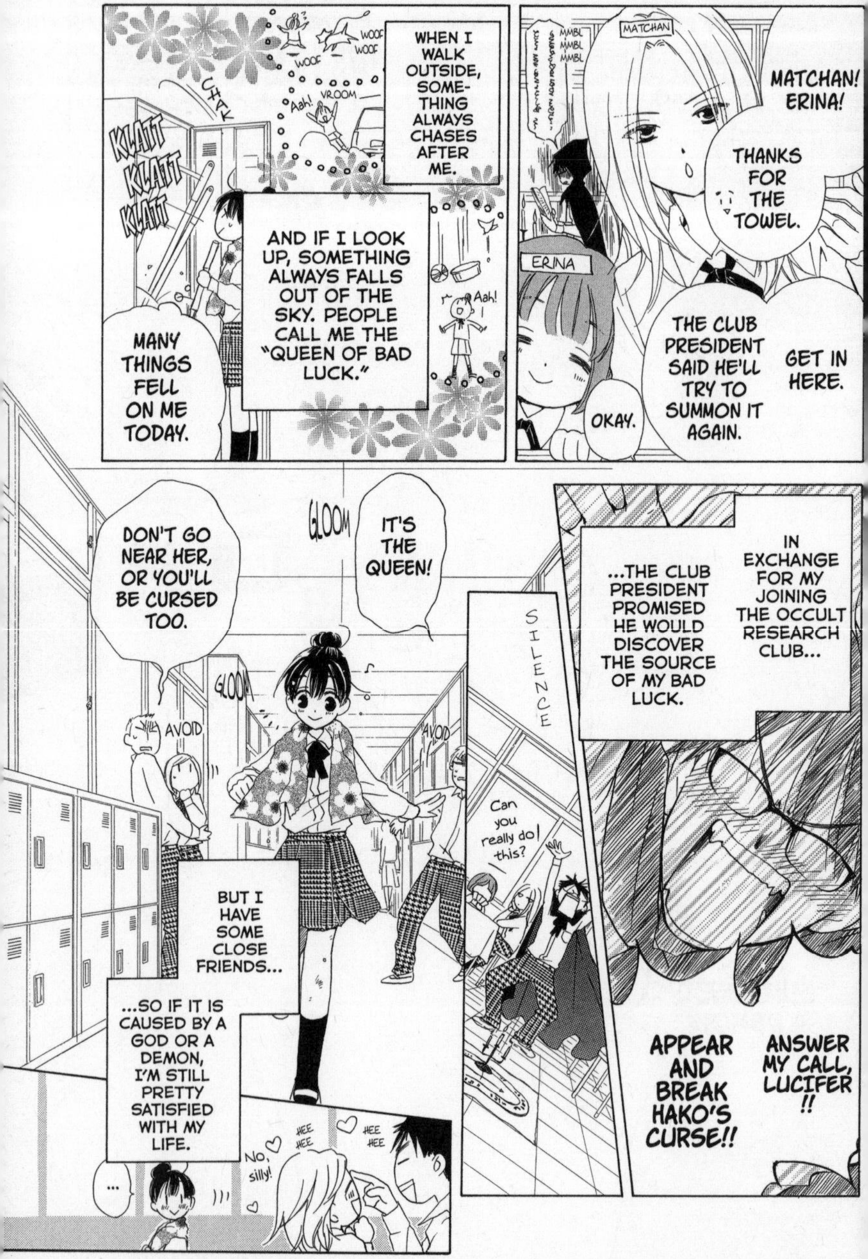
MMBL MMBL MMBL
MATCHAN
MATCHAN! ERINA!
THANKS FOR THE TOWEL.
ERINA
GET IN HERE.
THE CLUB PRESIDENT SAID HE'LL TRY TO SUMMON IT AGAIN.
OKAY.
WHEN I WALK OUTSIDE, SOMETHING ALWAYS CHASES AFTER ME.
WOOF WOOF
WOOF
VROOM
Aah!
CHAK
KLATT KLATT KLATT
AND IF I LOOK UP, SOMETHING ALWAYS FALLS OUT OF THE SKY. PEOPLE CALL ME THE "QUEEN OF BAD LUCK."
Aah!
MANY THINGS FELL ON ME TODAY.
IN EXCHANGE FOR MY JOINING THE OCCULT RESEARCH CLUB...
...THE CLUB PRESIDENT PROMISED HE WOULD DISCOVER THE SOURCE OF MY BAD LUCK.
ANSWER MY CALL, LUCIFER!!
APPEAR AND BREAK HAKO'S CURSE!!
SILENCE
Can you really do this?
IT'S THE QUEEN!
GLOOM
DON'T GO NEAR HER, OR YOU'LL BE CURSED TOO.
GLOOM
AVOID
AVOID
BUT I HAVE SOME CLOSE FRIENDS...
...SO IF IT IS CAUSED BY A GOD OR A DEMON, I'M STILL PRETTY SATISFIED WITH MY LIFE.
HEE HEE
HEE HEE
No, silly!
...

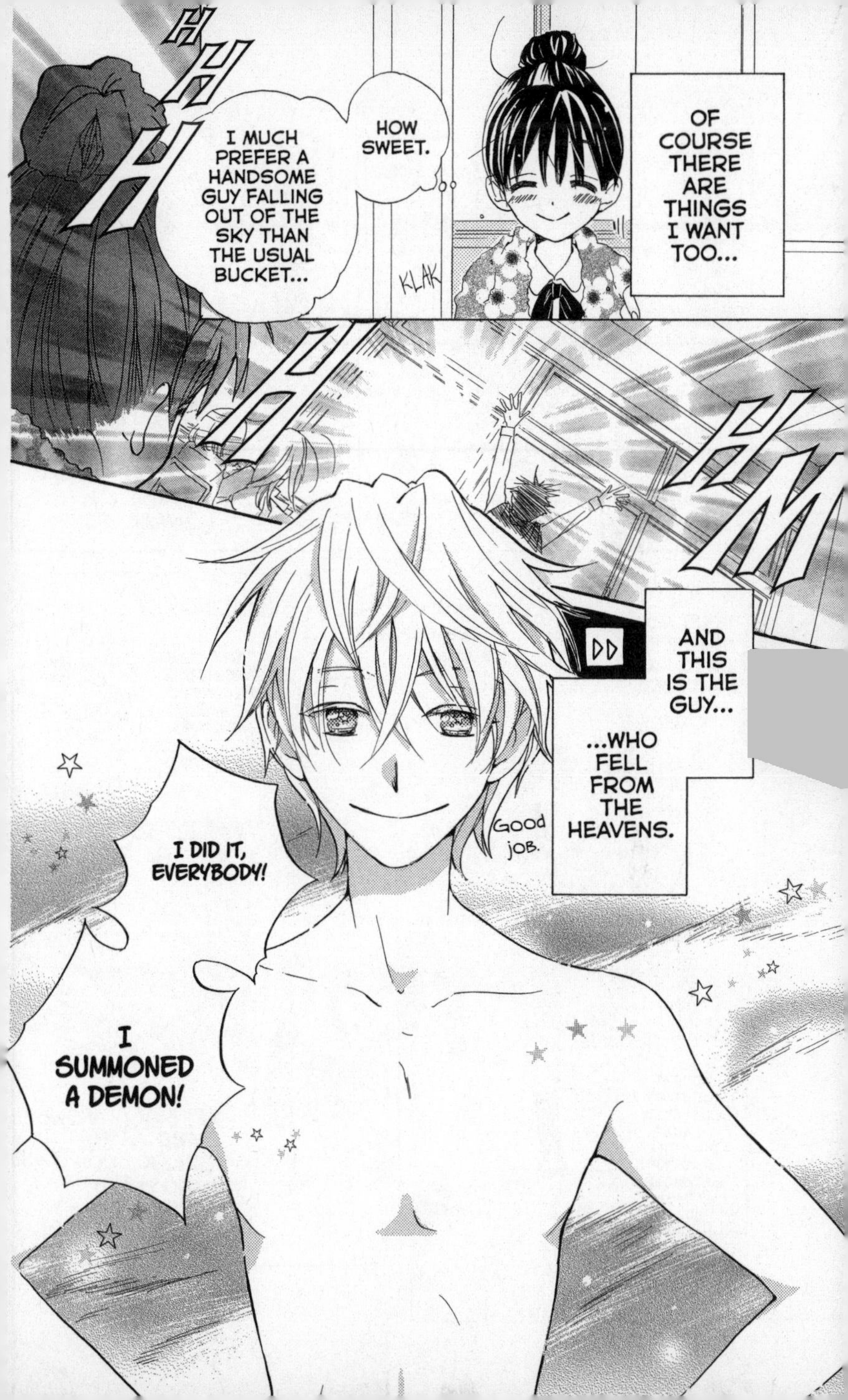
OF COURSE THERE ARE THINGS I WANT TOO...
HOW SWEET.
I MUCH PREFER A HANDSOME GUY FALLING OUT OF THE SKY THAN THE USUAL BUCKET...
KLAK
HHH
H
HM
AND THIS IS THE GUY...
...WHO FELL FROM THE HEAVENS.
Good job.
I DID IT, EVERYBODY!
I SUMMONED A DEMON!

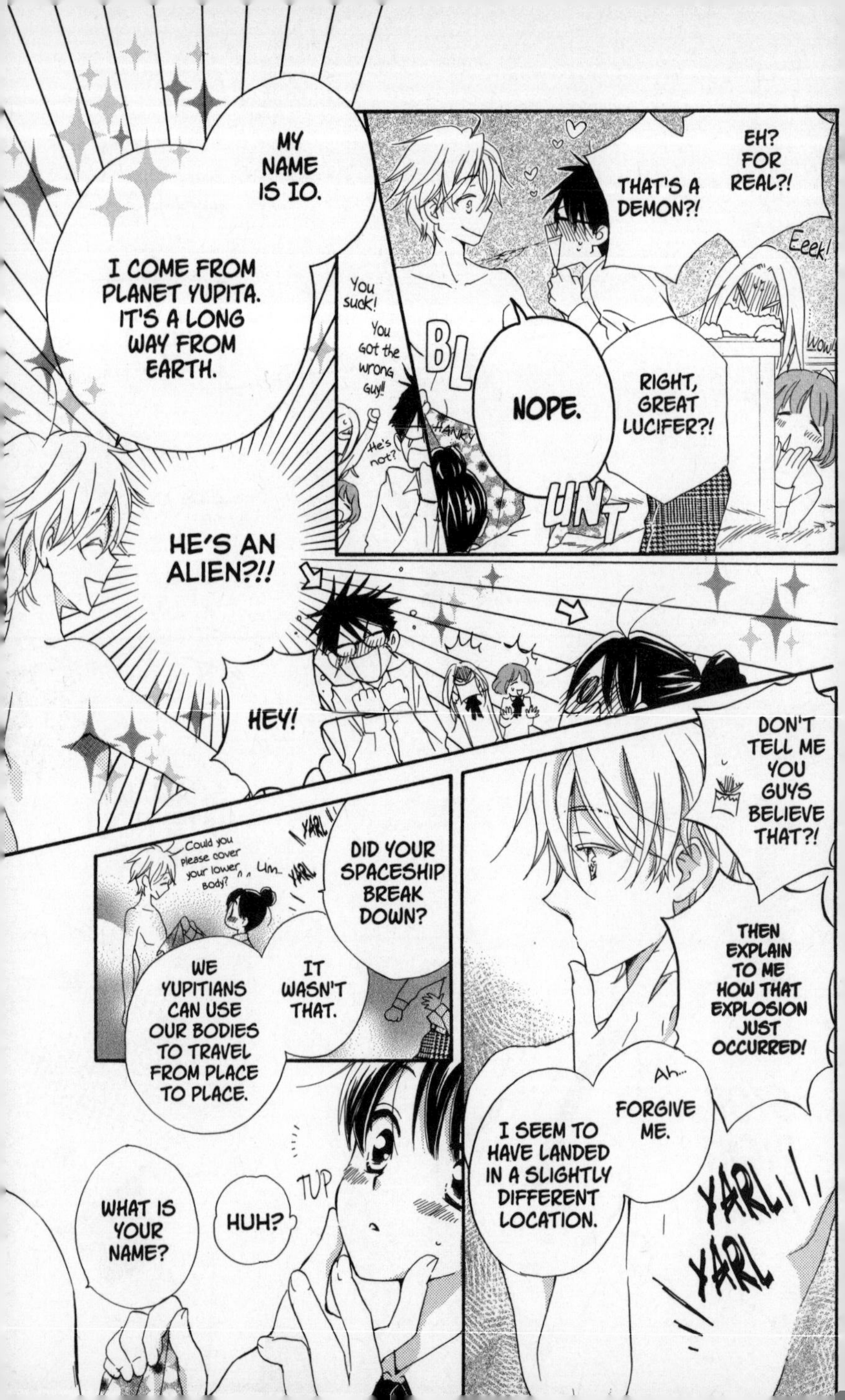
EH? FOR REAL?!
THAT'S A DEMON?!
Eeek!
Wow!
RIGHT, GREAT LUCIFER?!
NOPE.
BLUNT
You suck!
You got the wrong guy!!
He's not?
HANKY
MY NAME IS IO.
I COME FROM PLANET YUPITA. IT'S A LONG WAY FROM EARTH.
HE'S AN ALIEN?!!
HEY!
DON'T TELL ME YOU GUYS BELIEVE THAT?!
THEN EXPLAIN TO ME HOW THAT EXPLOSION JUST OCCURRED!
Ah...
FORGIVE ME.
I SEEM TO HAVE LANDED IN A SLIGHTLY DIFFERENT LOCATION.
YARL YARL
DID YOUR SPACESHIP BREAK DOWN?
YARL YARL
IT WASN'T THAT.
WE YUPITIANS CAN USE OUR BODIES TO TRAVEL FROM PLACE TO PLACE.
Could you please cover your lower body?
Um...
TUP
HUH?
WHAT IS YOUR NAME?

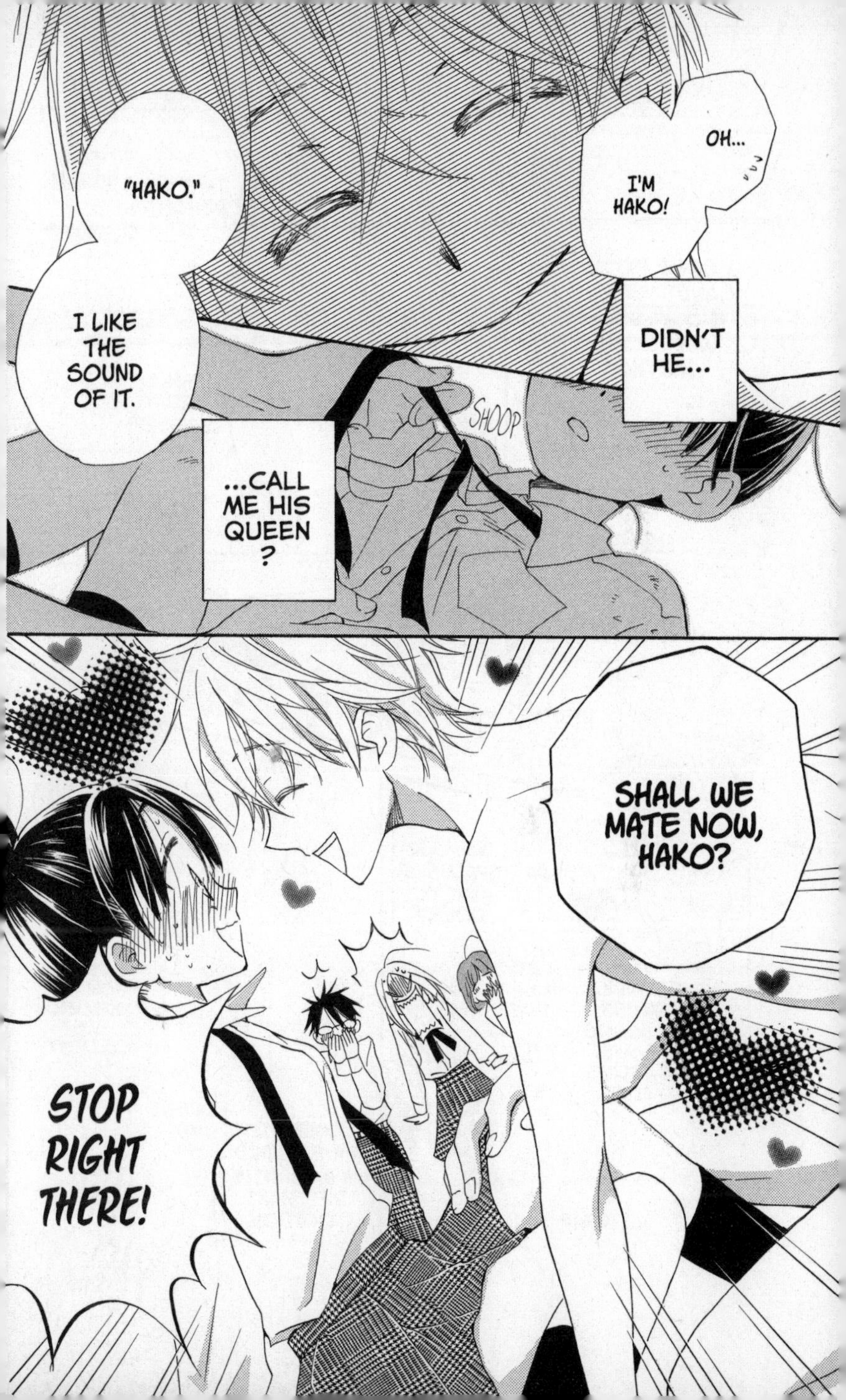
"HAKO."
I LIKE THE SOUND OF IT.
OH...
I'M HAKO!
DIDN'T HE...
...CALL ME HIS QUEEN ?
SHOOP
SHALL WE MATE NOW, HAKO?
STOP RIGHT THERE!

My 28th
Manga Volume

Hello everyone. And to those who are new, it's nice to meet you. I'm Tanaka.

COOL POSE

I have been drawing manga for a while now, and I've just realized that I have only two more volumes to go to reach my thirtieth volume overall. Wooo! For those who have bought all my works, thank you and I love you!!

If you're learning about me from this volume, thank you too! I will continue to work hard so I can create good manga that will make you want to return.

Well then, let's keep going.

VVOOOOSH

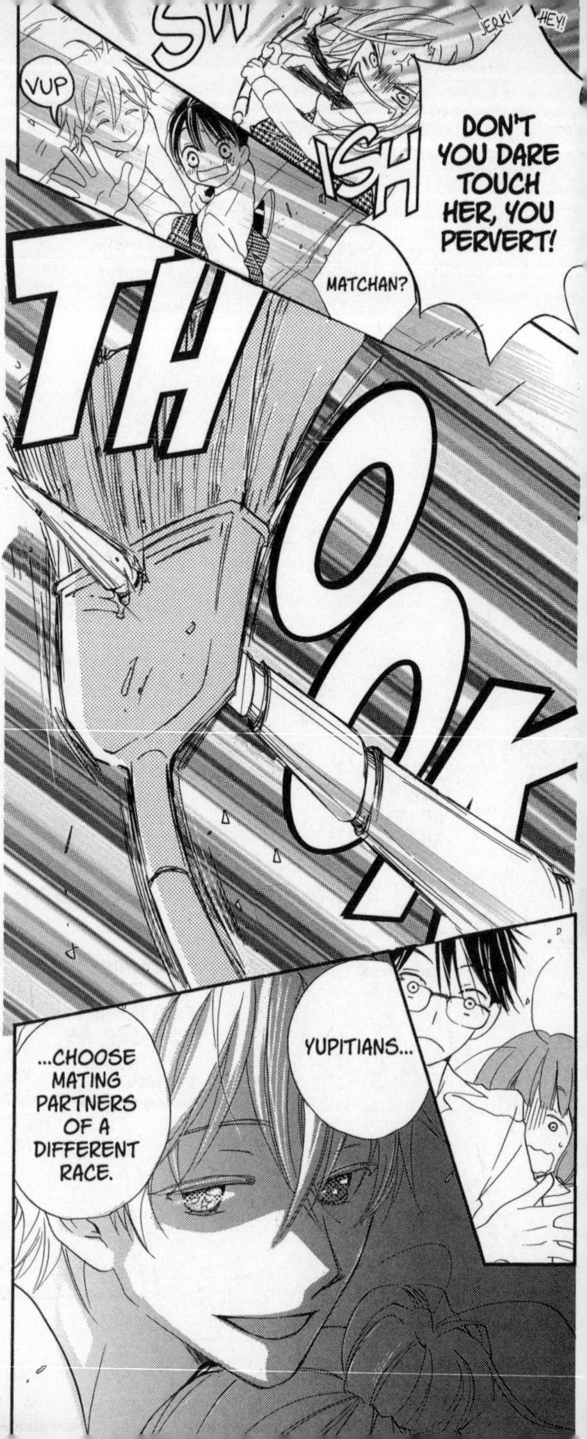
HEY!
JERK!
SW
ISH
VUP
DON'T YOU DARE TOUCH HER, YOU PERVERT!
MATCHAN?
THOOK
YUPITIANS...
...CHOOSE MATING PARTNERS OF A DIFFERENT RACE.

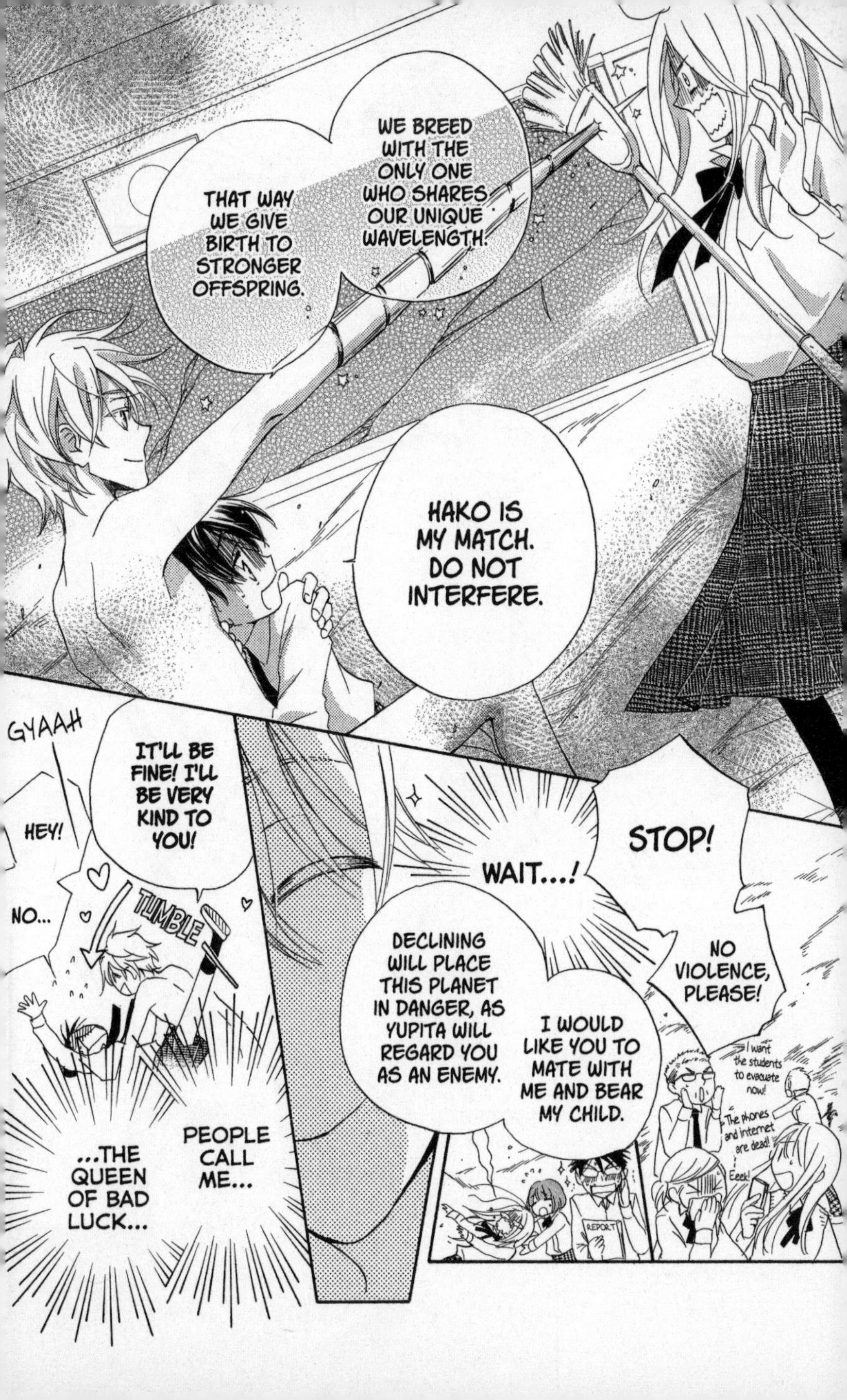
WE BREED WITH THE ONLY ONE WHO SHARES OUR UNIQUE WAVELENGTH.
THAT WAY WE GIVE BIRTH TO STRONGER OFFSPRING.
HAKO IS MY MATCH. DO NOT INTERFERE.
STOP!
WAIT...!
NO VIOLENCE, PLEASE!
I want the students to evacuate now!
The phones and internet are dead!
Eeek!
I WOULD LIKE YOU TO MATE WITH ME AND BEAR MY CHILD.
DECLINING WILL PLACE THIS PLANET IN DANGER, AS YUPITA WILL REGARD YOU AS AN ENEMY.
PEOPLE CALL ME...
...THE QUEEN OF BAD LUCK...
GYAAH
IT'LL BE FINE! I'LL BE VERY KIND TO YOU!
HEY!
NO...
TUMBLE
REPORT

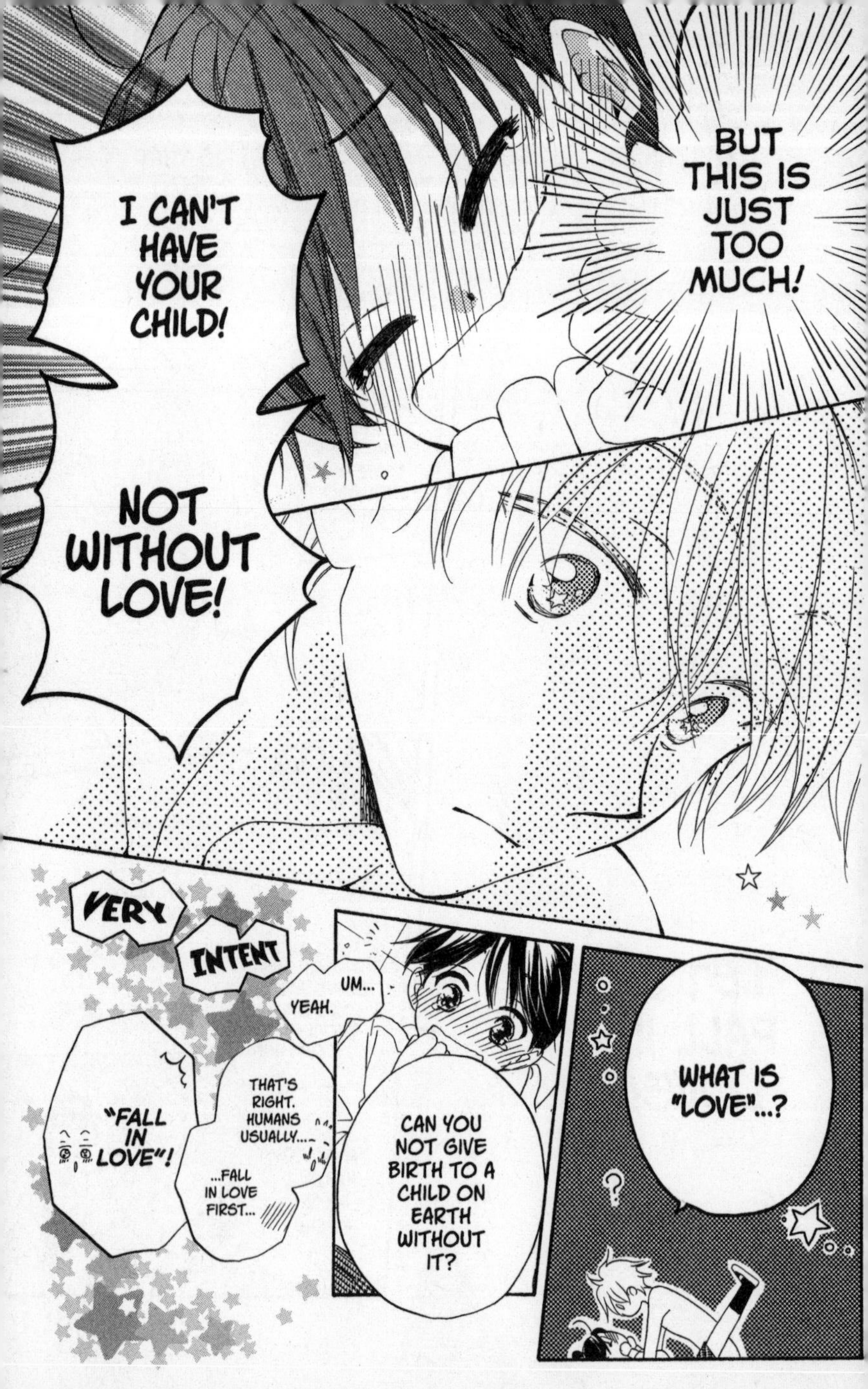
BUT THIS IS JUST TOO MUCH!
I CAN'T HAVE YOUR CHILD!
NOT WITHOUT LOVE!
WHAT IS "LOVE"...?
CAN YOU NOT GIVE BIRTH TO A CHILD ON EARTH WITHOUT IT?
UM...
YEAH.
VERY
INTENT
THAT'S RIGHT. HUMANS USUALLY...
...FALL IN LOVE FIRST...
"FALL IN LOVE"!

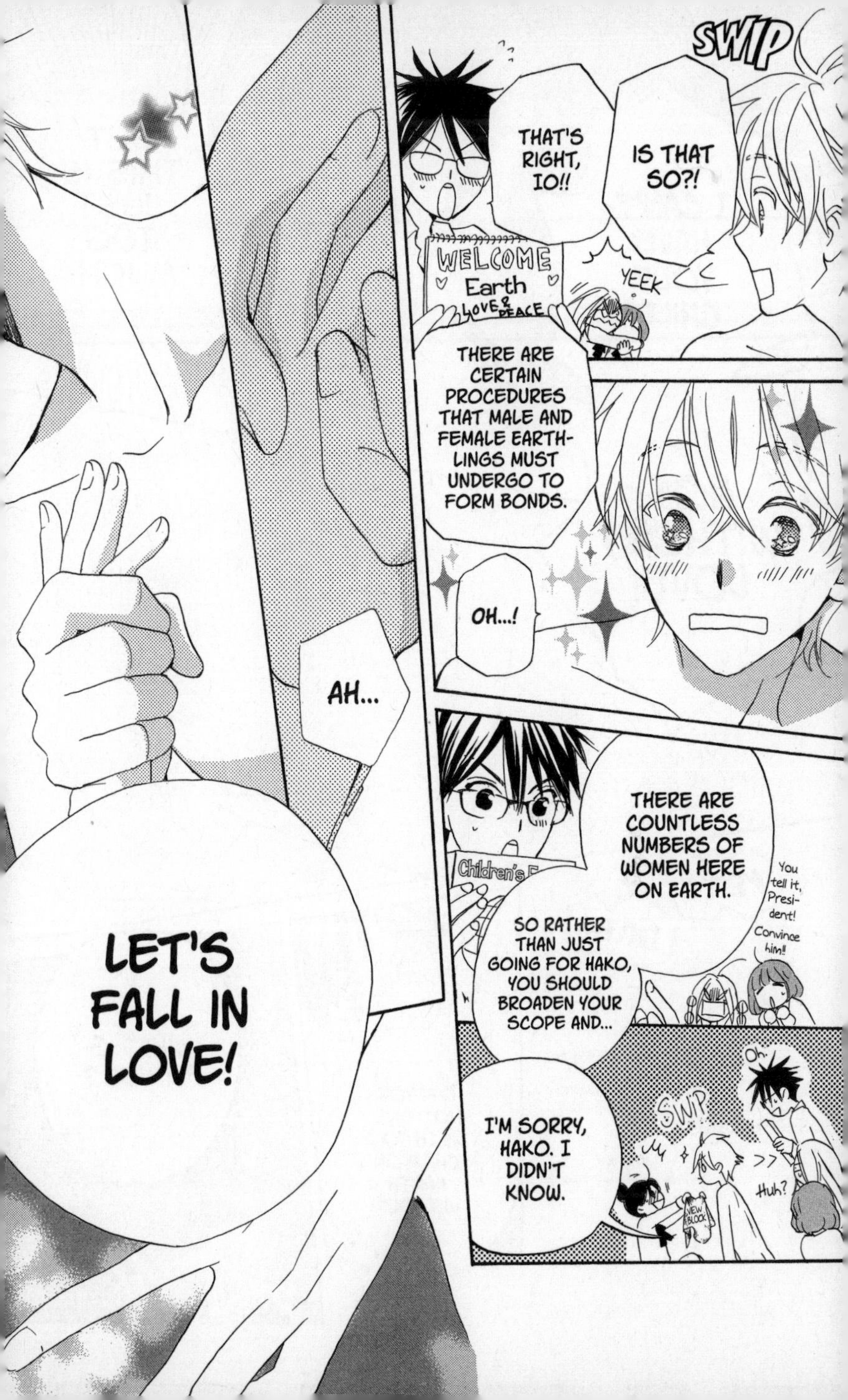
SWIP
IS THAT SO?!
THAT'S RIGHT, IO!!
WELCOME Earth LOVE & PEACE
YEEK
THERE ARE CERTAIN PROCEDURES THAT MALE AND FEMALE EARTH-LINGS MUST UNDERGO TO FORM BONDS.
OH...!
THERE ARE COUNTLESS NUMBERS OF WOMEN HERE ON EARTH.
You tell it, President! Convince him!!
SO RATHER THAN JUST GOING FOR HAKO, YOU SHOULD BROADEN YOUR SCOPE AND...
Oh.
SWIP
I'M SORRY, HAKO. I DIDN'T KNOW.
Huh?
AH...
LET'S FALL IN LOVE!

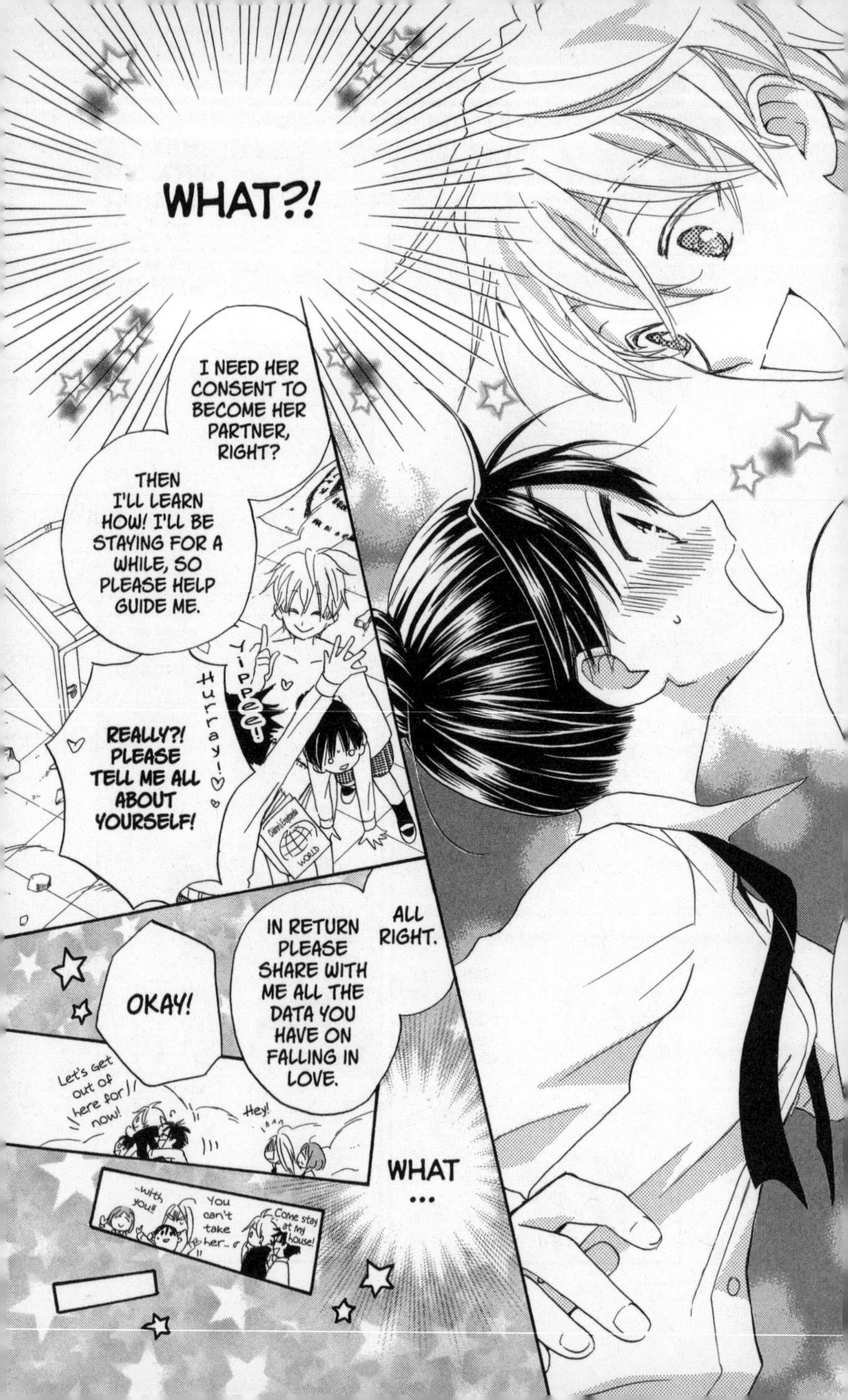
WHAT?!
I NEED HER CONSENT TO BECOME HER PARTNER, RIGHT?
THEN I'LL LEARN HOW! I'LL BE STAYING FOR A WHILE, SO PLEASE HELP GUIDE ME.
Yippee!
Hurray!
REALLY?! PLEASE TELL ME ALL ABOUT YOURSELF!
ALL RIGHT.
IN RETURN PLEASE SHARE WITH ME ALL THE DATA YOU HAVE ON FALLING IN LOVE.
OKAY!
Hey!
Let's get out of here for now!
Come stay at my house!
You can't take her...
-with you!!
WHAT ...

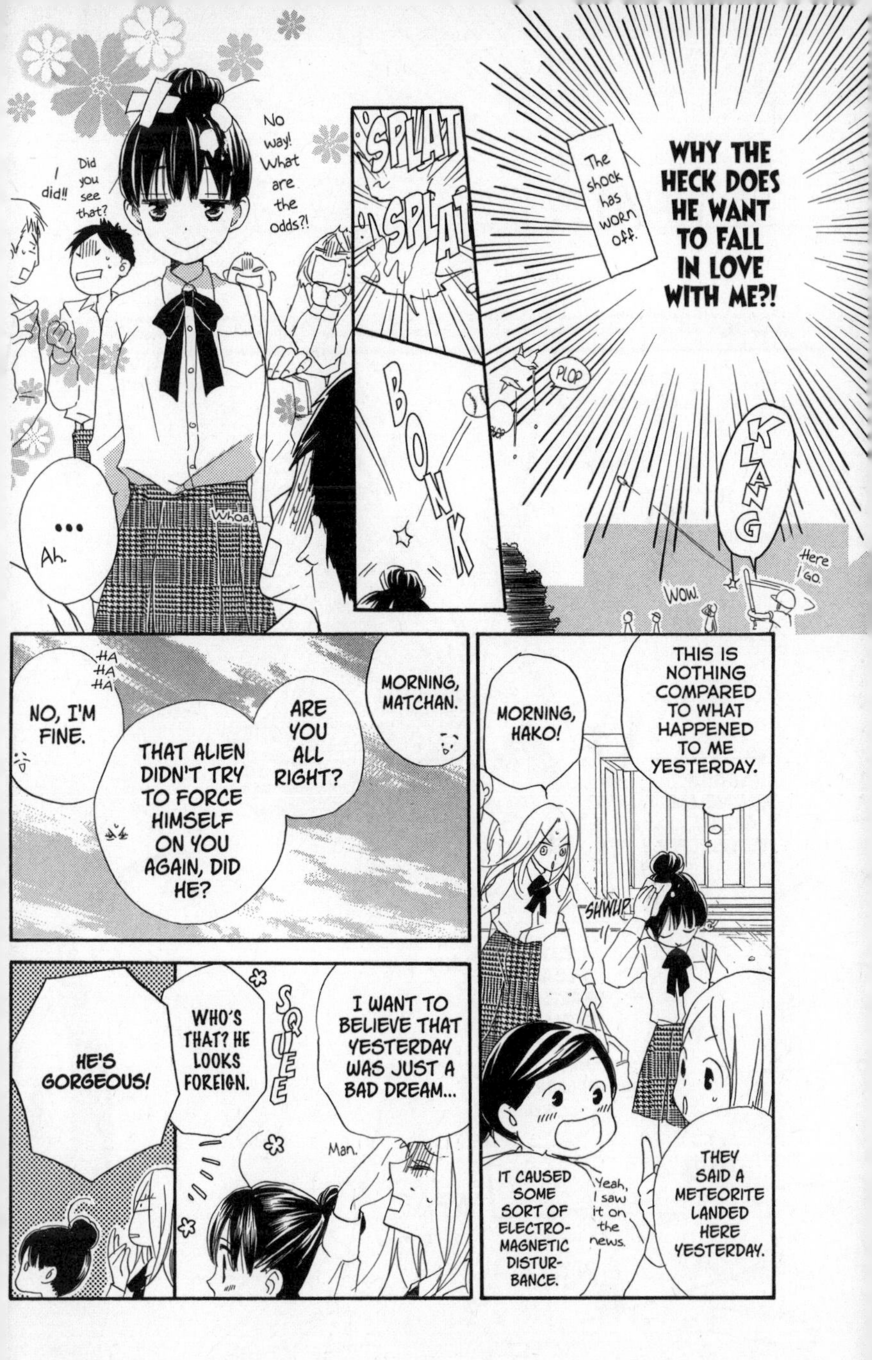
WHY THE HECK DOES HE WANT TO FALL IN LOVE WITH ME?!
The shock has worn off.
PLOP
KLANG
Here I go.
Wow.
SPLAT
SPLAT
BONK
No way! What are the odds?!
Did you see that?
I did!!
Whoa
...
Ah.
THIS IS NOTHING COMPARED TO WHAT HAPPENED TO ME YESTERDAY.
MORNING, HAKO!
SHWUP
THEY SAID A METEORITE LANDED HERE YESTERDAY.
Yeah, I saw it on the news.
IT CAUSED SOME SORT OF ELECTRO-MAGNETIC DISTUR-BANCE.
MORNING, MATCHAN.
ARE YOU ALL RIGHT?
THAT ALIEN DIDN'T TRY TO FORCE HIMSELF ON YOU AGAIN, DID HE?
HA HA HA
NO, I'M FINE.
I WANT TO BELIEVE THAT YESTERDAY WAS JUST A BAD DREAM...
Man.
SQUEE
WHO'S THAT? HE LOOKS FOREIGN.
HE'S GORGEOUS!

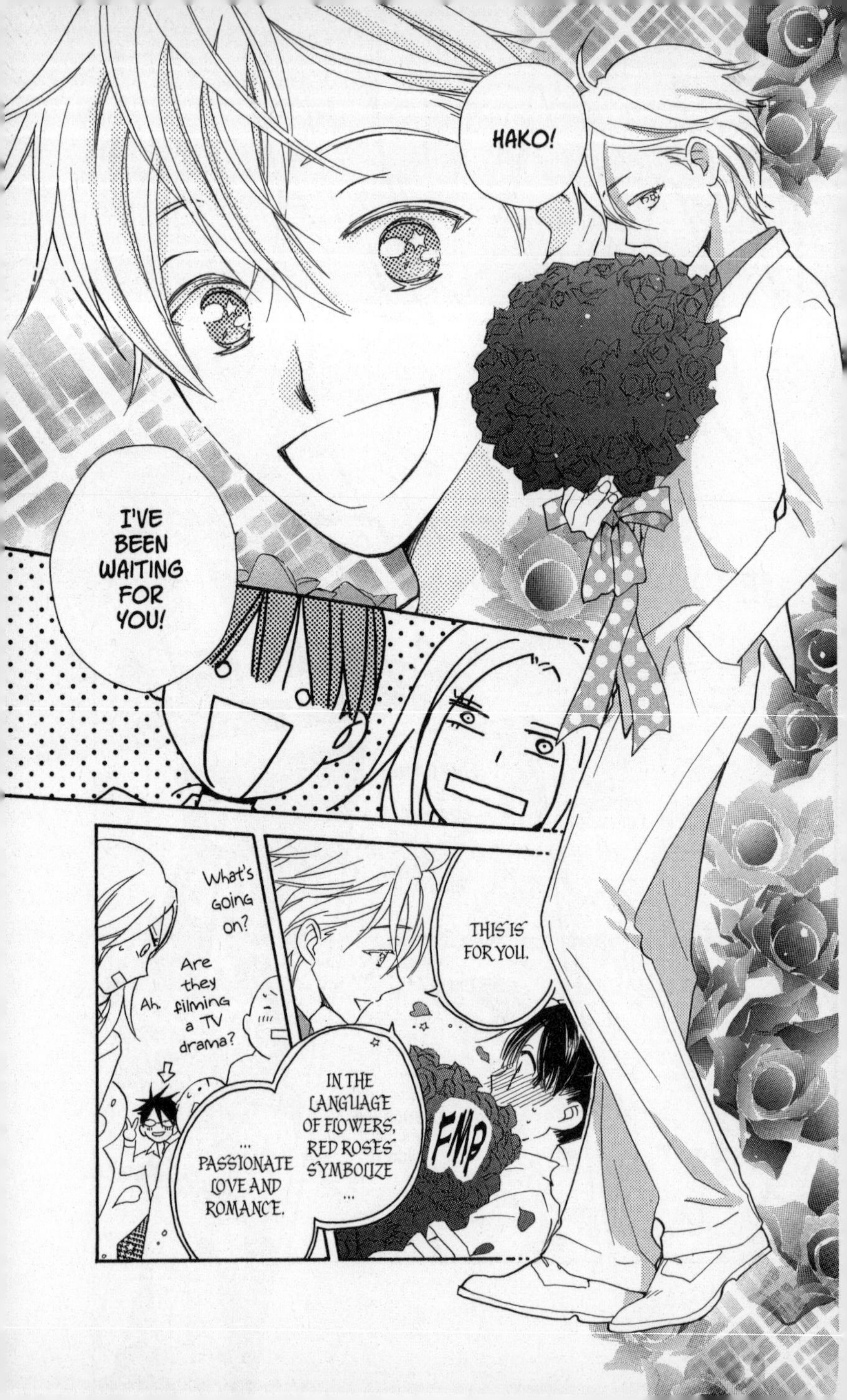
HAKO!
I'VE BEEN WAITING FOR YOU!
THIS IS FOR YOU.
IN THE LANGUAGE OF FLOWERS, RED ROSES SYMBOLIZE ...
... PASSIONATE LOVE AND ROMANCE.
FMP
What's going on?
Are they filming a TV drama?
Ah.

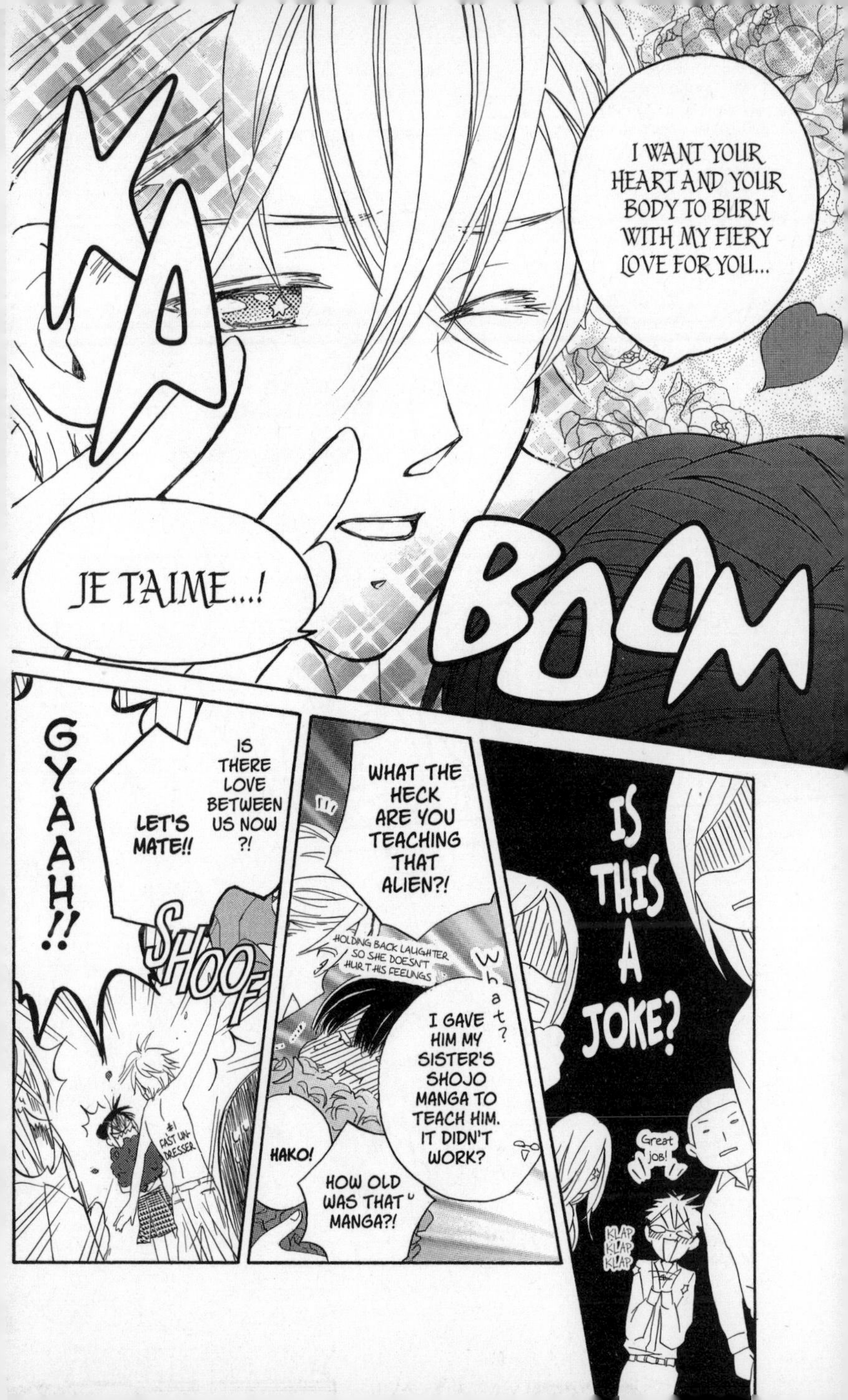
I WANT YOUR HEART AND YOUR BODY TO BURN WITH MY FIERY LOVE FOR YOU...
KA
JE T'AIME...!
BOOM
IS THIS A JOKE?
Great job!
KLAP KLAP KLAP
WHAT THE HECK ARE YOU TEACHING THAT ALIEN?!
What?
HOLDING BACK LAUGHTER SO SHE DOESN'T HURT HIS FEELINGS
I GAVE HIM MY SISTER'S SHOJO MANGA TO TEACH HIM. IT DIDN'T WORK?
HAKO!
HOW OLD WAS THAT MANGA?!
IS THERE LOVE BETWEEN US NOW ?!
LET'S MATE!!
GYAAH!!
SHOOF
#1 FAST UN-DRESSER

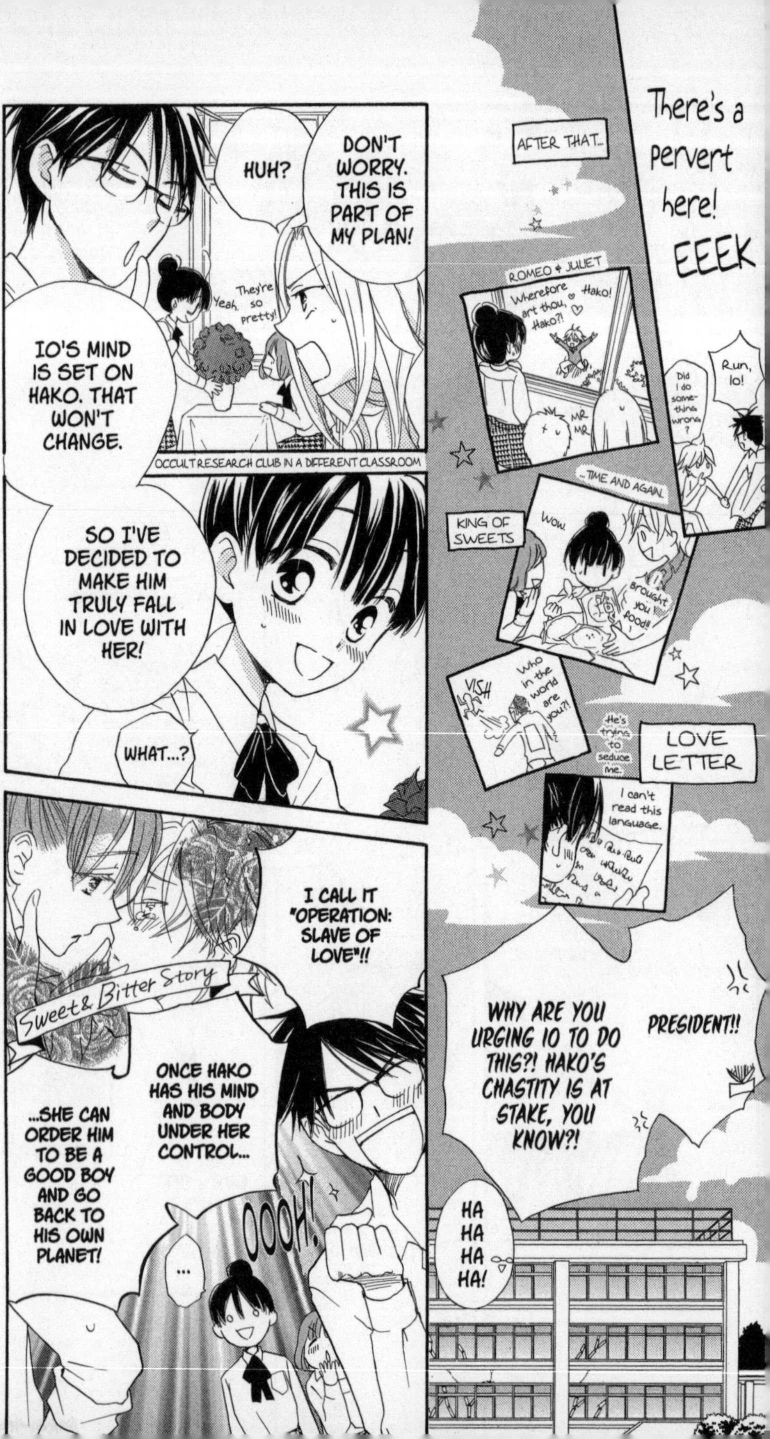
There's a pervert here!
EEEK
AFTER THAT...
ROMEO & JULIET
Wherefore art thou, Hako?!
Hako! ♡
MR MR
Run, Io!
Did I do something wrong?
...TIME AND AGAIN
KING OF SWEETS
Wow.
Brought you food!!
VISH
Who in the world are you?!
He's trying to seduce me.
LOVE LETTER
I can't read this language.
PRESIDENT!!
WHY ARE YOU URGING IO TO DO THIS?! HAKO'S CHASTITY IS AT STAKE, YOU KNOW?!
HA HA HA HA!
DON'T WORRY. THIS IS PART OF MY PLAN!
HUH?
They're so pretty!
Yeah.
IO'S MIND IS SET ON HAKO. THAT WON'T CHANGE.
OCCULT RESEARCH CLUB IN A DIFFERENT CLASSROOM
SO I'VE DECIDED TO MAKE HIM TRULY FALL IN LOVE WITH HER!
WHAT...?
I CALL IT "OPERATION: SLAVE OF LOVE"!!
Sweet & Bitter Story
ONCE HAKO HAS HIS MIND AND BODY UNDER HER CONTROL...
...SHE CAN ORDER HIM TO BE A GOOD BOY AND GO BACK TO HIS OWN PLANET!
OOOH!
...

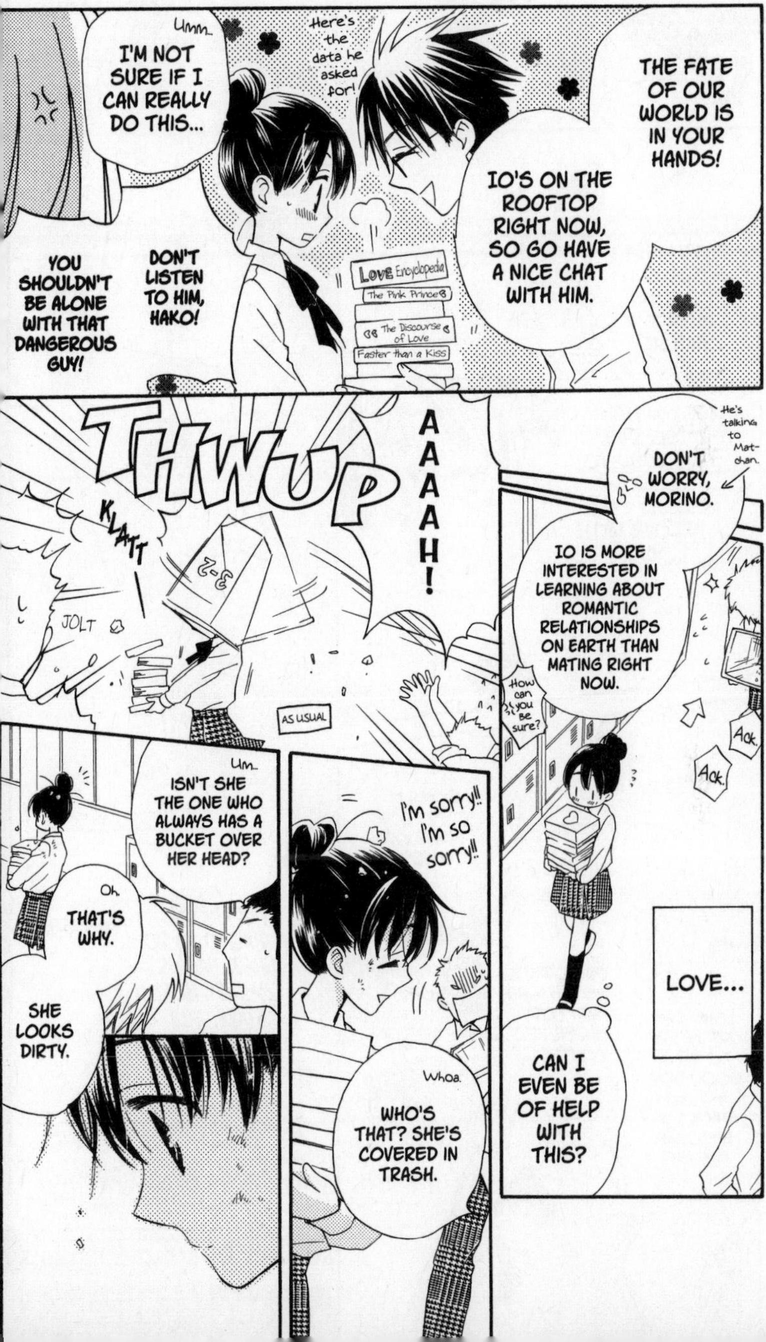
THE FATE OF OUR WORLD IS IN YOUR HANDS!
IO'S ON THE ROOFTOP RIGHT NOW, SO GO HAVE A NICE CHAT WITH HIM.
Here's the data he asked for!
LOVE Encyclopedia
The Pink Prince
The Discourse of Love
Faster than a Kiss
Umm...
I'M NOT SURE IF I CAN REALLY DO THIS...
DON'T LISTEN TO HIM, HAKO!
YOU SHOULDN'T BE ALONE WITH THAT DANGEROUS GUY!
He's talking to Mat-chan.
DON'T WORRY, MORINO.
IO IS MORE INTERESTED IN LEARNING ABOUT ROMANTIC RELATIONSHIPS ON EARTH THAN MATING RIGHT NOW.
How can you be sure?
Ack.
Ack.
LOVE...
CAN I EVEN BE OF HELP WITH THIS?
THWUP
AAAAAH!
KLATT
3-2
JOLT
AS USUAL
I'm sorry!! I'm so sorry!!
Whoa.
WHO'S THAT? SHE'S COVERED IN TRASH.
Um...
ISN'T SHE THE ONE WHO ALWAYS HAS A BUCKET OVER HER HEAD?
Oh.
THAT'S WHY.
SHE LOOKS DIRTY.

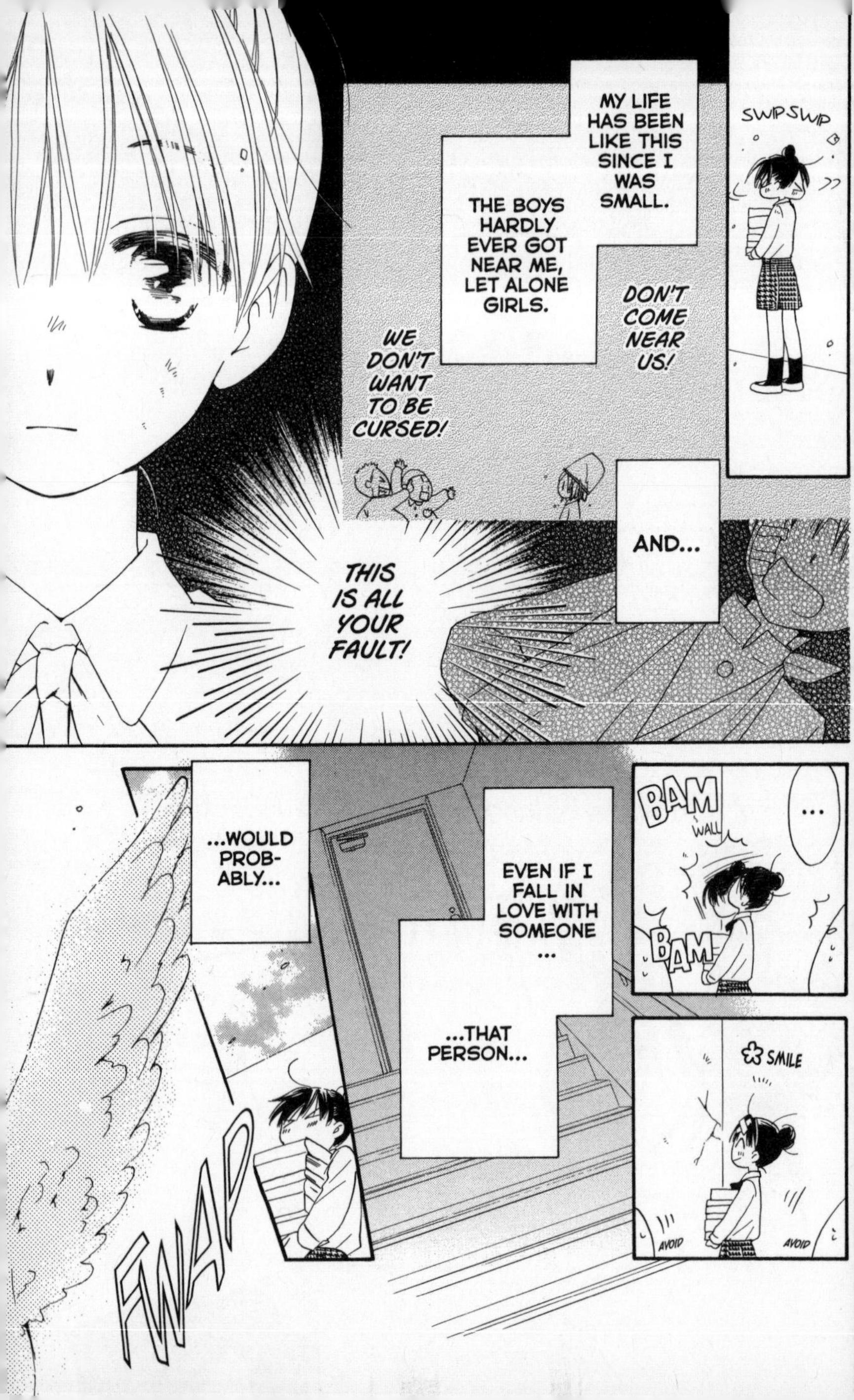
SWIPSWIP
MY LIFE HAS BEEN LIKE THIS SINCE I WAS SMALL.
THE BOYS HARDLY EVER GOT NEAR ME, LET ALONE GIRLS.
DON'T COME NEAR US!
WE DON'T WANT TO BE CURSED!
AND...
THIS IS ALL YOUR FAULT!
...
BAM
WALL
BAM
SMILE
AVOID
AVOID
EVEN IF I FALL IN LOVE WITH SOMEONE ...
...THAT PERSON...
...WOULD PROBABLY...
FWAP

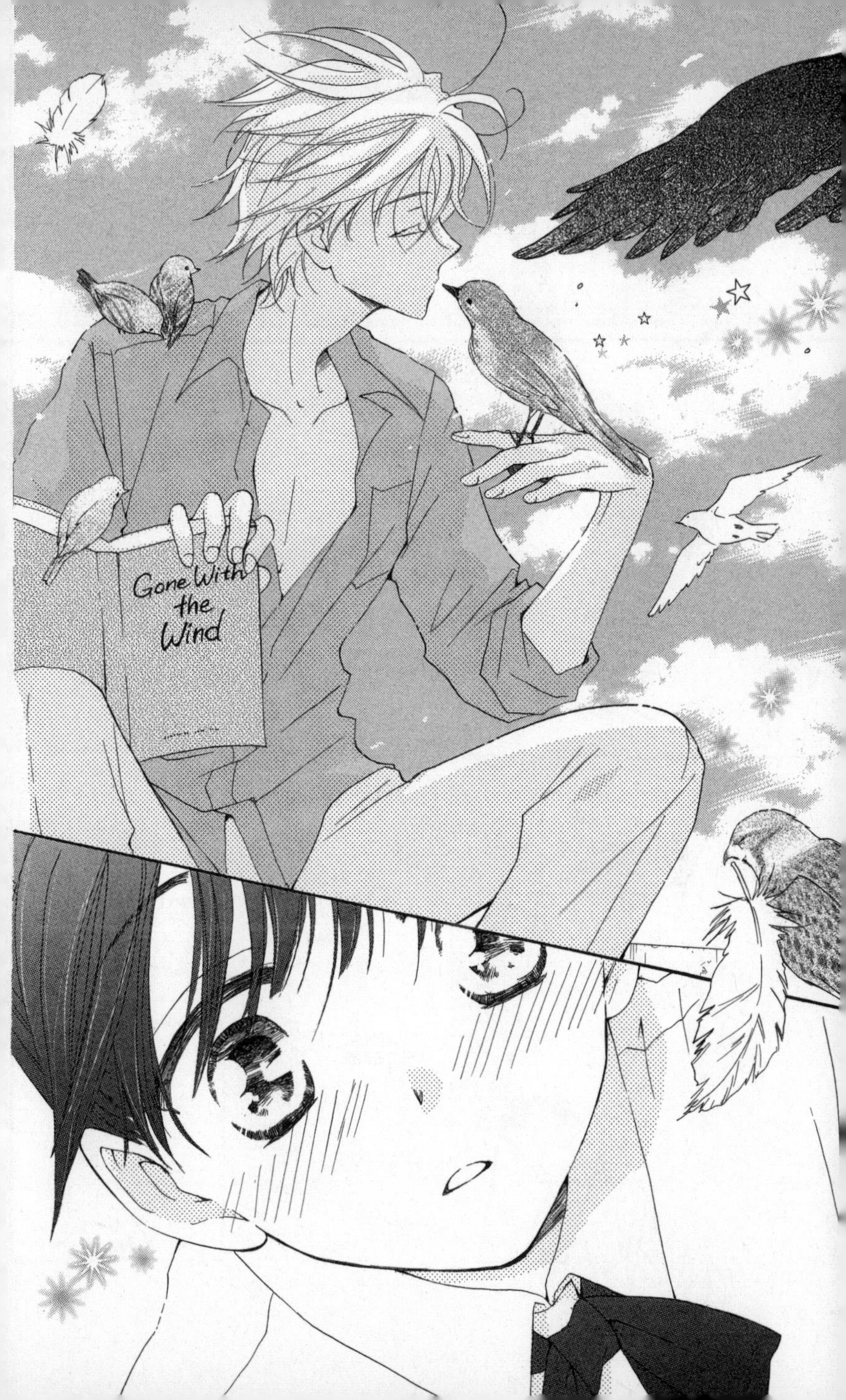
Gone With the Wind

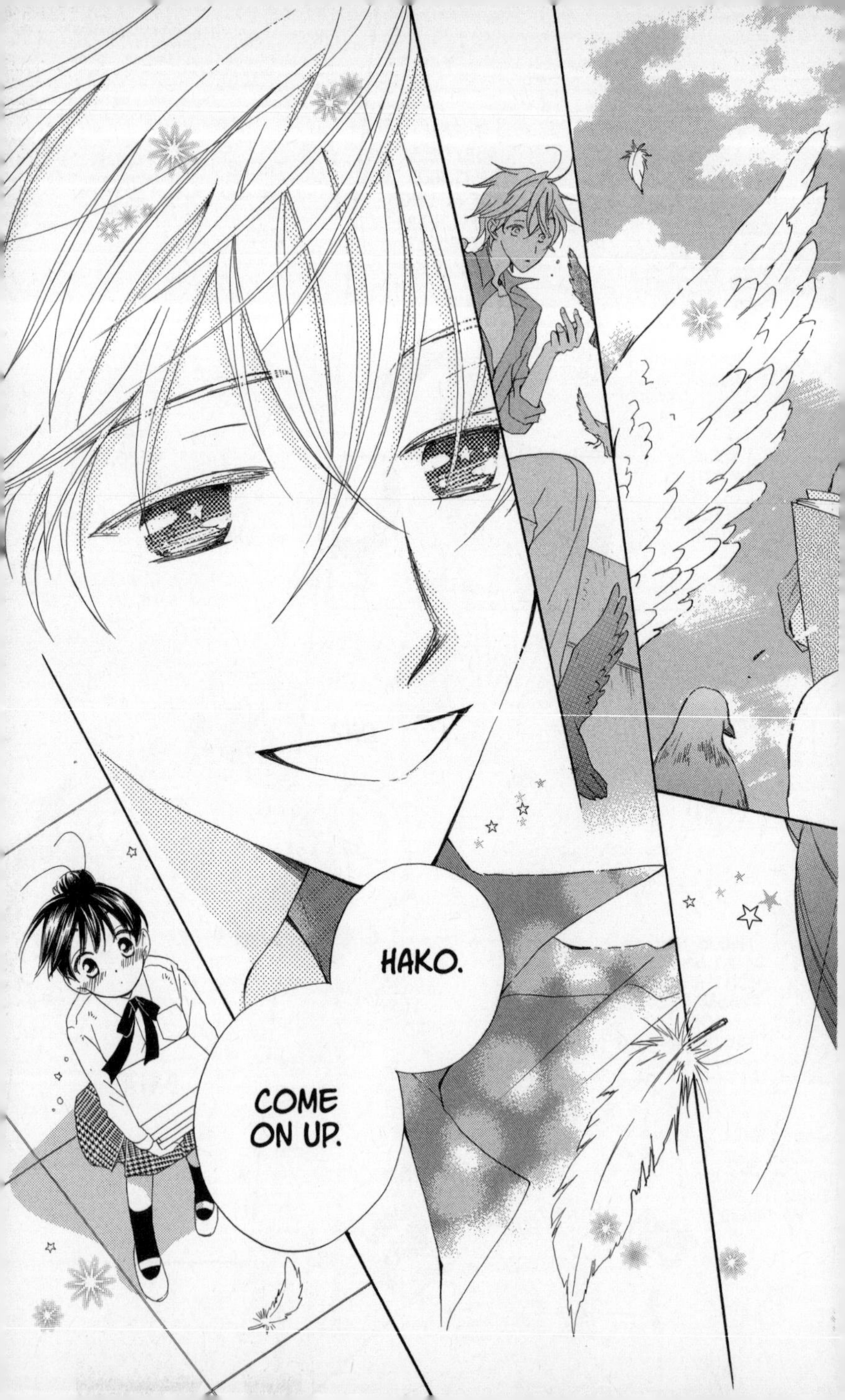
HAKO.
COME ON UP.

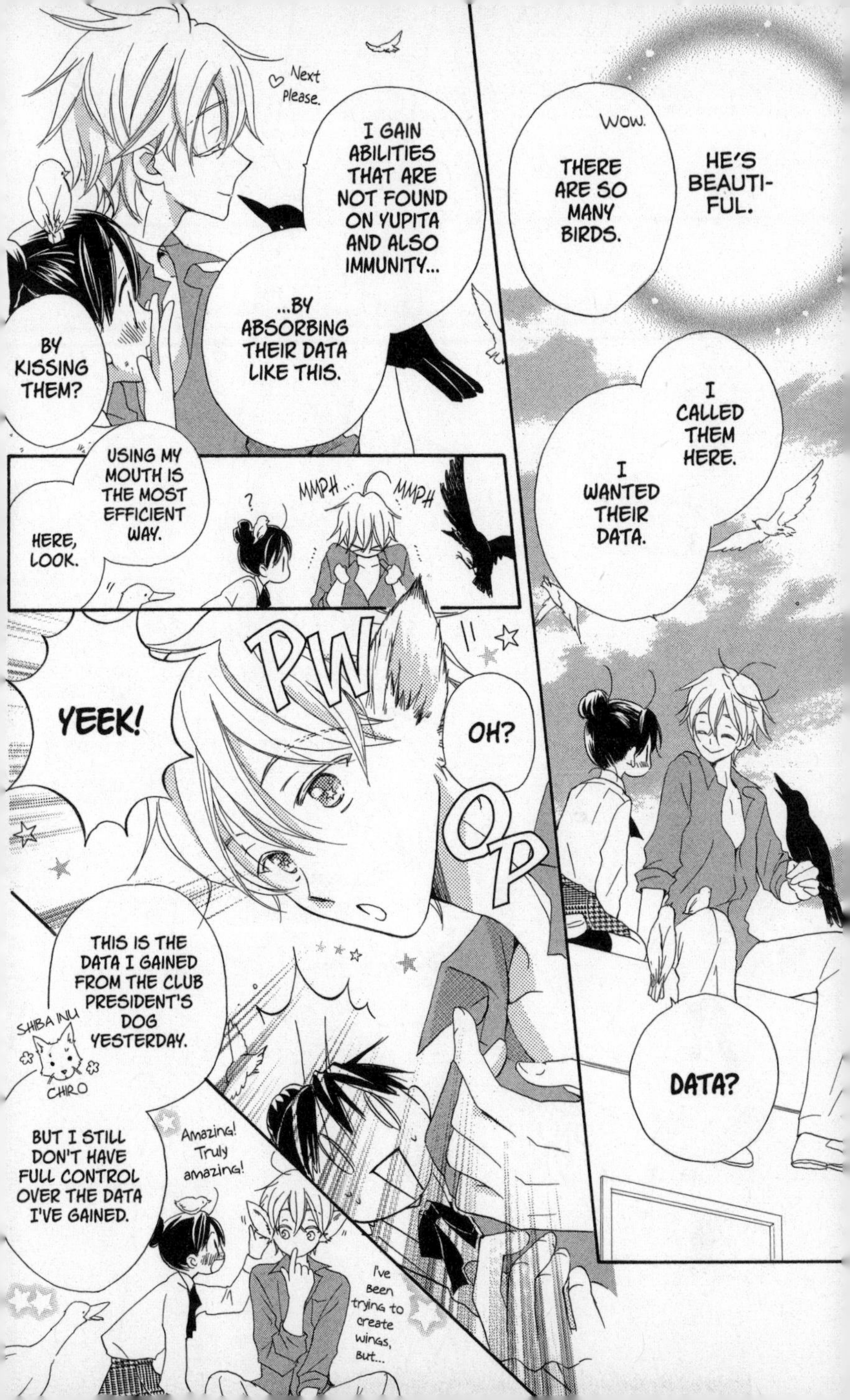
HE'S BEAUTI-FUL.
WOW.
THERE ARE SO MANY BIRDS.
I CALLED THEM HERE.
I WANTED THEIR DATA.
DATA?
Next please.
I GAIN ABILITIES THAT ARE NOT FOUND ON YUPITA AND ALSO IMMUNITY...
...BY ABSORBING THEIR DATA LIKE THIS.
BY KISSING THEM?
MMPH
MMPH...
?
USING MY MOUTH IS THE MOST EFFICIENT WAY.
HERE, LOOK.
OH?
PWOP
YEEK!
THIS IS THE DATA I GAINED FROM THE CLUB PRESIDENT'S DOG YESTERDAY.
SHIBA INU
CHIRO
I've been trying to create wings, but...
Amazing! Truly amazing!
BUT I STILL DON'T HAVE FULL CONTROL OVER THE DATA I'VE GAINED.

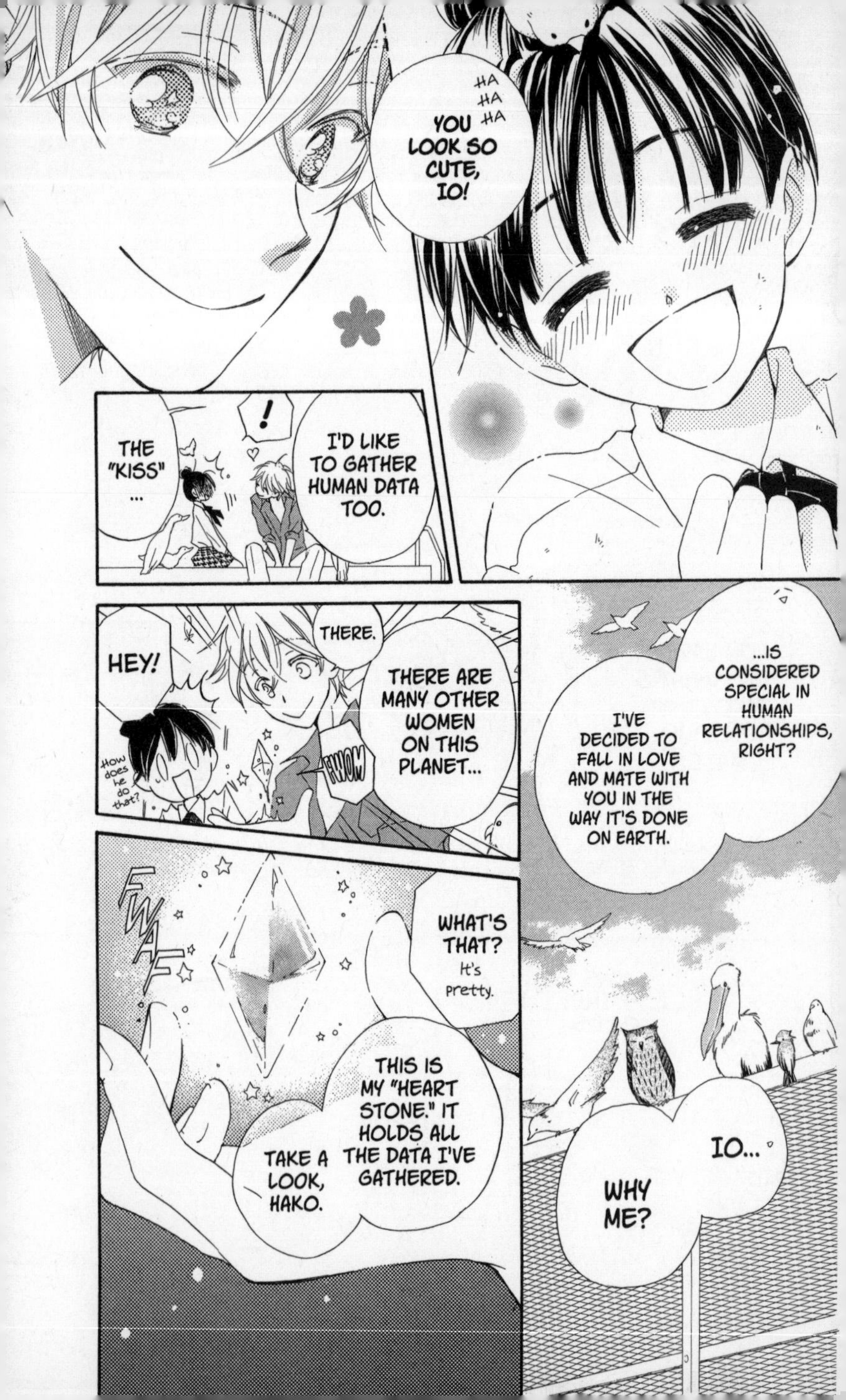

HA HA HA
YOU LOOK SO CUTE, IO!
!
I'D LIKE TO GATHER HUMAN DATA TOO.
THE "KISS" ...
...IS CONSIDERED SPECIAL IN HUMAN RELATIONSHIPS, RIGHT?
I'VE DECIDED TO FALL IN LOVE AND MATE WITH YOU IN THE WAY IT'S DONE ON EARTH.
IO...
WHY ME?
THERE.
THERE ARE MANY OTHER WOMEN ON THIS PLANET...
FWOM
HEY!
How does he do that?
WHAT'S THAT? It's pretty.
THIS IS MY "HEART STONE." IT HOLDS ALL THE DATA I'VE GATHERED.
TAKE A LOOK, HAKO.
FWAF

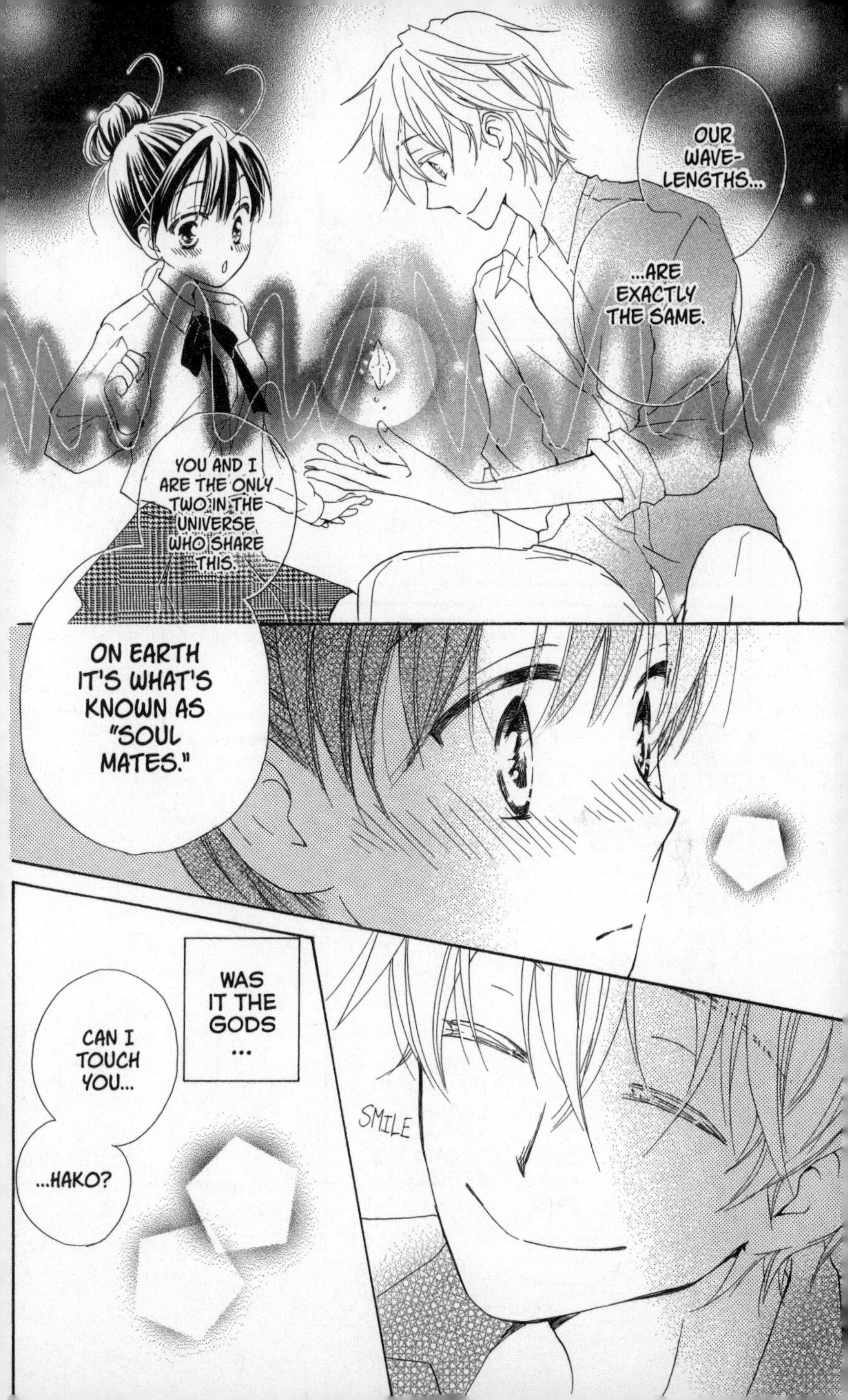
OUR WAVE-LENGTHS...
...ARE EXACTLY THE SAME.
YOU AND I ARE THE ONLY TWO IN THE UNIVERSE WHO SHARE THIS.
ON EARTH IT'S WHAT'S KNOWN AS "SOUL MATES."
WAS IT THE GODS ...
SMILE
CAN I TOUCH YOU...
...HAKO?

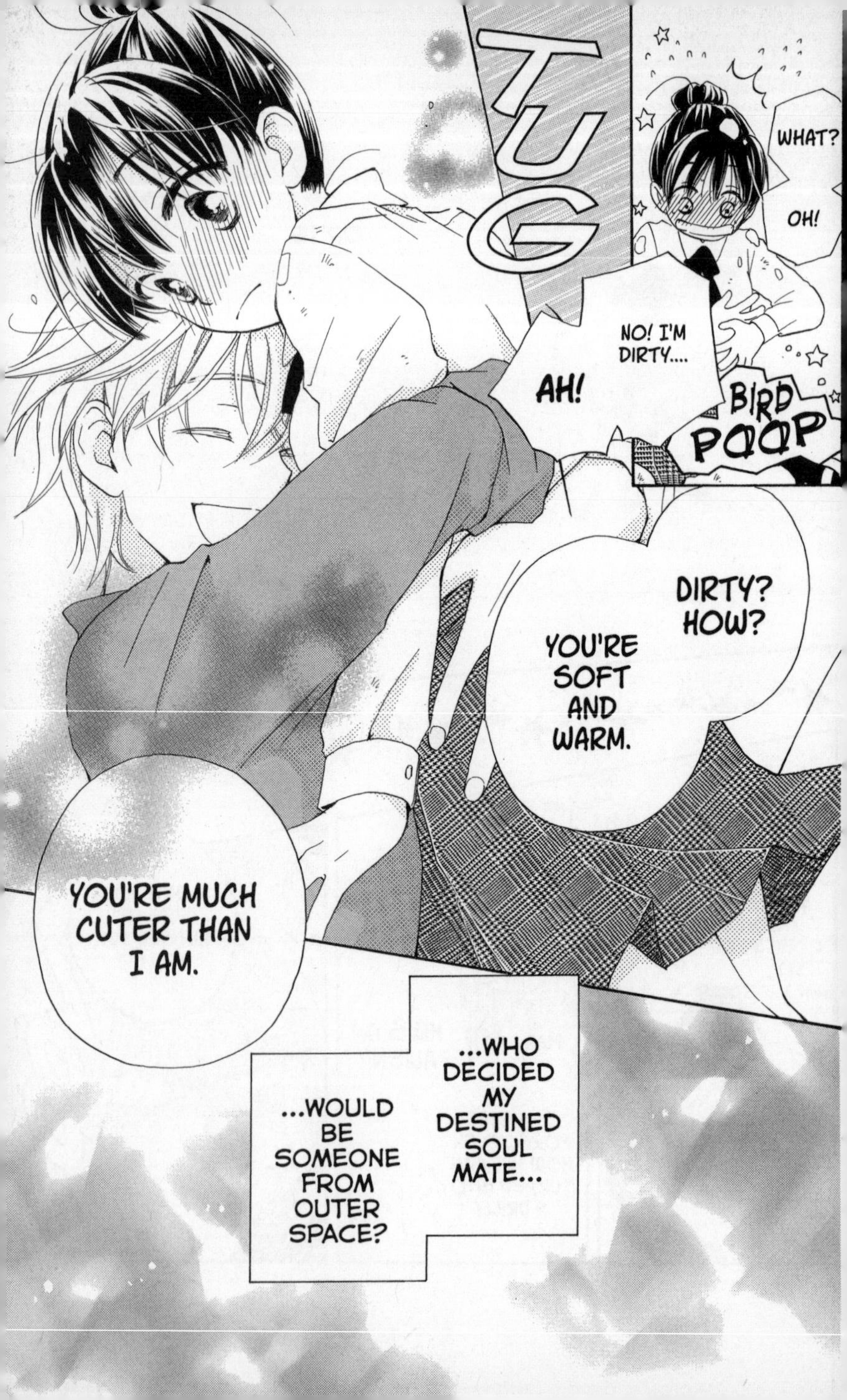
WHAT?
OH!
BIRD POOP
NO! I'M DIRTY....
TUG
AH!
DIRTY? HOW?
YOU'RE SOFT AND WARM.
YOU'RE MUCH CUTER THAN I AM.
...WHO DECIDED MY DESTINED SOUL MATE...
...WOULD BE SOMEONE FROM OUTER SPACE?

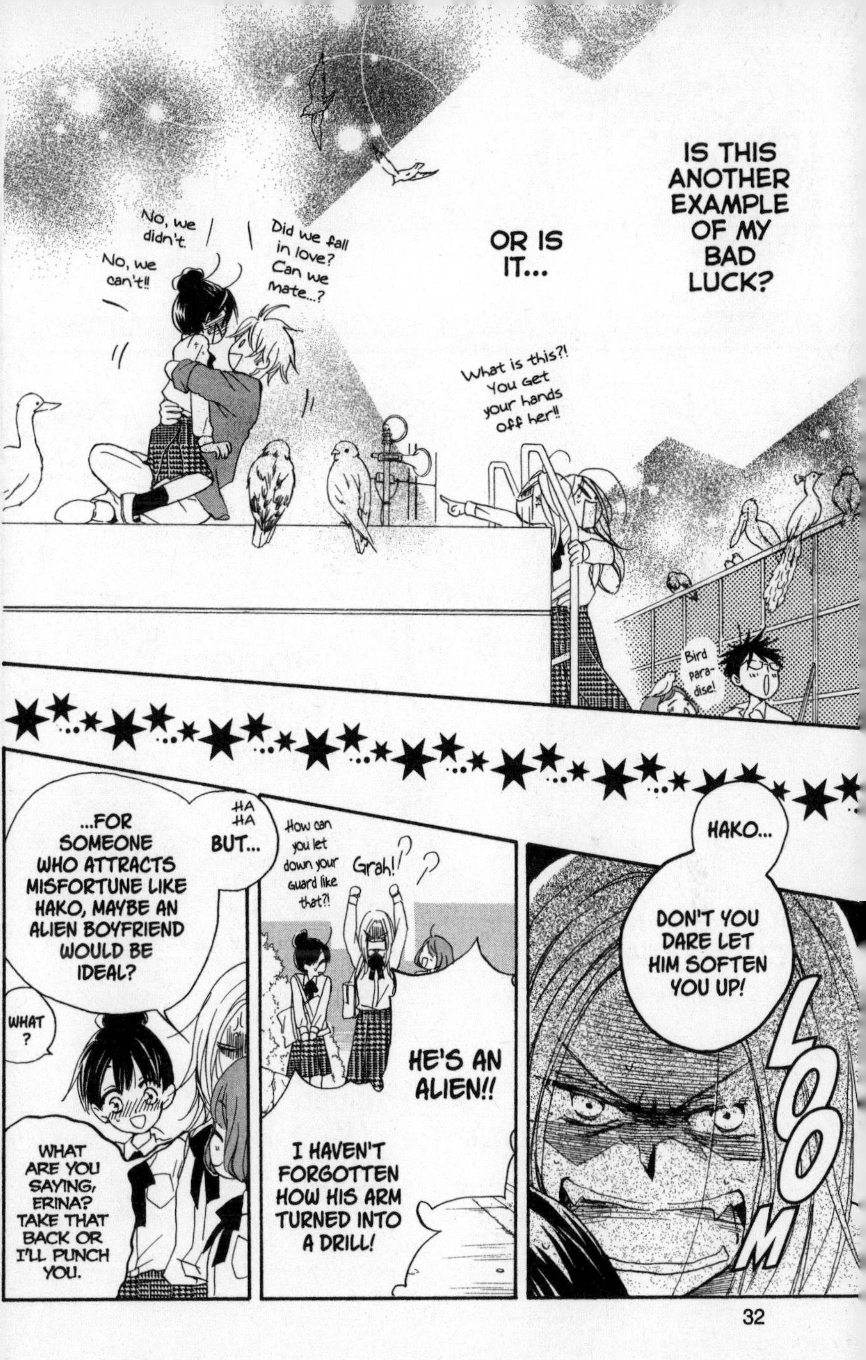
IS THIS ANOTHER EXAMPLE OF MY BAD LUCK?
OR IS IT...
Did we fall in love? Can we mate...?
No, we didn't.
No, we can't!!
What is this?! You get your hands off her!!
Bird paradise!
HAKO...
DON'T YOU DARE LET HIM SOFTEN YOU UP!
LOOM
Grah!
How can you let down your guard like that?!
HE'S AN ALIEN!!
I HAVEN'T FORGOTTEN HOW HIS ARM TURNED INTO A DRILL!
HA HA
BUT...
...FOR SOMEONE WHO ATTRACTS MISFORTUNE LIKE HAKO, MAYBE AN ALIEN BOYFRIEND WOULD BE IDEAL?
WHAT?
WHAT ARE YOU SAYING, ERINA? TAKE THAT BACK OR I'LL PUNCH YOU.

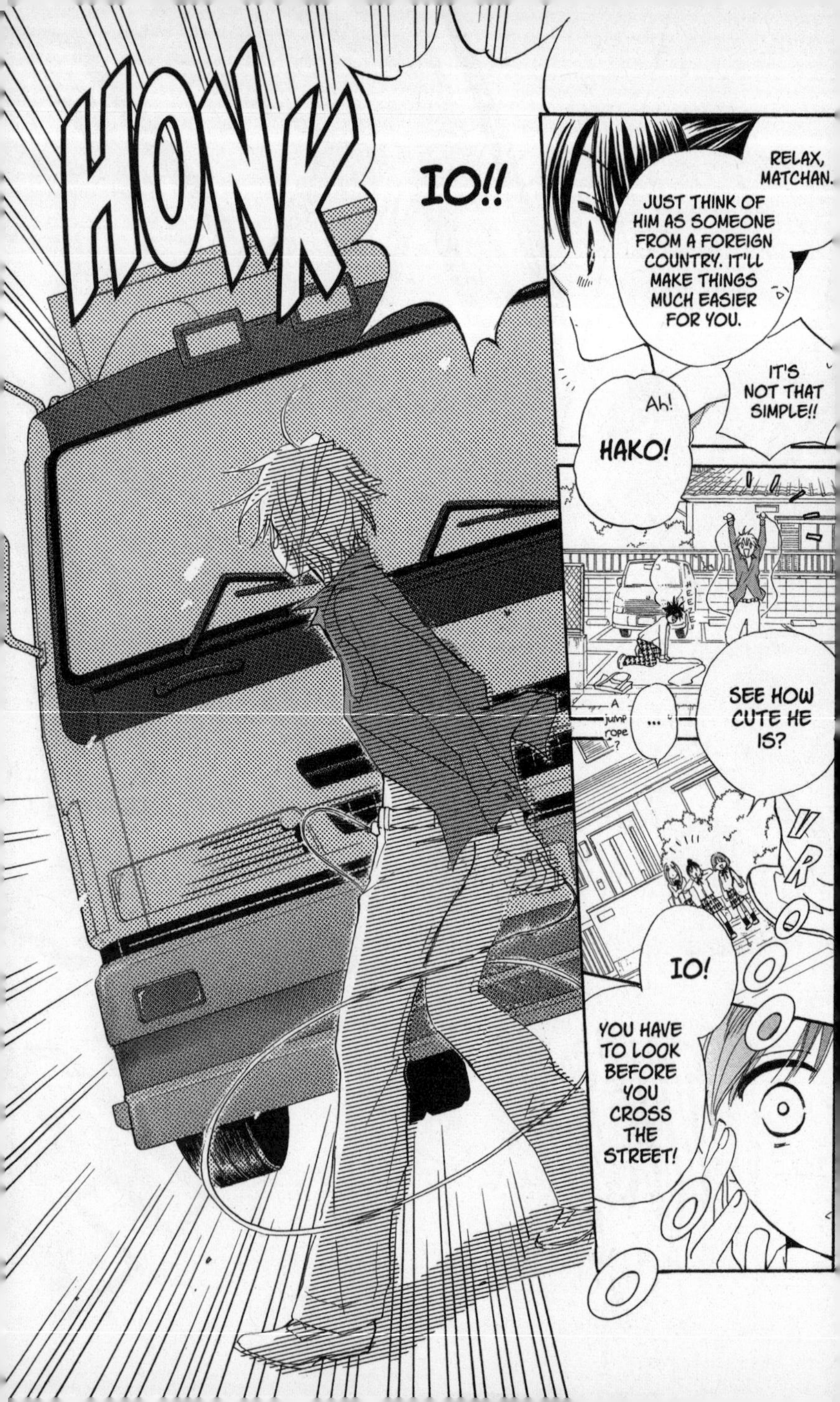
RELAX, MATCHAN.
JUST THINK OF HIM AS SOMEONE FROM A FOREIGN COUNTRY. IT'LL MAKE THINGS MUCH EASIER FOR YOU.
IT'S NOT THAT SIMPLE!!
Ah!
HAKO!
SEE HOW CUTE HE IS?
...
A jump rope?
VROOOOOO
IO!
YOU HAVE TO LOOK BEFORE YOU CROSS THE STREET!
HONK
IO!!

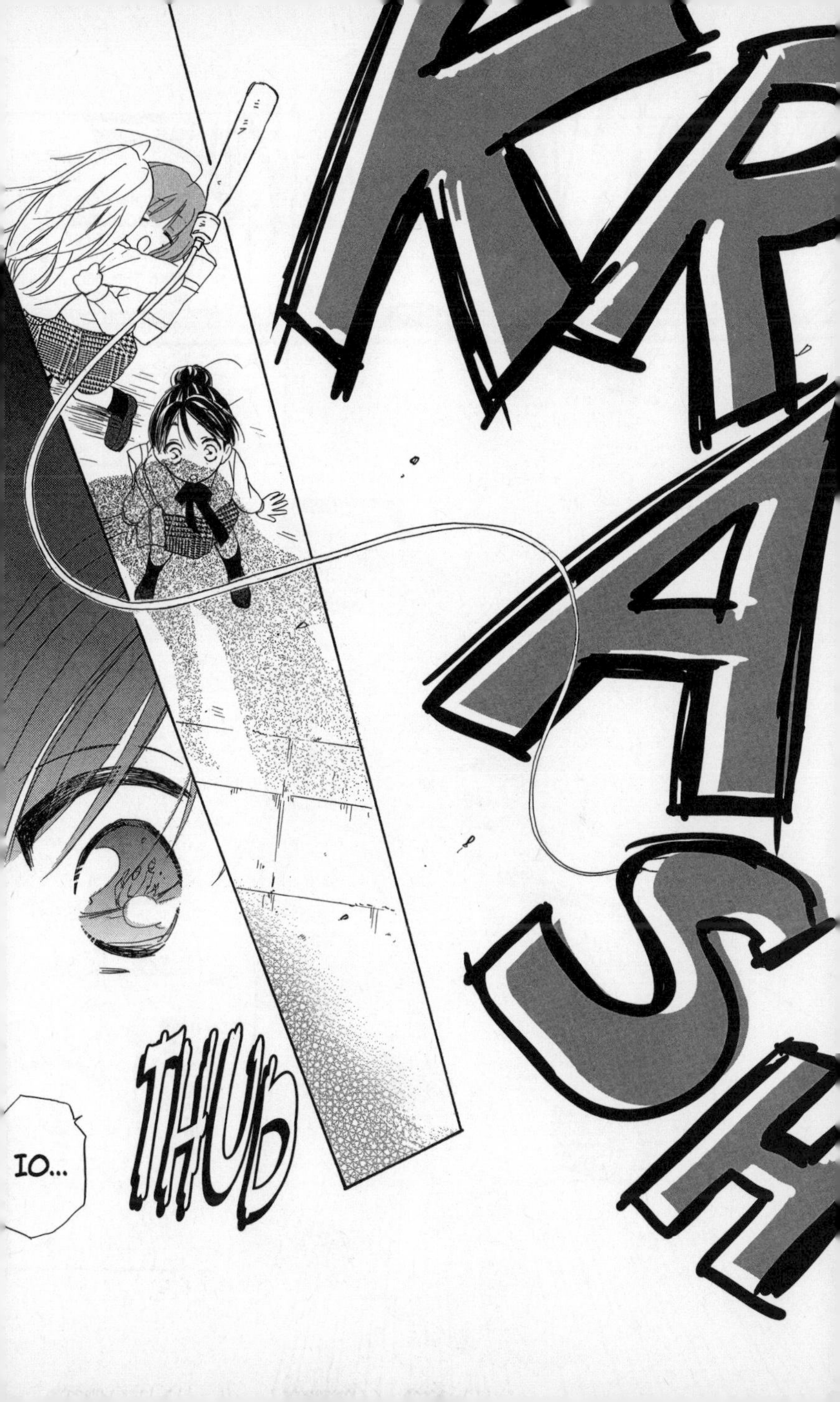
THUD
IO...

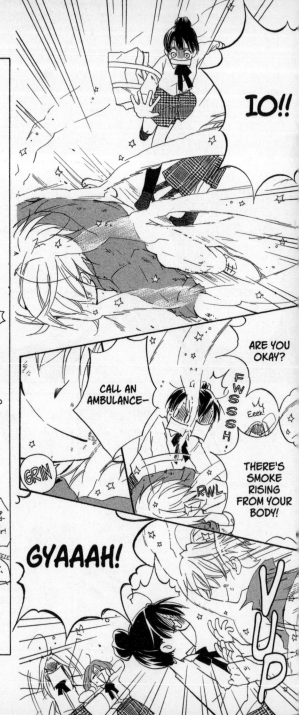

Time Out 1

After my last series I was able to take a longer break. I took the opportunity to go traveling.

October: Hawaii (office trip)

November: Italy (with my mother)

December: Shikoku Prefecture, Seto Inlands (alone)

Too much traveling?!

But it was so much fun! Everyone on the Hawaii trip was active and a bargain hunter, so we ignored the high-end shopping and spent every day swimming, swimming, swimming in the sea.

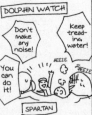

DOLPHIN WATCH

Don't make any noise!

Keep tread-ing water!

You can do it!

WHEEZE

WHEEZE

SPARTAN

I ate a lot, but I didn't gain any weight thanks to that.

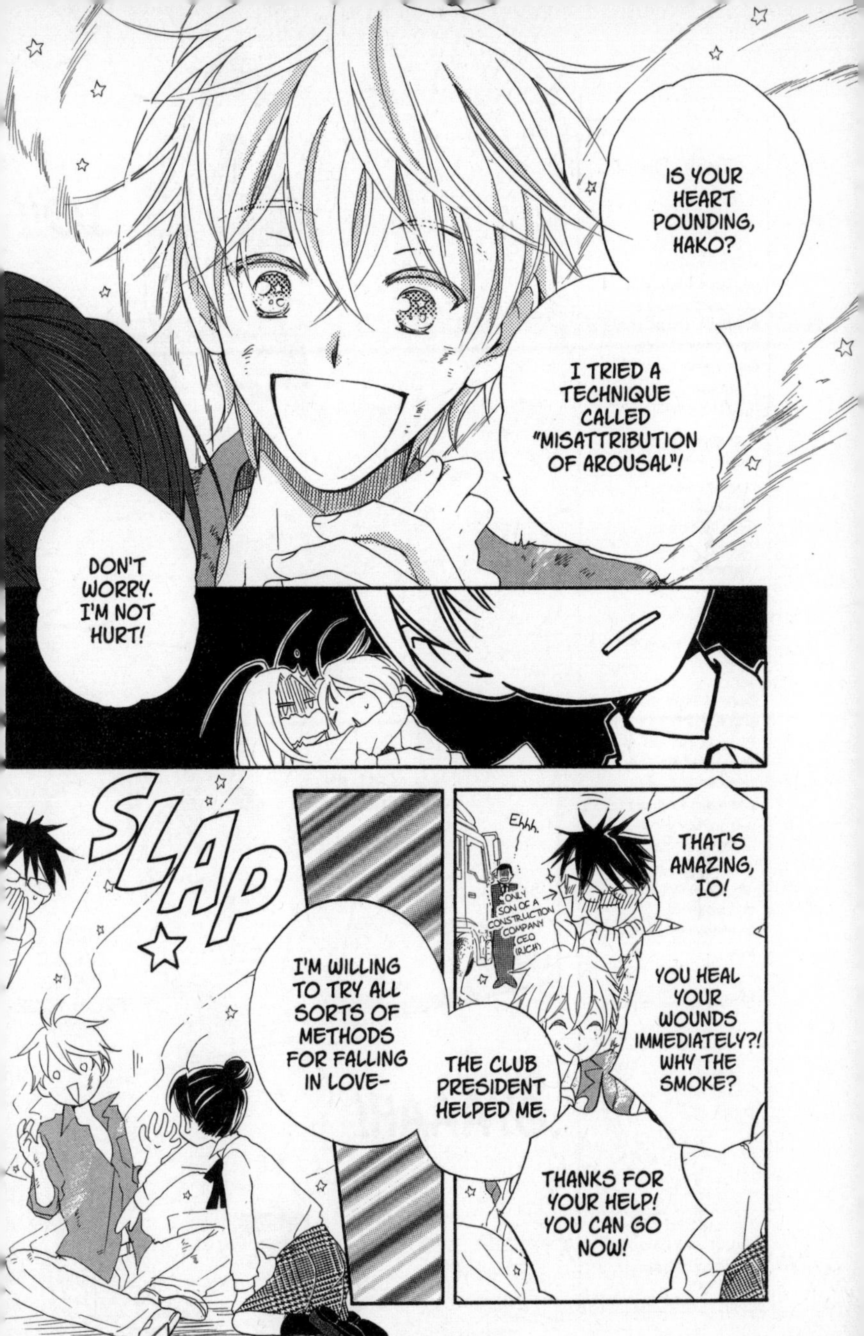
IS YOUR HEART POUNDING, HAKO?
I TRIED A TECHNIQUE CALLED "MISATTRIBUTION OF AROUSAL"!
DON'T WORRY. I'M NOT HURT!
THAT'S AMAZING, IO!
YOU HEAL YOUR WOUNDS IMMEDIATELY?! WHY THE SMOKE?
Ehhh.
ONLY SON OF A CONSTRUCTION COMPANY CEO (RICH)
THE CLUB PRESIDENT HELPED ME.
THANKS FOR YOUR HELP! YOU CAN GO NOW!
SLAP
I'M WILLING TO TRY ALL SORTS OF METHODS FOR FALLING IN LOVE-

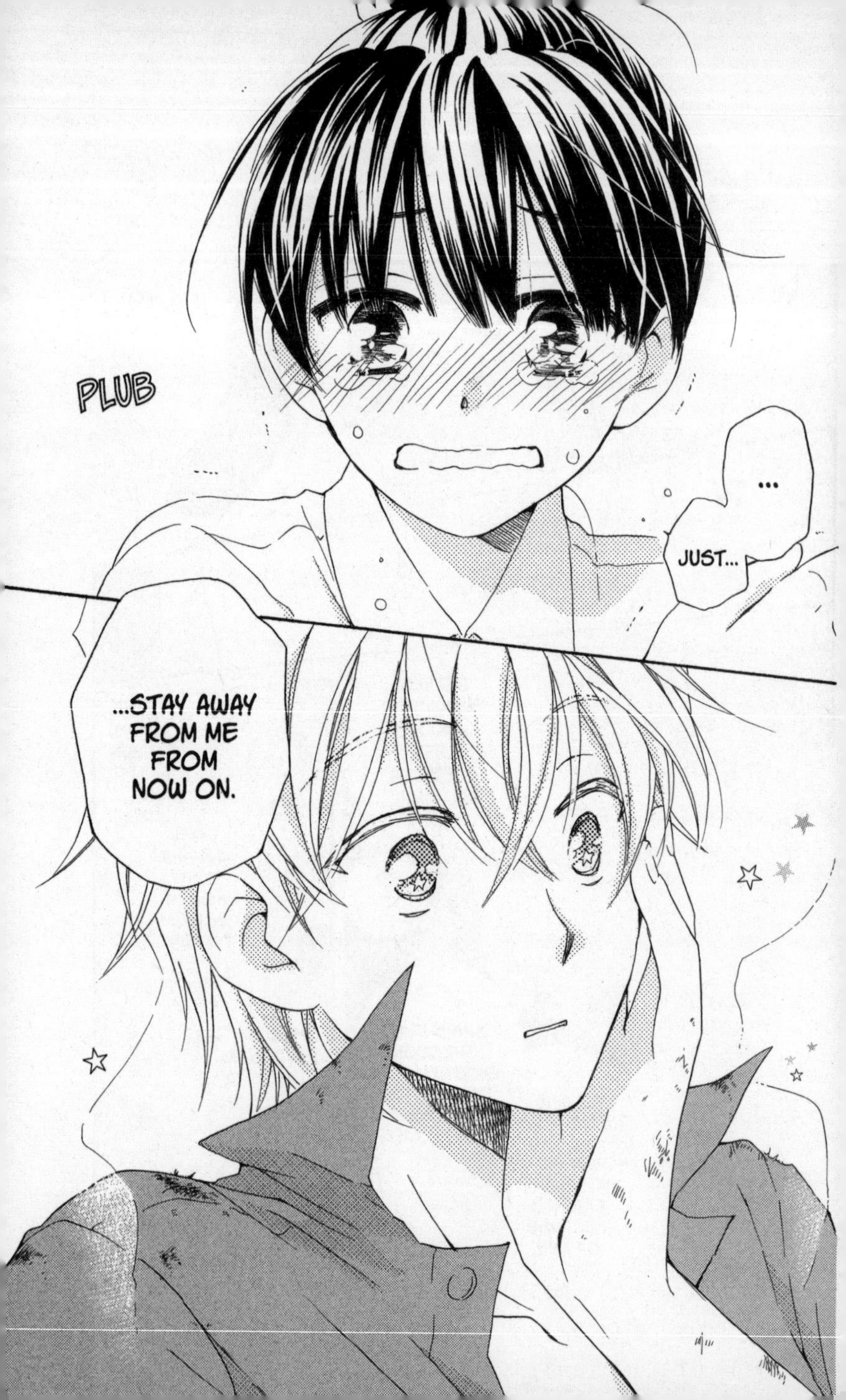
...
JUST...
PLUB
....
...STAY AWAY FROM ME FROM NOW ON.

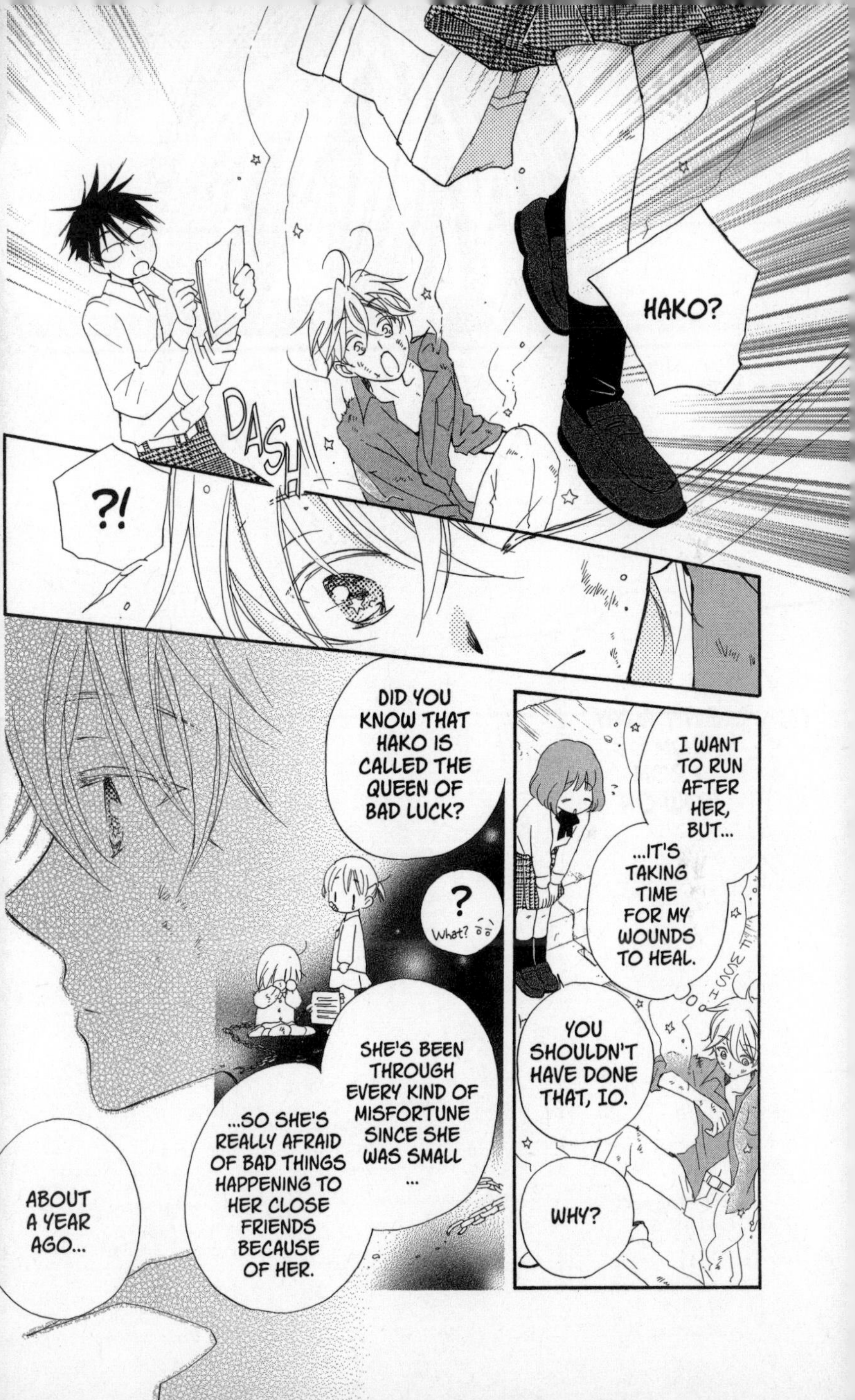
HAKO?
DASH
?!
I WANT TO RUN AFTER HER, BUT...
...IT'S TAKING TIME FOR MY WOUNDS TO HEAL.
YOU SHOULDN'T HAVE DONE THAT, IO.
WHY?
DID YOU KNOW THAT HAKO IS CALLED THE QUEEN OF BAD LUCK?
?
What?
SHE'S BEEN THROUGH EVERY KIND OF MISFORTUNE SINCE SHE WAS SMALL...
...SO SHE'S REALLY AFRAID OF BAD THINGS HAPPENING TO HER CLOSE FRIENDS BECAUSE OF HER.
ABOUT A YEAR AGO...

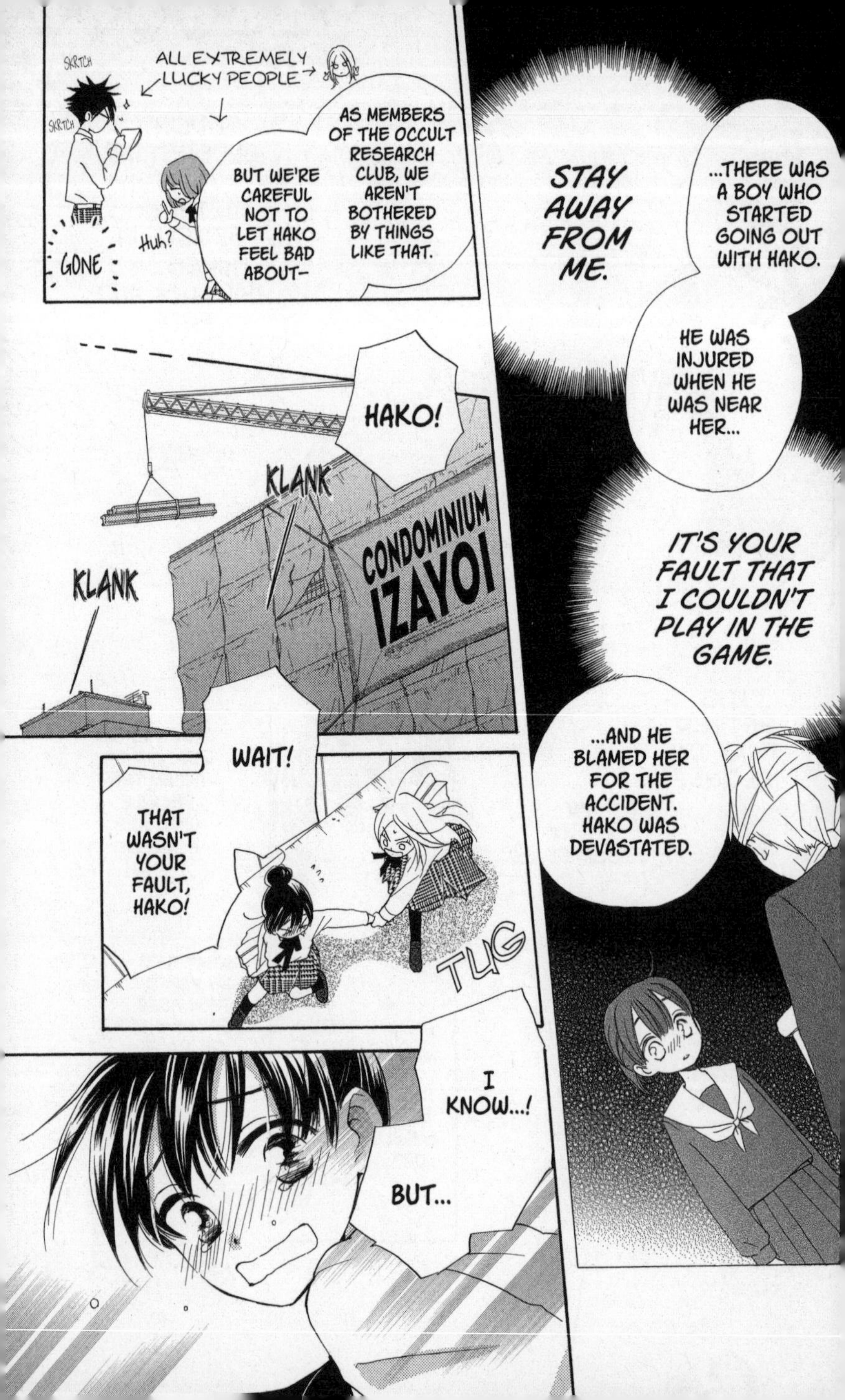
...THERE WAS A BOY WHO STARTED GOING OUT WITH HAKO.
STAY AWAY FROM ME.
HE WAS INJURED WHEN HE WAS NEAR HER...
IT'S YOUR FAULT THAT I COULDN'T PLAY IN THE GAME.
...AND HE BLAMED HER FOR THE ACCIDENT. HAKO WAS DEVASTATED.
AS MEMBERS OF THE OCCULT RESEARCH CLUB, WE AREN'T BOTHERED BY THINGS LIKE THAT.
BUT WE'RE CAREFUL NOT TO LET HAKO FEEL BAD ABOUT-
ALL EXTREMELY LUCKY PEOPLE
SKRTCH
SKRTCH
Huh?
GONE
HAKO!
KLANK
CONDOMINIUM IZAYOI
KLANK
WAIT!
THAT WASN'T YOUR FAULT, HAKO!
TUG
I KNOW...!
BUT...

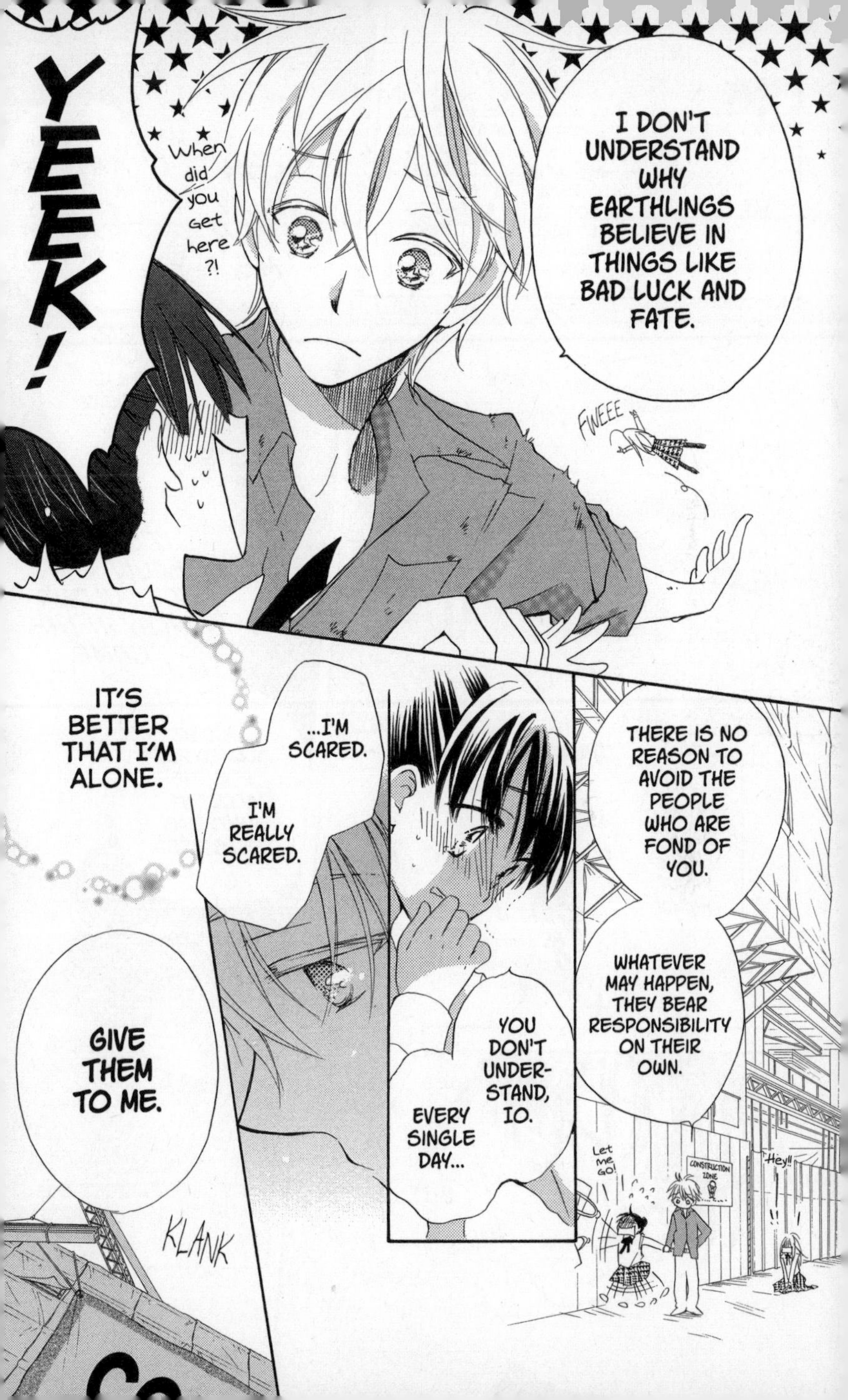
I DON'T UNDERSTAND WHY EARTHLINGS BELIEVE IN THINGS LIKE BAD LUCK AND FATE.
FWEEE
YEEK!
When did you get here?!
THERE IS NO REASON TO AVOID THE PEOPLE WHO ARE FOND OF YOU.
WHATEVER MAY HAPPEN, THEY BEAR RESPONSIBILITY ON THEIR OWN.
Hey!!
CONSTRUCTION ZONE
Let me GO!
...I'M SCARED.
I'M REALLY SCARED.
YOU DON'T UNDER-STAND, IO.
EVERY SINGLE DAY...
IT'S BETTER THAT I'M ALONE.
GIVE THEM TO ME.
KLANK

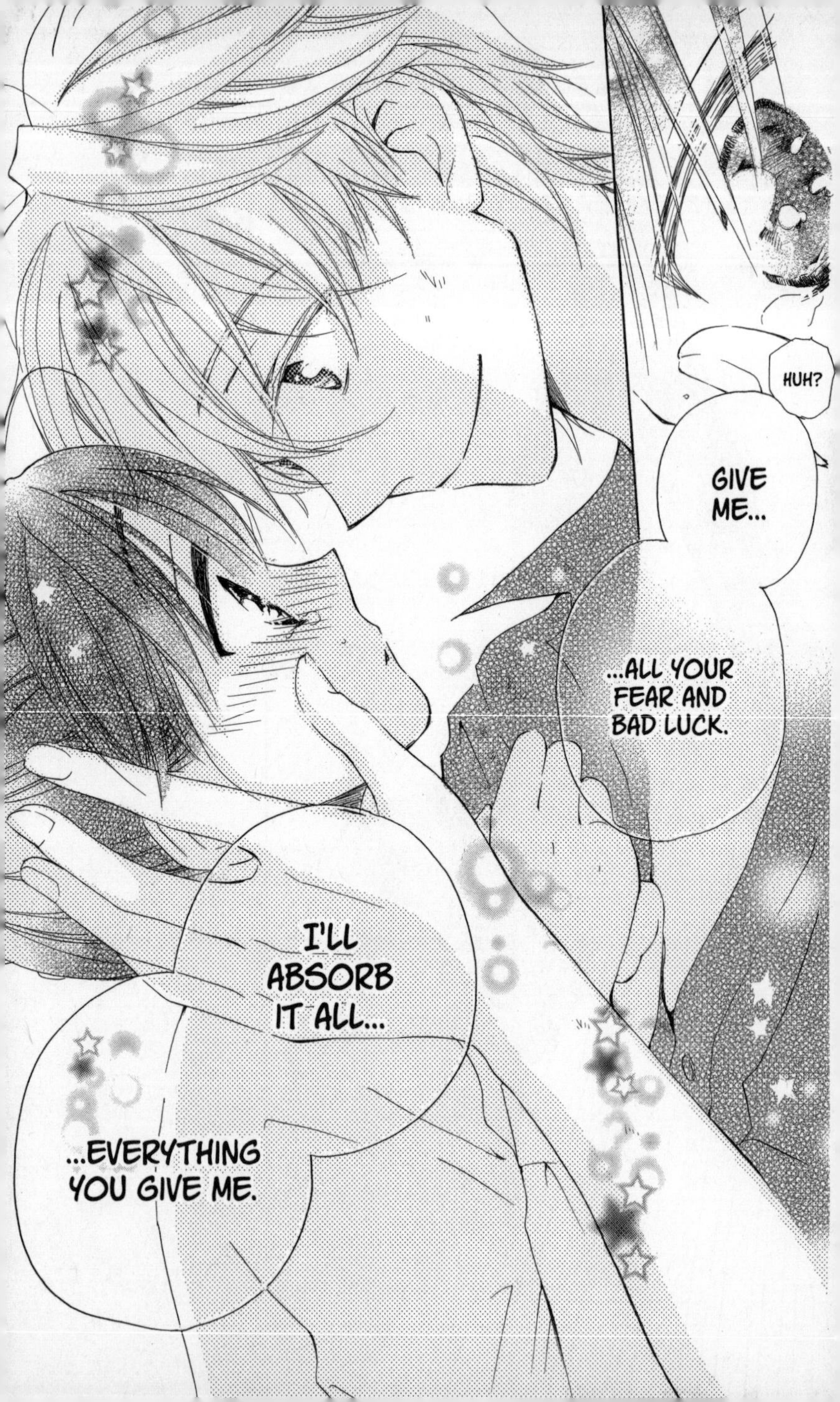
HUH?
GIVE ME...
...ALL YOUR FEAR AND BAD LUCK.
I'LL ABSORB IT ALL...
...EVERYTHING YOU GIVE ME.

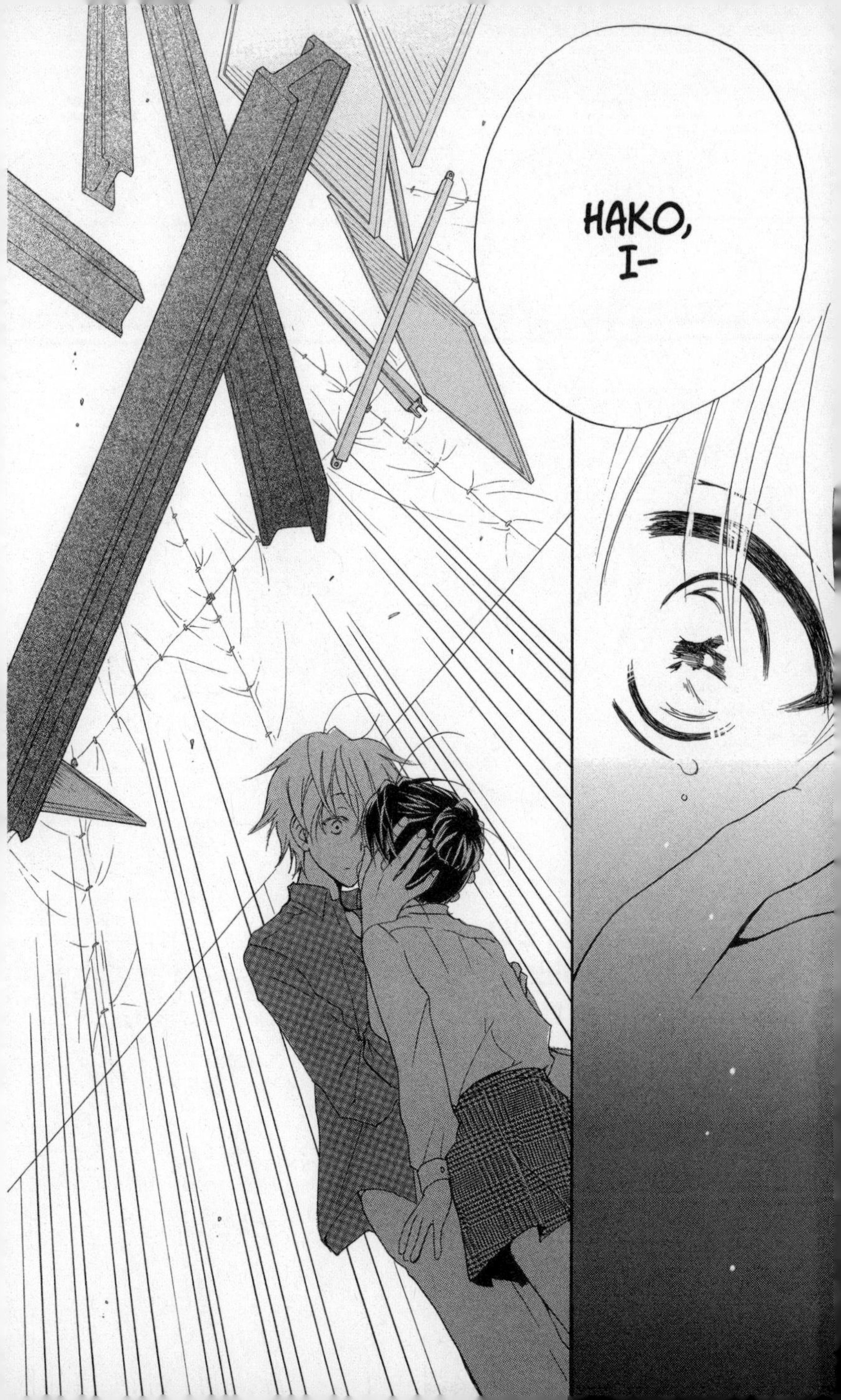
HAKO, I-

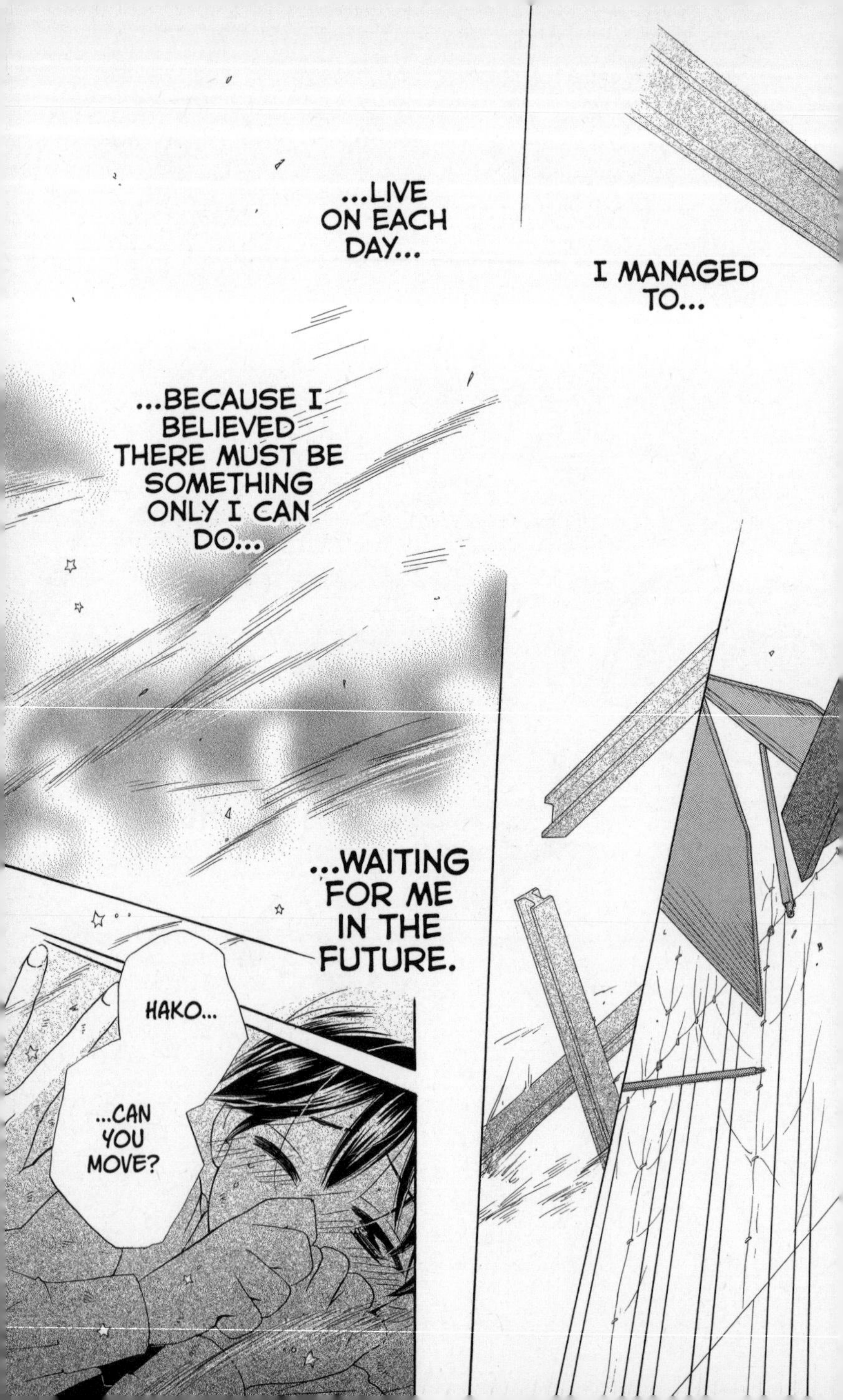
I MANAGED TO...
...LIVE ON EACH DAY...
...BECAUSE I BELIEVED THERE MUST BE SOMETHING ONLY I CAN DO...
...WAITING FOR ME IN THE FUTURE.
HAKO...
...CAN YOU MOVE?

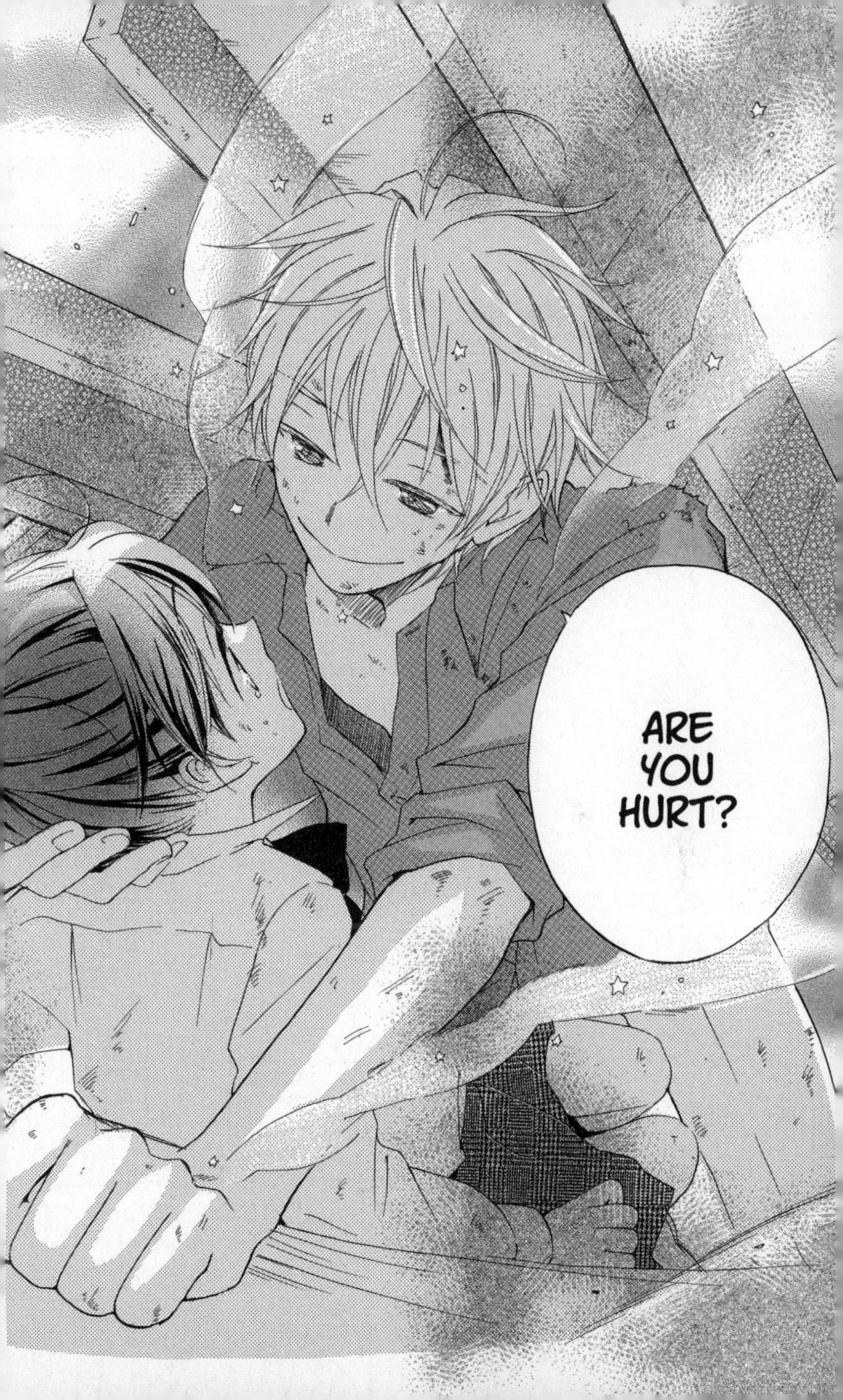
ARE YOU HURT?

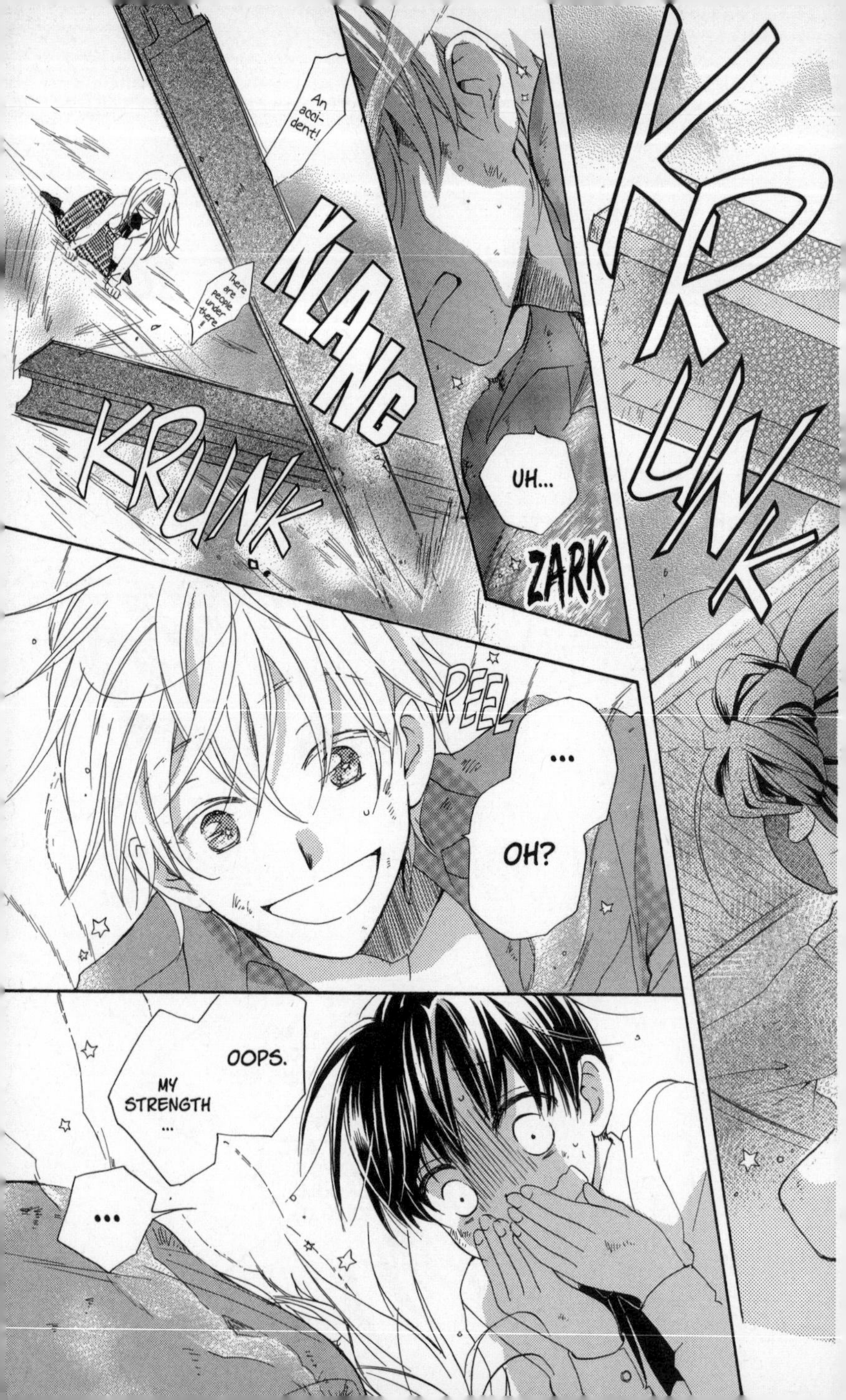
KRUNK
UH...
ZARK
An accident!
There are people under there!!
KLANG
KRUNK
REEL
...
OH?
OOPS.
MY STRENGTH...
...

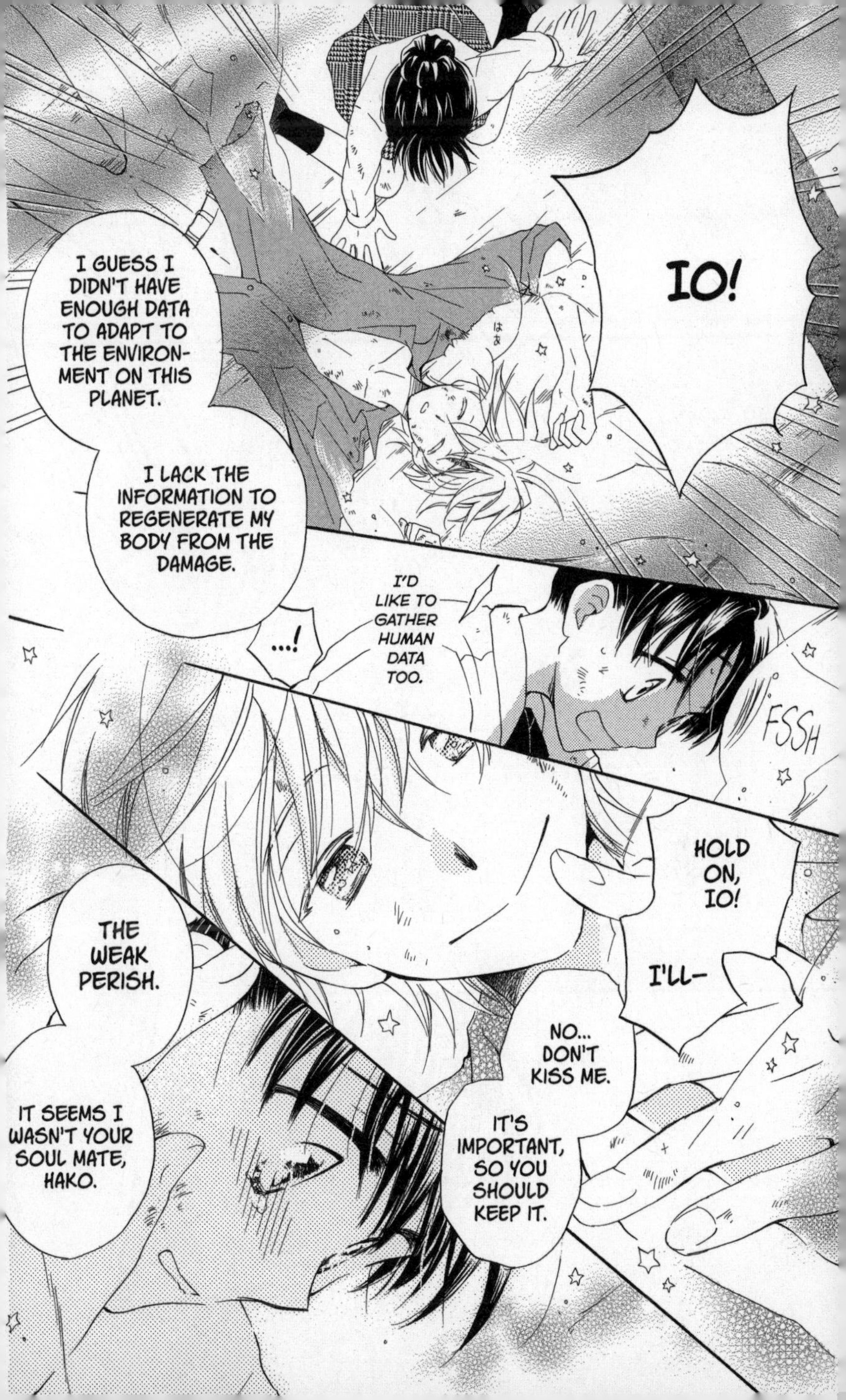
IO!
I GUESS I DIDN'T HAVE ENOUGH DATA TO ADAPT TO THE ENVIRON-MENT ON THIS PLANET.
I LACK THE INFORMATION TO REGENERATE MY BODY FROM THE DAMAGE.
FSSH
I'D LIKE TO GATHER HUMAN DATA TOO.
...!
HOLD ON, IO!
I'LL-
NO... DON'T KISS ME.
IT'S IMPORTANT, SO YOU SHOULD KEEP IT.
THE WEAK PERISH.
IT SEEMS I WASN'T YOUR SOUL MATE, HAKO.

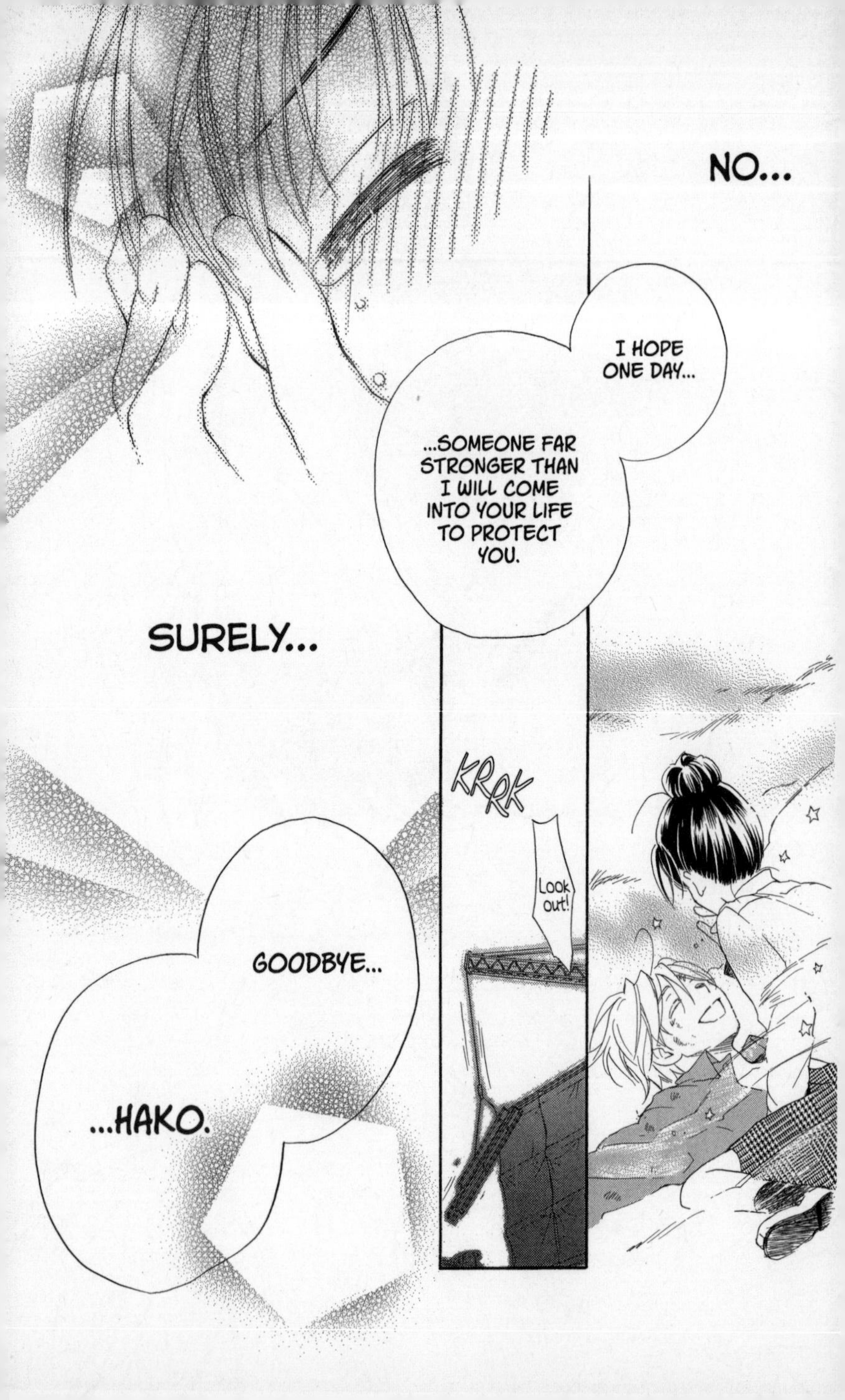
NO...
I HOPE ONE DAY...
...SOMEONE FAR STRONGER THAN I WILL COME INTO YOUR LIFE TO PROTECT YOU.
KRRK
Look out!
SURELY...
GOODBYE...
...HAKO.

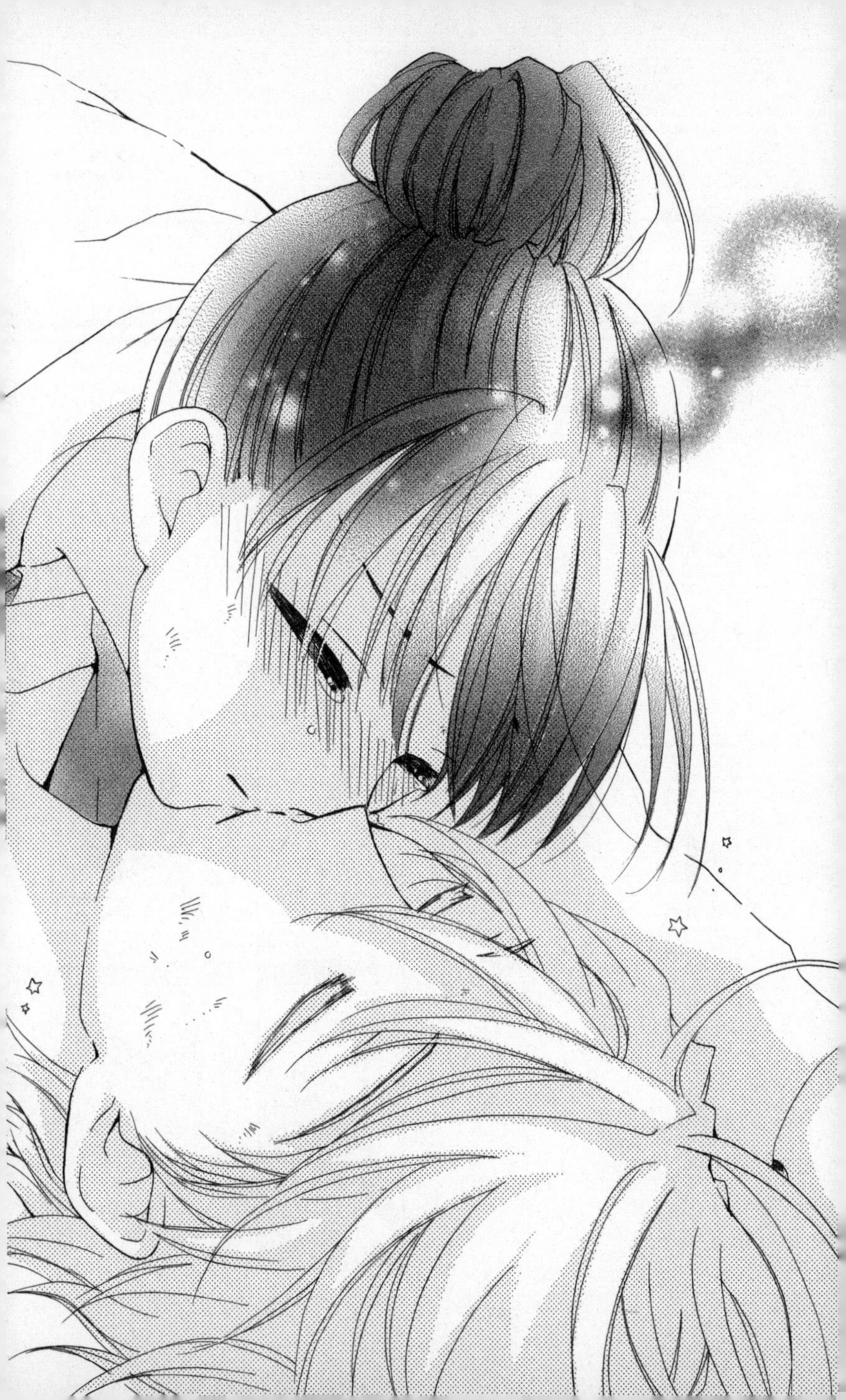

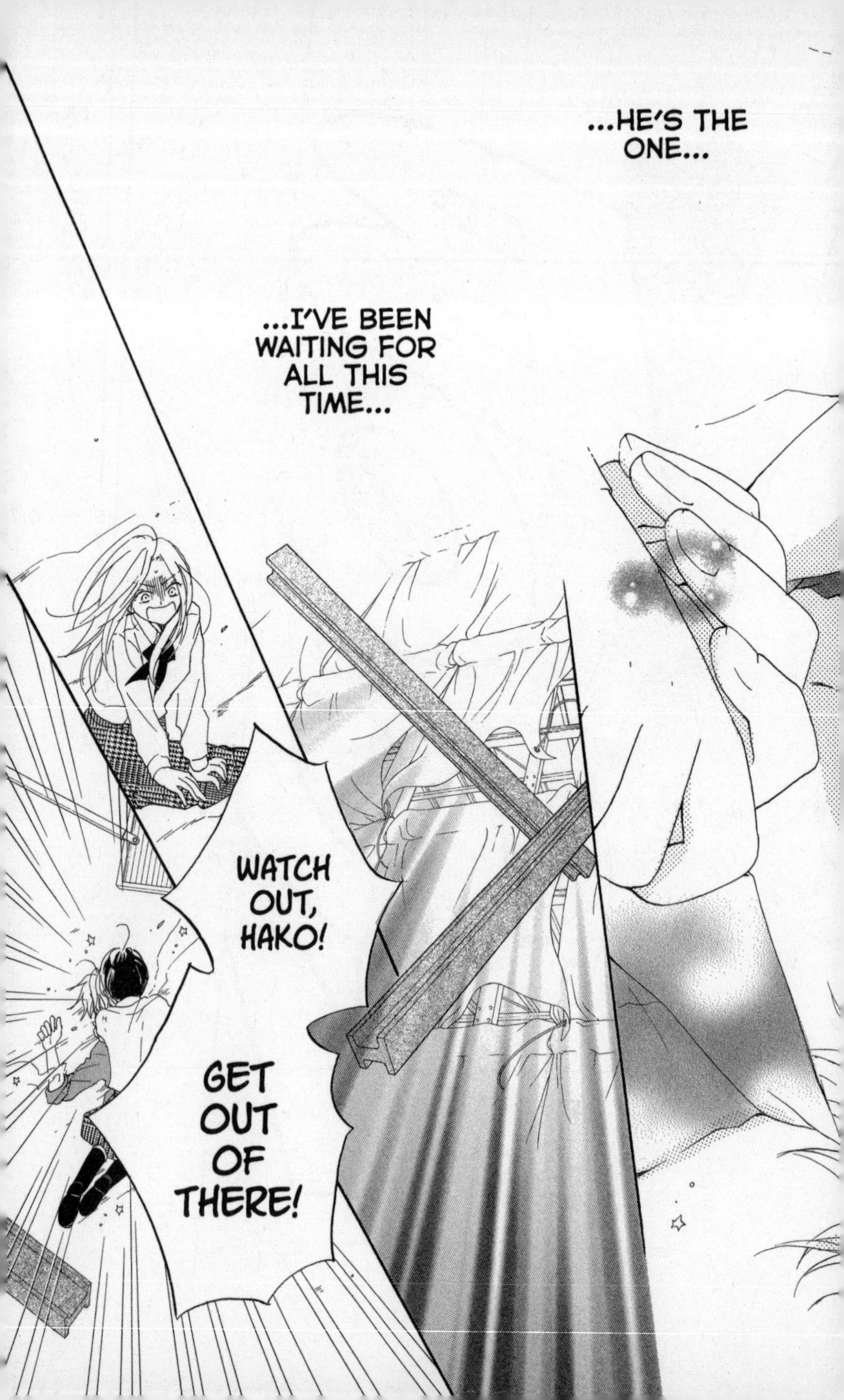
...HE'S THE ONE...
...I'VE BEEN WAITING FOR ALL THIS TIME...
WATCH OUT, HAKO!
GET OUT OF THERE!

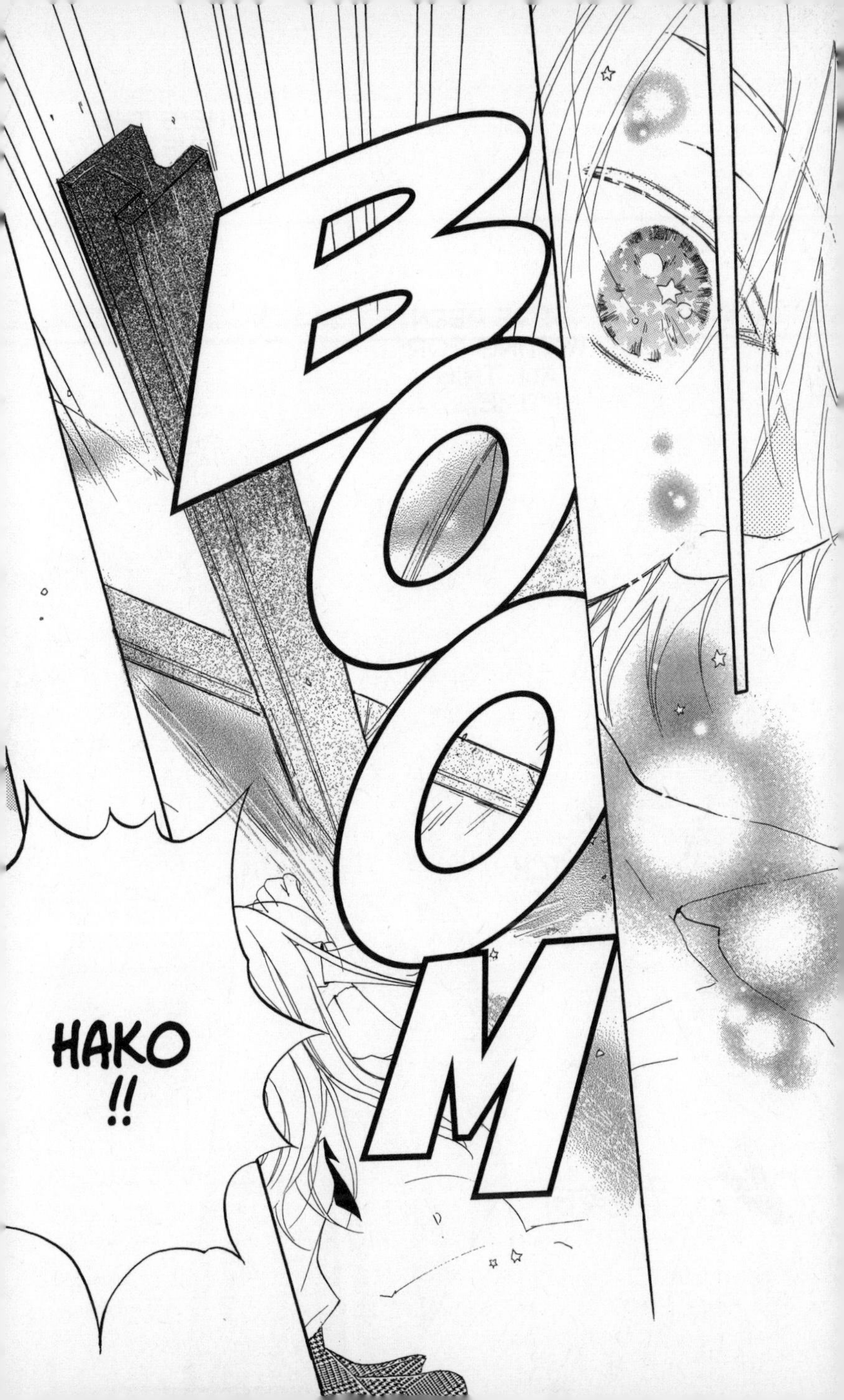
BOOM
HAKO !!

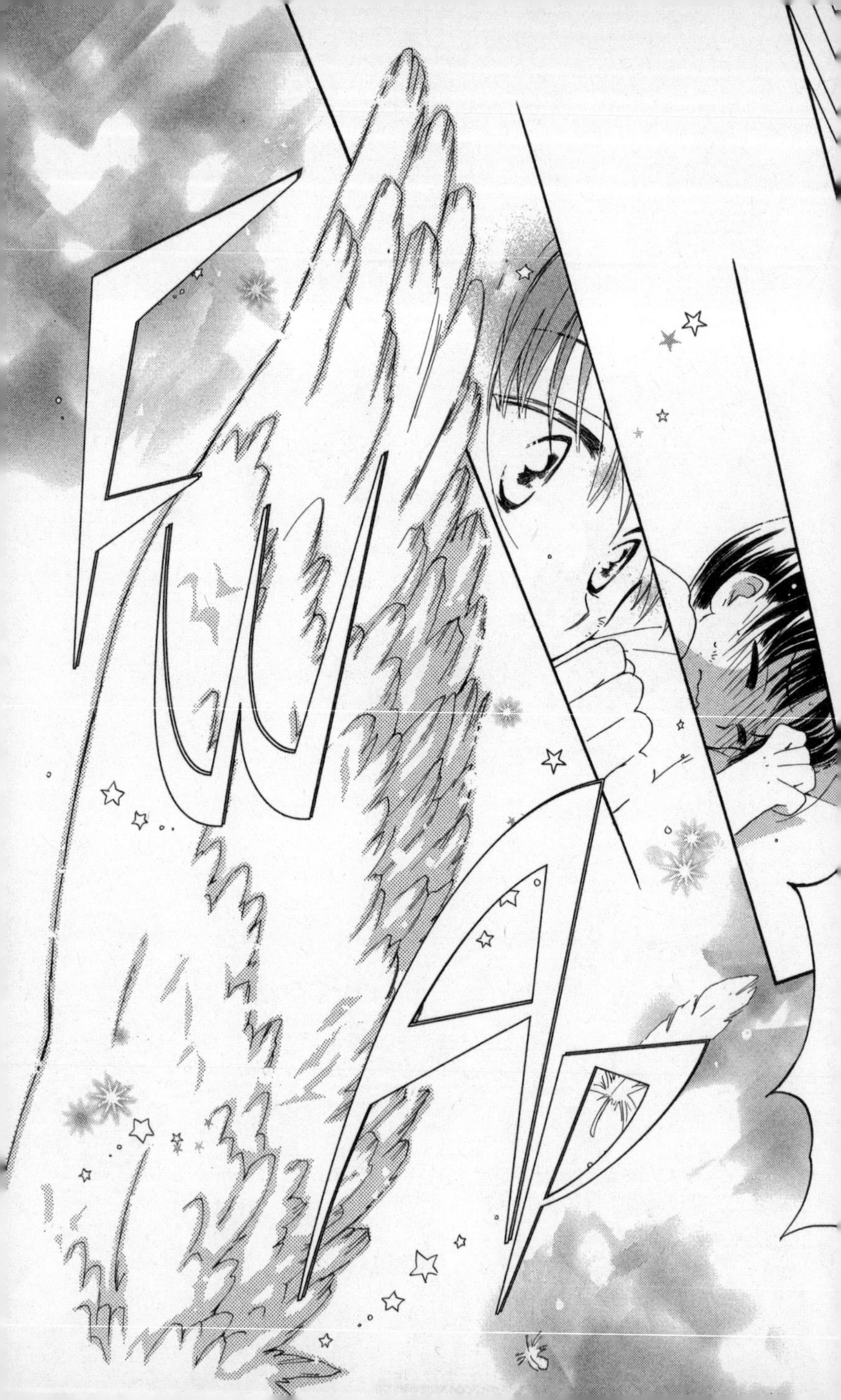
FWAA

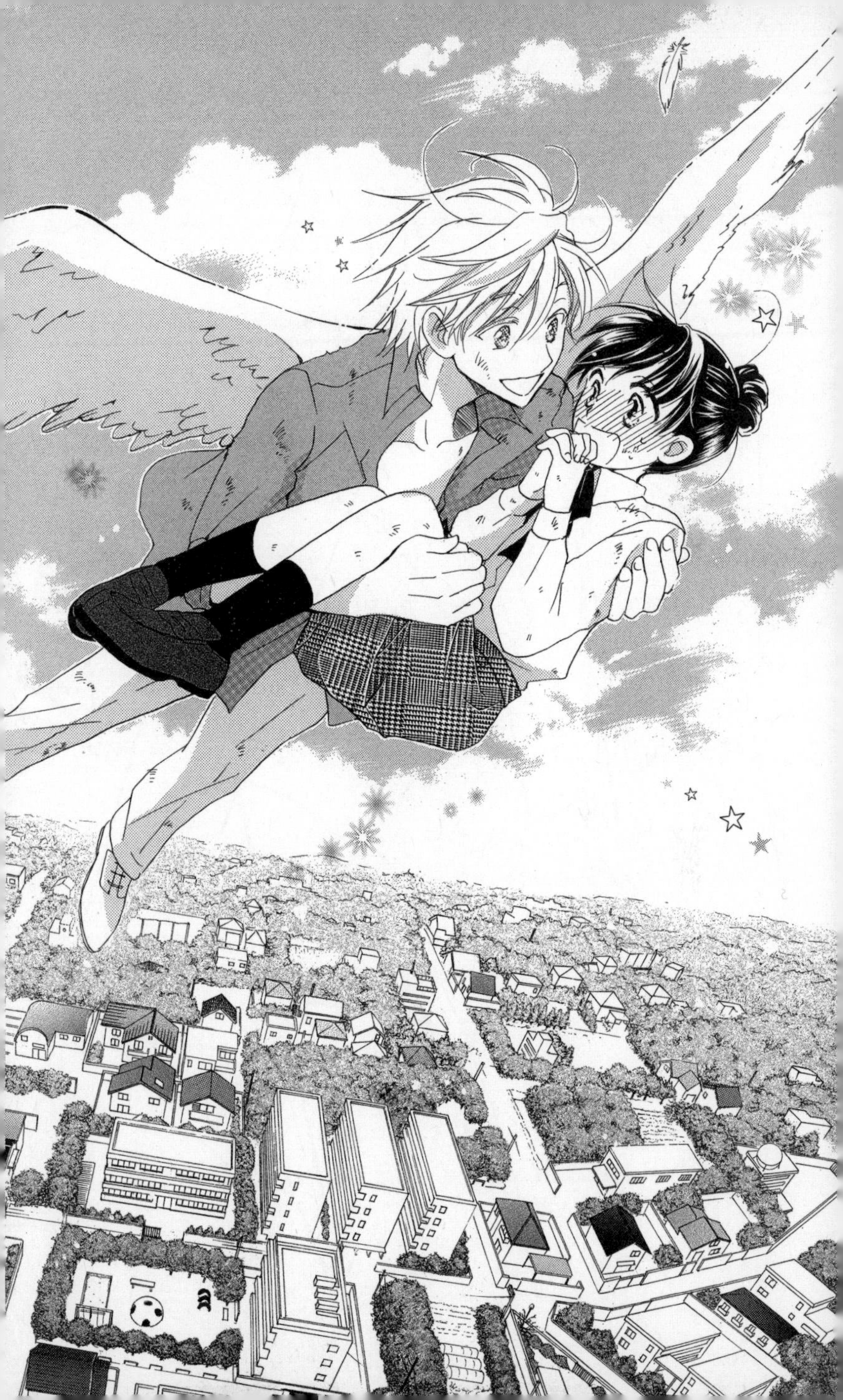

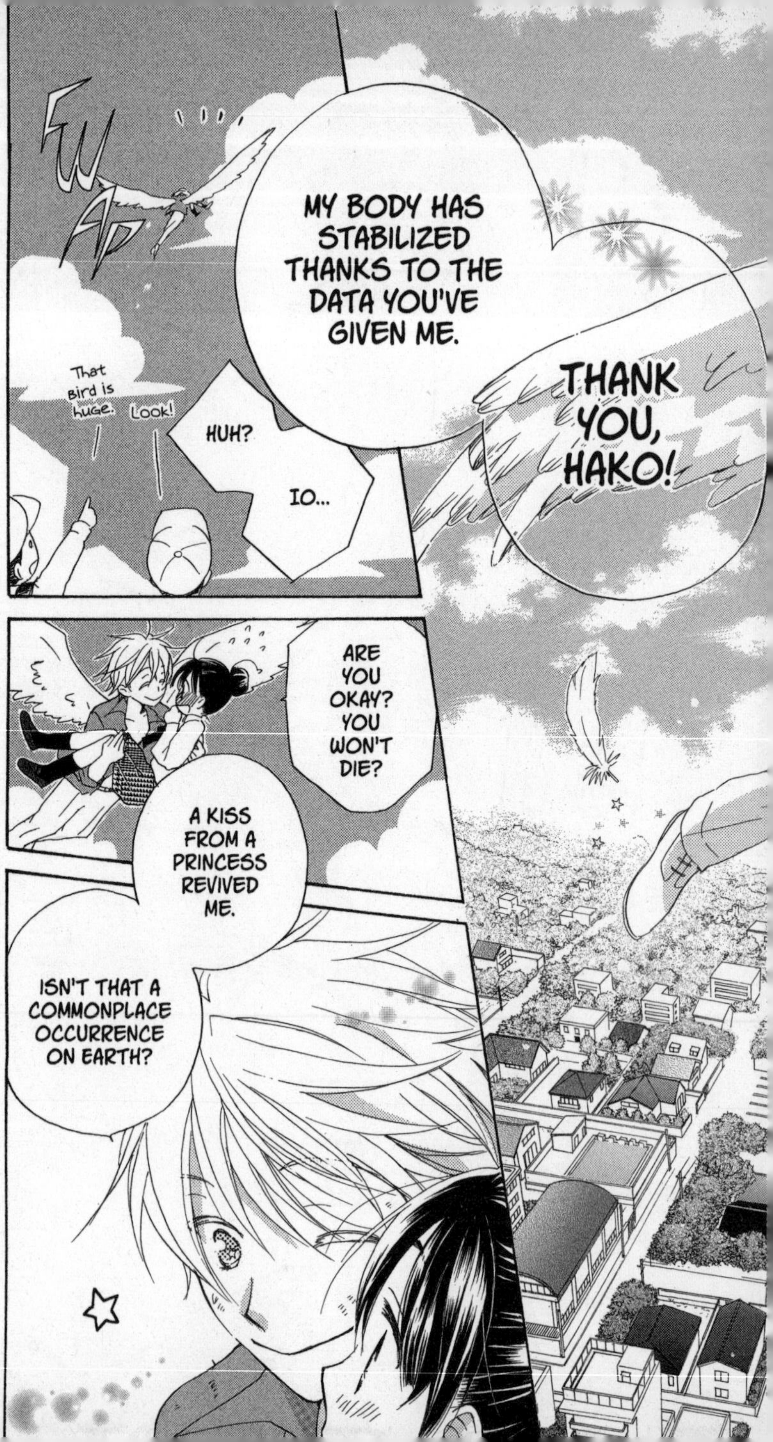
MY BODY HAS STABILIZED THANKS TO THE DATA YOU'VE GIVEN ME.
THANK YOU, HAKO!
FWAP
Look!
That bird is huge.
HUH?
IO...
ARE YOU OKAY? YOU WON'T DIE?
A KISS FROM A PRINCESS REVIVED ME.
ISN'T THAT A COMMONPLACE OCCURRENCE ON EARTH?

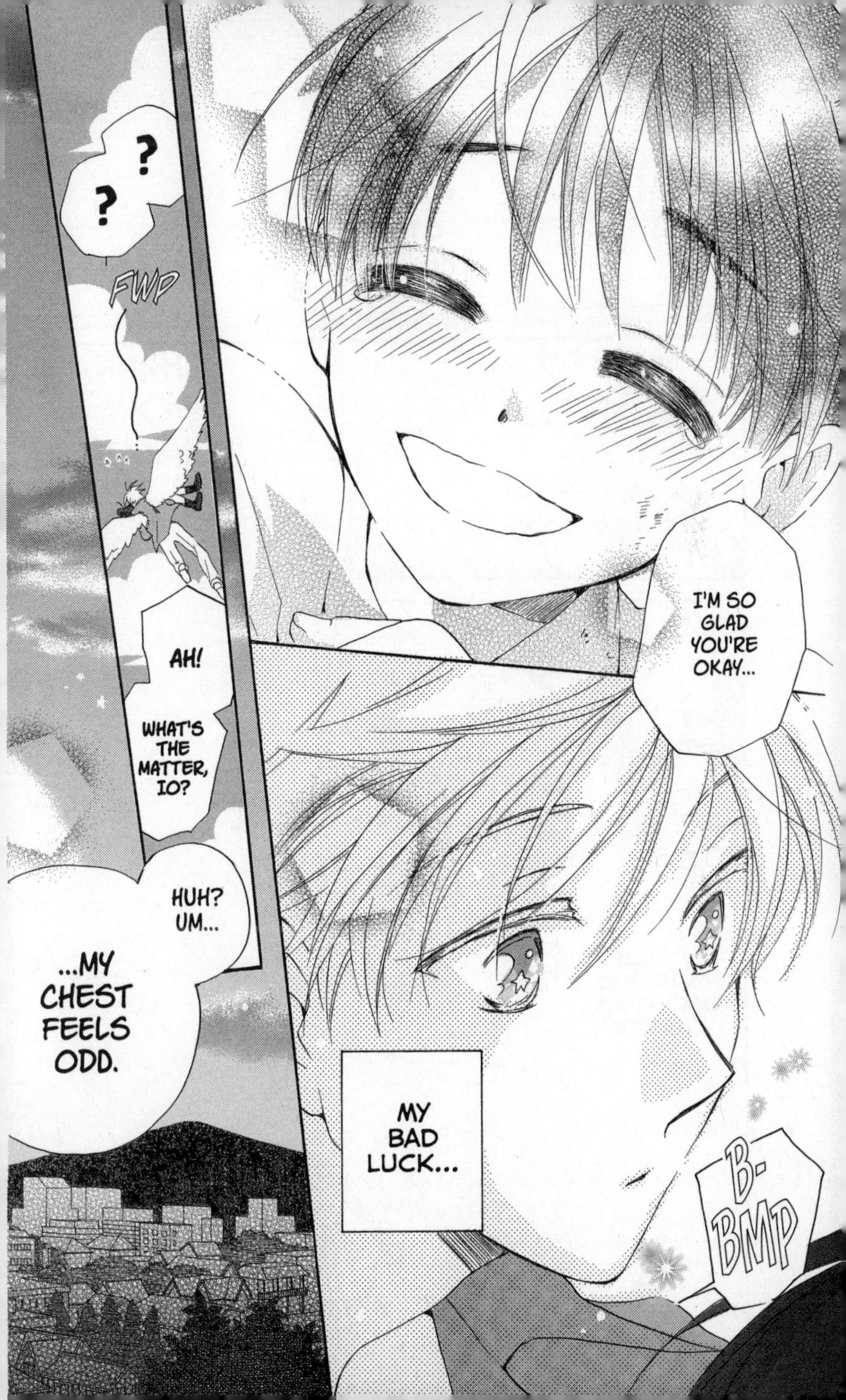
I'M SO GLAD YOU'RE OKAY...
MY BAD LUCK...
B-BMP
? ?
FWP
AH!
WHAT'S THE MATTER, IO?
HUH? UM...
...MY CHEST FEELS ODD.

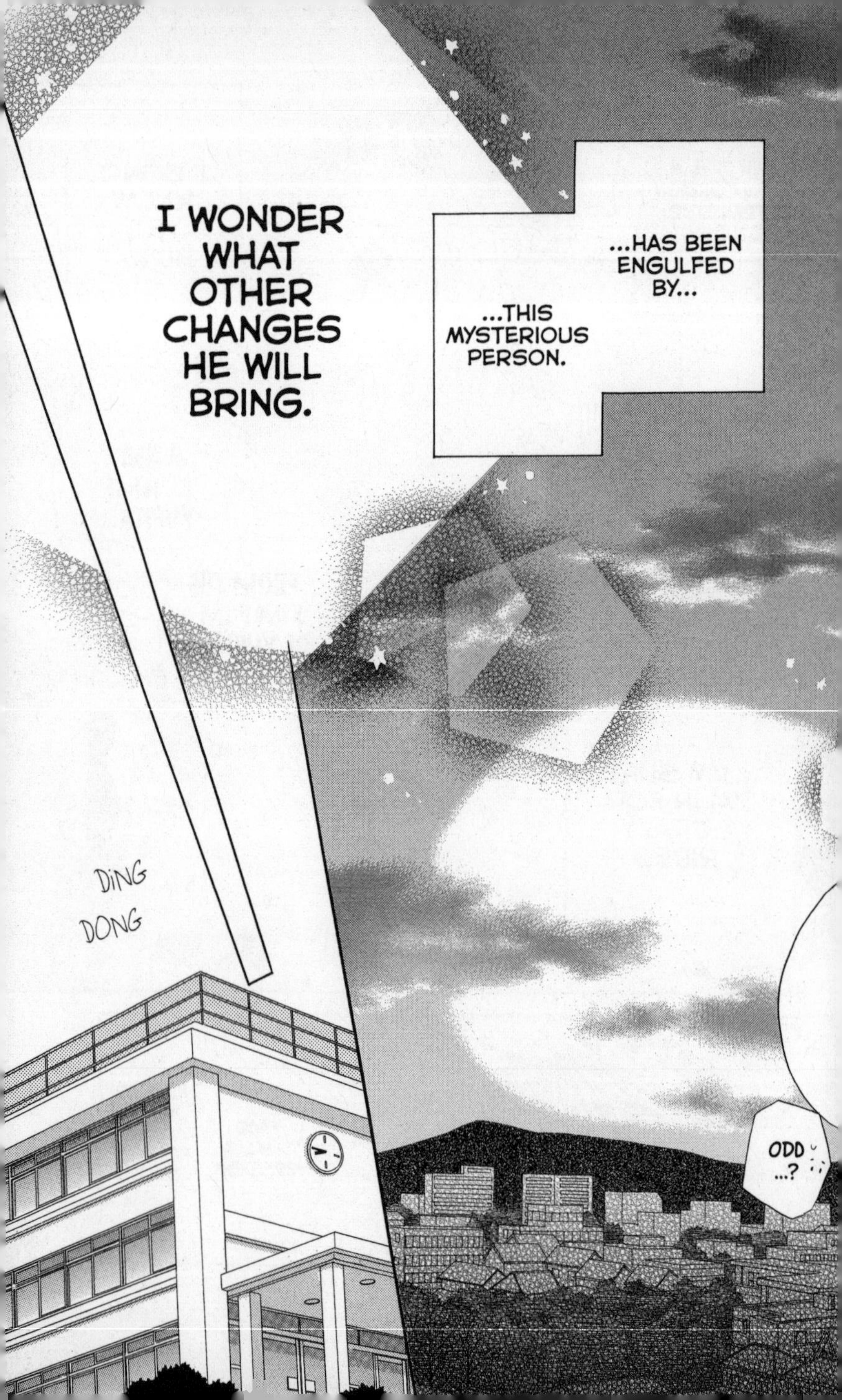
...HAS BEEN ENGULFED BY...
...THIS MYSTERIOUS PERSON.
I WONDER WHAT OTHER CHANGES HE WILL BRING.
ODD ...?
DING DONG

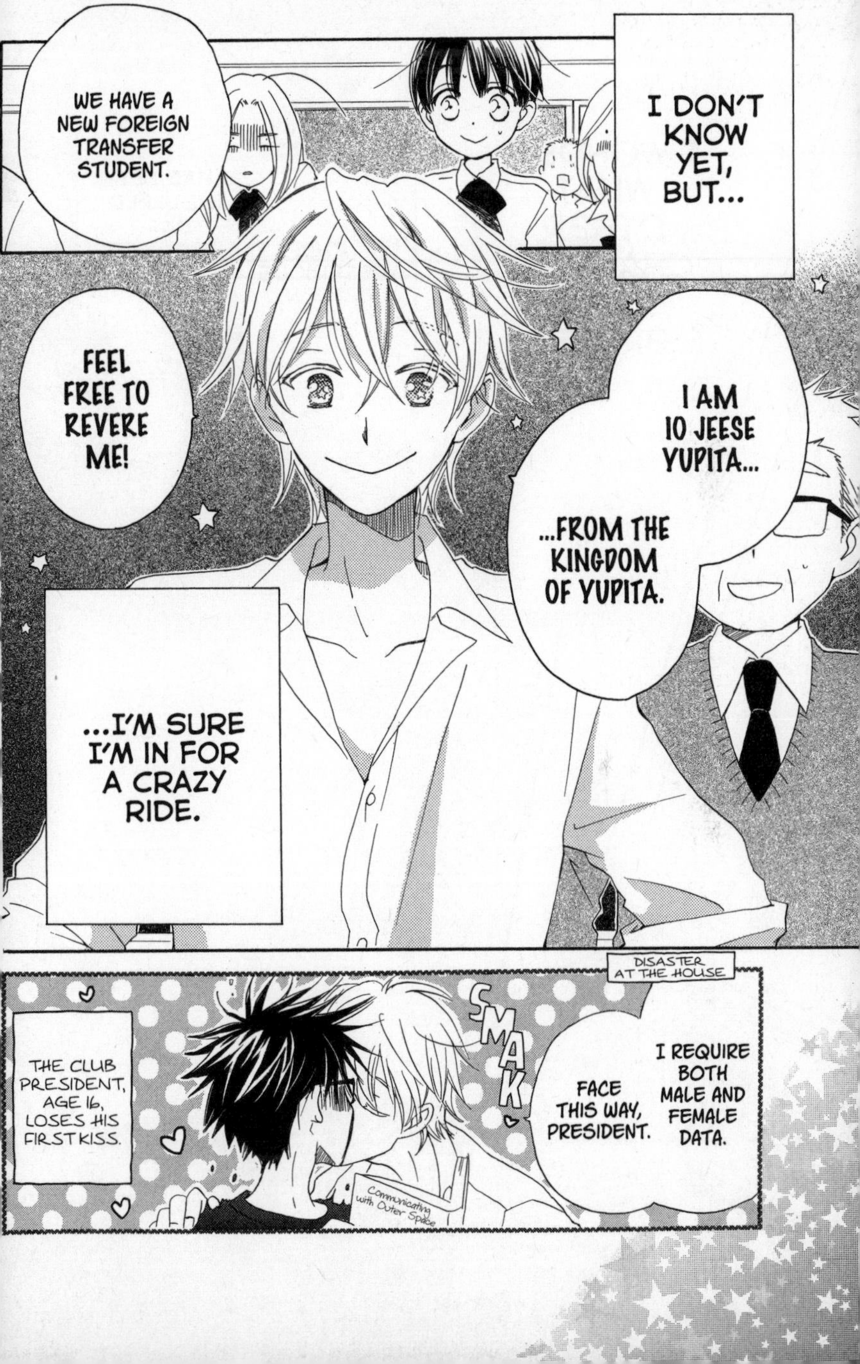
I DON'T KNOW YET, BUT...
WE HAVE A NEW FOREIGN TRANSFER STUDENT.
I AM IO JEESE YUPITA...
...FROM THE KINGDOM OF YUPITA.
FEEL FREE TO REVERE ME!
...I'M SURE I'M IN FOR A CRAZY RIDE.
DISASTER AT THE HOUSE
I REQUIRE BOTH MALE AND FEMALE DATA.
FACE THIS WAY, PRESIDENT.
SMAK
Communicating with Outer Space
THE CLUB PRESIDENT, AGE 16, LOSES HIS FIRST KISS.

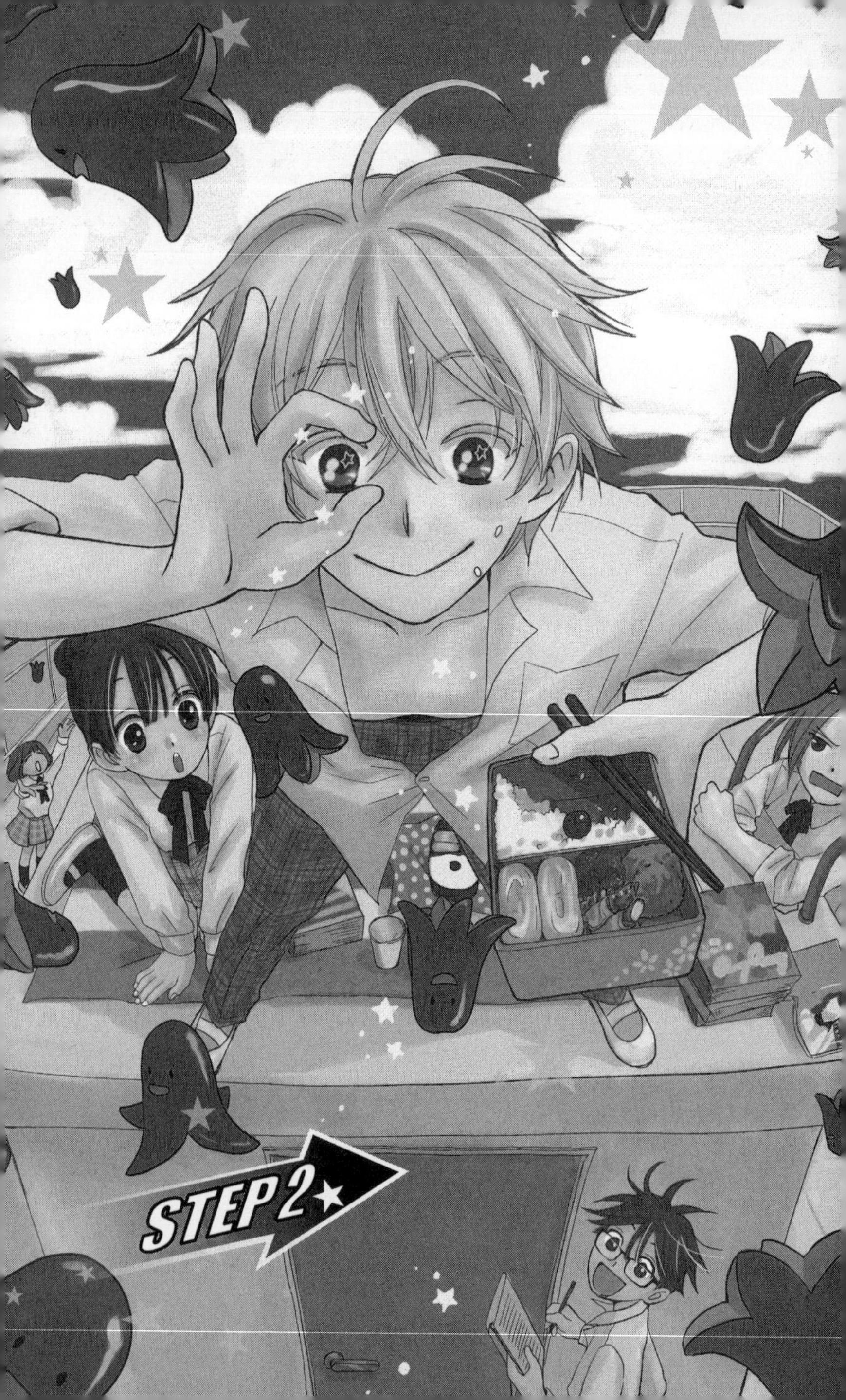
STEP 2★

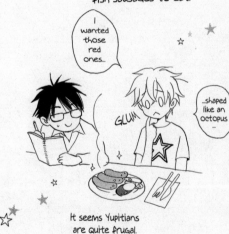

THE PRESIDENT'S OBSERVATION DIARY

I gave him some gourmet fish sausages to eat.

I wanted those red ones...

...shaped like an octopus—

GLUM

It seems Yupitians are quite frugal.

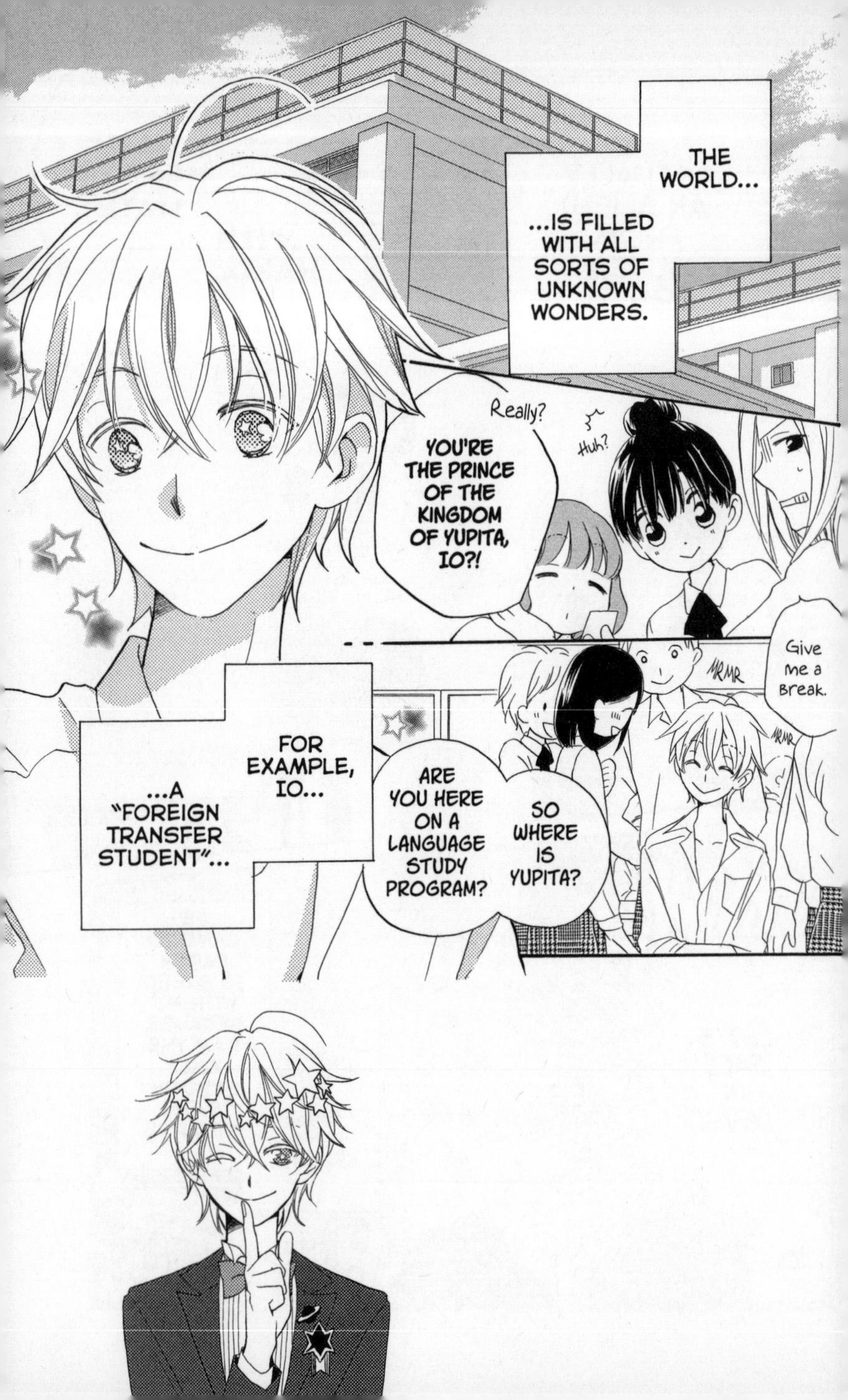
THE WORLD...
...IS FILLED WITH ALL SORTS OF UNKNOWN WONDERS.
Huh?
Really?
YOU'RE THE PRINCE OF THE KINGDOM OF YUPITA, IO?!
Give me a break.
MRMR
MRMR
SO WHERE IS YUPITA?
ARE YOU HERE ON A LANGUAGE STUDY PROGRAM?
FOR EXAMPLE, IO...
...A "FOREIGN TRANSFER STUDENT"...

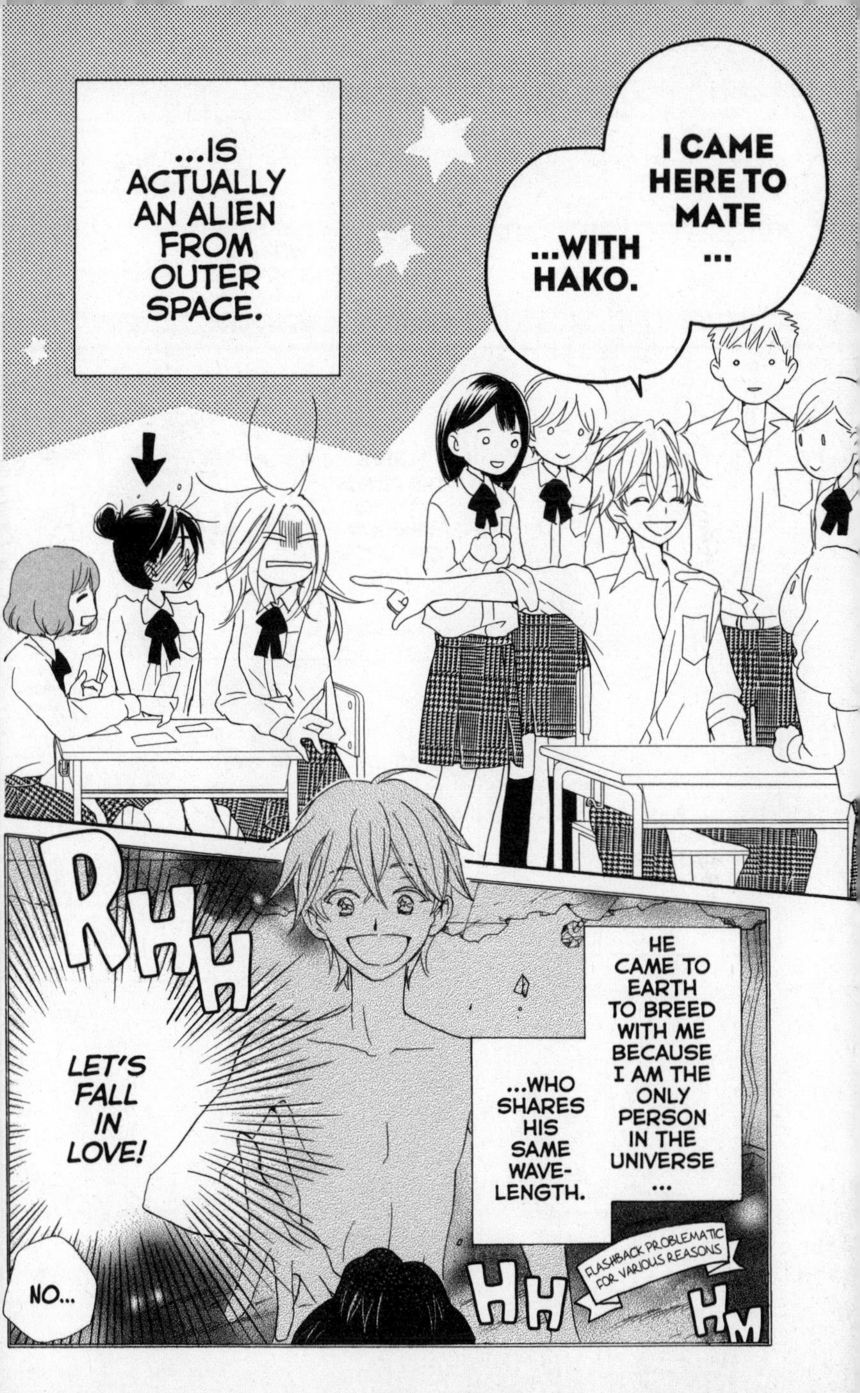
I CAME HERE TO MATE ...
...WITH HAKO.
...IS ACTUALLY AN ALIEN FROM OUTER SPACE.
HE CAME TO EARTH TO BREED WITH ME BECAUSE I AM THE ONLY PERSON IN THE UNIVERSE ...
...WHO SHARES HIS SAME WAVE-LENGTH.
FLASHBACK PROBLEMATIC FOR VARIOUS REASONS
RHHH
LET'S FALL IN LOVE!
HH
HM
NO...

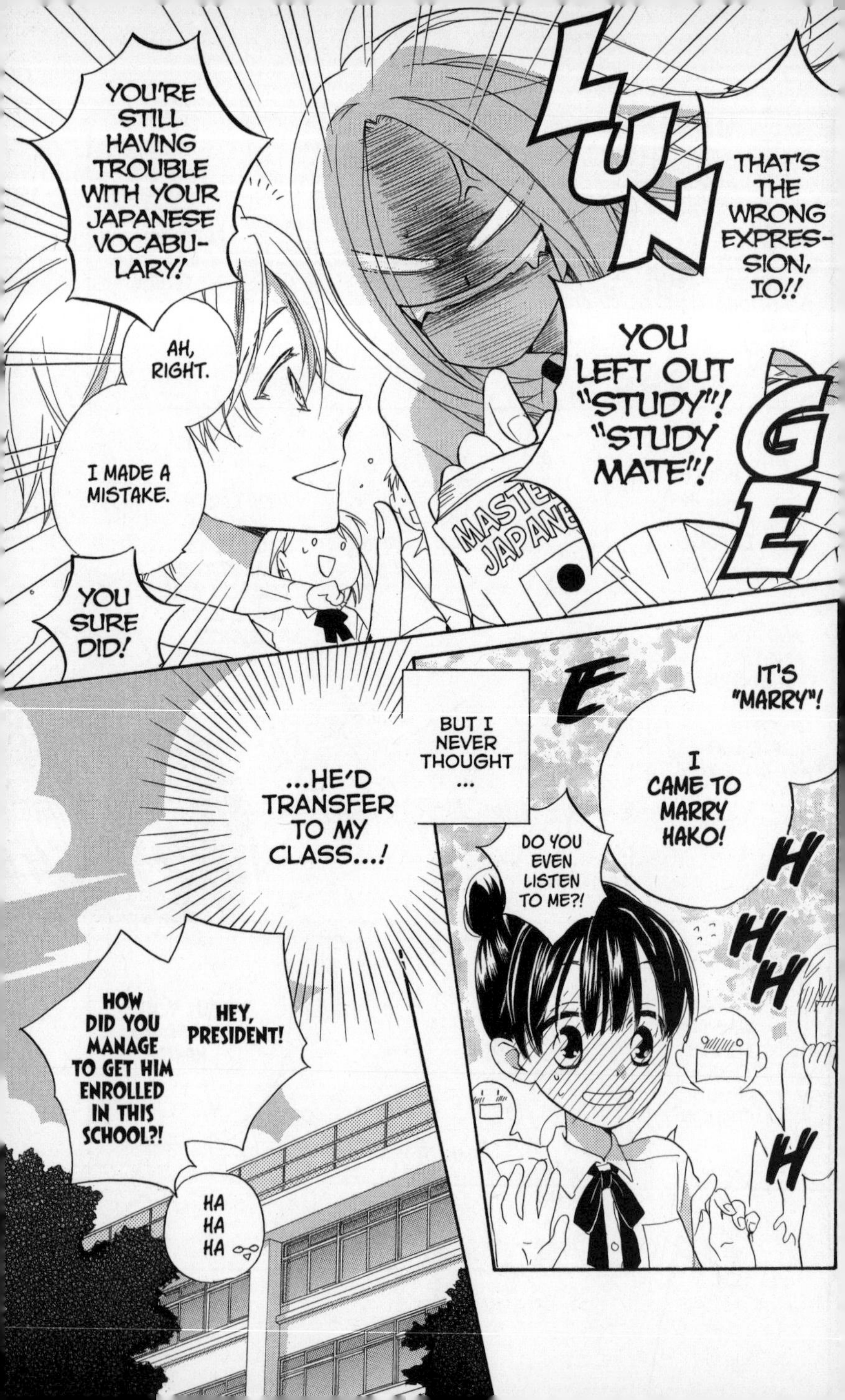
THAT'S THE WRONG EXPRESSION, IO!!
LUN
YOU LEFT OUT "STUDY"! "STUDY MATE"!
GE
YOU'RE STILL HAVING TROUBLE WITH YOUR JAPANESE VOCABULARY!
AH, RIGHT.
I MADE A MISTAKE.
YOU SURE DID!
IT'S "MARRY"!
I CAME TO MARRY HAKO!
E
HHHHH
DO YOU EVEN LISTEN TO ME?!
BUT I NEVER THOUGHT...
...HE'D TRANSFER TO MY CLASS...!
HEY, PRESIDENT!
HOW DID YOU MANAGE TO GET HIM ENROLLED IN THIS SCHOOL?!
HA HA HA

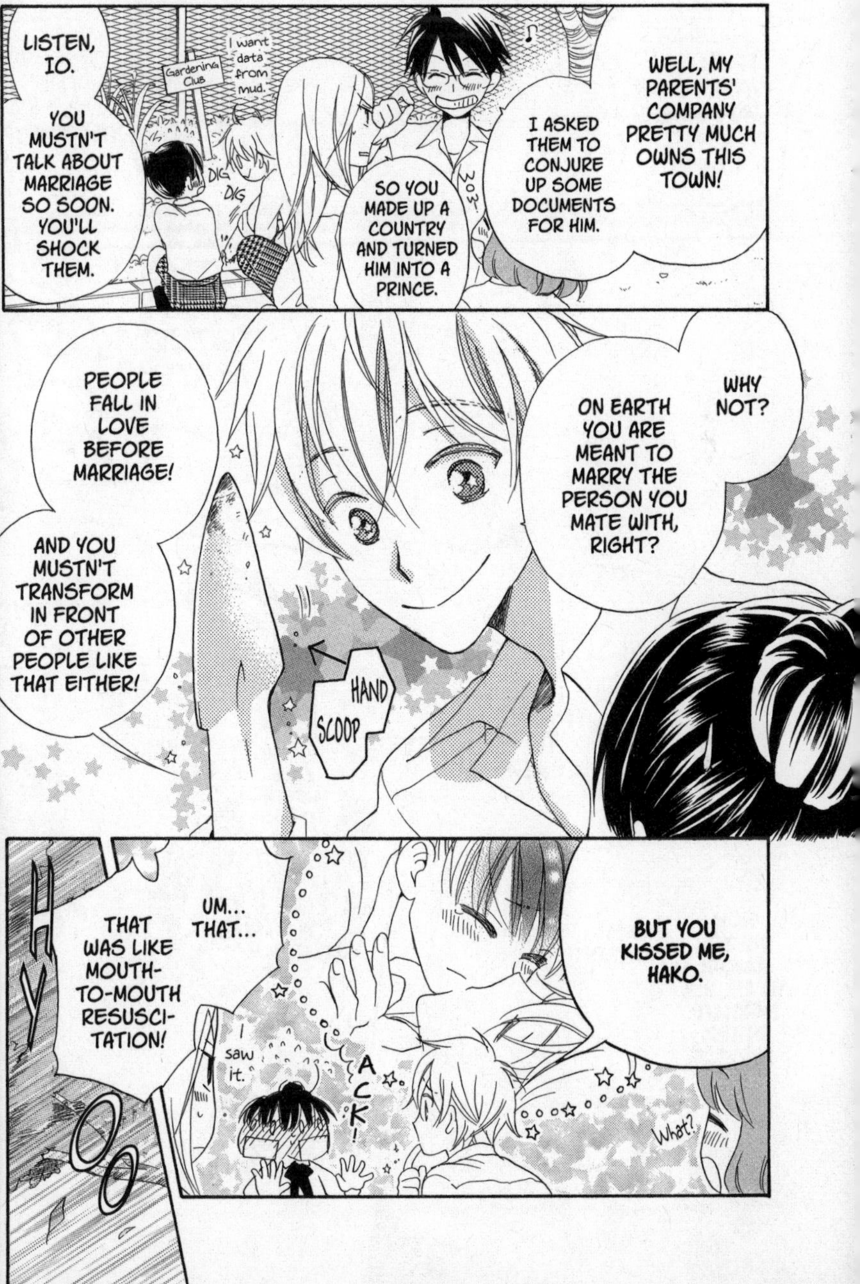
WELL, MY PARENTS' COMPANY PRETTY MUCH OWNS THIS TOWN!
I ASKED THEM TO CONJURE UP SOME DOCUMENTS FOR HIM.
SO YOU MADE UP A COUNTRY AND TURNED HIM INTO A PRINCE.
I want data from mud.
Gardening Club
DIG
DIG
LISTEN, IO.
YOU MUSTN'T TALK ABOUT MARRIAGE SO SOON. YOU'LL SHOCK THEM.
WHY NOT?
ON EARTH YOU ARE MEANT TO MARRY THE PERSON YOU MATE WITH, RIGHT?
HAND SCOOP
PEOPLE FALL IN LOVE BEFORE MARRIAGE!
AND YOU MUSTN'T TRANSFORM IN FRONT OF OTHER PEOPLE LIKE THAT EITHER!
BUT YOU KISSED ME, HAKO.
What?
ACK!
UM... THAT...
I saw it.
THAT WAS LIKE MOUTH-TO-MOUTH RESUSCITATION!
HYOO

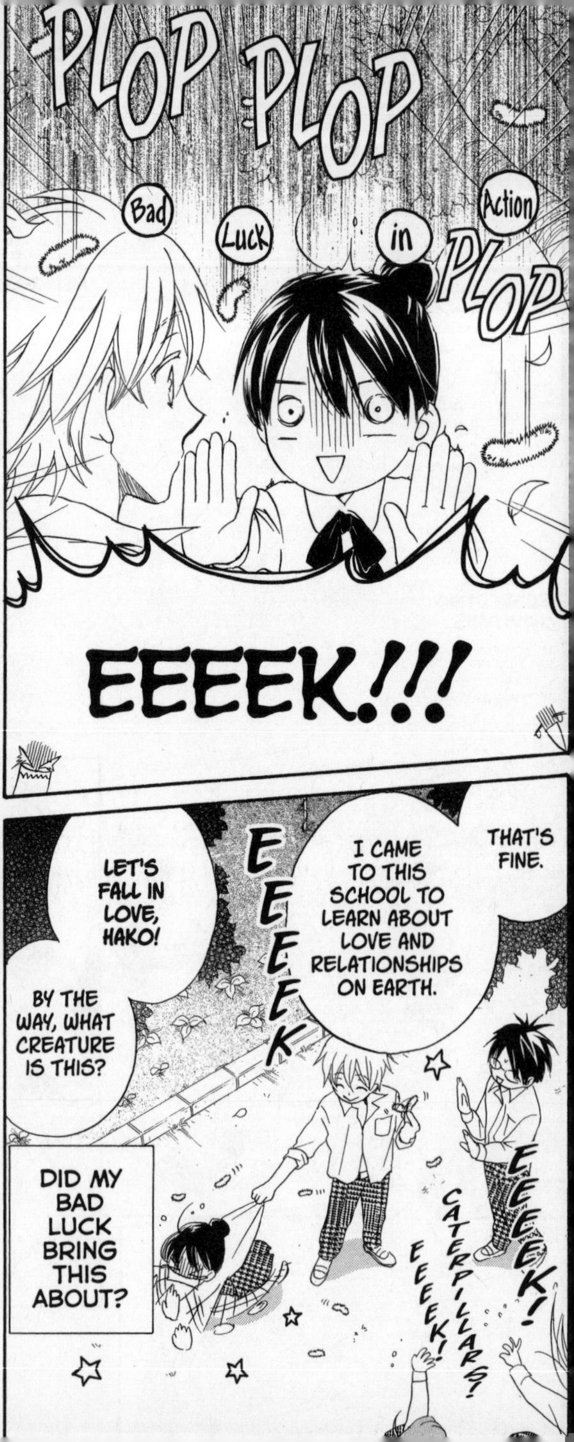
PLOP PLOP
Bad Luck in Action
PLOP
EEEEK!!!
THAT'S FINE.
I CAME TO THIS SCHOOL TO LEARN ABOUT LOVE AND RELATIONSHIPS ON EARTH.
EEEEEK
LET'S FALL IN LOVE, HAKO!
BY THE WAY, WHAT CREATURE IS THIS?
EEEEK!
CATERPILLARS!
EEEEK!
DID MY BAD LUCK BRING THIS ABOUT?

Time Out 2

My tour of Italy was a pretty busy since we travelled south from Milano → Venice → Florence → Rome. But it was my first time in Europe, so it was a very fulfilling and exciting experience.

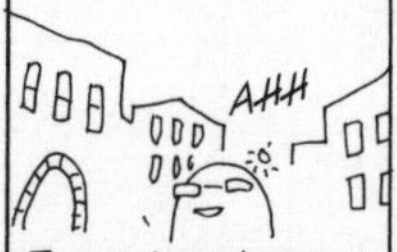
AHH

Everywhere I looked it was like being in a picture book. I was totally enchanted. But I was met by an awful lightning storm in Rome...

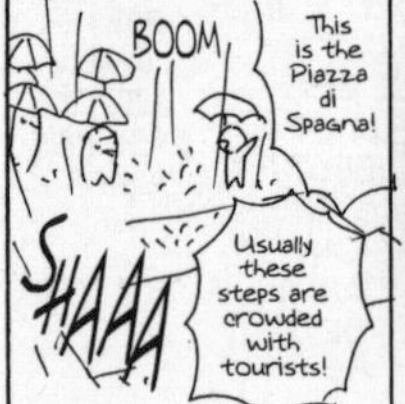
BOOM
This is the Piazza di Spagna!
SHAAA
Usually these steps are crowded with tourists!

The place was deserted...

I liked Florence the most of all the cities I visited. It's a small city without too much traffic, so I was able to relax and enjoy sightseeing. I wish I could've spent a whole day looking around the Uffizi Gallery.

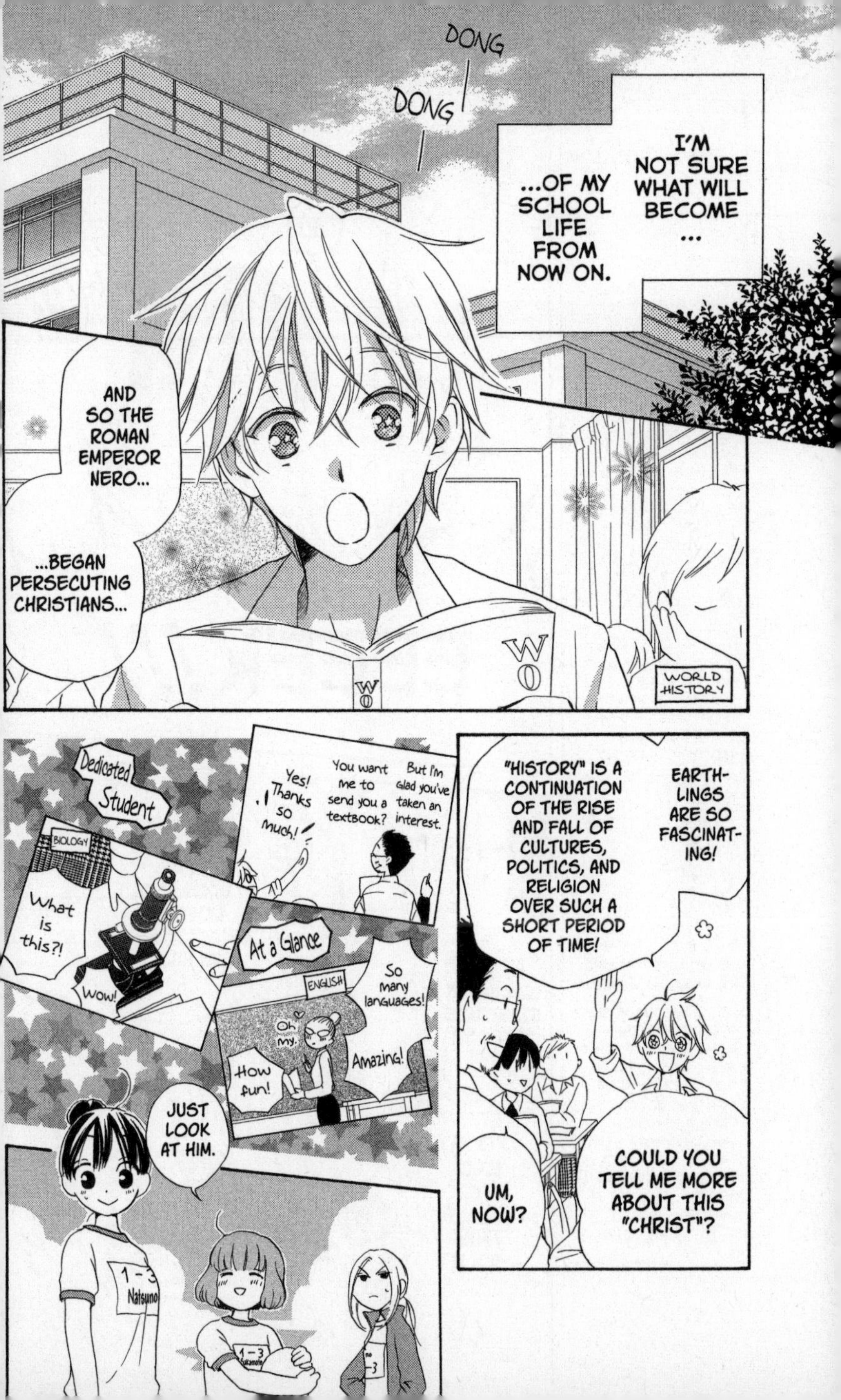
DONG
DONG
I'M NOT SURE WHAT WILL BECOME...
...OF MY SCHOOL LIFE FROM NOW ON.
AND SO THE ROMAN EMPEROR NERO...
...BEGAN PERSECUTING CHRISTIANS...
WORLD HISTORY
EARTH-LINGS ARE SO FASCINAT-ING!
"HISTORY" IS A CONTINUATION OF THE RISE AND FALL OF CULTURES, POLITICS, AND RELIGION OVER SUCH A SHORT PERIOD OF TIME!
COULD YOU TELL ME MORE ABOUT THIS "CHRIST"?
UM, NOW?
Dedicated Student
But I'm Glad you've taken an interest.
You want me to send you a textbook?
Yes! Thanks so much!
BIOLOGY
What is this?!
Wow!
At a Glance
ENGLISH
So many languages!
Amazing!
Oh my.
How fun!
JUST LOOK AT HIM.
1-3 Natsuno
1-3 Sakamoto

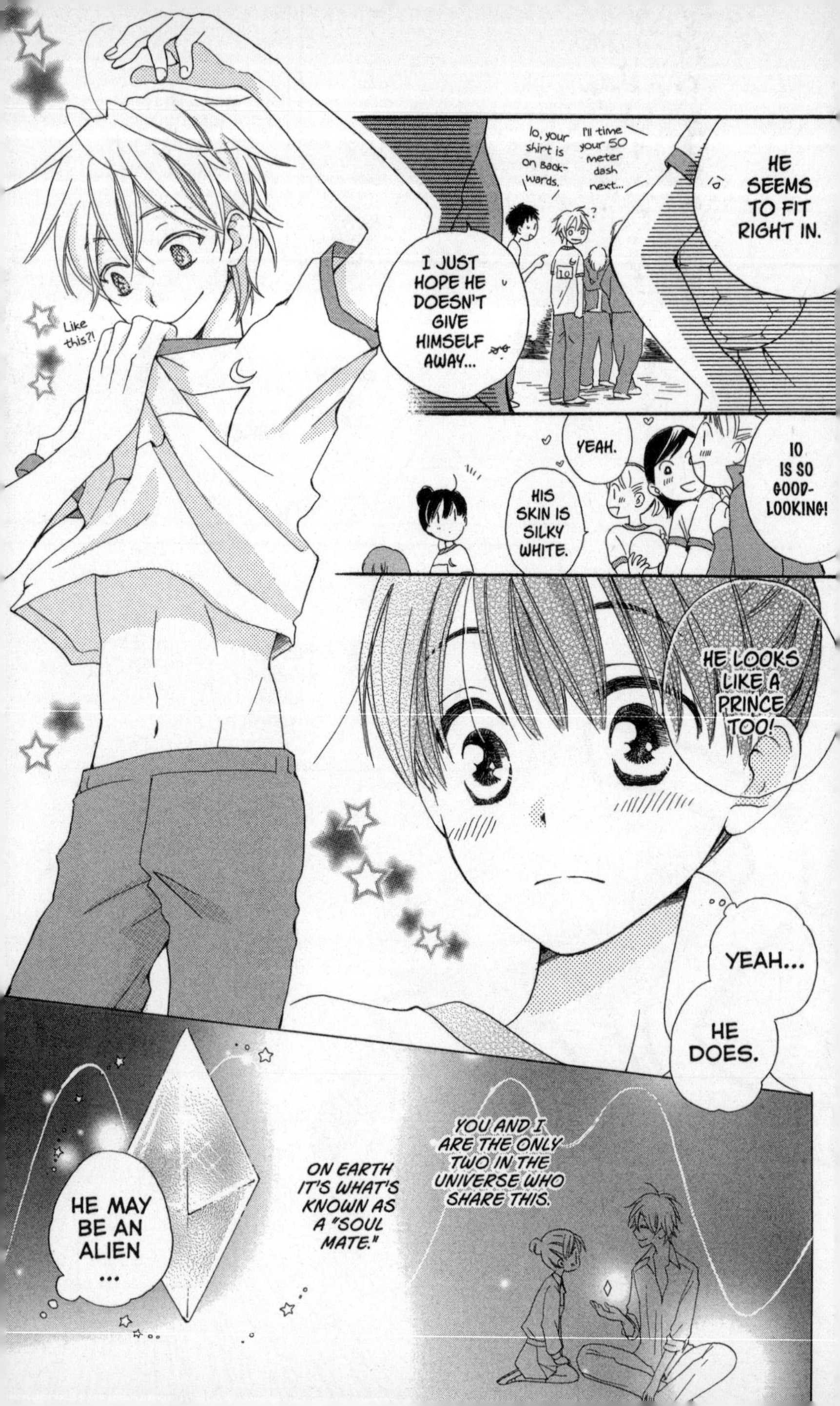
HE SEEMS TO FIT RIGHT IN.
I'll time your 50 meter dash next...
Io, your shirt is on backwards.
I JUST HOPE HE DOESN'T GIVE HIMSELF AWAY...
IO IS SO GOOD-LOOKING!
YEAH.
HIS SKIN IS SILKY WHITE.
HE LOOKS LIKE A PRINCE TOO!
YEAH...
HE DOES.
Like this?!
YOU AND I ARE THE ONLY TWO IN THE UNIVERSE WHO SHARE THIS.
ON EARTH IT'S WHAT'S KNOWN AS A "SOUL MATE."
HE MAY BE AN ALIEN ...

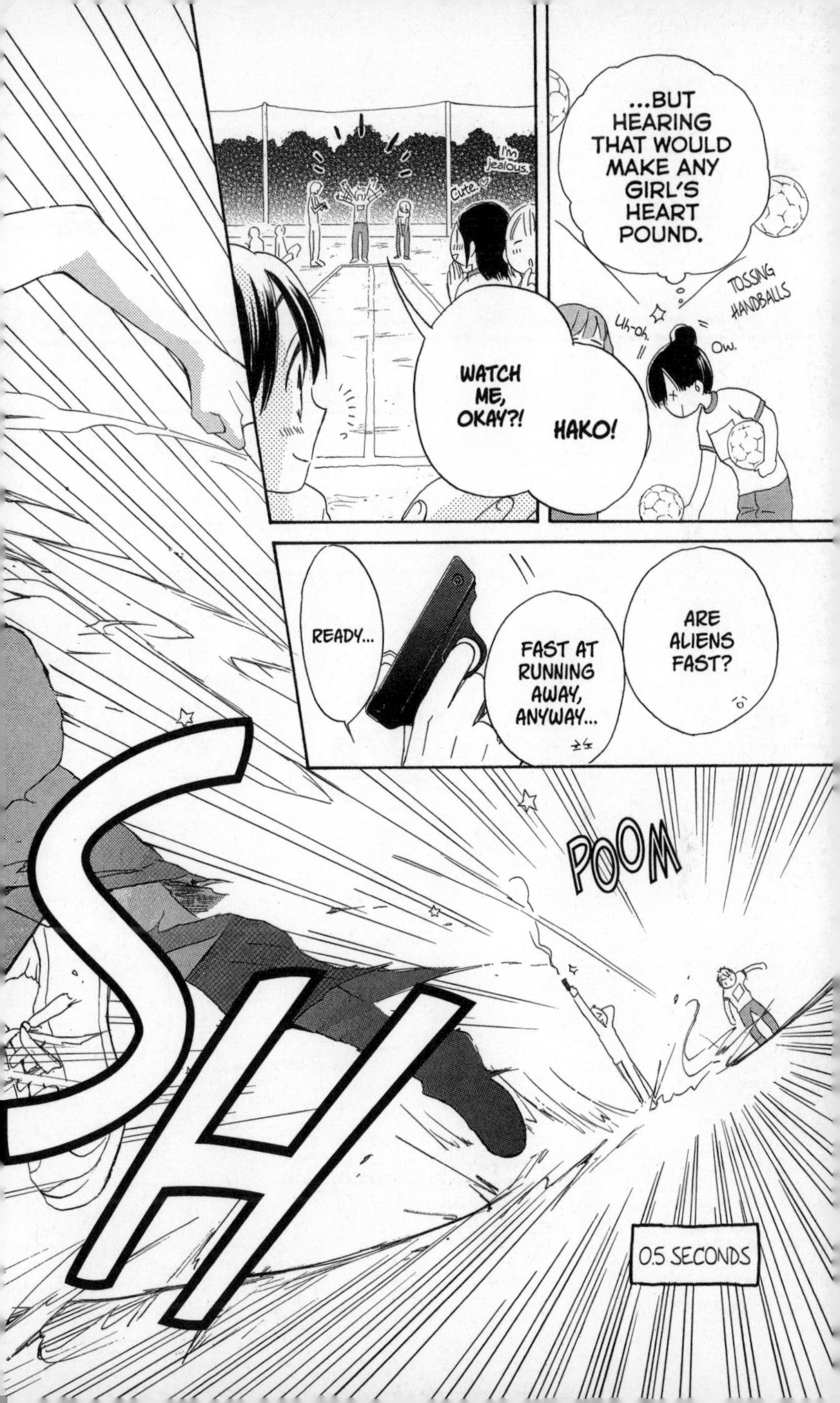
...BUT HEARING THAT WOULD MAKE ANY GIRL'S HEART POUND.
TOSSING HANDBALLS
Ow.
Uh-oh.
I'm jealous.
Cute.
WATCH ME, OKAY?!
HAKO!
ARE ALIENS FAST?
FAST AT RUNNING AWAY, ANYWAY...
READY...
POOM
SH
0.5 SECONDS

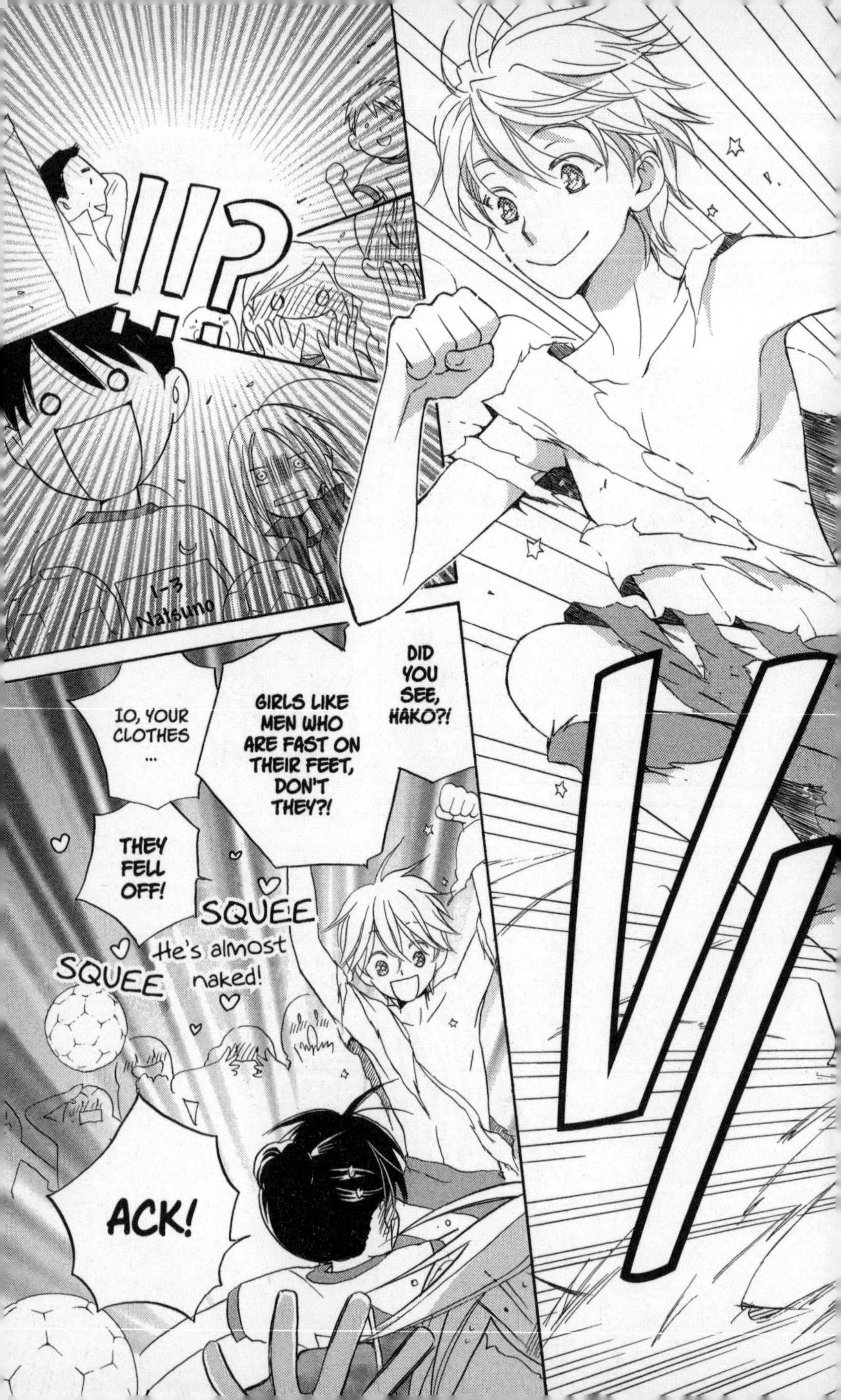
!!?
1-3
Natsuno
DID YOU SEE, HAKO?!
GIRLS LIKE MEN WHO ARE FAST ON THEIR FEET, DON'T THEY?!
IO, YOUR CLOTHES ...
THEY FELL OFF!
SQUEE
He's almost naked!
SQUEE
ACK!

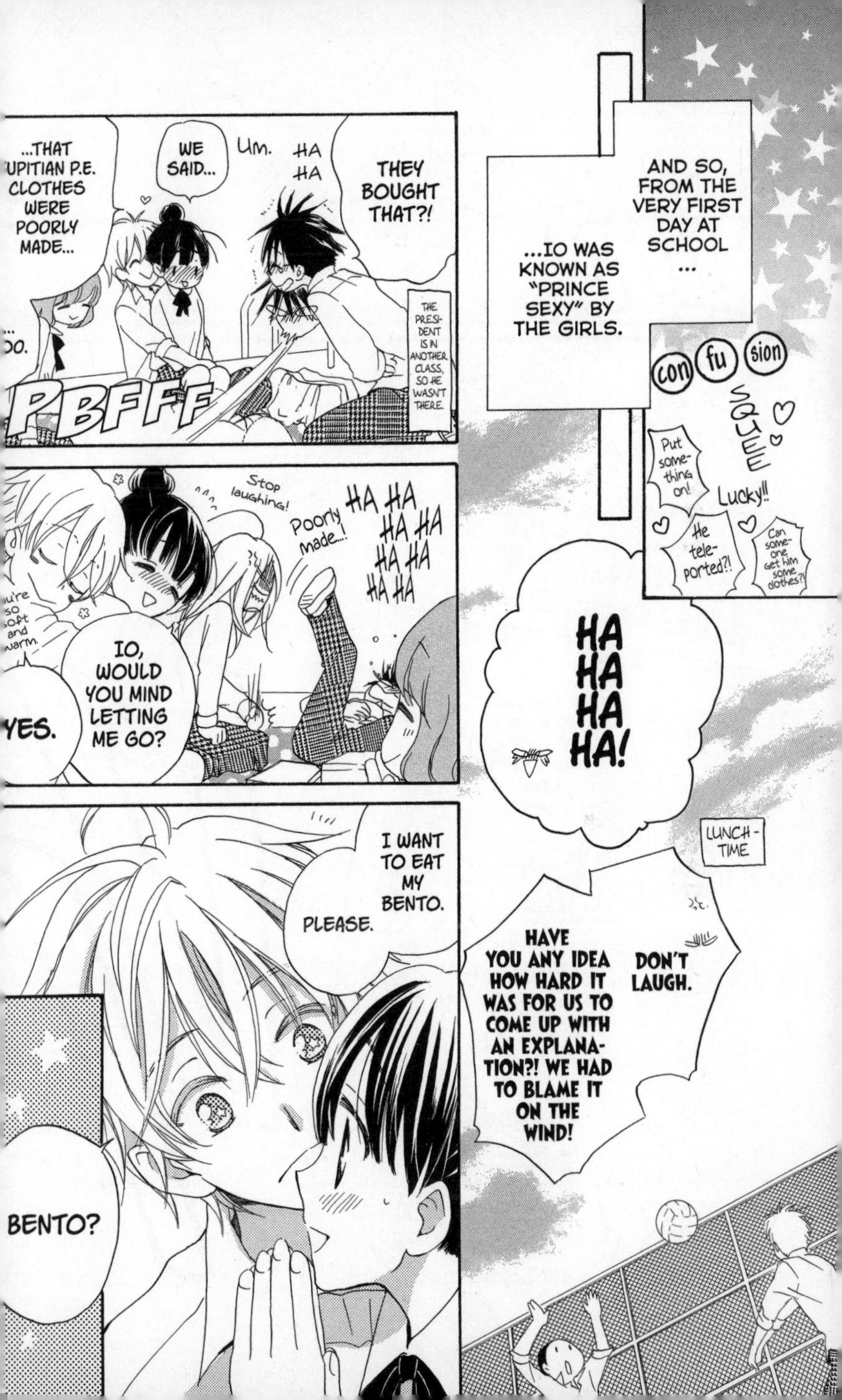
AND SO, FROM THE VERY FIRST DAY AT SCHOOL ...
...IO WAS KNOWN AS "PRINCE SEXY" BY THE GIRLS.
con fu sion
SQUEE
Put something on!
Lucky!!
He teleported?!
Can someone get him some clothes?!
HA HA HA HA!
LUNCH-TIME
DON'T LAUGH.
HAVE YOU ANY IDEA HOW HARD IT WAS FOR US TO COME UP WITH AN EXPLANATION?! WE HAD TO BLAME IT ON THE WIND!
THEY BOUGHT THAT?!
HA HA
Um.
WE SAID...
...THAT UPITIAN P.E. CLOTHES WERE POORLY MADE...
... DO.
THE PRESIDENT IS IN ANOTHER CLASS, SO HE WASN'T THERE.
PBFFF
HA HA HA HA HA HA HA HA
Poorly made...!
Stop laughing!
IO, WOULD YOU MIND LETTING ME GO?
YES.
u're so soft and warm.
I WANT TO EAT MY BENTO.
PLEASE.
BENTO?

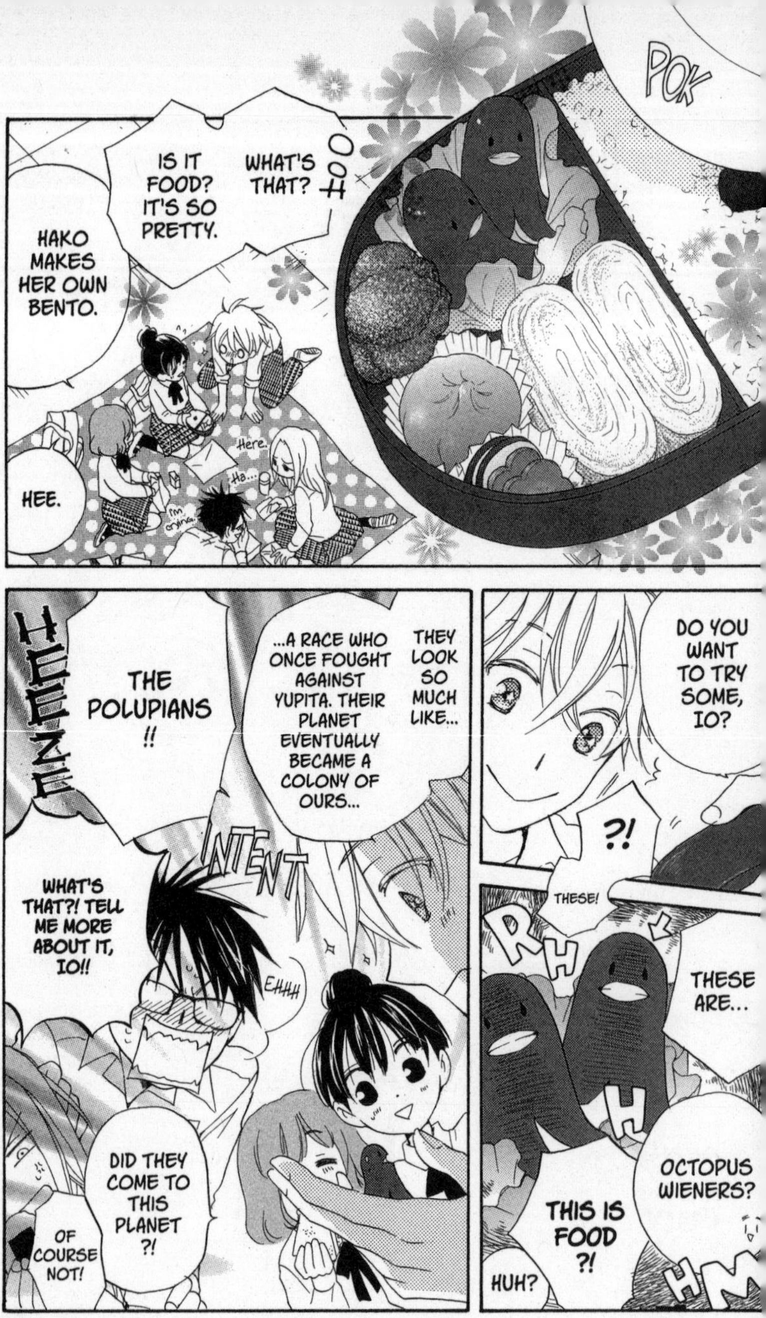
POK
OOH
WHAT'S THAT?
IS IT FOOD? IT'S SO PRETTY.
HAKO MAKES HER OWN BENTO.
Here.
Ha...
I'm crying.
HEE.
DO YOU WANT TO TRY SOME, IO?
?!
THESE!
RHH
THESE ARE...
OCTOPUS WIENERS?
HM
THIS IS FOOD ?!
HUH?
THEY LOOK SO MUCH LIKE...
...A RACE WHO ONCE FOUGHT AGAINST YUPITA. THEIR PLANET EVENTUALLY BECAME A COLONY OF OURS...
THE POLUPIANS !!
INTENT
WHAT'S THAT?! TELL ME MORE ABOUT IT, IO!!
EHHH
DID THEY COME TO THIS PLANET ?!
OF COURSE NOT!

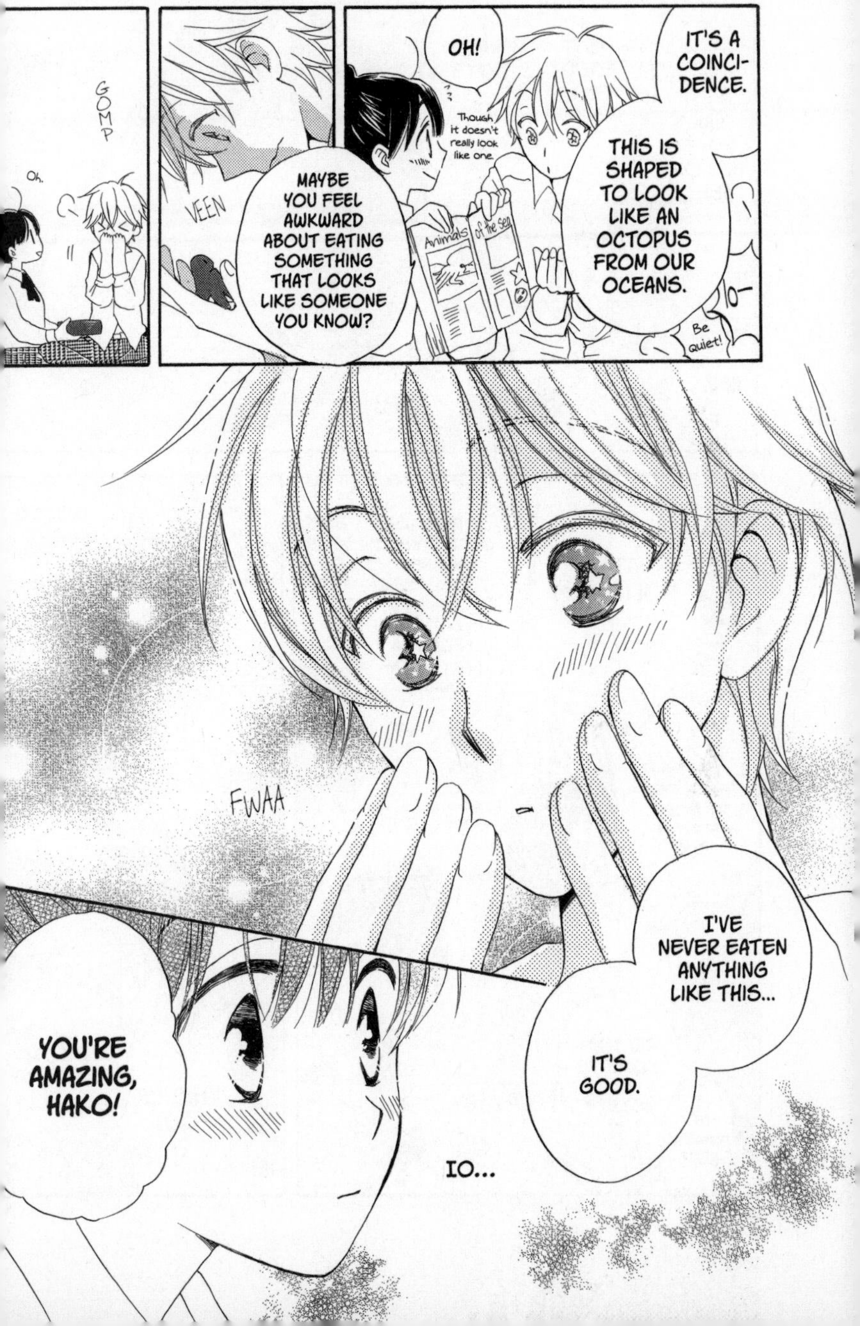
IT'S A COINCIDENCE.
OH!
THIS IS SHAPED TO LOOK LIKE AN OCTOPUS FROM OUR OCEANS.
Though it doesn't really look like one.
Animals of the sea
Io—
Be Quiet!
MAYBE YOU FEEL AWKWARD ABOUT EATING SOMETHING THAT LOOKS LIKE SOMEONE YOU KNOW?
VEEN
GOMP
Oh.
FWAA
I'VE NEVER EATEN ANYTHING LIKE THIS...
IT'S GOOD.
IO...
YOU'RE AMAZING, HAKO!

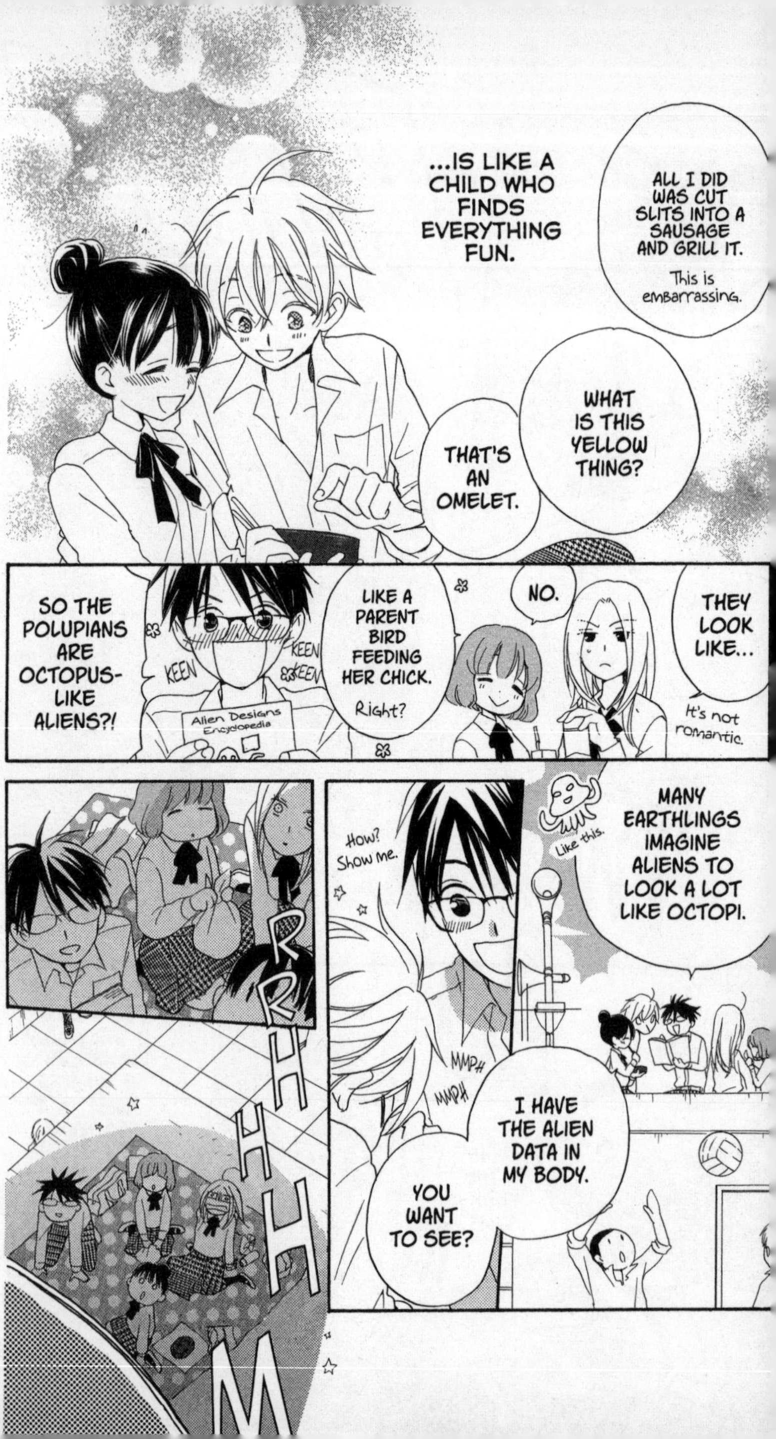
ALL I DID WAS CUT SLITS INTO A SAUSAGE AND GRILL IT.
This is embarrassing.
...IS LIKE A CHILD WHO FINDS EVERYTHING FUN.
WHAT IS THIS YELLOW THING?
THAT'S AN OMELET.
THEY LOOK LIKE...
It's not romantic.
NO.
LIKE A PARENT BIRD FEEDING HER CHICK.
Right?
KEEN KEEN KEEN
SO THE POLUPIANS ARE OCTOPUS-LIKE ALIENS?!
Alien Designs Encyclopedia
MANY EARTHLINGS IMAGINE ALIENS TO LOOK A LOT LIKE OCTOPI.
Like this.
How? Show me.
I HAVE THE ALIEN DATA IN MY BODY.
YOU WANT TO SEE?
MMPH MMPH
RRHHHHM

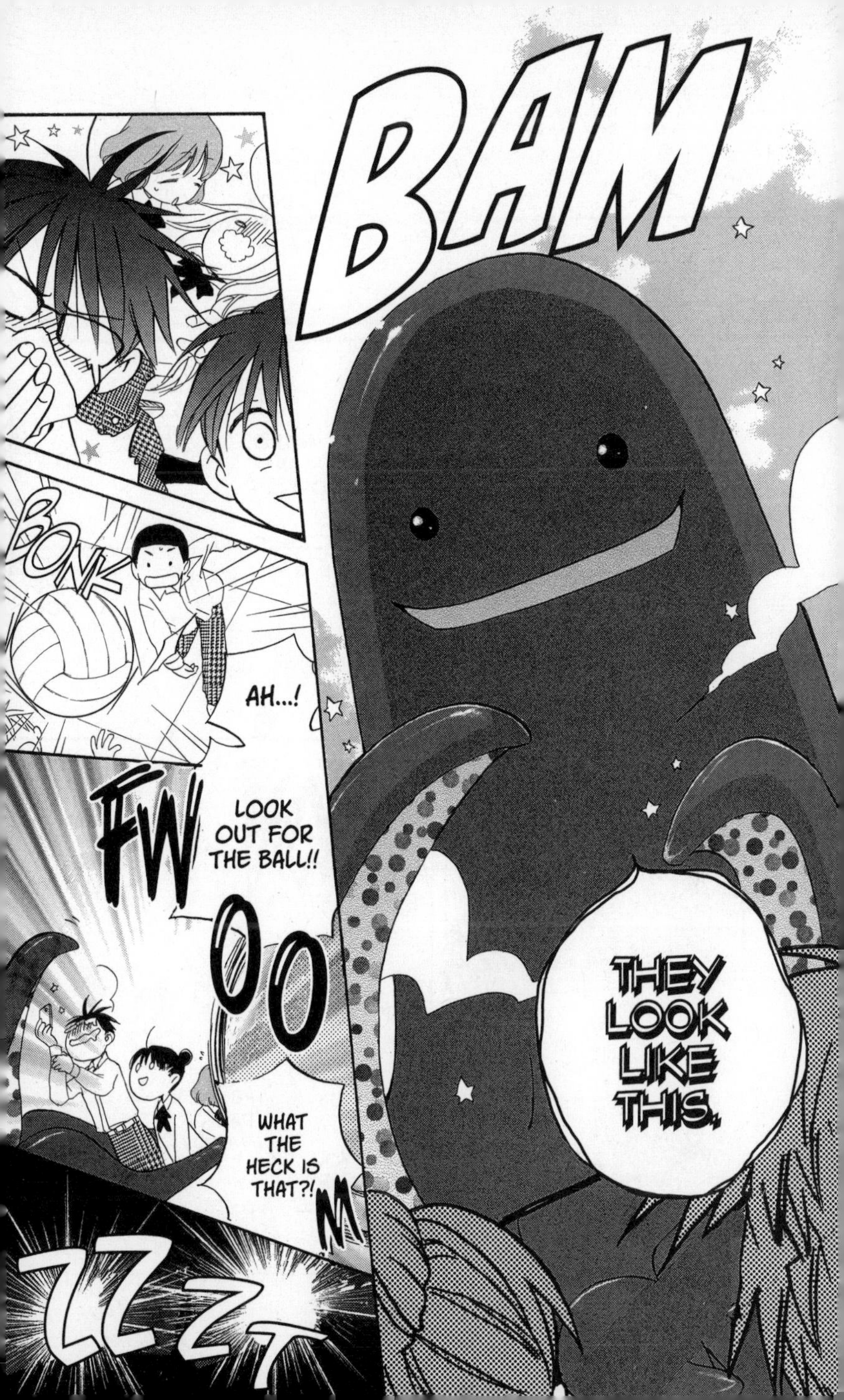
BAM
THEY LOOK LIKE THIS.
BONK
AH...!
FWOOOM
LOOK OUT FOR THE BALL!!
WHAT THE HECK IS THAT?!
ZZZT

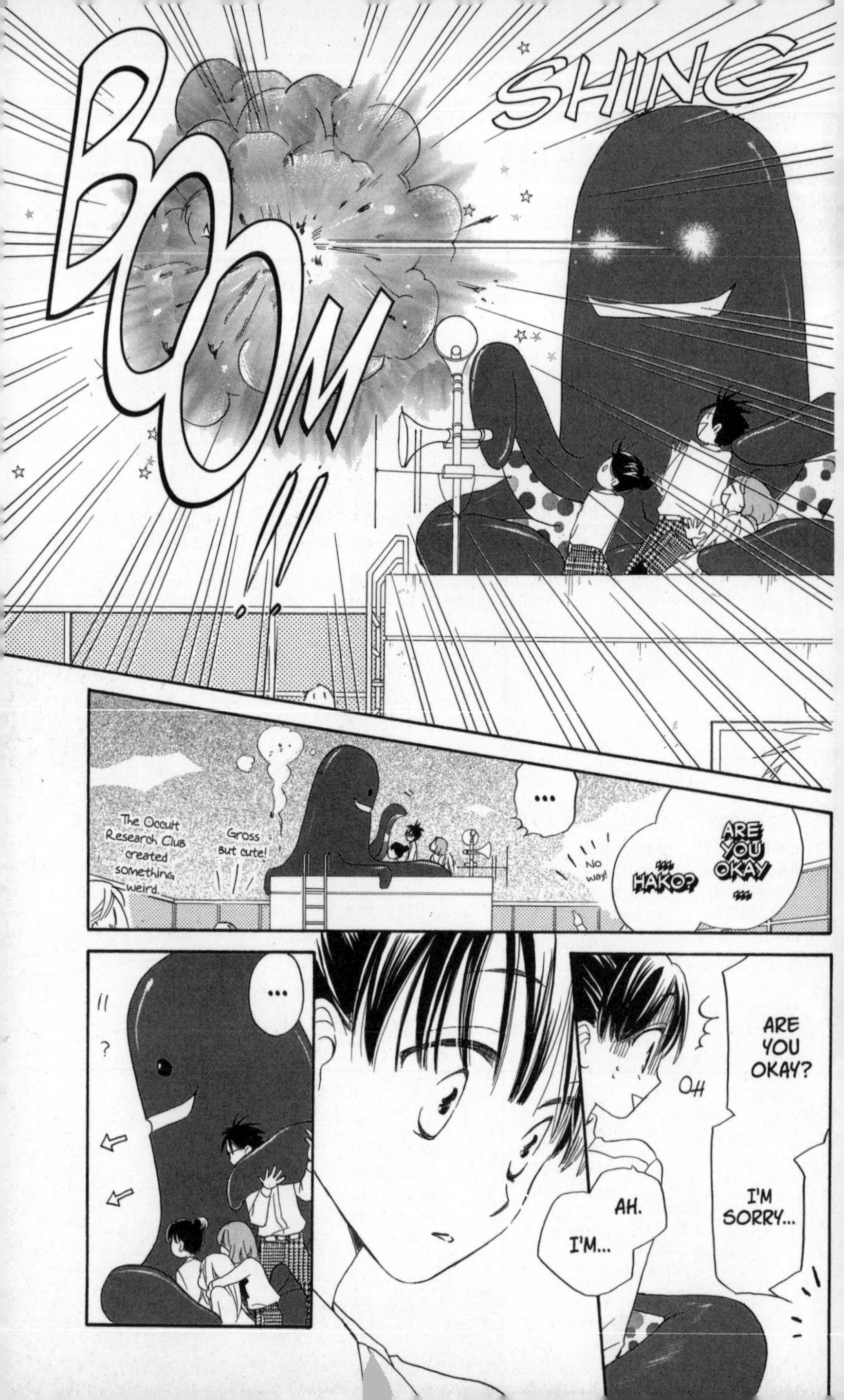

SHING
BOOM!!
HAKO? ARE YOU OKAY
...
No way!
Gross but cute!
The Occult Research Club created something weird.
ARE YOU OKAY?
I'M SORRY...
OH
AH.
I'M...
...

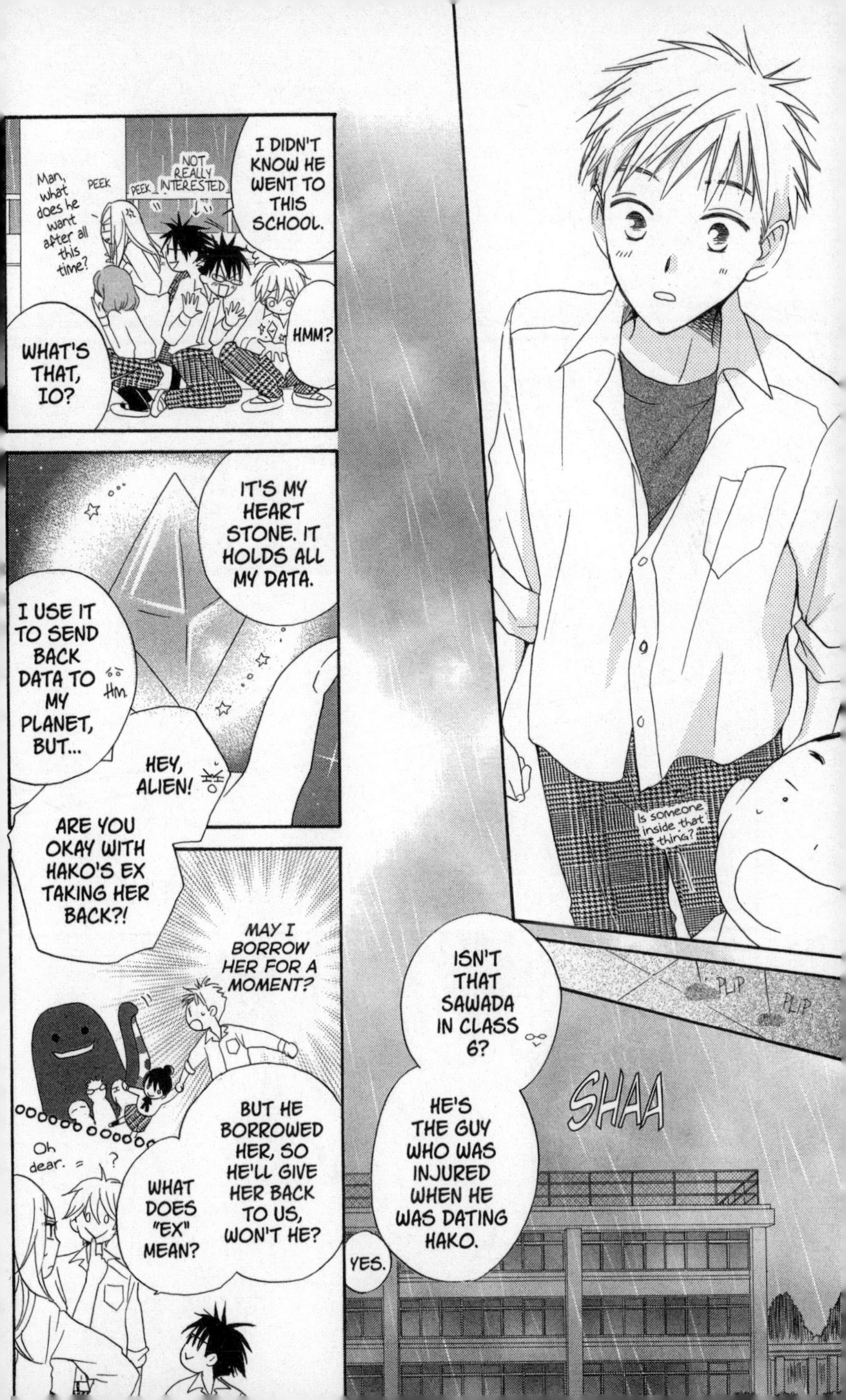
Is someone inside that thing?
PLIP
PLIP
ISN'T THAT SAWADA IN CLASS 6?
SHAA
HE'S THE GUY WHO WAS INJURED WHEN HE WAS DATING HAKO.
YES.
I DIDN'T KNOW HE WENT TO THIS SCHOOL.
NOT REALLY INTERESTED
PEEK
PEEK
Man, what does he want after all this time?
HMM?
WHAT'S THAT, IO?
IT'S MY HEART STONE. IT HOLDS ALL MY DATA.
I USE IT TO SEND BACK DATA TO MY PLANET, BUT...
Hm.
HEY, ALIEN!
ARE YOU OKAY WITH HAKO'S EX TAKING HER BACK?!
MAY I BORROW HER FOR A MOMENT?
BUT HE BORROWED HER, SO HE'LL GIVE HER BACK TO US, WON'T HE?
WHAT DOES "EX" MEAN?
Oh dear.

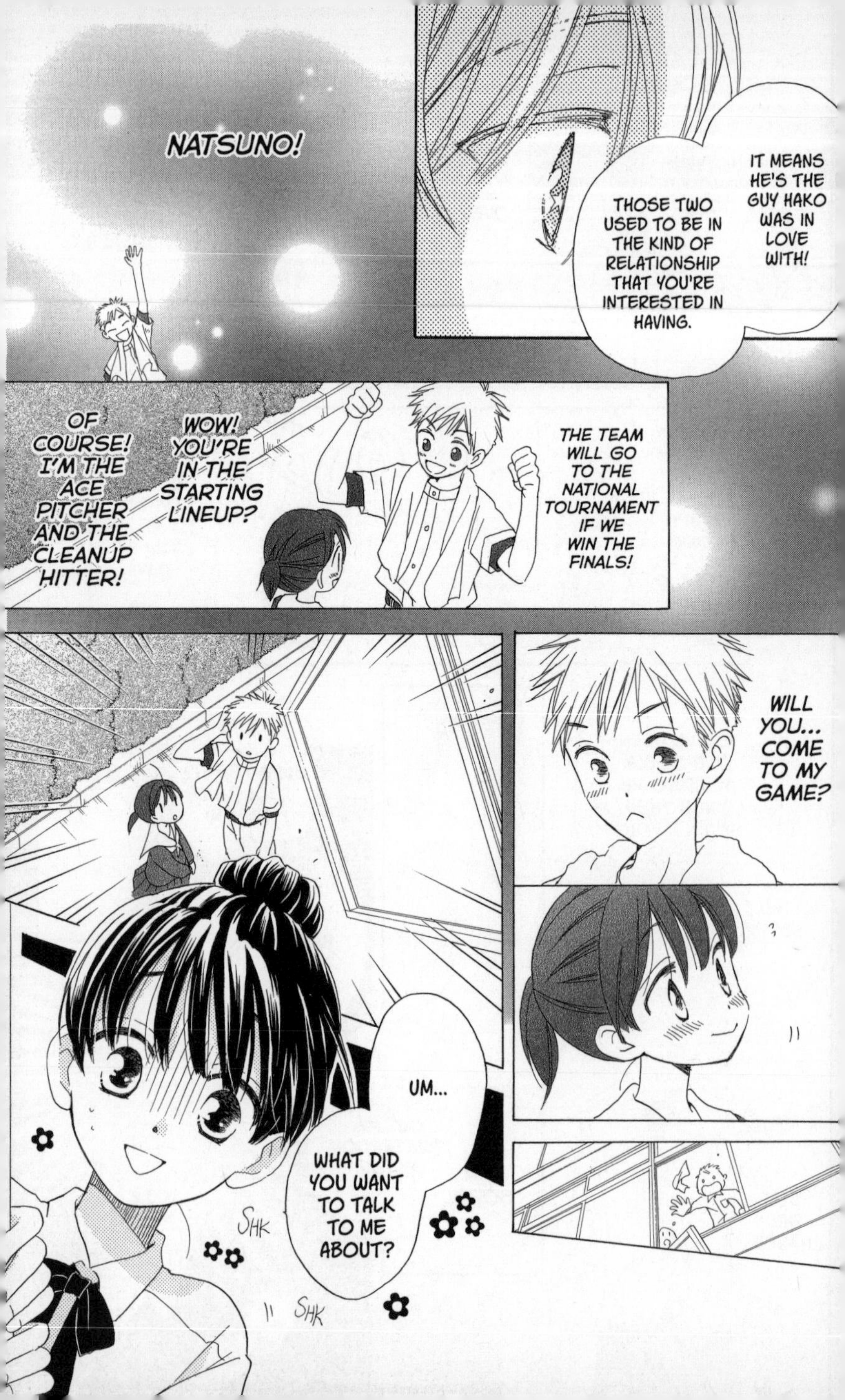
THOSE TWO USED TO BE IN THE KIND OF RELATIONSHIP THAT YOU'RE INTERESTED IN HAVING.
IT MEANS HE'S THE GUY HAKO WAS IN LOVE WITH!
NATSUNO!
THE TEAM WILL GO TO THE NATIONAL TOURNAMENT IF WE WIN THE FINALS!
WOW! YOU'RE IN THE STARTING LINEUP?
OF COURSE! I'M THE ACE PITCHER AND THE CLEANUP HITTER!
WILL YOU... COME TO MY GAME?
UM...
WHAT DID YOU WANT TO TALK TO ME ABOUT?
SHK
SHK

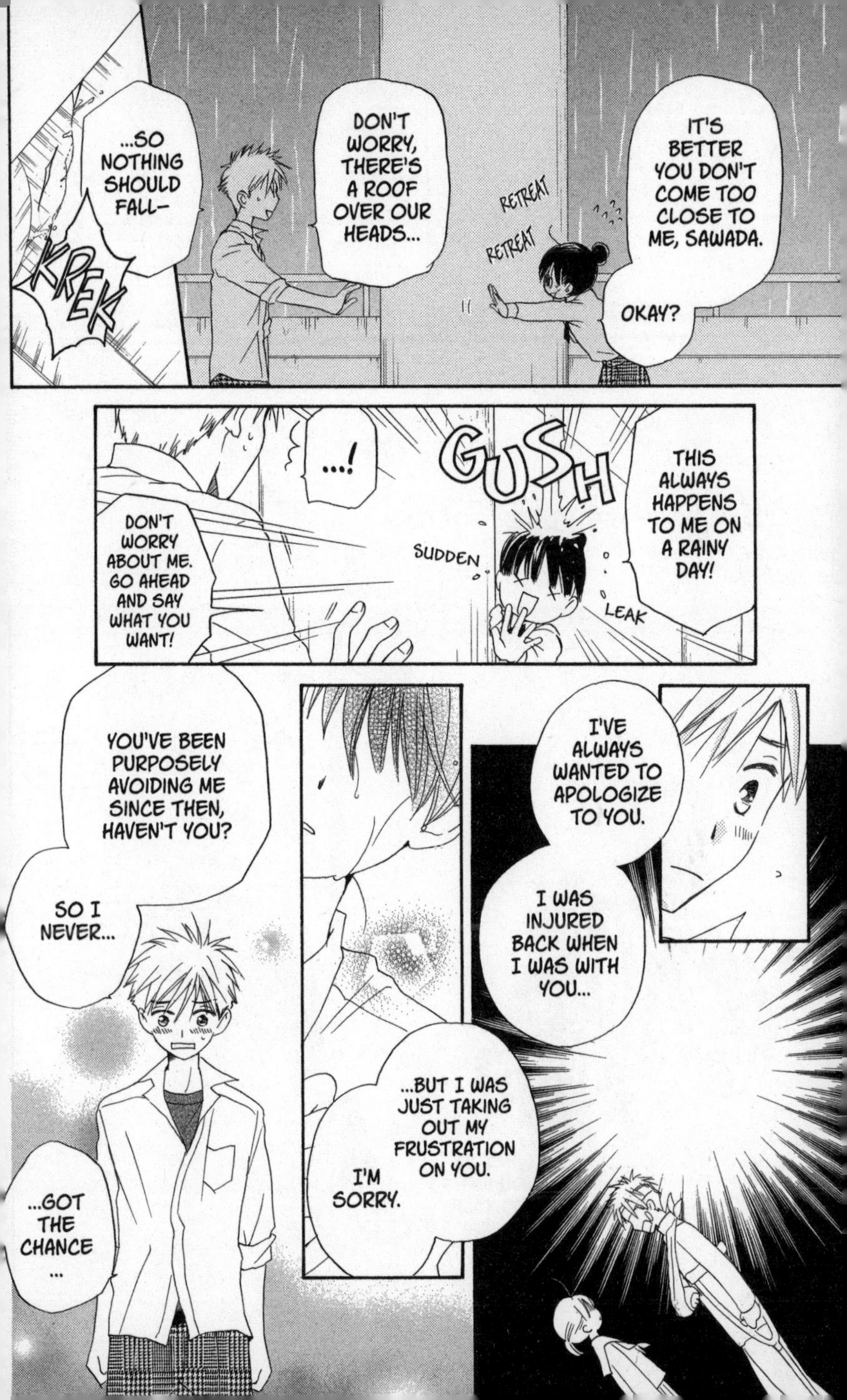
IT'S BETTER YOU DON'T COME TOO CLOSE TO ME, SAWADA.
OKAY?
RETREAT
RETREAT
DON'T WORRY, THERE'S A ROOF OVER OUR HEADS...
...SO NOTHING SHOULD FALL—
KREK
THIS ALWAYS HAPPENS TO ME ON A RAINY DAY!
GUSH
SUDDEN
LEAK
...!
DON'T WORRY ABOUT ME. GO AHEAD AND SAY WHAT YOU WANT!
I'VE ALWAYS WANTED TO APOLOGIZE TO YOU.
I WAS INJURED BACK WHEN I WAS WITH YOU...
...BUT I WAS JUST TAKING OUT MY FRUSTRATION ON YOU.
I'M SORRY.
YOU'VE BEEN PURPOSELY AVOIDING ME SINCE THEN, HAVEN'T YOU?
SO I NEVER...
...GOT THE CHANCE ...

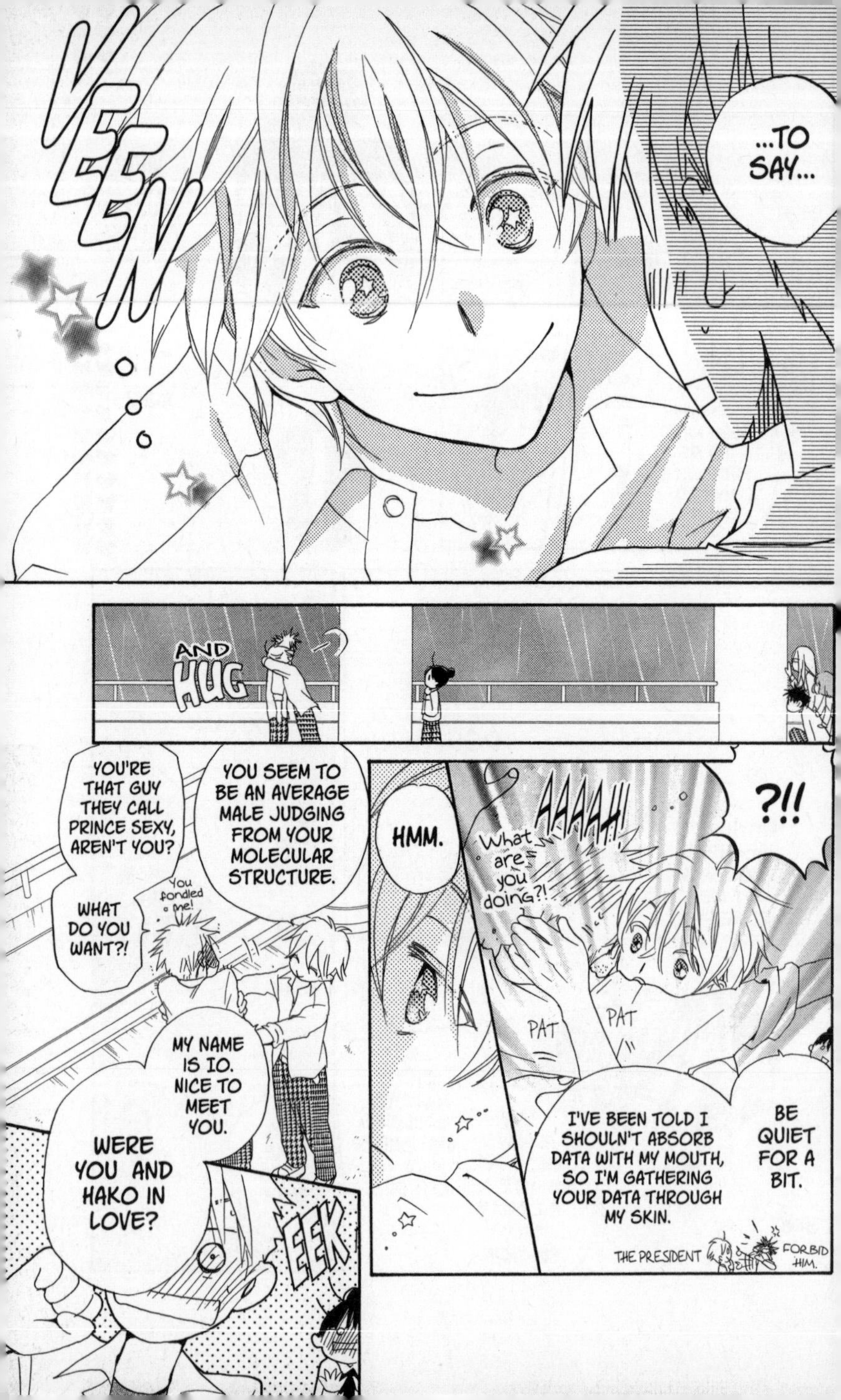
...TO SAY...
VEEN
AND HUG
?!!
AAAAH!
What are you doing?!
HMM.
PAT
PAT
BE QUIET FOR A BIT.
I'VE BEEN TOLD I SHOULN'T ABSORB DATA WITH MY MOUTH, SO I'M GATHERING YOUR DATA THROUGH MY SKIN.
THE PRESIDENT FORBID HIM.
YOU SEEM TO BE AN AVERAGE MALE JUDGING FROM YOUR MOLECULAR STRUCTURE.
YOU'RE THAT GUY THEY CALL PRINCE SEXY, AREN'T YOU?
You fondled me!
WHAT DO YOU WANT?!
MY NAME IS IO. NICE TO MEET YOU.
EEK
WERE YOU AND HAKO IN LOVE?

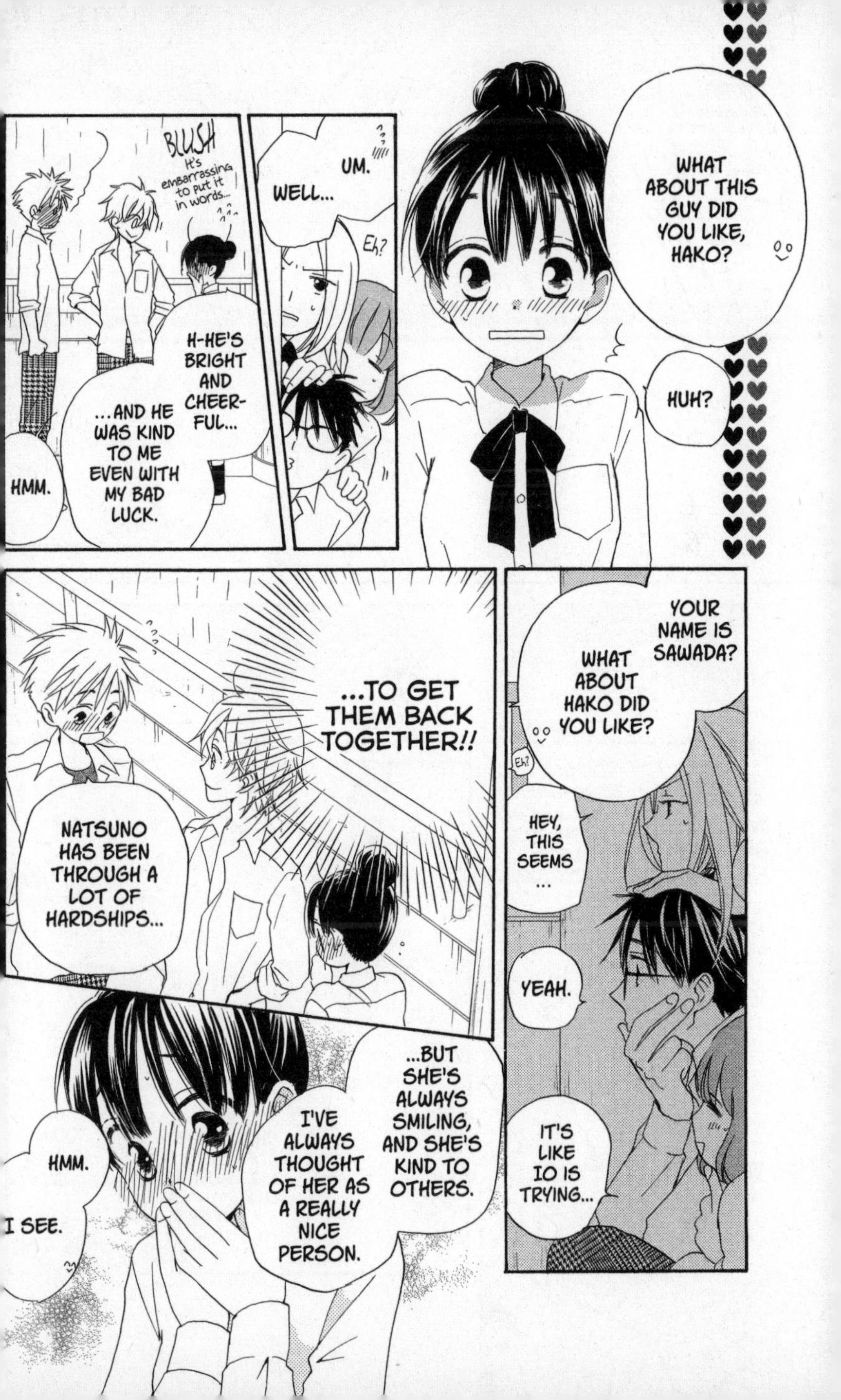
WHAT ABOUT THIS GUY DID YOU LIKE, HAKO?
HUH?
UM.
WELL...
Eh?
BLUSH
It's embarrassing to put it in words...
H-HE'S BRIGHT AND CHEERFUL...
...AND HE WAS KIND TO ME EVEN WITH MY BAD LUCK.
HMM.
YOUR NAME IS SAWADA?
WHAT ABOUT HAKO DID YOU LIKE?
Eh?
HEY, THIS SEEMS...
YEAH.
IT'S LIKE IO IS TRYING...
...TO GET THEM BACK TOGETHER!!
NATSUNO HAS BEEN THROUGH A LOT OF HARDSHIPS...
...BUT SHE'S ALWAYS SMILING, AND SHE'S KIND TO OTHERS.
I'VE ALWAYS THOUGHT OF HER AS A REALLY NICE PERSON.
HMM.
I SEE.

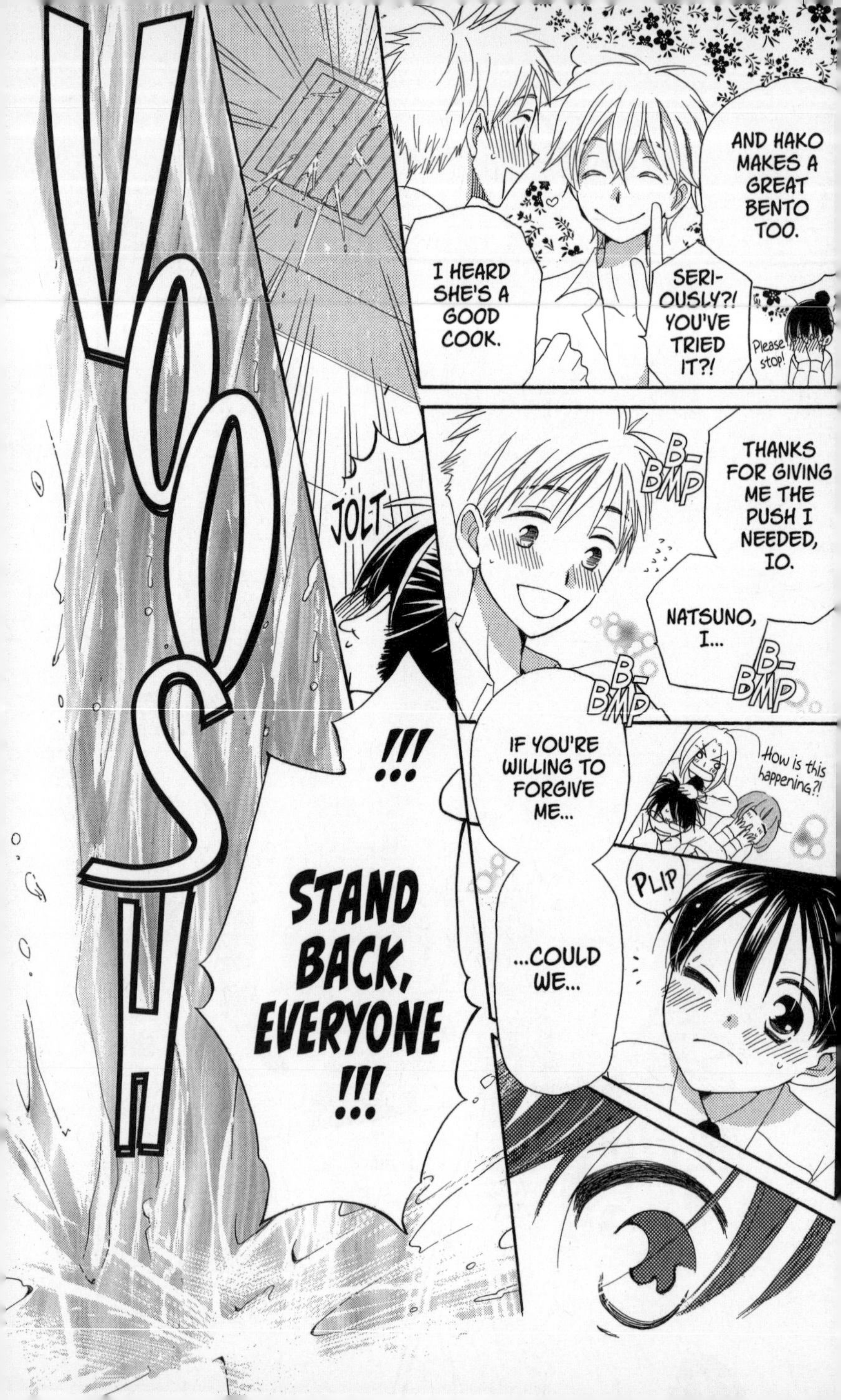

AND HAKO MAKES A GREAT BENTO TOO.
Please stop!
SERI-OUSLY?! YOU'VE TRIED IT?!
I HEARD SHE'S A GOOD COOK.
THANKS FOR GIVING ME THE PUSH I NEEDED, IO.
B-BMP
NATSUNO, I...
B-BMP
B-BMP
How is this happening?!
IF YOU'RE WILLING TO FORGIVE ME...
PLIP
...COULD WE...
JOLT
!!!
STAND BACK, EVERYONE!!!
VOOSH

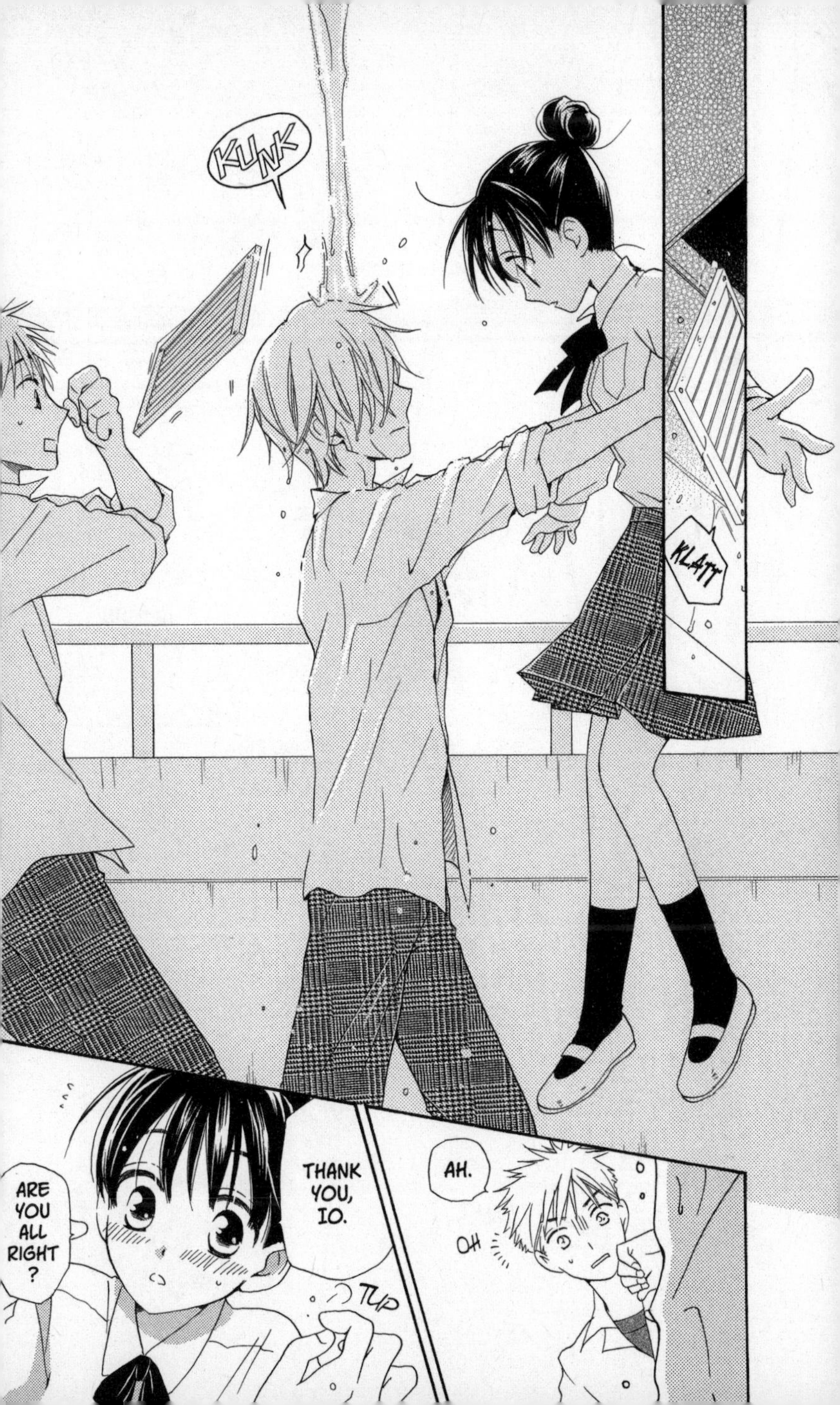
KUNK
KLATT
AH.
OH
THANK YOU, IO.
ARE YOU ALL RIGHT?
TUP

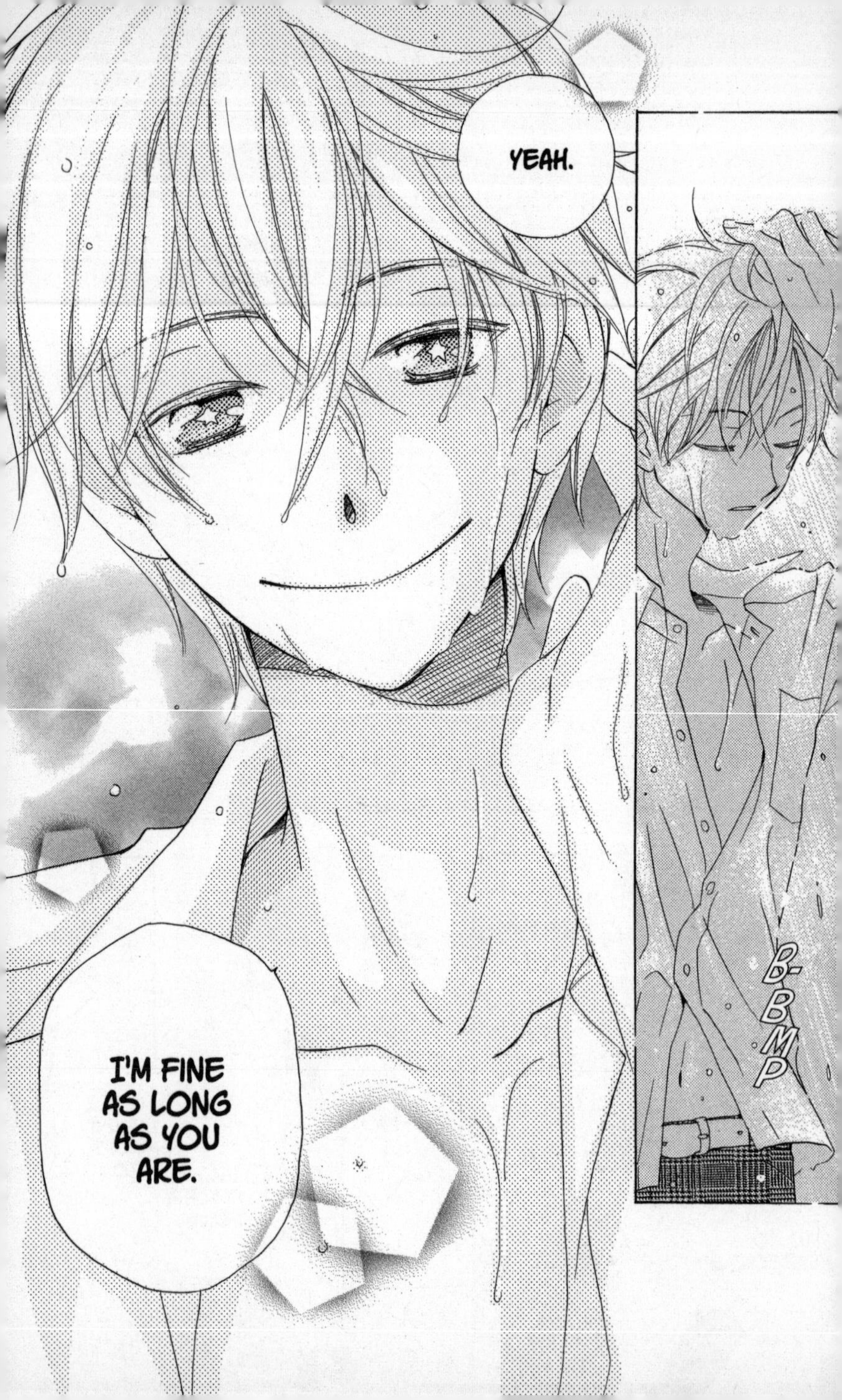
YEAH.
I'M FINE AS LONG AS YOU ARE.
B-BMP

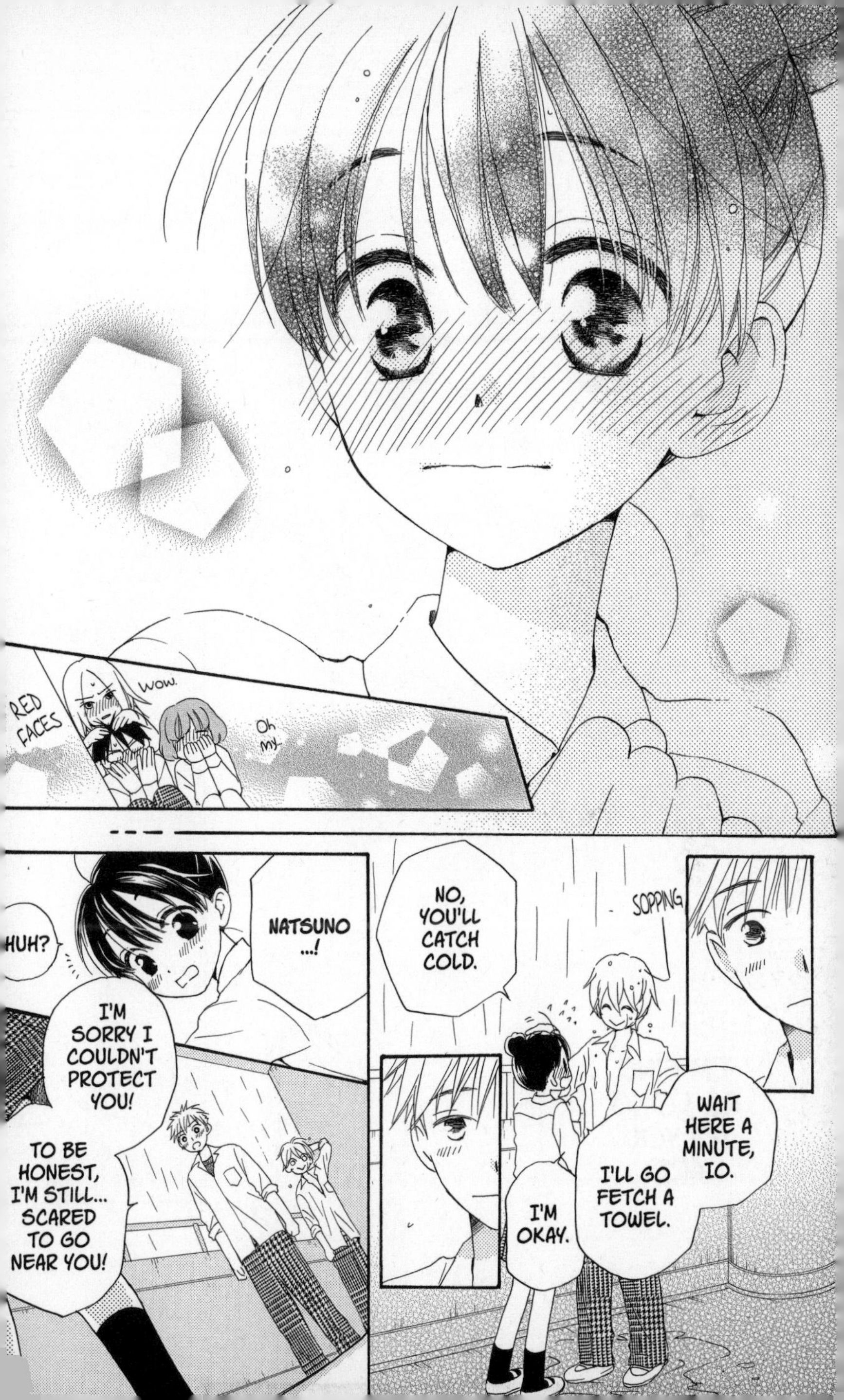
Oh my...
WOW.
RED FACES
SOPPING
WAIT HERE A MINUTE, IO.
I'LL GO FETCH A TOWEL.
I'M OKAY.
NO, YOU'LL CATCH COLD.
NATSUNO ...!
HUH?
I'M SORRY I COULDN'T PROTECT YOU!
TO BE HONEST, I'M STILL... SCARED TO GO NEAR YOU!

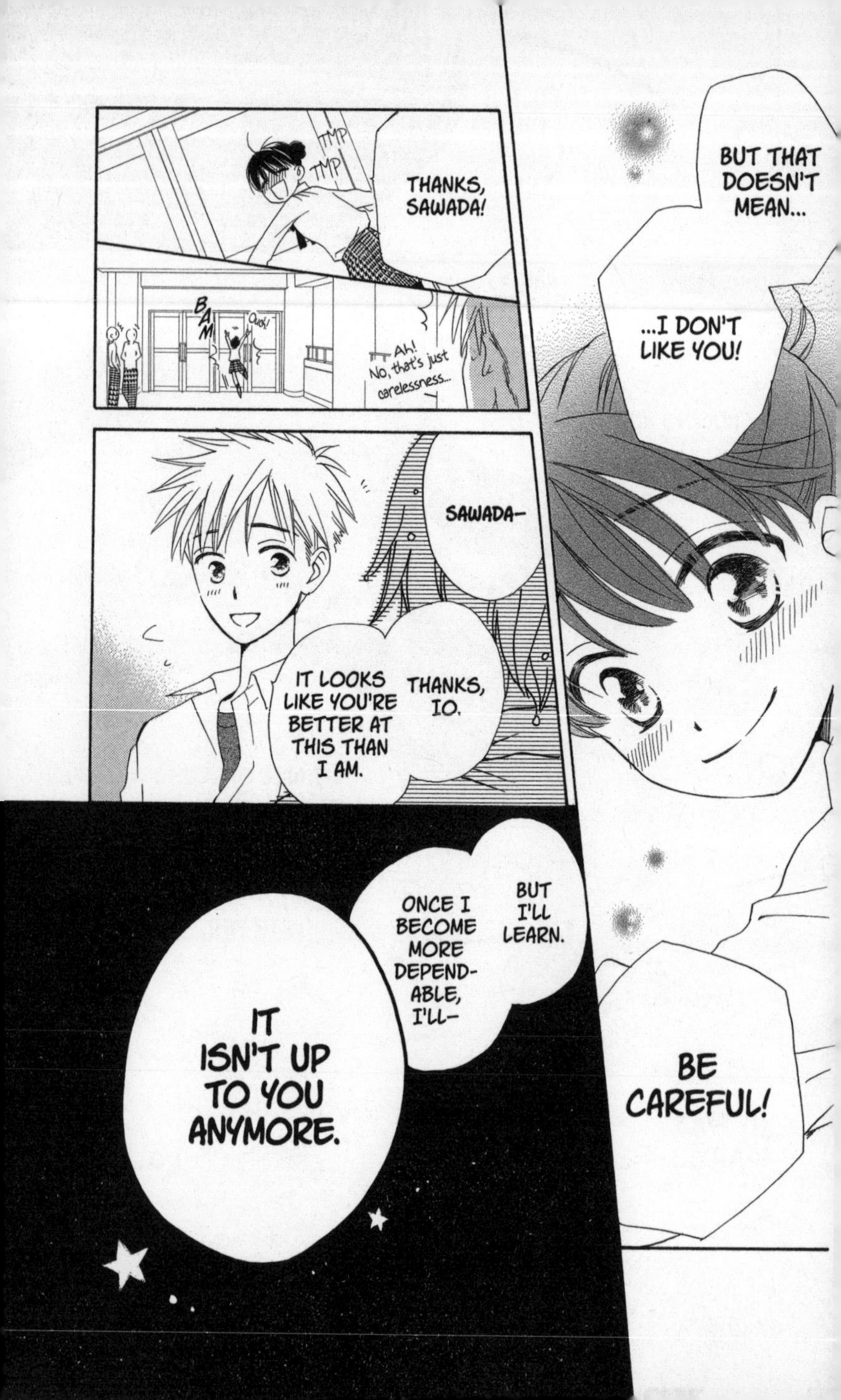
BUT THAT DOESN'T MEAN...
...I DON'T LIKE YOU!
BE CAREFUL!
THANKS, SAWADA!
TMP TMP
Ah! No, that's just carelessness...
BAM
Ouch!
SAWADA-
THANKS, IO.
IT LOOKS LIKE YOU'RE BETTER AT THIS THAN I AM.
BUT I'LL LEARN.
ONCE I BECOME MORE DEPEND-ABLE, I'LL-
IT ISN'T UP TO YOU ANYMORE.

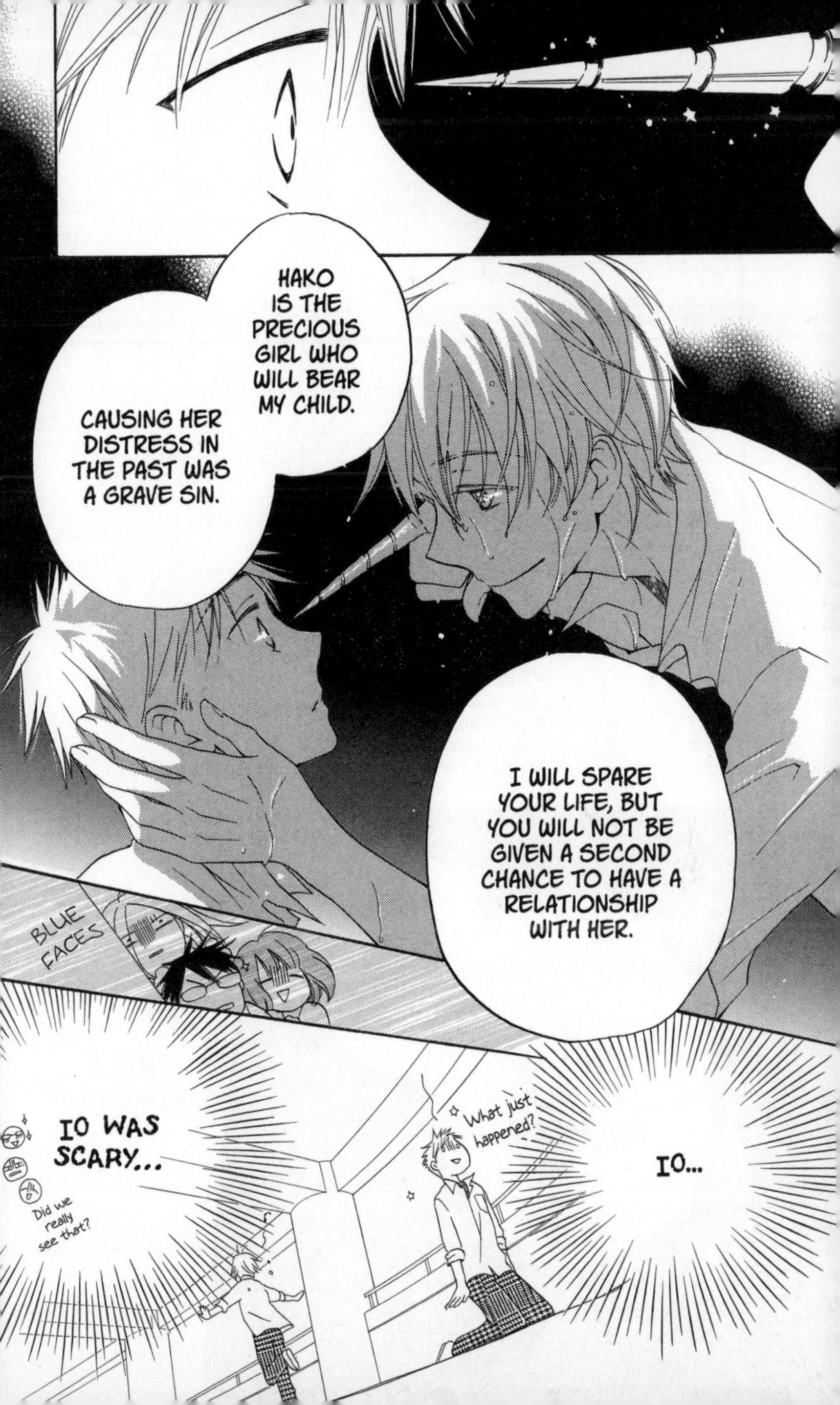
HAKO IS THE PRECIOUS GIRL WHO WILL BEAR MY CHILD.
CAUSING HER DISTRESS IN THE PAST WAS A GRAVE SIN.
I WILL SPARE YOUR LIFE, BUT YOU WILL NOT BE GIVEN A SECOND CHANCE TO HAVE A RELATIONSHIP WITH HER.
BLUE FACES
IO...
What just happened?
IO WAS SCARY...
Did we really see that?

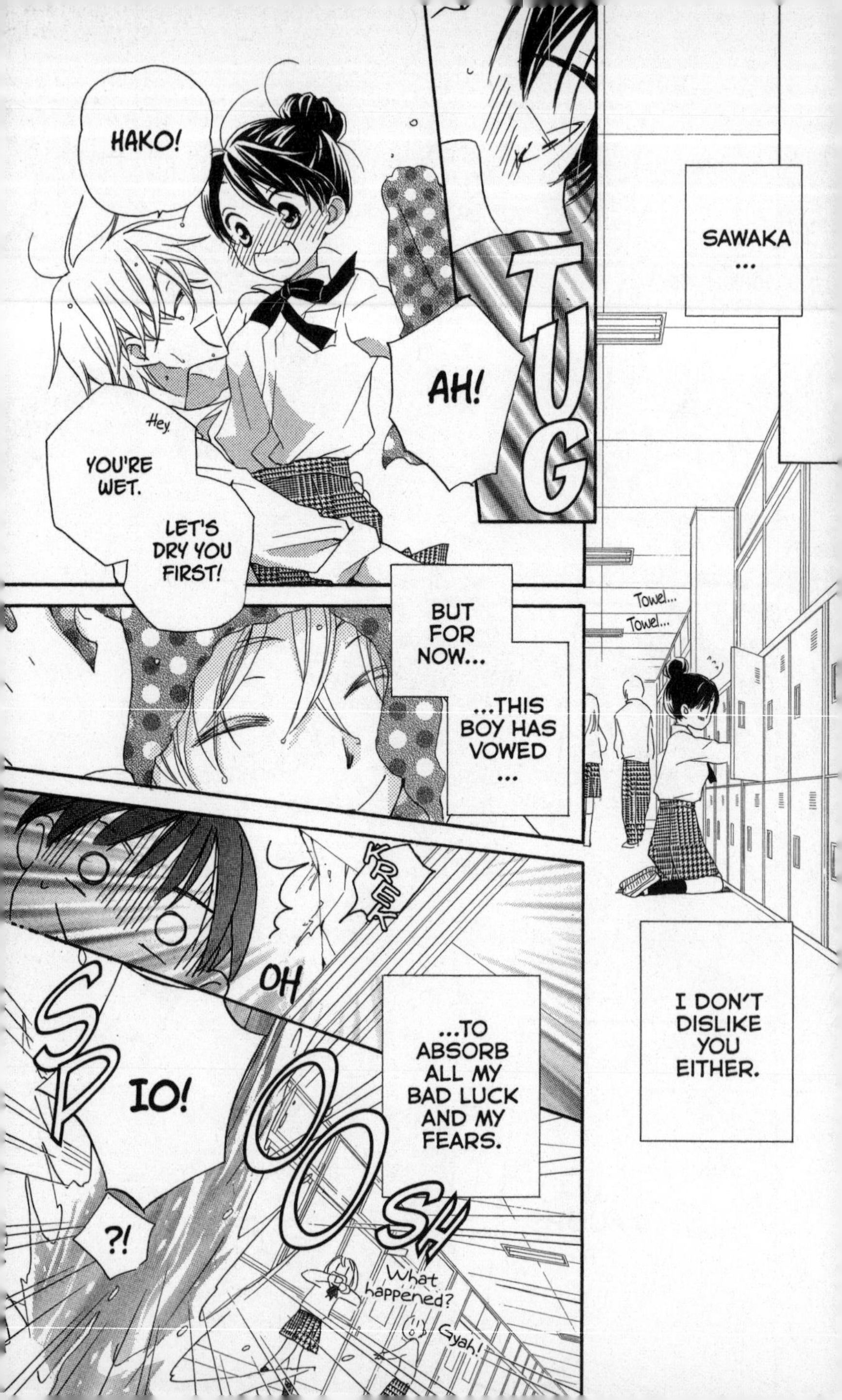
SAWAKA ...
Towel...
Towel...
I DON'T DISLIKE YOU EITHER.
TUG
AH!
HAKO!
Hey.
YOU'RE WET.
LET'S DRY YOU FIRST!
BUT FOR NOW...
...THIS BOY HAS VOWED ...
KREK
OH
...TO ABSORB ALL MY BAD LUCK AND MY FEARS.
SPOOSH
IO!
?!
What happened?
Gyah!

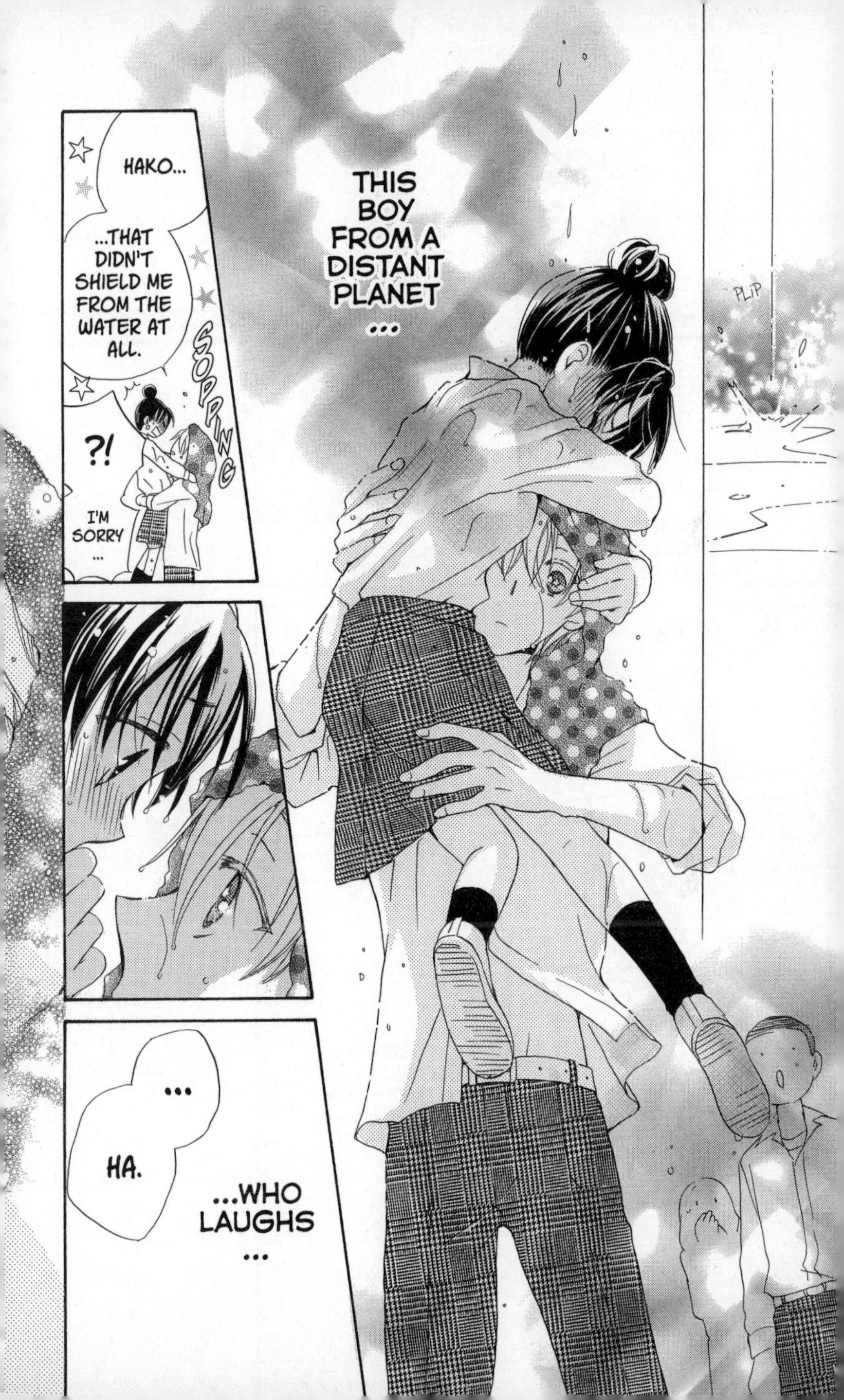
THIS BOY FROM A DISTANT PLANET ...
PLIP
HAKO...
...THAT DIDN'T SHIELD ME FROM THE WATER AT ALL.
SOPPING
?!
I'M SORRY ...
...
HA.
...WHO LAUGHS ...

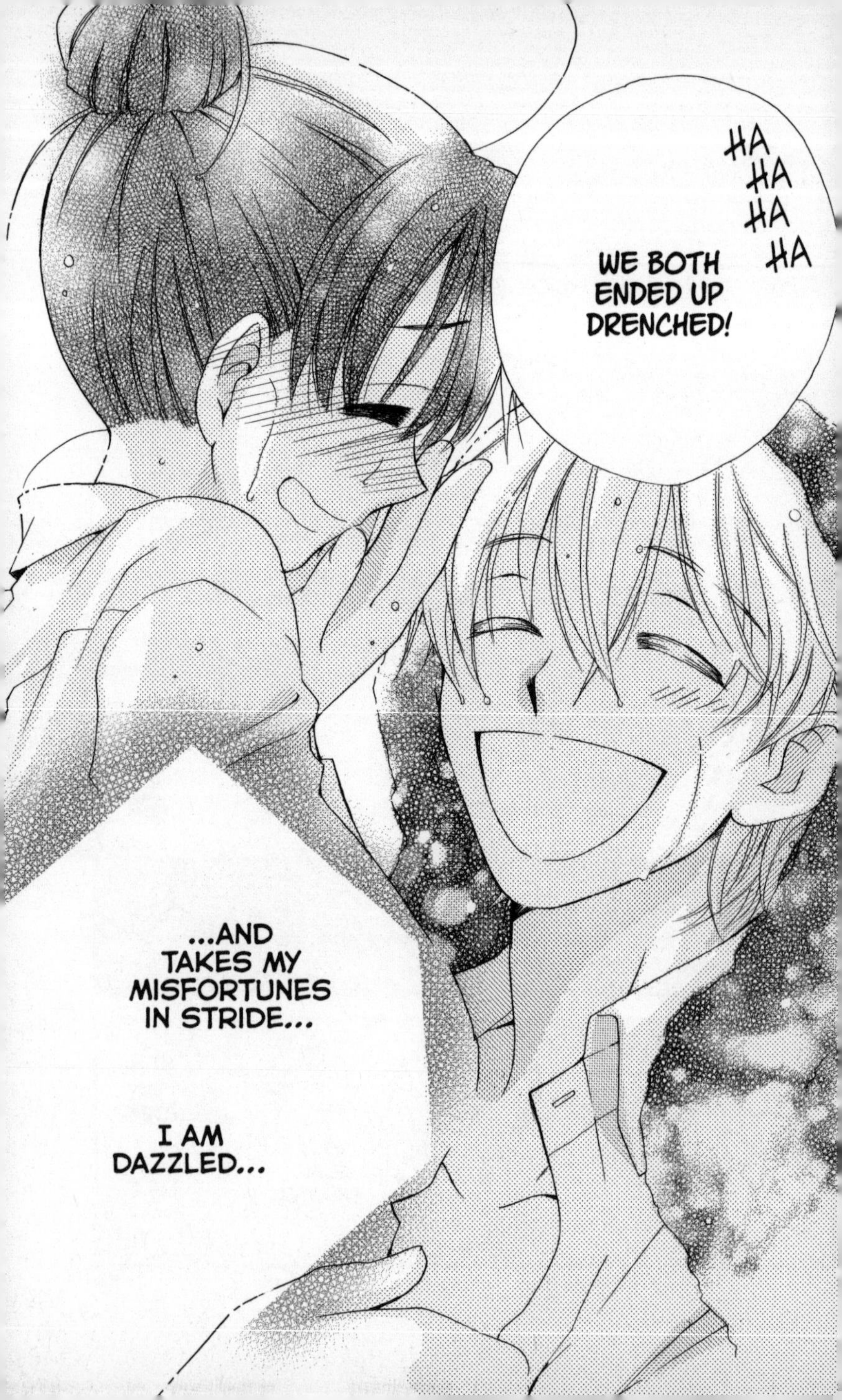
HA HA HA HA
WE BOTH ENDED UP DRENCHED!
...AND TAKES MY MISFORTUNES IN STRIDE...
I AM DAZZLED...

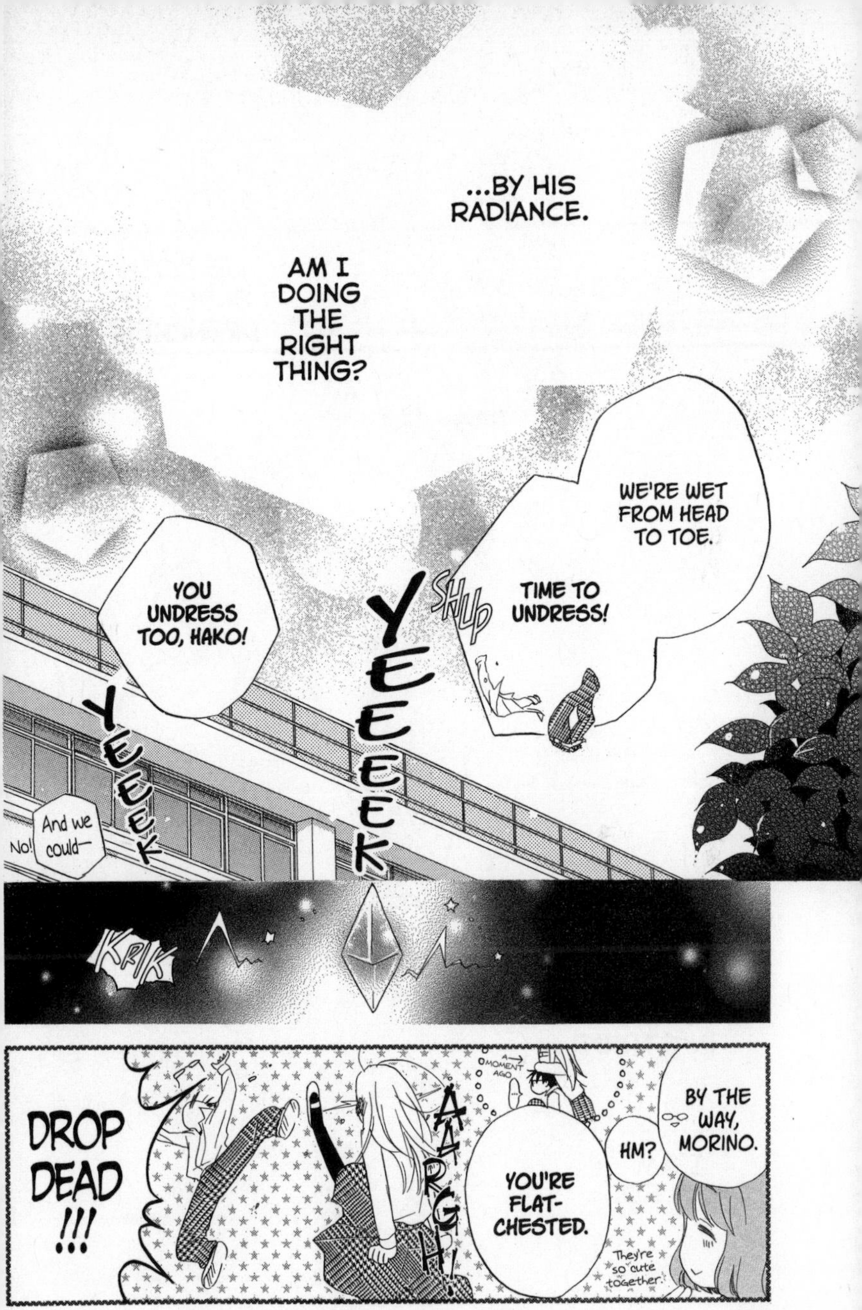
...BY HIS RADIANCE.
AM I DOING THE RIGHT THING?
WE'RE WET FROM HEAD TO TOE.
TIME TO UNDRESS!
SHUP
YEEEEK
YOU UNDRESS TOO, HAKO!
YEEEEK
And we could—
No!
KRIK
BY THE WAY, MORINO.
A MOMENT AGO
HM?
YOU'RE FLAT-CHESTED.
They're so cute together.
AARGH!
DROP DEAD!!!

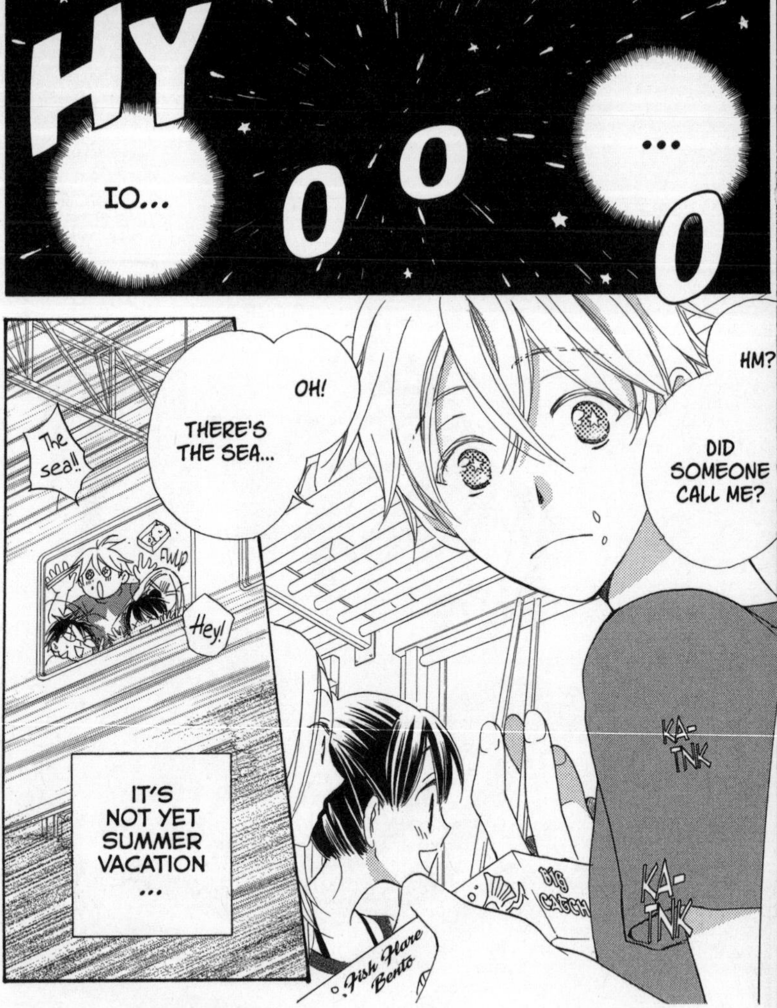
HYOOOO
...
IO...
HM?
DID SOMEONE CALL ME?
OH!
THERE'S THE SEA...
KA-TNK
KA-TNK
BIG CATCH
Fish Flare Bento
The sea!!
Hey!
IT'S NOT YET SUMMER VACATION ...

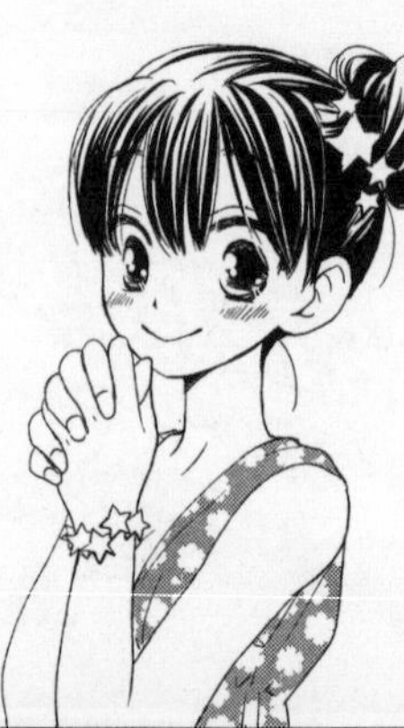

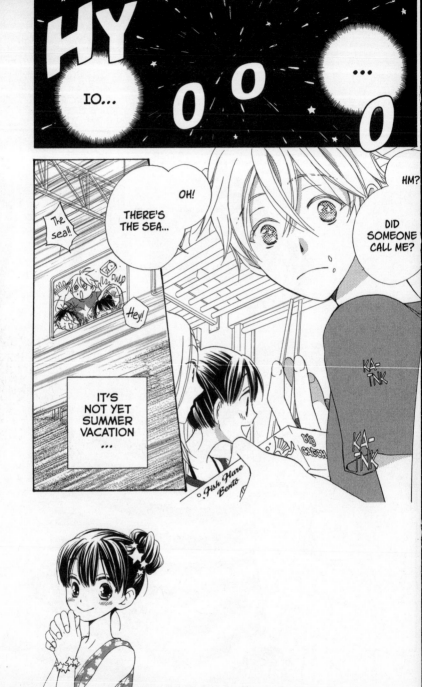

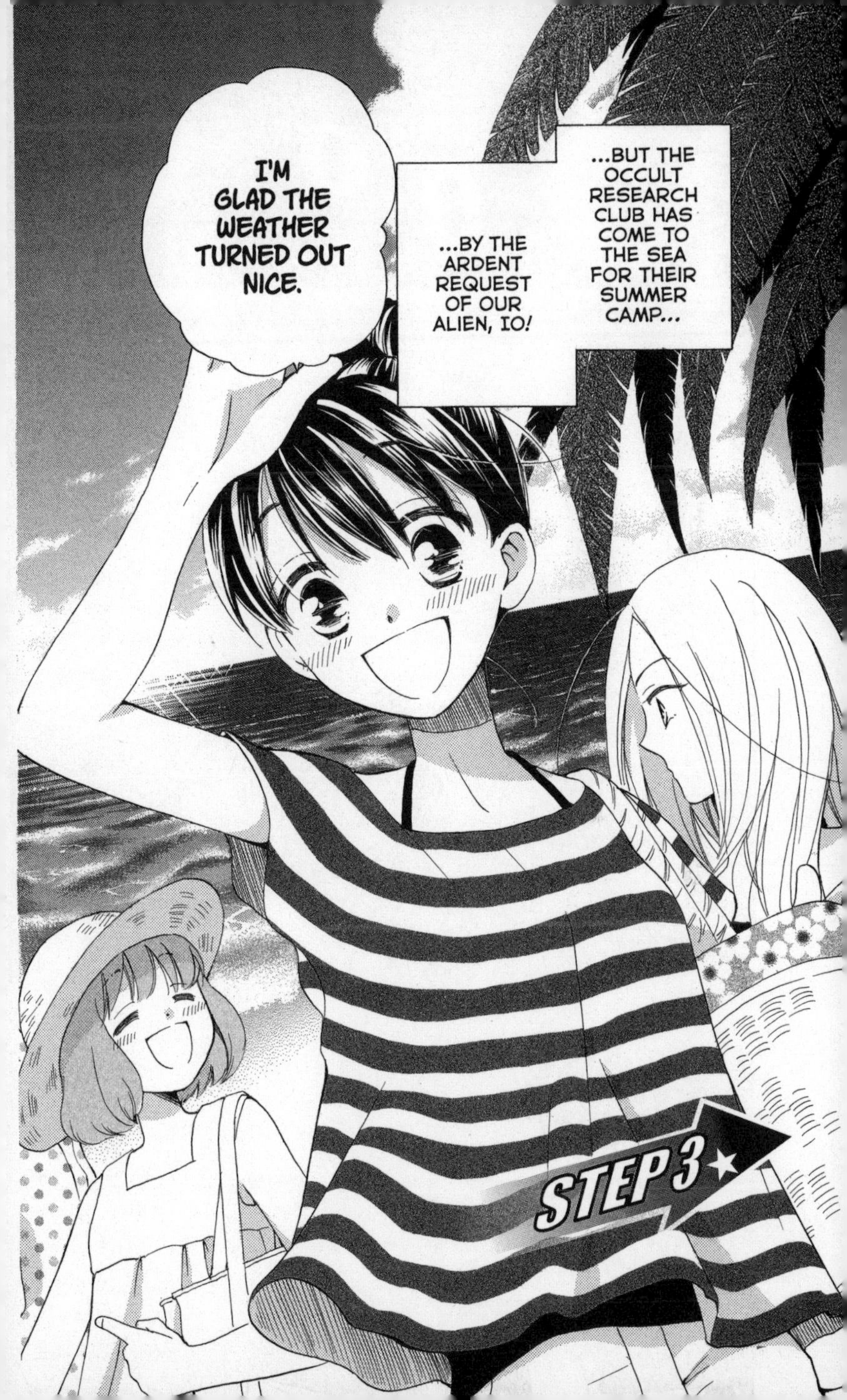
...BUT THE OCCULT RESEARCH CLUB HAS COME TO THE SEA FOR THEIR SUMMER CAMP...
...BY THE ARDENT REQUEST OF OUR ALIEN, IO!
I'M GLAD THE WEATHER TURNED OUT NICE.
STEP 3 ★

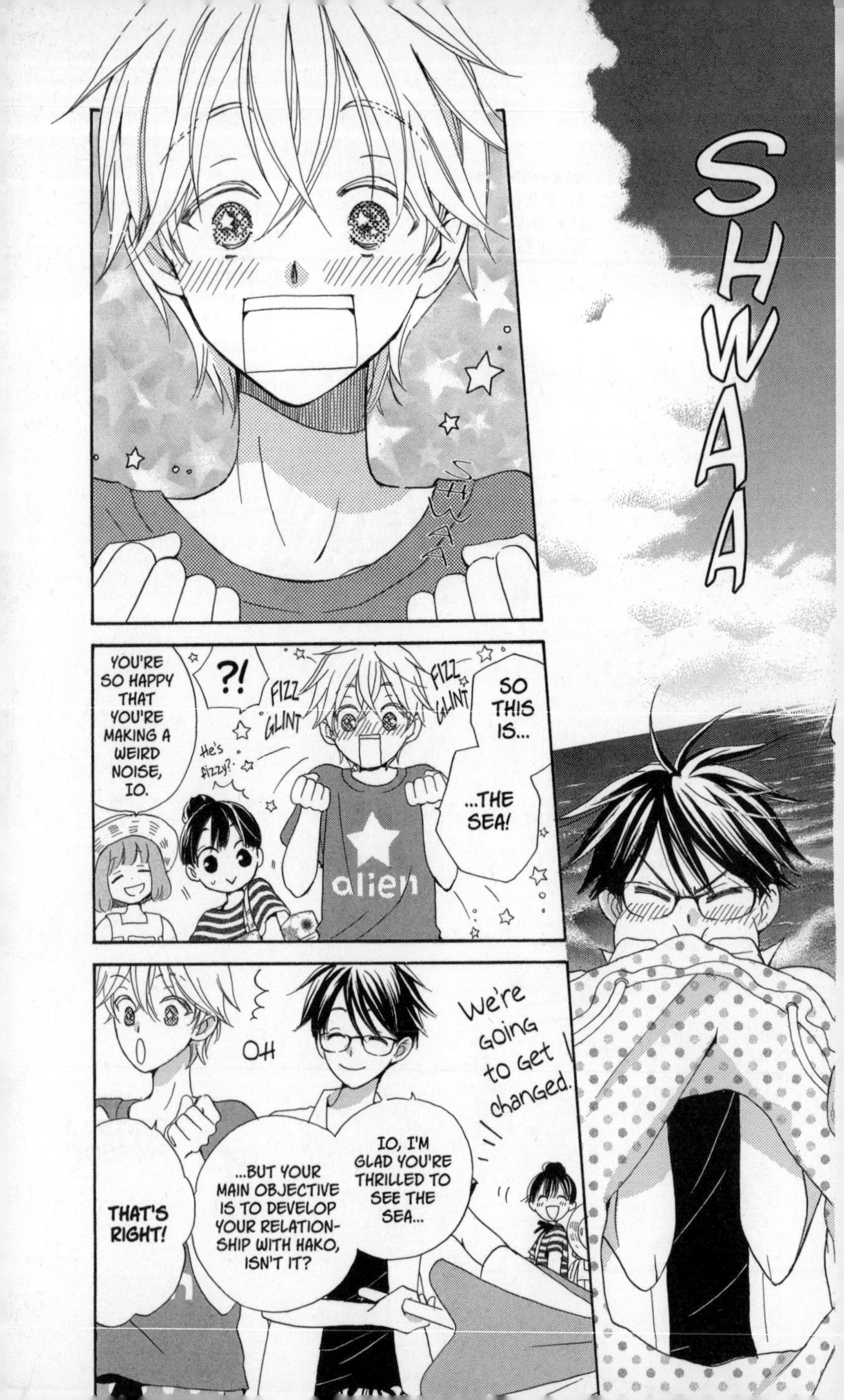
SHWAA
SHWAA
FIZZ GLINT
SO THIS IS...
...THE SEA!
FIZZ GLINT
?!
YOU'RE SO HAPPY THAT YOU'RE MAKING A WEIRD NOISE, IO.
He's fizzy?
We're going to get changed.
OH
IO, I'M GLAD YOU'RE THRILLED TO SEE THE SEA...
...BUT YOUR MAIN OBJECTIVE IS TO DEVELOP YOUR RELATIONSHIP WITH HAKO, ISN'T IT?
THAT'S RIGHT!

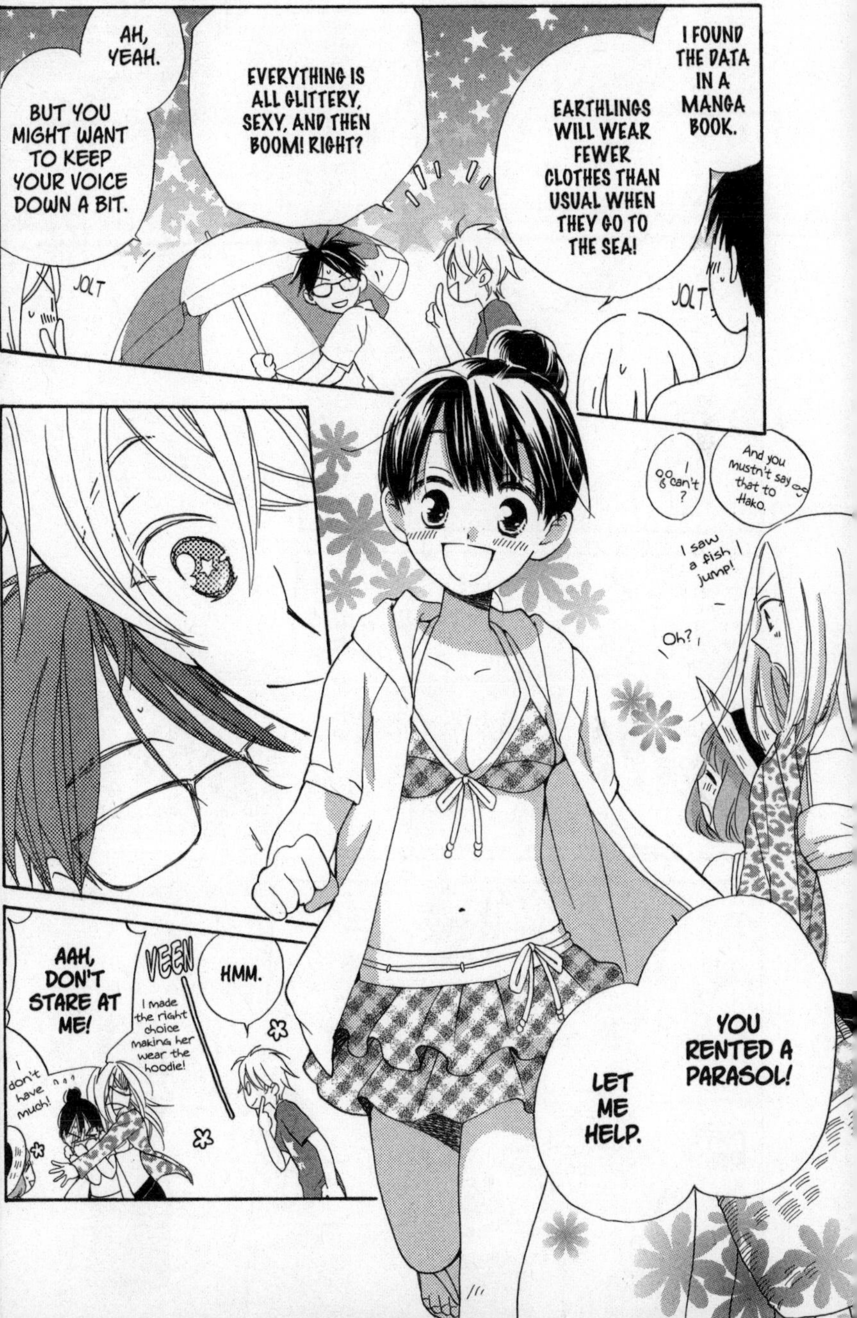
I FOUND THE DATA IN A MANGA BOOK.
EARTHLINGS WILL WEAR FEWER CLOTHES THAN USUAL WHEN THEY GO TO THE SEA!
JOLT
EVERYTHING IS ALL GLITTERY, SEXY, AND THEN BOOM! RIGHT?
AH, YEAH.
BUT YOU MIGHT WANT TO KEEP YOUR VOICE DOWN A BIT.
JOLT
And you mustn't say that to Hako.
I can't?
I saw a fish jump!
Oh?
YOU RENTED A PARASOL!
LET ME HELP.
HMM.
VEEN
I made the right choice making her wear the hoodie!
AAH, DON'T STARE AT ME!
I don't have much!

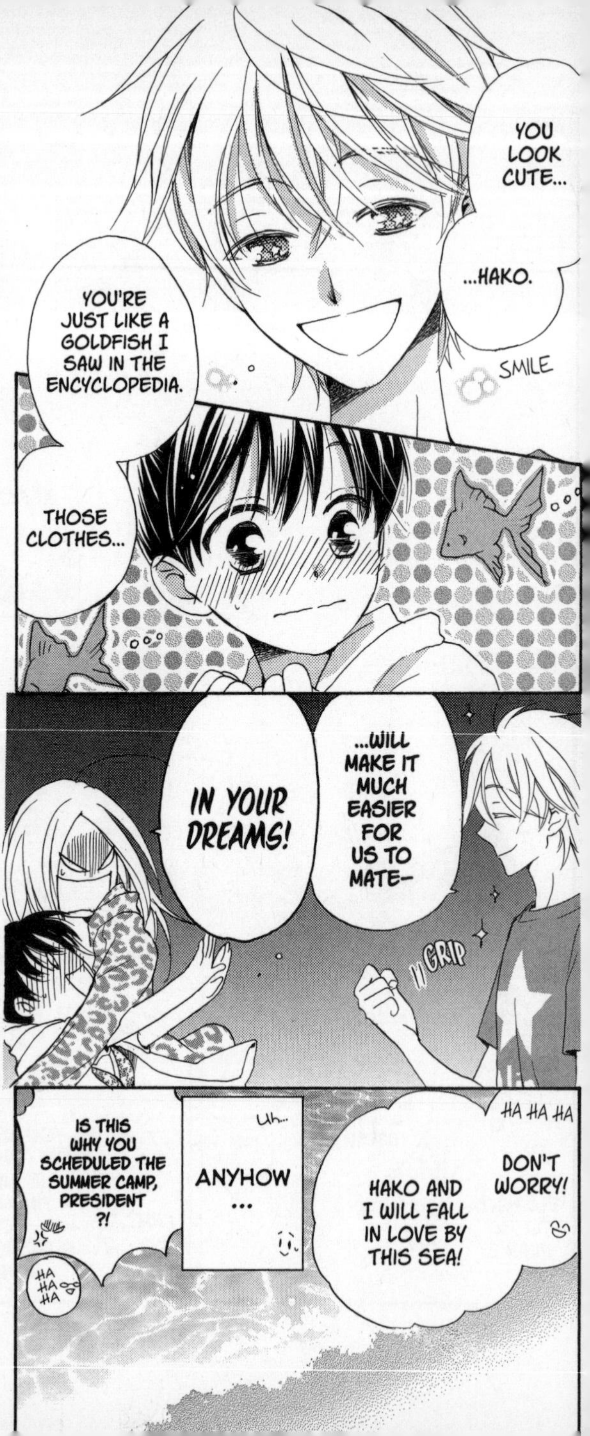
YOU LOOK CUTE...
...HAKO.
SMILE
YOU'RE JUST LIKE A GOLDFISH I SAW IN THE ENCYCLOPEDIA.
THOSE CLOTHES...
...WILL MAKE IT MUCH EASIER FOR US TO MATE-
IN YOUR DREAMS!
GRIP
HA HA HA
DON'T WORRY!
HAKO AND I WILL FALL IN LOVE BY THIS SEA!
Uh...
ANYHOW ...
IS THIS WHY YOU SCHEDULED THE SUMMER CAMP, PRESIDENT ?!
HA HA HA

Digitize

For the Met-Pri series I started to color my illustrations on my computer. I had been practicing with it on the coming next chapter illustrations.

I have only a vague understanding of what I'm supposed to do, so I've made mistakes and had all sorts of trouble, but I'm enjoying learning this new program.

I create the single color illustrations on my computer too, but like I wrote above, I don't have a full grasp on what I'm doing yet. The other day, I sent an 8 x 8 cm illustration, but for some odd reason, I had set the size to 8 x 8 mm by mistake, and that made the editor laugh.

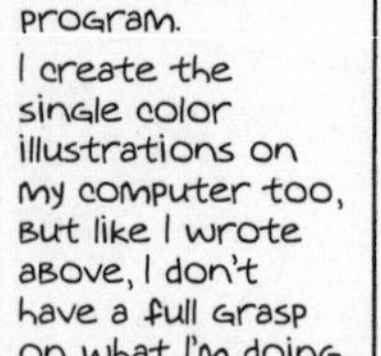
HA HA HA HA
AH HA HA HA
A grain of rice...
It's like a grain of rice!
Really?
AH HA HA HA
I'm really sorry.

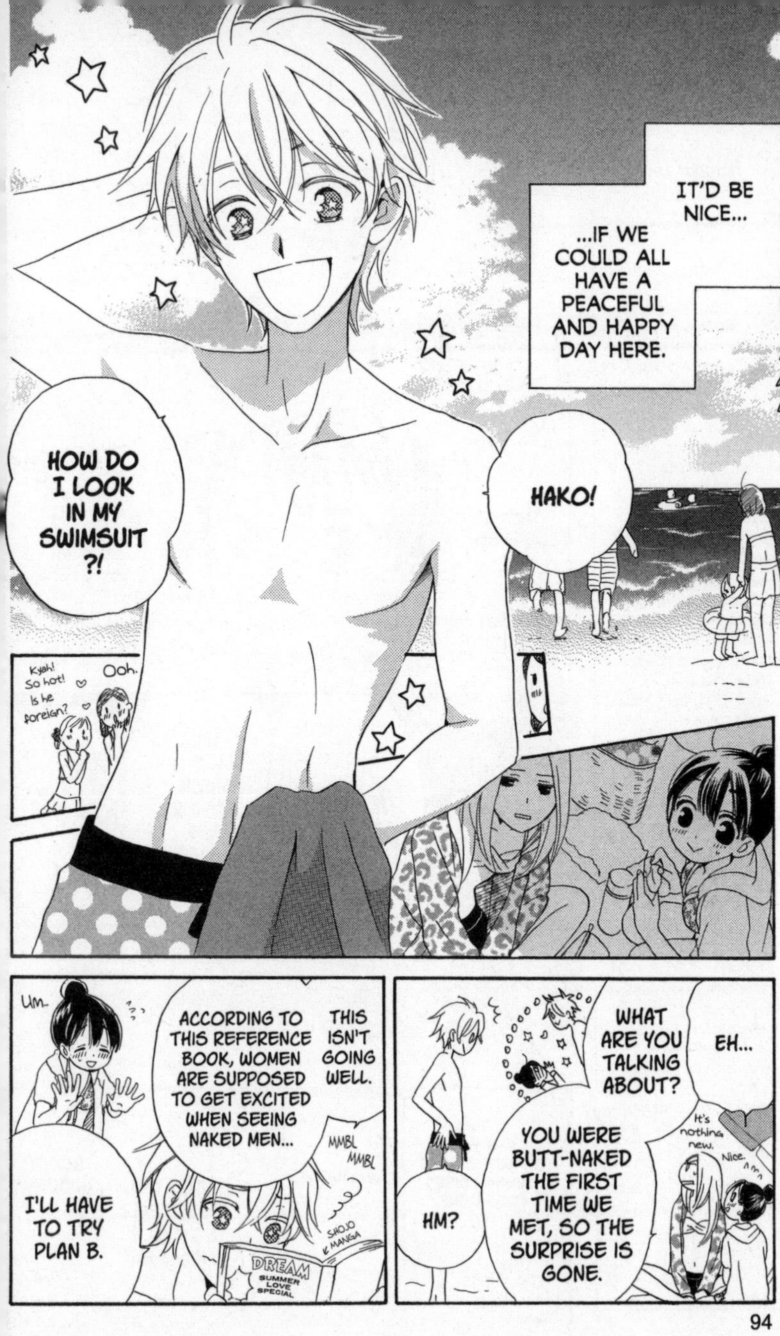
IT'D BE NICE...
...IF WE COULD ALL HAVE A PEACEFUL AND HAPPY DAY HERE.
SHWAAA
HAKO!
HOW DO I LOOK IN MY SWIMSUIT?!
Ooh.
Kyah! So hot! Is he foreign?
EH...
WHAT ARE YOU TALKING ABOUT?
It's nothing new.
Nice.
YOU WERE BUTT-NAKED THE FIRST TIME WE MET, SO THE SURPRISE IS GONE.
HM?
THIS ISN'T GOING WELL.
ACCORDING TO THIS REFERENCE BOOK, WOMEN ARE SUPPOSED TO GET EXCITED WHEN SEEING NAKED MEN...
Um.
MMBL MMBL
SHOJO MANGA
DREAM SUMMER LOVE SPECIAL
I'LL HAVE TO TRY PLAN B.

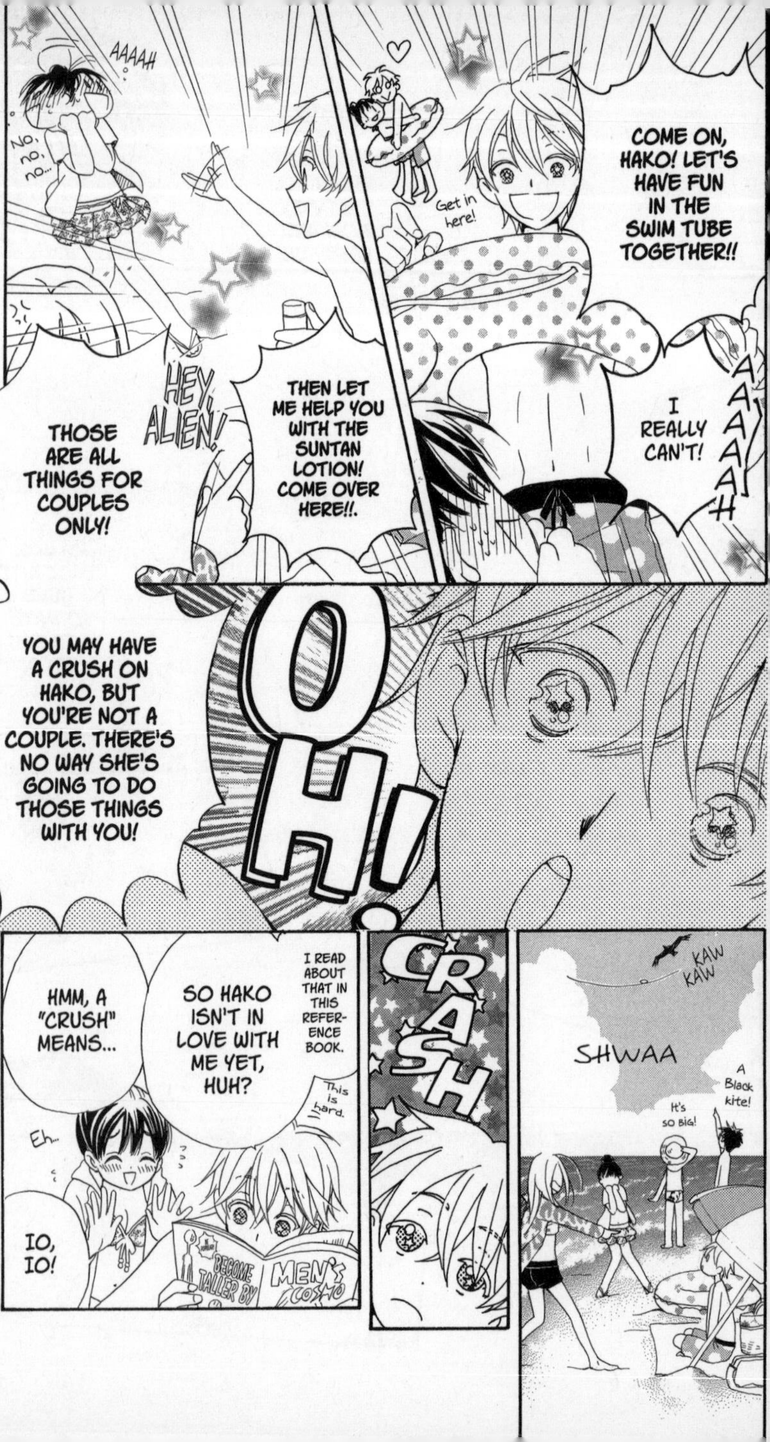
COME ON, HAKO! LET'S HAVE FUN IN THE SWIM TUBE TOGETHER!!
Get in here!
I REALLY CAN'T!
AAAAAH
AAAAH
No, no, no...
THEN LET ME HELP YOU WITH THE SUNTAN LOTION! COME OVER HERE!!.
HEY, ALIEN!
THOSE ARE ALL THINGS FOR COUPLES ONLY!
YOU MAY HAVE A CRUSH ON HAKO, BUT YOU'RE NOT A COUPLE. THERE'S NO WAY SHE'S GOING TO DO THOSE THINGS WITH YOU!
OH!
KAW KAW
SHWAA
A Black kite!
It's so big!
CRASH
I READ ABOUT THAT IN THIS REFERENCE BOOK.
SO HAKO ISN'T IN LOVE WITH ME YET, HUH?
This is hard.
HMM, A "CRUSH" MEANS...
Eh...
IO, IO!
BECOME TALLER BY
MEN'S COSMO

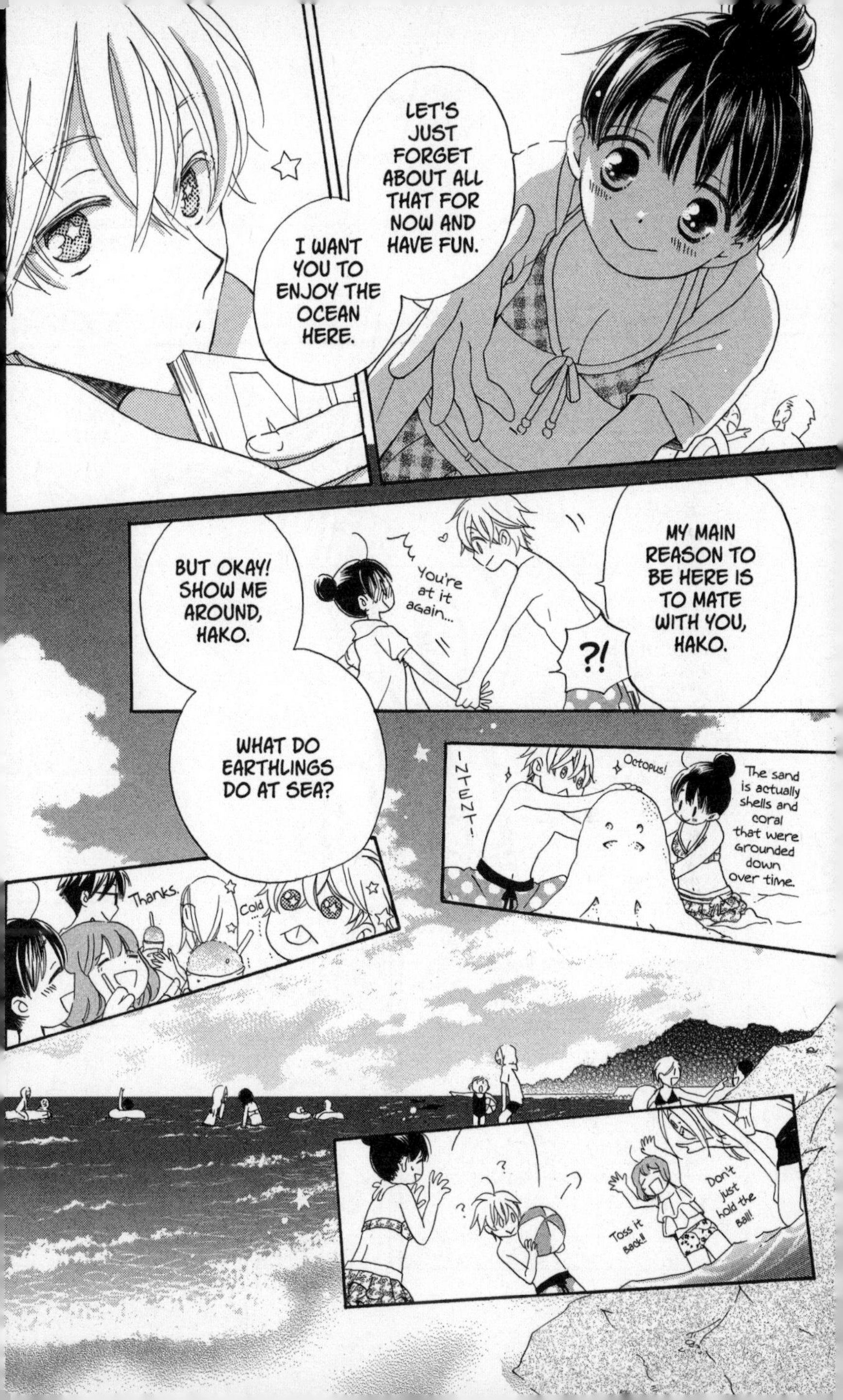
LET'S JUST FORGET ABOUT ALL THAT FOR NOW AND HAVE FUN.
I WANT YOU TO ENJOY THE OCEAN HERE.
MY MAIN REASON TO BE HERE IS TO MATE WITH YOU, HAKO.
?!
You're at it again...
BUT OKAY! SHOW ME AROUND, HAKO.
WHAT DO EARTHLINGS DO AT SEA?
The sand is actually shells and coral that were grounded down over time.
Octopus!
INTENT
Cold...
Thanks.
Don't just hold the ball!
Toss it back!!

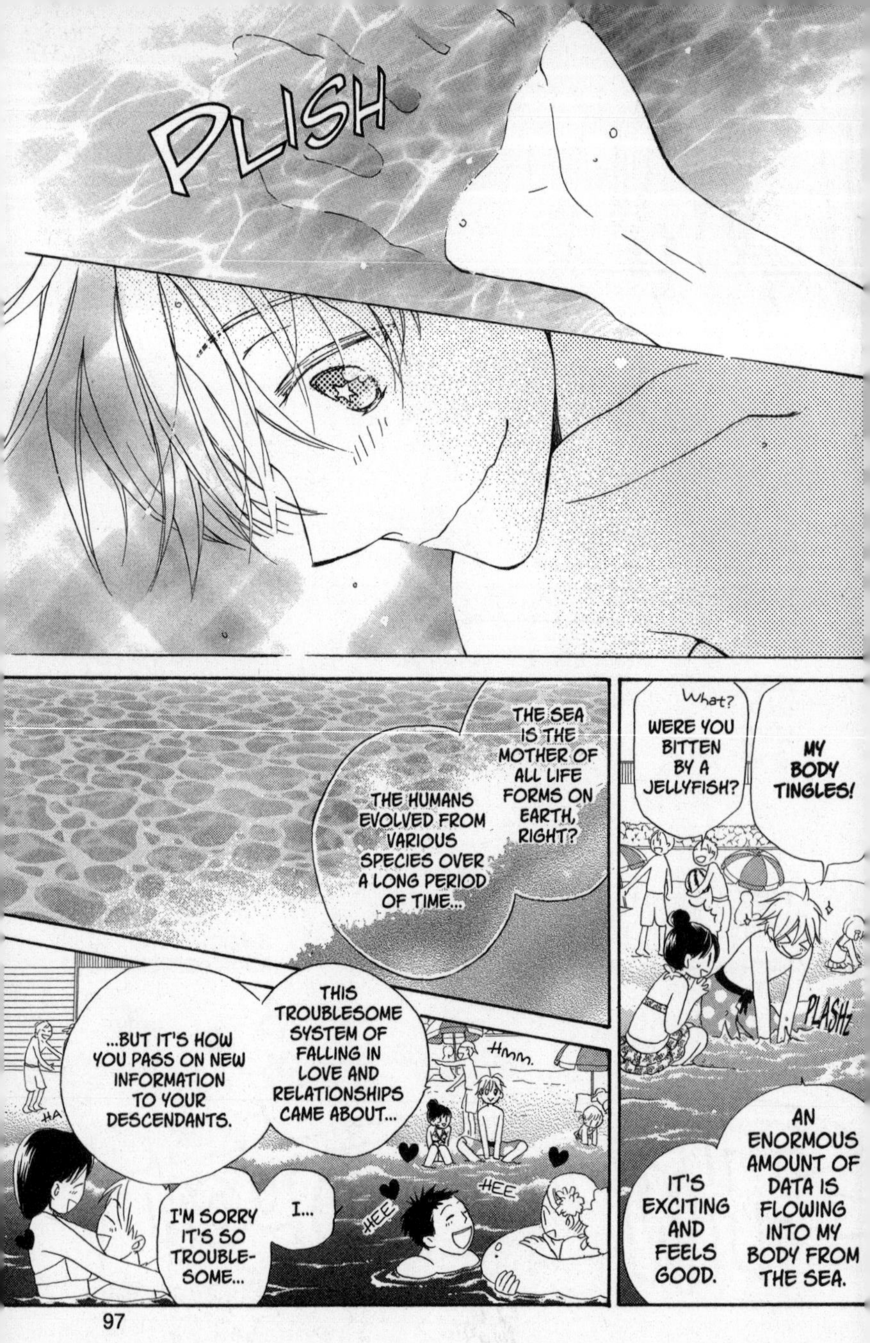
PLISH
MY BODY TINGLES!
What?
WERE YOU BITTEN BY A JELLYFISH?
PLASHz
AN ENORMOUS AMOUNT OF DATA IS FLOWING INTO MY BODY FROM THE SEA.
IT'S EXCITING AND FEELS GOOD.
THE SEA IS THE MOTHER OF ALL LIFE FORMS ON EARTH, RIGHT?
THE HUMANS EVOLVED FROM VARIOUS SPECIES OVER A LONG PERIOD OF TIME...
THIS TROUBLESOME SYSTEM OF FALLING IN LOVE AND RELATIONSHIPS CAME ABOUT...
...BUT IT'S HOW YOU PASS ON NEW INFORMATION TO YOUR DESCENDANTS.
Hmm.
HA
HEE
HEE
I...
I'M SORRY IT'S SO TROUBLE-SOME...

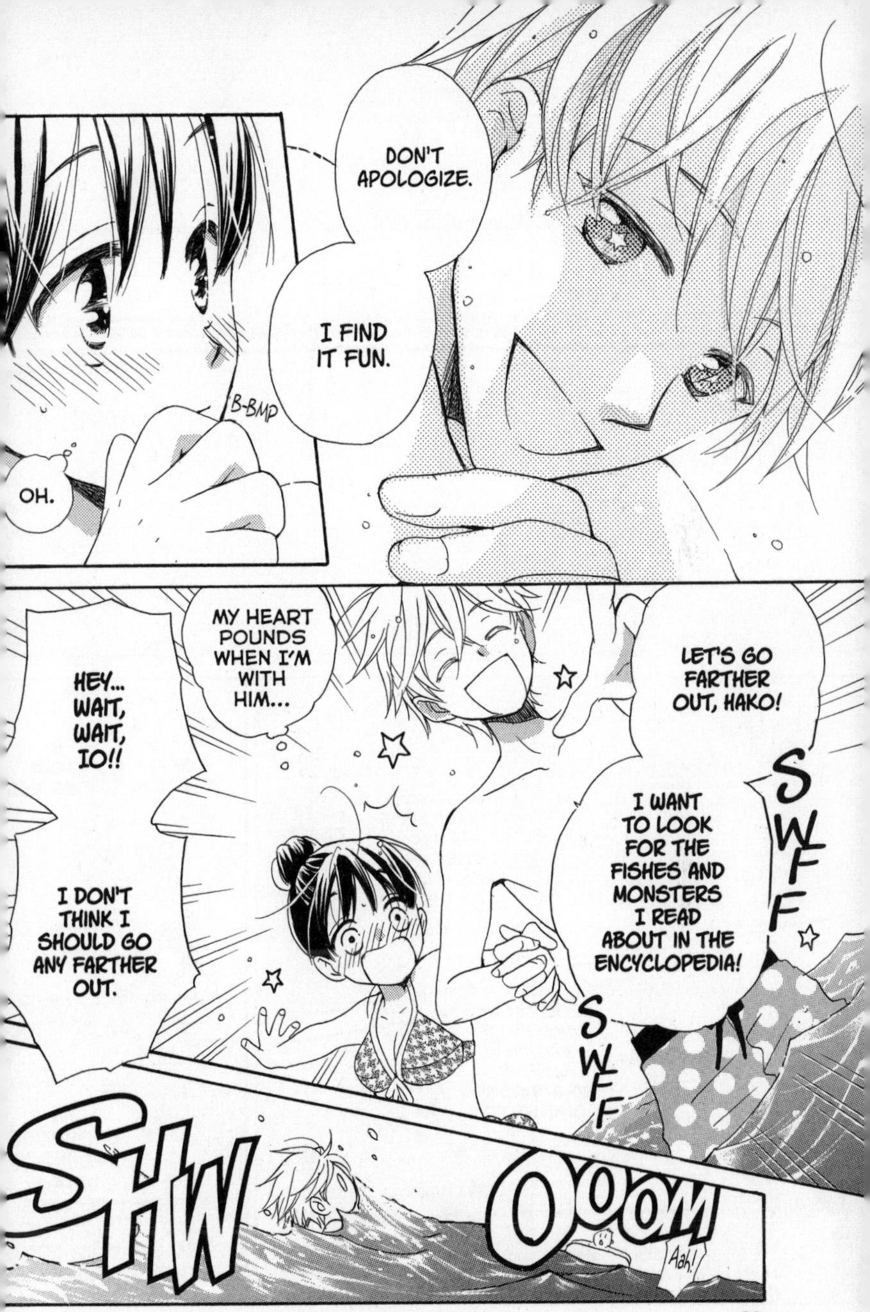
DON'T APOLOGIZE.
I FIND IT FUN.
B-BMP
OH.
LET'S GO FARTHER OUT, HAKO!
I WANT TO LOOK FOR THE FISHES AND MONSTERS I READ ABOUT IN THE ENCYCLOPEDIA!
SWFF
SWFF
MY HEART POUNDS WHEN I'M WITH HIM...
HEY... WAIT, WAIT, IO!!
I DON'T THINK I SHOULD GO ANY FARTHER OUT.
SHWOOOM
Aah!

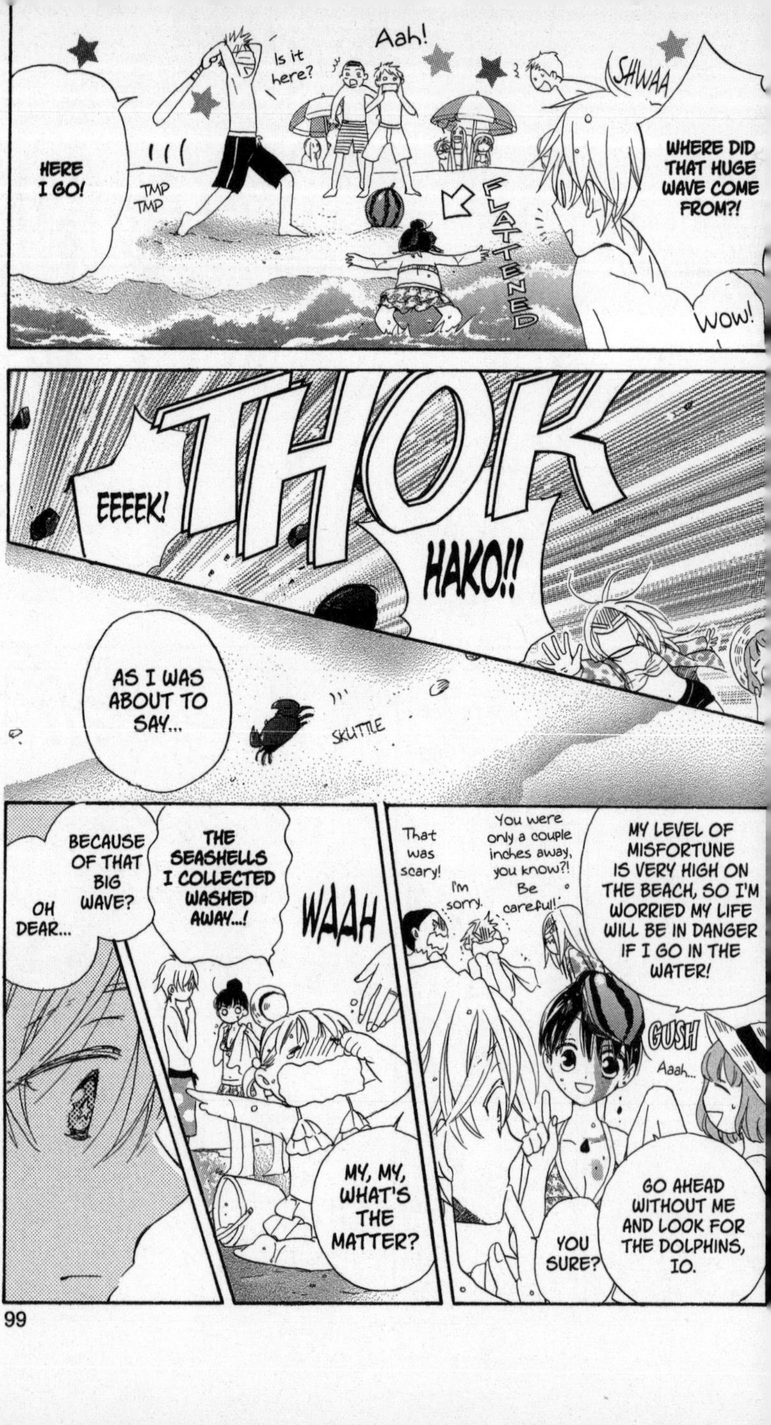
SHWAA
WHERE DID THAT HUGE WAVE COME FROM?!
WOW!
FLATTENED
Aah!
Is it here?
TMP TMP
HERE I GO!
HAKO!!
THOK
EEEEK!
SKUTTLE
AS I WAS ABOUT TO SAY...
MY LEVEL OF MISFORTUNE IS VERY HIGH ON THE BEACH, SO I'M WORRIED MY LIFE WILL BE IN DANGER IF I GO IN THE WATER!
You were only a couple inches away, you know?! Be careful!!
I'm sorry.
That was scary!
GUSH
Aaah...
GO AHEAD WITHOUT ME AND LOOK FOR THE DOLPHINS, IO.
YOU SURE?
THE SEASHELLS I COLLECTED WASHED AWAY...!
WAAH
MY, MY, WHAT'S THE MATTER?
BECAUSE OF THAT BIG WAVE?
OH DEAR...

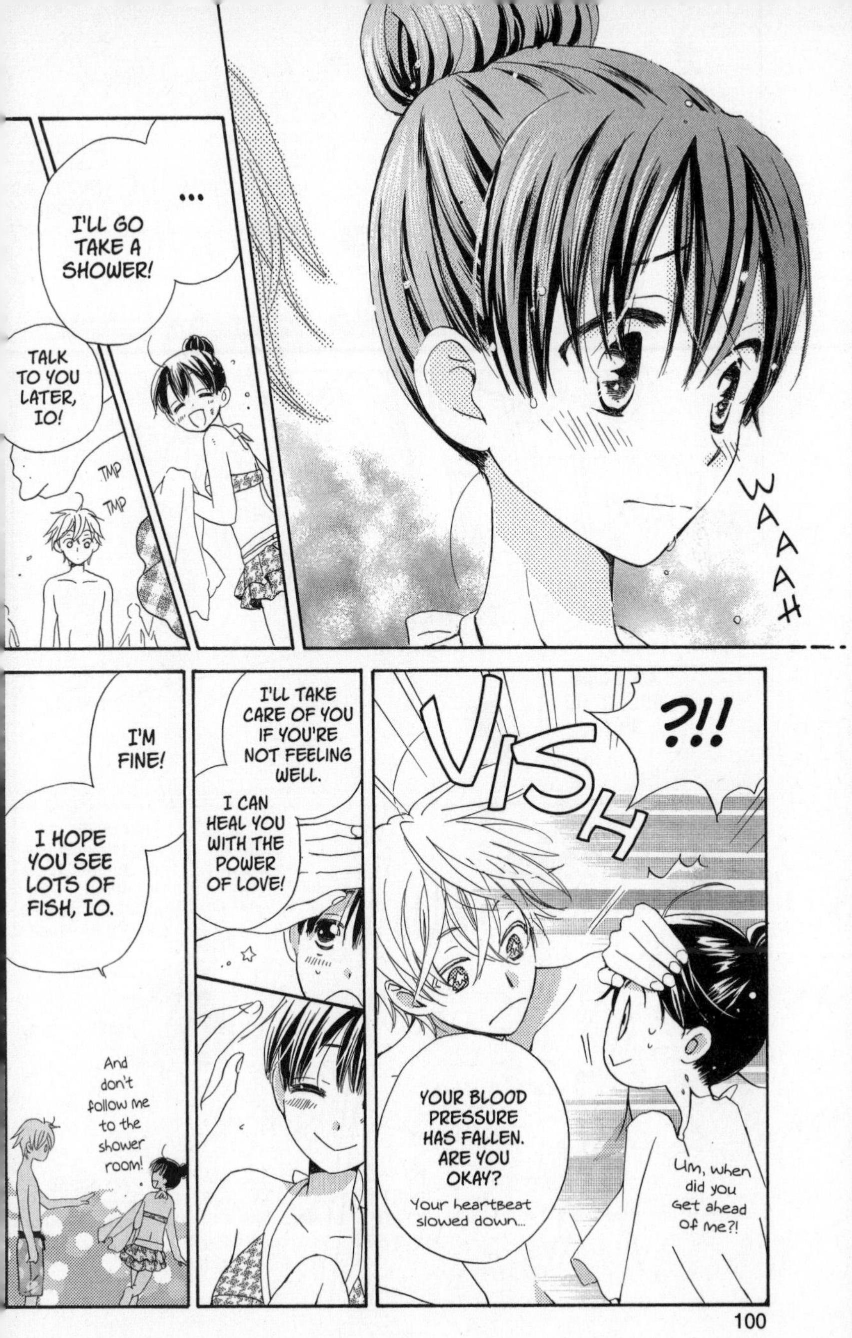
WAAAH
...
I'LL GO TAKE A SHOWER!
TALK TO YOU LATER, IO!
TMP
TMP
?!!
VISH
YOUR BLOOD PRESSURE HAS FALLEN. ARE YOU OKAY?
Your heartbeat slowed down...
Um, when did you get ahead of me?!
I'LL TAKE CARE OF YOU IF YOU'RE NOT FEELING WELL.
I CAN HEAL YOU WITH THE POWER OF LOVE!
I'M FINE!
I HOPE YOU SEE LOTS OF FISH, IO.
And don't follow me to the shower room!

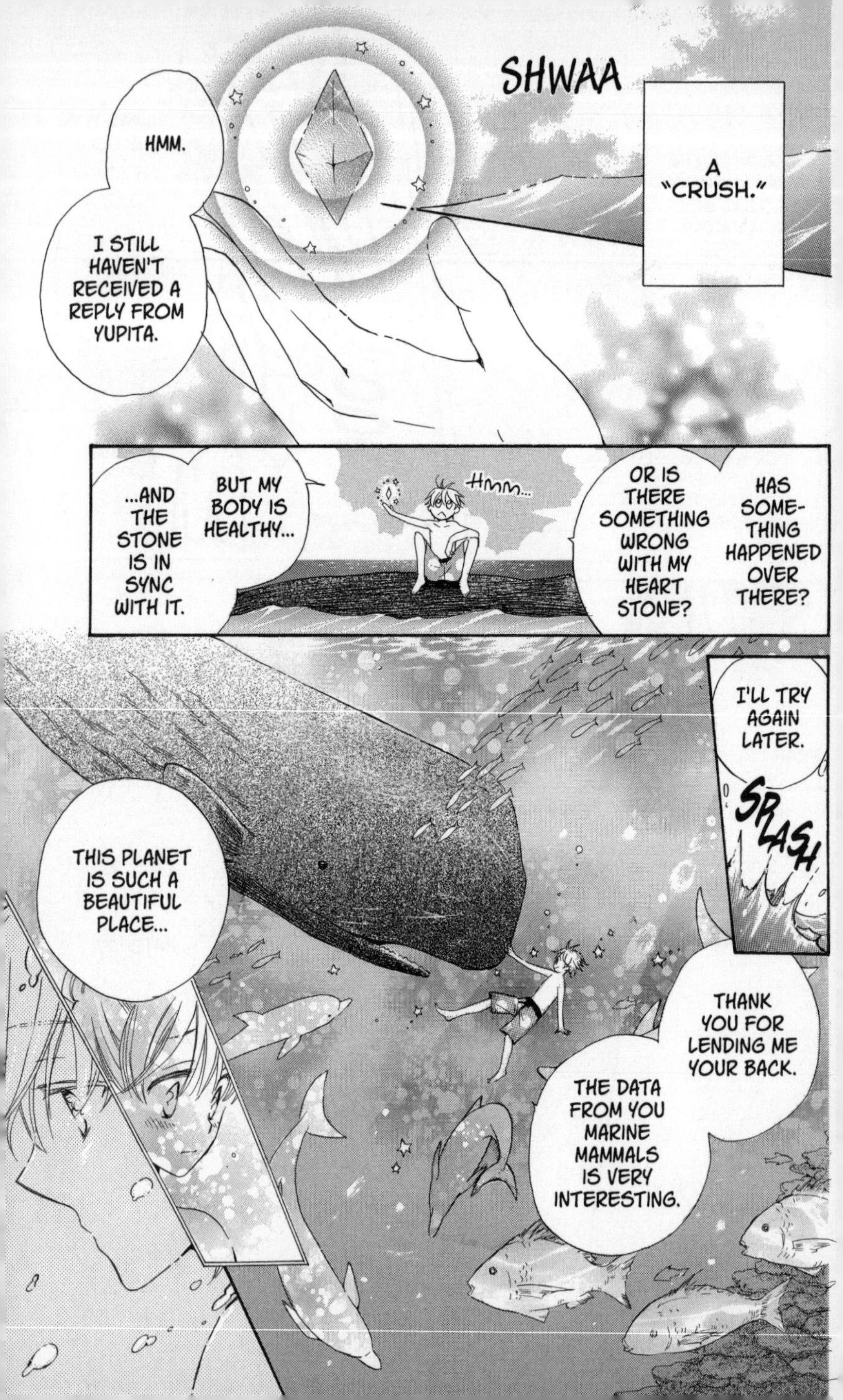
SHWAA
A "CRUSH."
HMM.
I STILL HAVEN'T RECEIVED A REPLY FROM YUPITA.
HAS SOMETHING HAPPENED OVER THERE?
OR IS THERE SOMETHING WRONG WITH MY HEART STONE?
Hmm...
BUT MY BODY IS HEALTHY...
...AND THE STONE IS IN SYNC WITH IT.
I'LL TRY AGAIN LATER.
SPLASH
THANK YOU FOR LENDING ME YOUR BACK.
THE DATA FROM YOU MARINE MAMMALS IS VERY INTERESTING.
THIS PLANET IS SUCH A BEAUTIFUL PLACE...

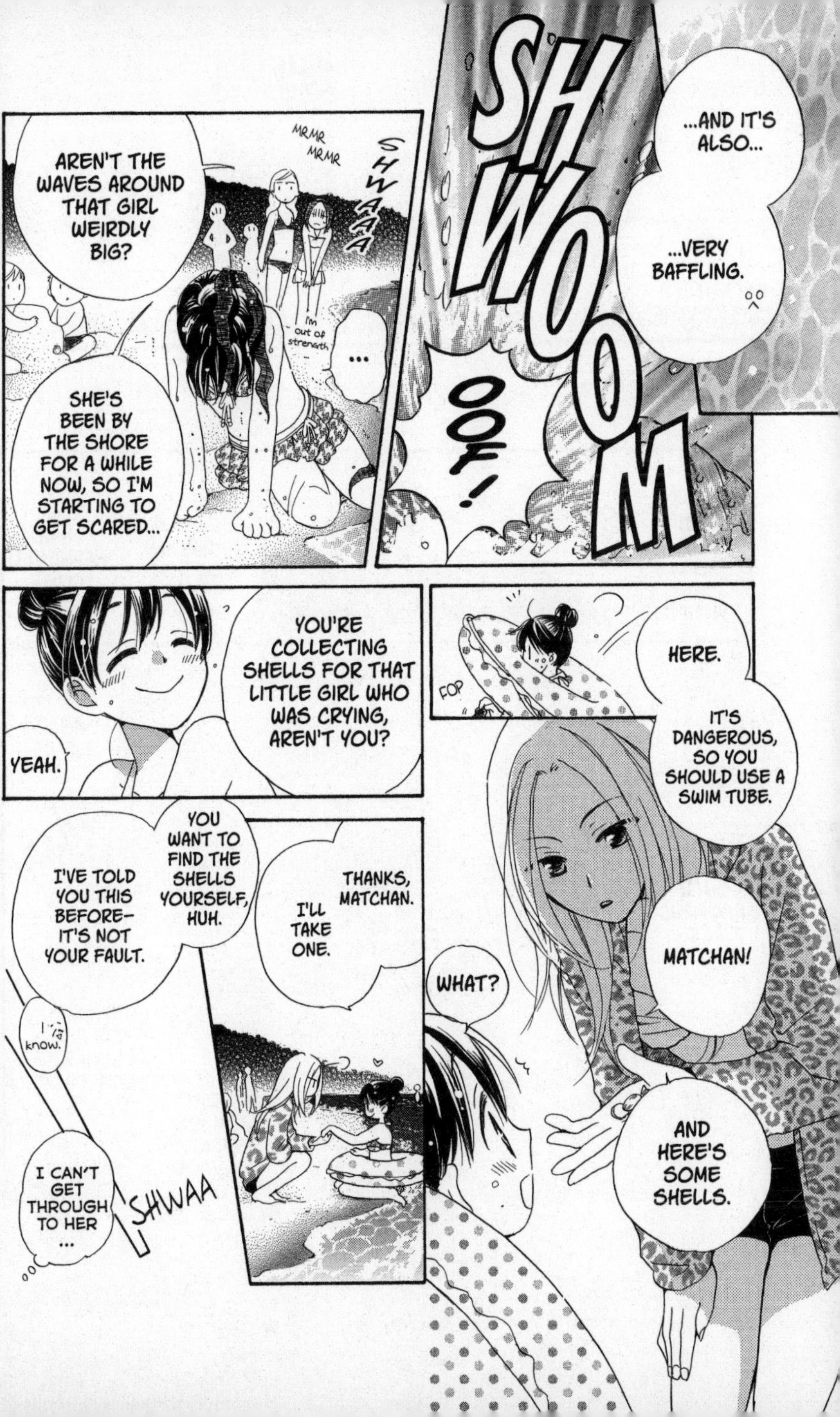
...AND IT'S ALSO...
...VERY BAFFLING.
SHWOOM
OOF!
SHWAAA
MRMR MRMR
AREN'T THE WAVES AROUND THAT GIRL WEIRDLY BIG?
SHE'S BEEN BY THE SHORE FOR A WHILE NOW, SO I'M STARTING TO GET SCARED...
I'm out of strength...
...
HERE.
FOP
YOU'RE COLLECTING SHELLS FOR THAT LITTLE GIRL WHO WAS CRYING, AREN'T YOU?
YEAH.
IT'S DANGEROUS, SO YOU SHOULD USE A SWIM TUBE.
MATCHAN!
WHAT?
AND HERE'S SOME SHELLS.
THANKS, MATCHAN.
I'LL TAKE ONE.
YOU WANT TO FIND THE SHELLS YOURSELF, HUH.
I'VE TOLD YOU THIS BEFORE- IT'S NOT YOUR FAULT.
I know.
SHWAA
I CAN'T GET THROUGH TO HER...

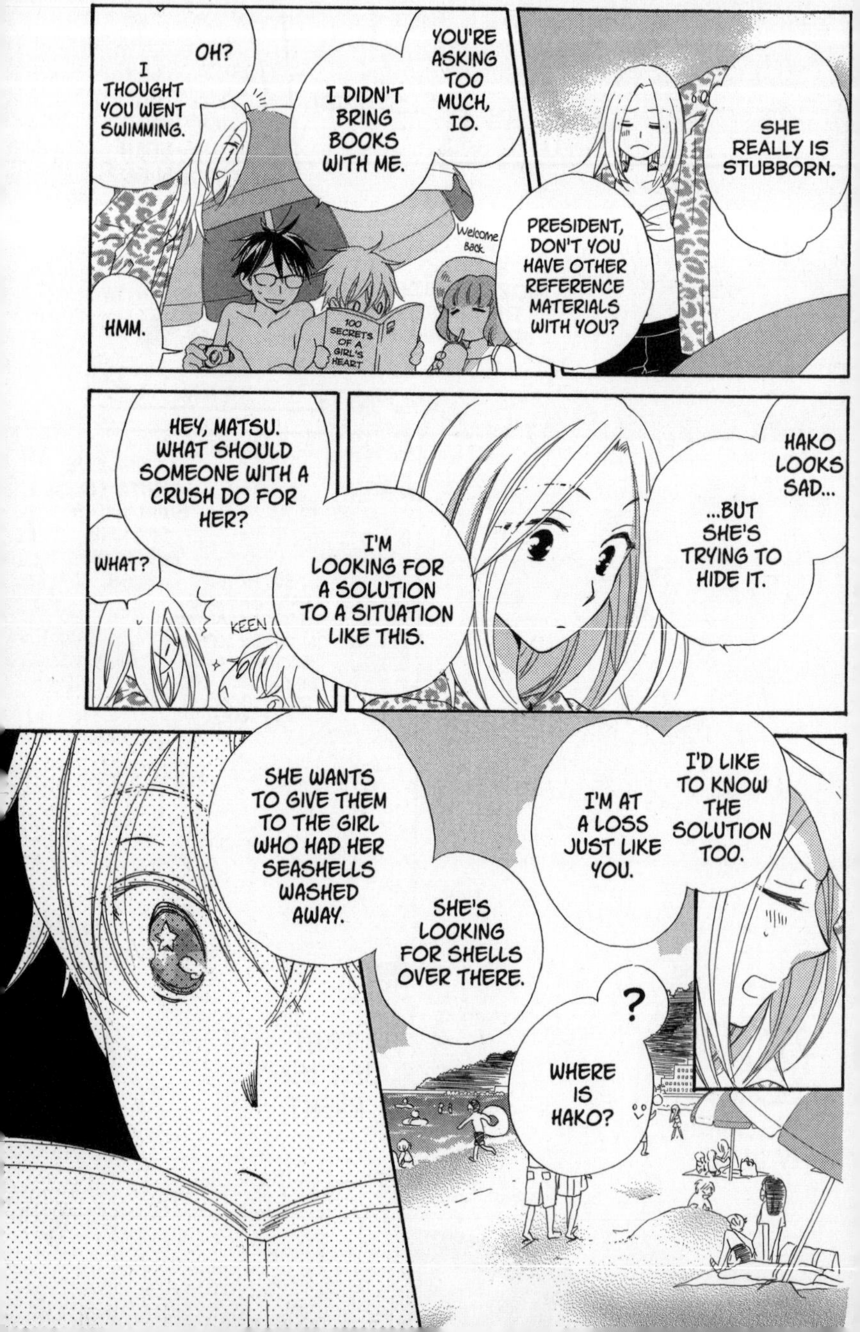
SHE REALLY IS STUBBORN.
PRESIDENT, DON'T YOU HAVE OTHER REFERENCE MATERIALS WITH YOU?
YOU'RE ASKING TOO MUCH, IO.
I DIDN'T BRING BOOKS WITH ME.
OH?
I THOUGHT YOU WENT SWIMMING.
Welcome Back
100 SECRETS OF A GIRL'S HEART
HMM.
HAKO LOOKS SAD...
...BUT SHE'S TRYING TO HIDE IT.
HEY, MATSU. WHAT SHOULD SOMEONE WITH A CRUSH DO FOR HER?
I'M LOOKING FOR A SOLUTION TO A SITUATION LIKE THIS.
WHAT?
KEEN
I'D LIKE TO KNOW THE SOLUTION TOO.
I'M AT A LOSS JUST LIKE YOU.
?
WHERE IS HAKO?
SHE'S LOOKING FOR SHELLS OVER THERE.
SHE WANTS TO GIVE THEM TO THE GIRL WHO HAD HER SEASHELLS WASHED AWAY.

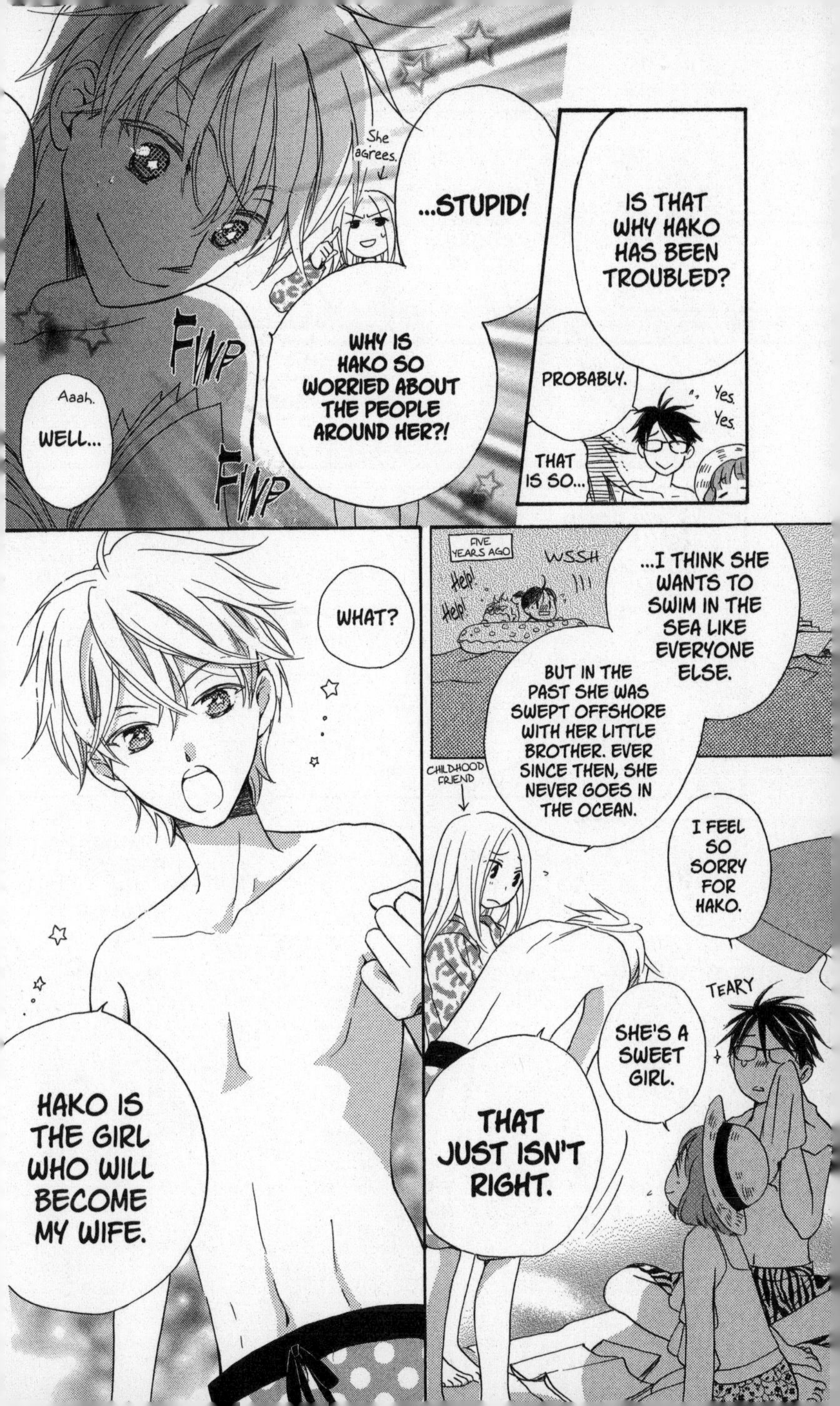
IS THAT WHY HAKO HAS BEEN TROUBLED?
PROBABLY.
Yes. Yes.
THAT IS SO...
...STUPID!
She agrees.
WHY IS HAKO SO WORRIED ABOUT THE PEOPLE AROUND HER?!
FWP
Aaah.
WELL...
FWP
FIVE YEARS AGO
WSSH
Help!
Help!
...I THINK SHE WANTS TO SWIM IN THE SEA LIKE EVERYONE ELSE.
BUT IN THE PAST SHE WAS SWEPT OFFSHORE WITH HER LITTLE BROTHER. EVER SINCE THEN, SHE NEVER GOES IN THE OCEAN.
CHILDHOOD FRIEND
I FEEL SO SORRY FOR HAKO.
TEARY
SHE'S A SWEET GIRL.
THAT JUST ISN'T RIGHT.
WHAT?
HAKO IS THE GIRL WHO WILL BECOME MY WIFE.

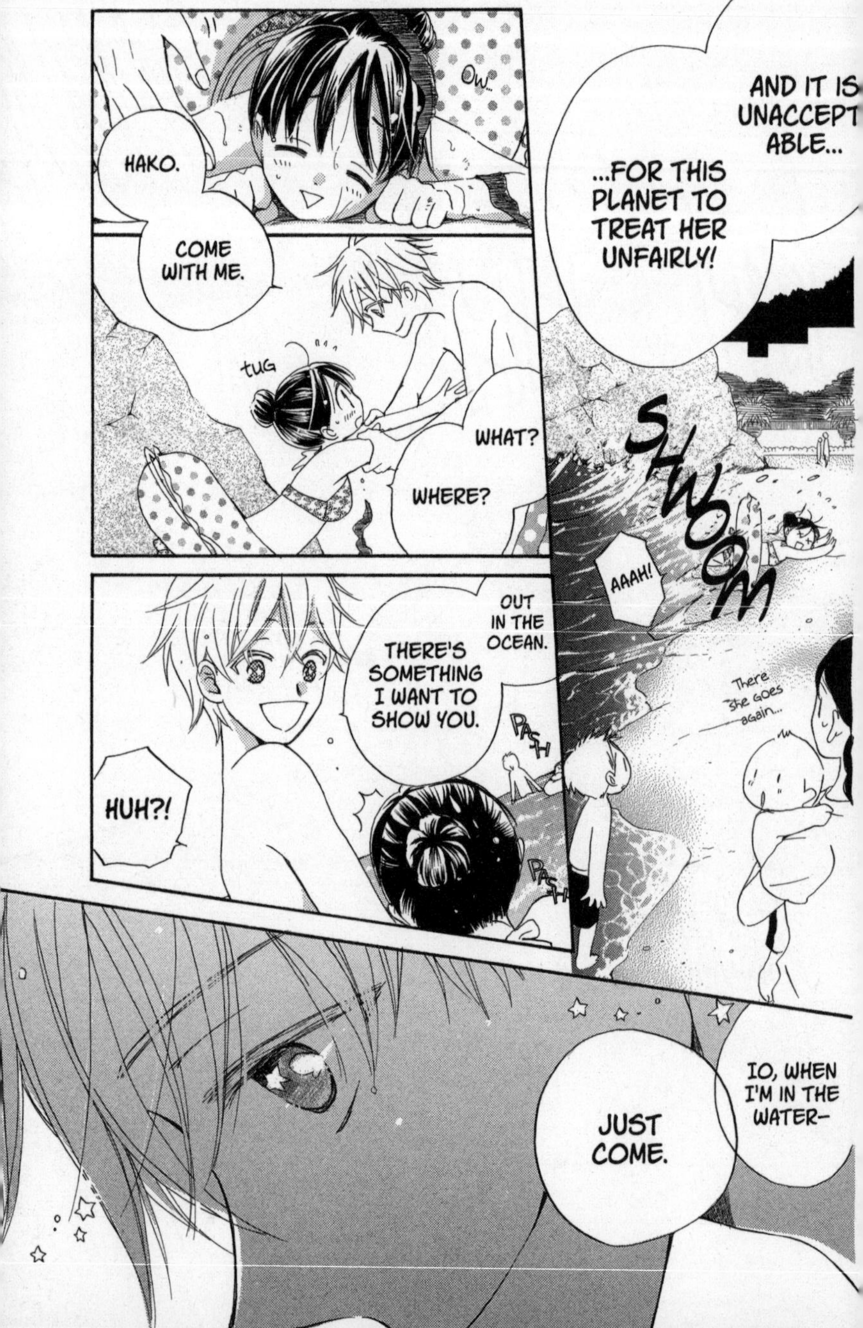
AND IT IS UNACCEPTABLE...
...FOR THIS PLANET TO TREAT HER UNFAIRLY!
SHWOOM
AAAH!
There she goes again...
Ow...
HAKO.
COME WITH ME.
tug
WHAT?
WHERE?
OUT IN THE OCEAN.
THERE'S SOMETHING I WANT TO SHOW YOU.
PASH
HUH?!
PASH
IO, WHEN I'M IN THE WATER—
JUST COME.

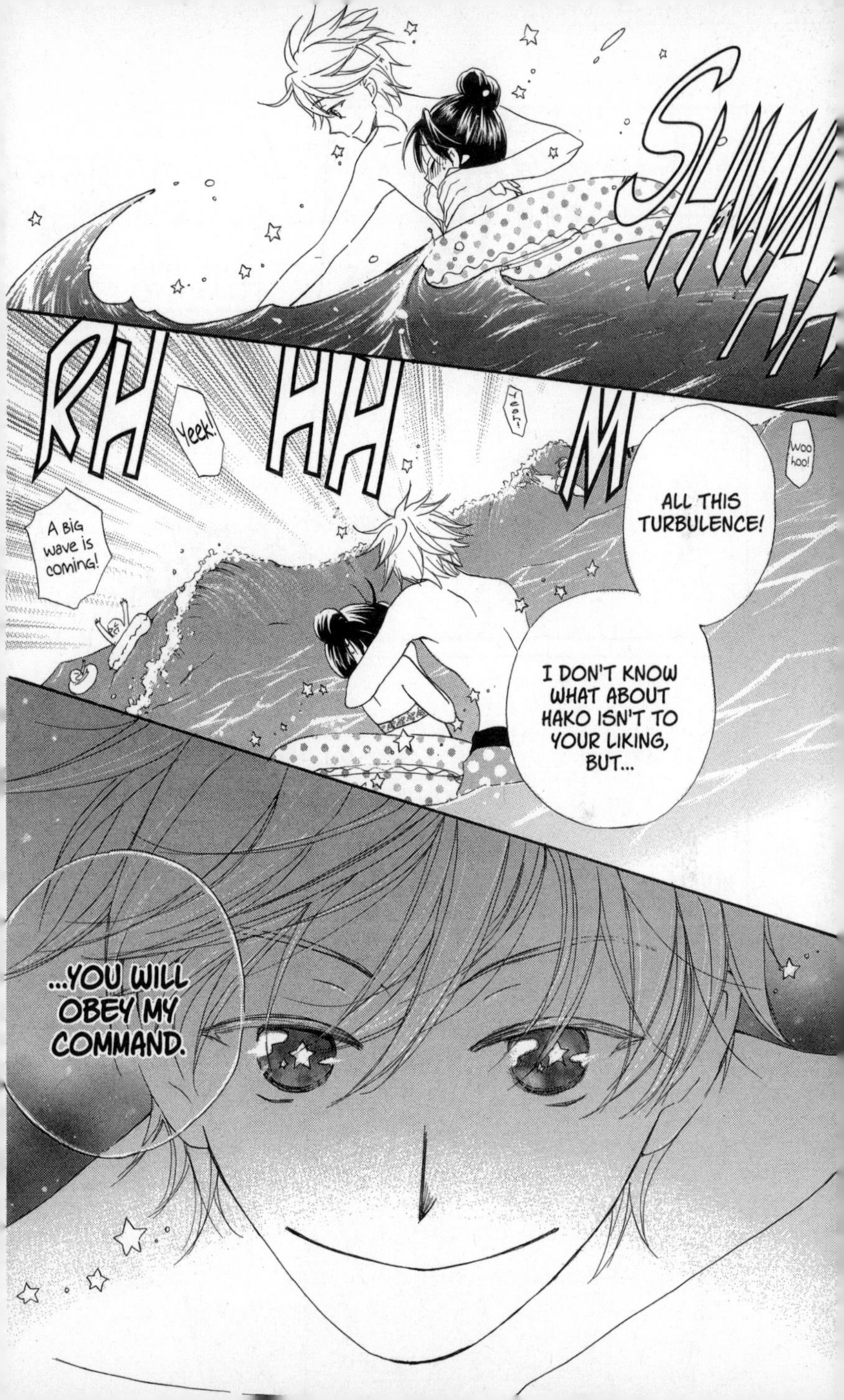
SHWAA
RHHHHM
Woo hoo!
ALL THIS TURBULENCE!
Yeah!
Yeek!
A BIG wave is coming!
I DON'T KNOW WHAT ABOUT HAKO ISN'T TO YOUR LIKING, BUT...
...YOU WILL OBEY MY COMMAND.

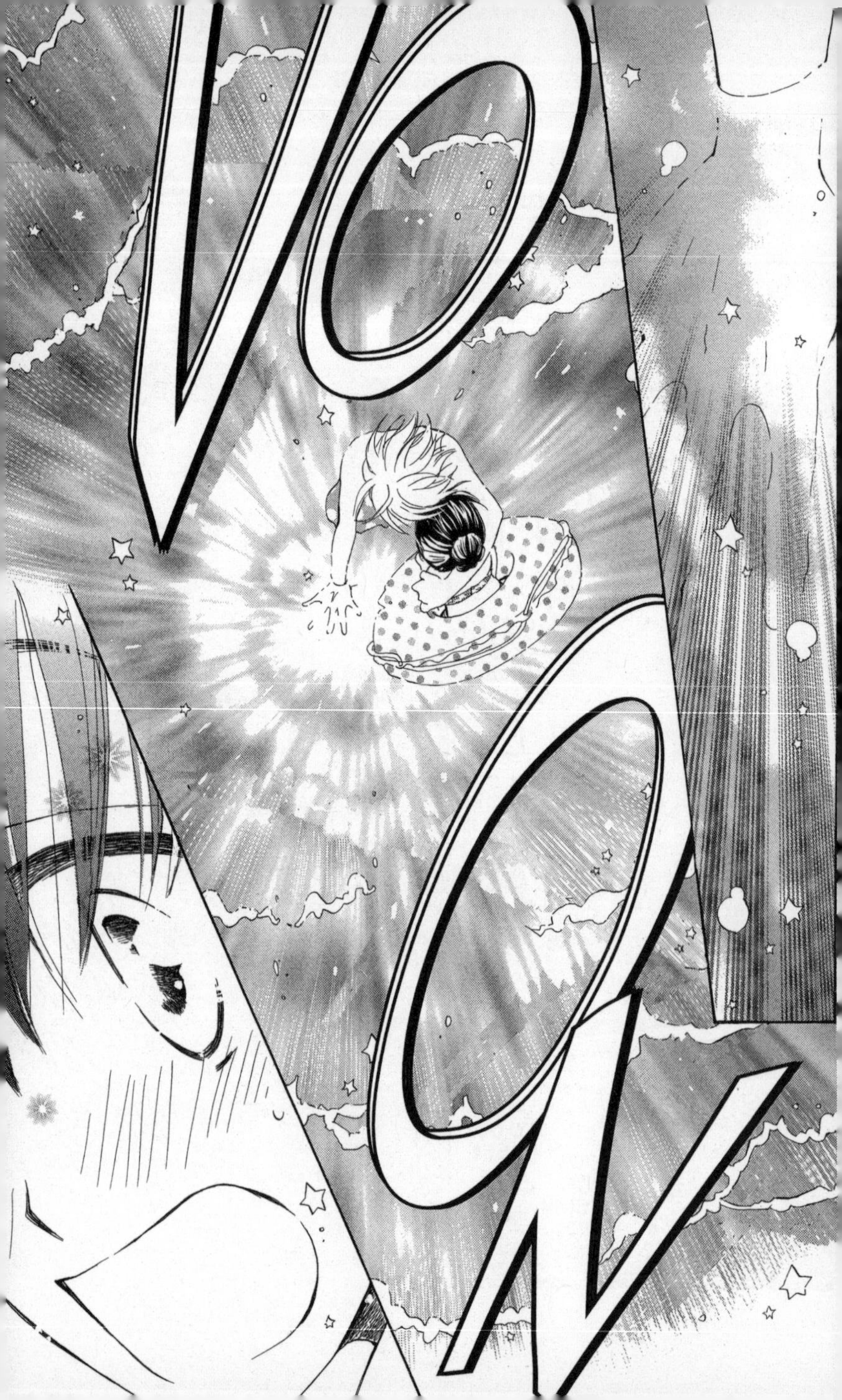
VOOOM

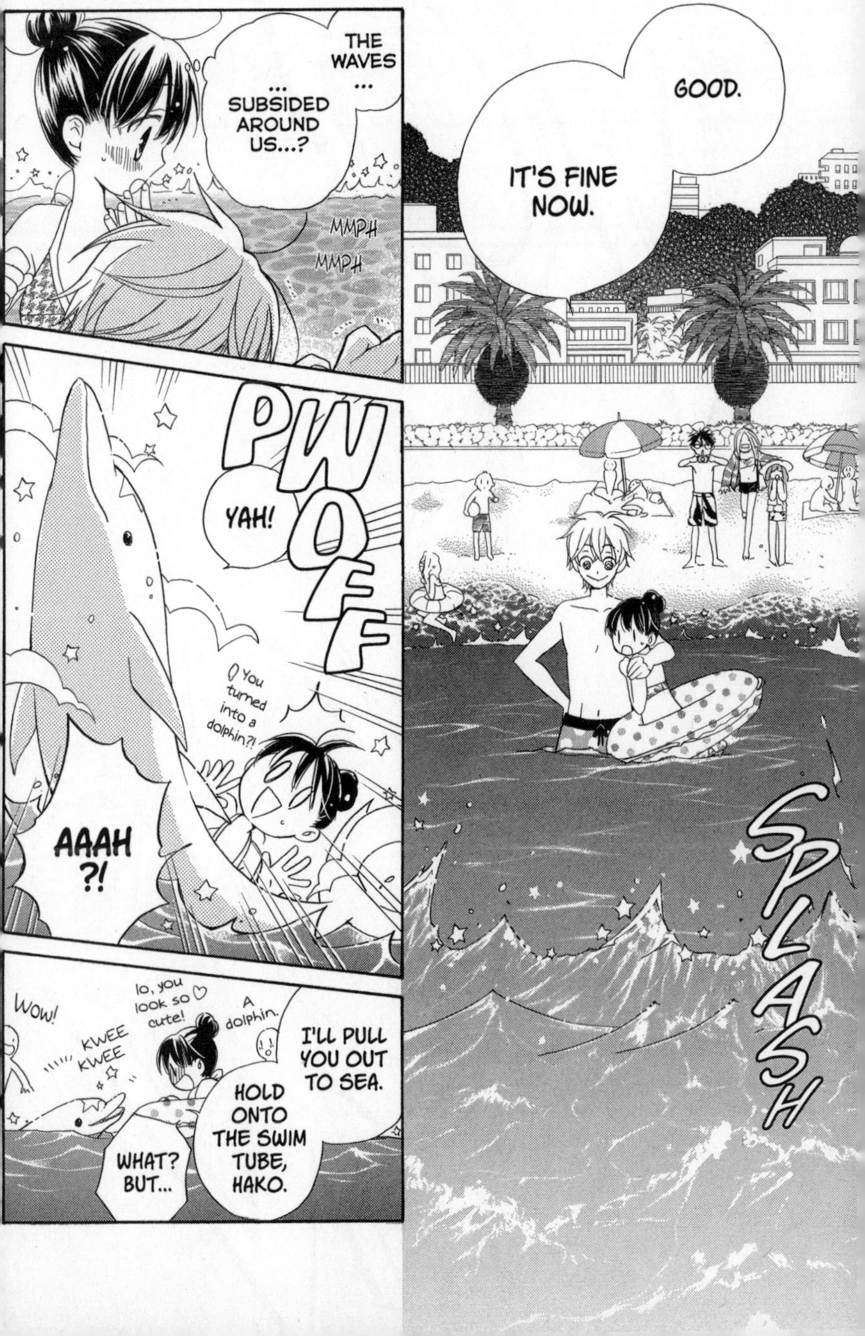
GOOD.
IT'S FINE NOW.
SPLASH
THE WAVES ... SUBSIDED AROUND US...?
MMPH MMPH
PWOFF
YAH!
You turned into a dolphin?!
AAAH ?!
I'LL PULL YOU OUT TO SEA.
HOLD ONTO THE SWIM TUBE, HAKO.
A dolphin.
Io, you look so cute!
WOW!
KWEE KWEE
WHAT? BUT...

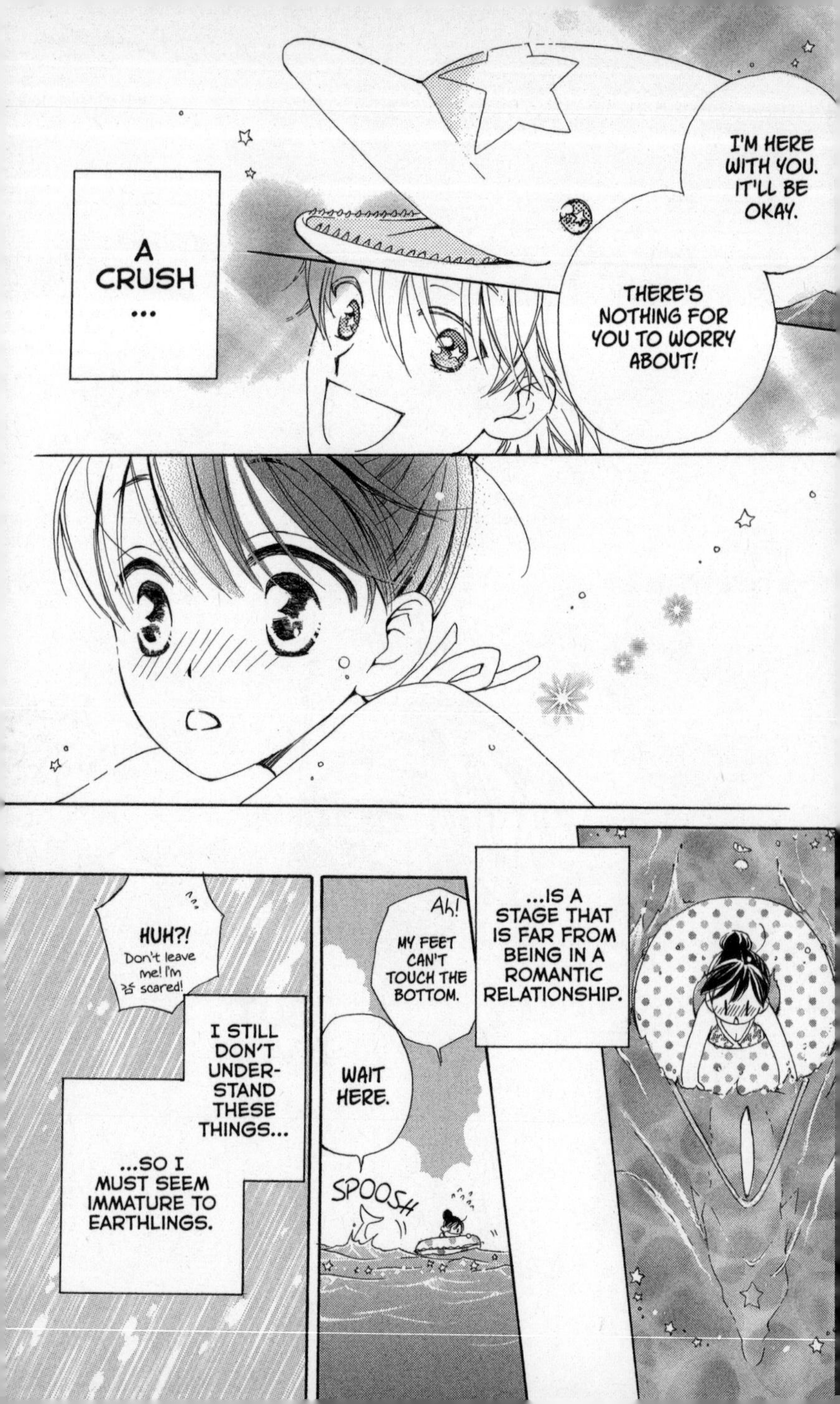
I'M HERE WITH YOU. IT'LL BE OKAY.
THERE'S NOTHING FOR YOU TO WORRY ABOUT!
A CRUSH ...
...IS A STAGE THAT IS FAR FROM BEING IN A ROMANTIC RELATIONSHIP.
Ah!
MY FEET CAN'T TOUCH THE BOTTOM.
WAIT HERE.
SPOOSH
HUH?!
Don't leave me! I'm scared!
I STILL DON'T UNDER-STAND THESE THINGS...
...SO I MUST SEEM IMMATURE TO EARTHLINGS.

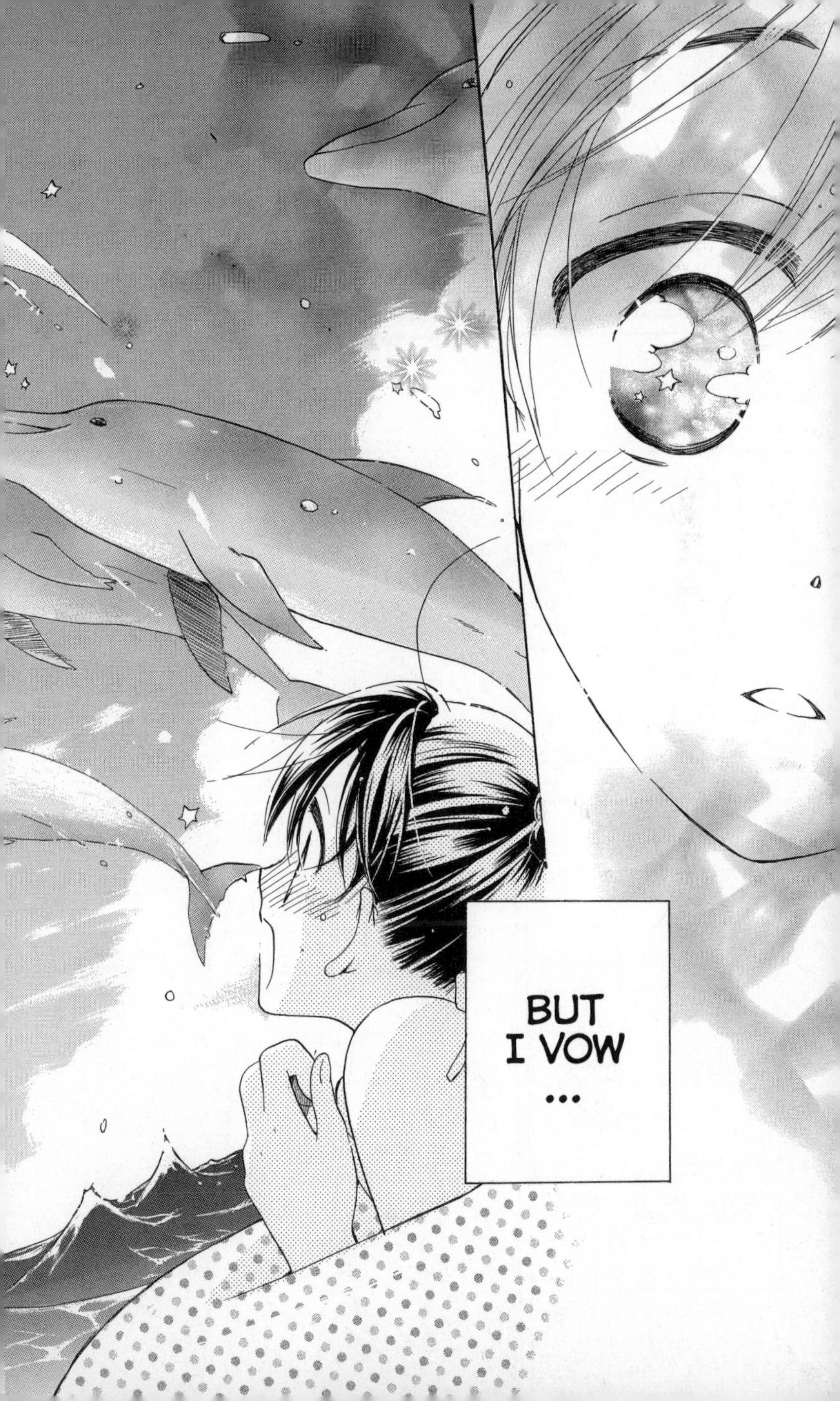
BUT I VOW ...

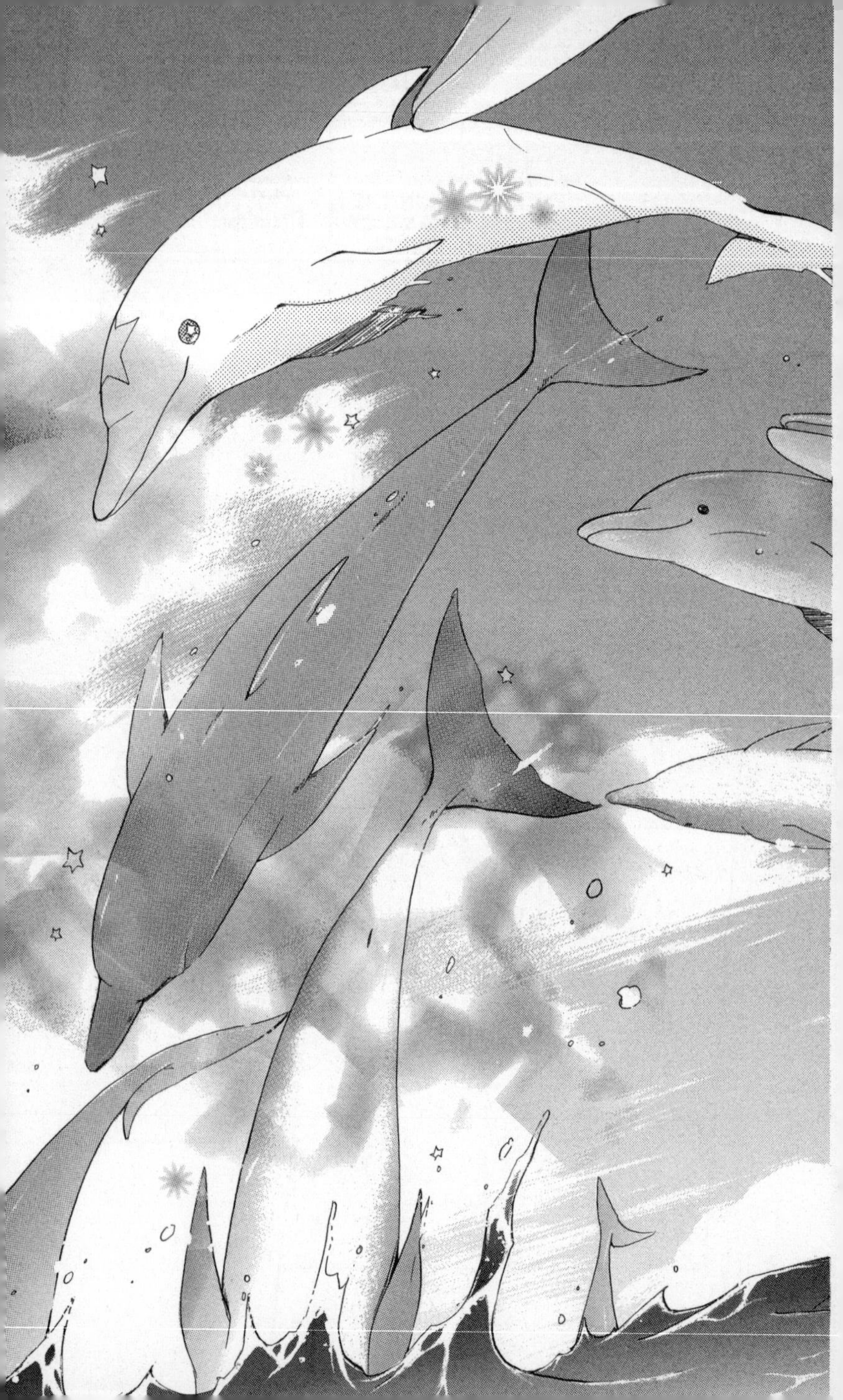

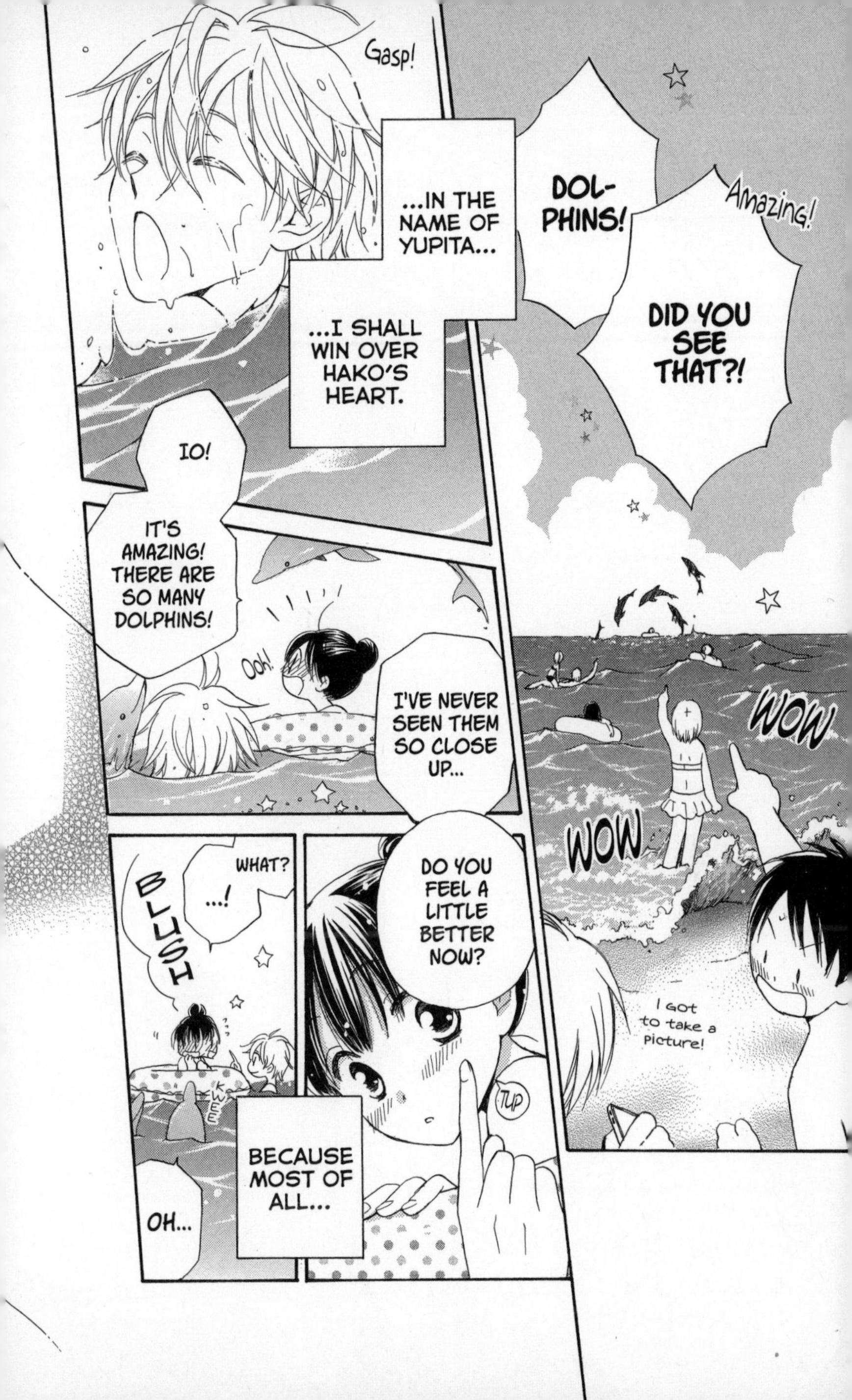
DOL-PHINS!
Amazing!
DID YOU SEE THAT?!
WOW
WOW
I got to take a picture!
Gasp!
...IN THE NAME OF YUPITA...
...I SHALL WIN OVER HAKO'S HEART.
IO!
IT'S AMAZING! THERE ARE SO MANY DOLPHINS!
Ooh!
I'VE NEVER SEEN THEM SO CLOSE UP...
DO YOU FEEL A LITTLE BETTER NOW?
TUP
BECAUSE MOST OF ALL...
WHAT?
...!
BLUSH
KWEE
OH...

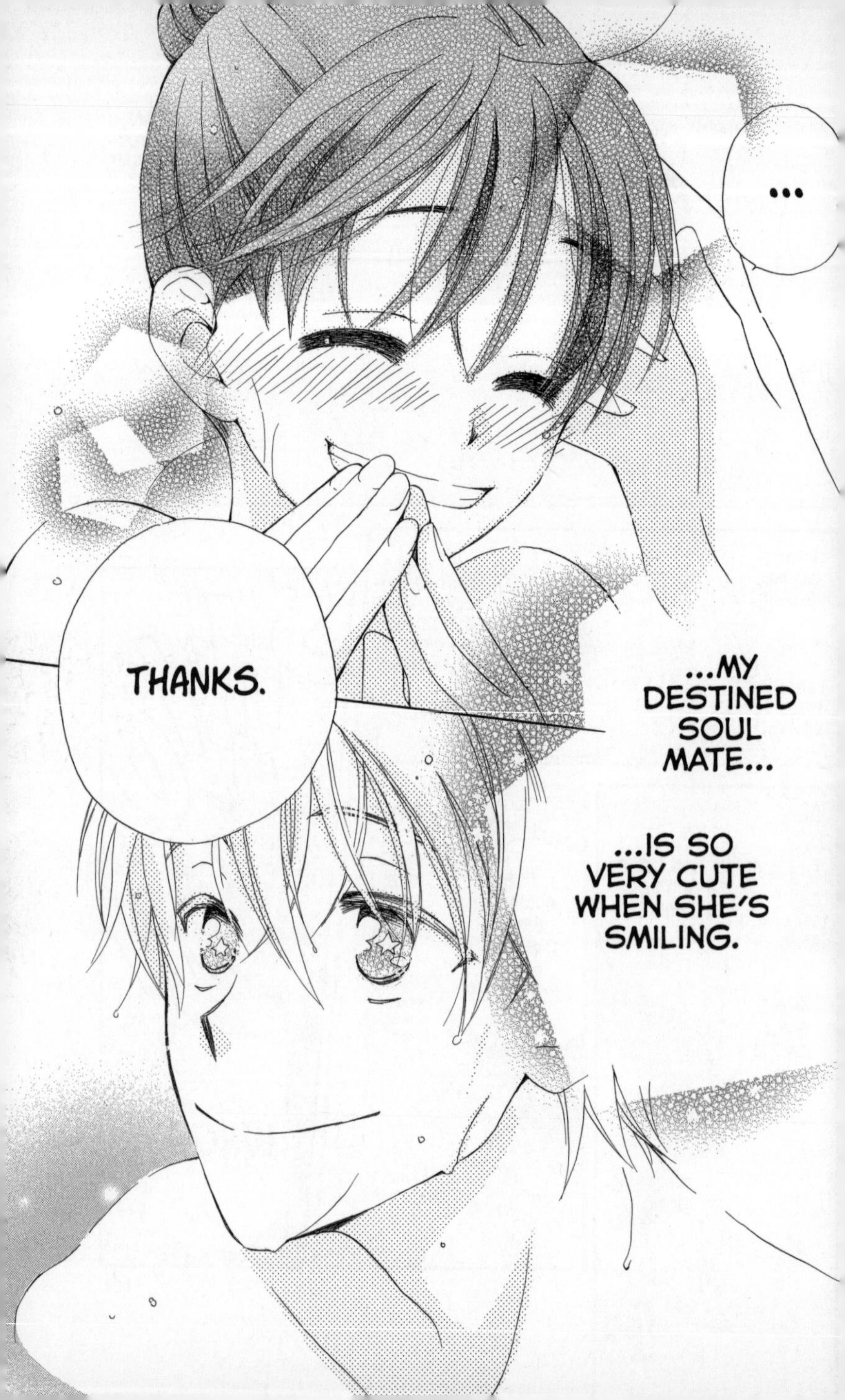
...
...MY DESTINED SOUL MATE...
...IS SO VERY CUTE WHEN SHE'S SMILING.
THANKS.

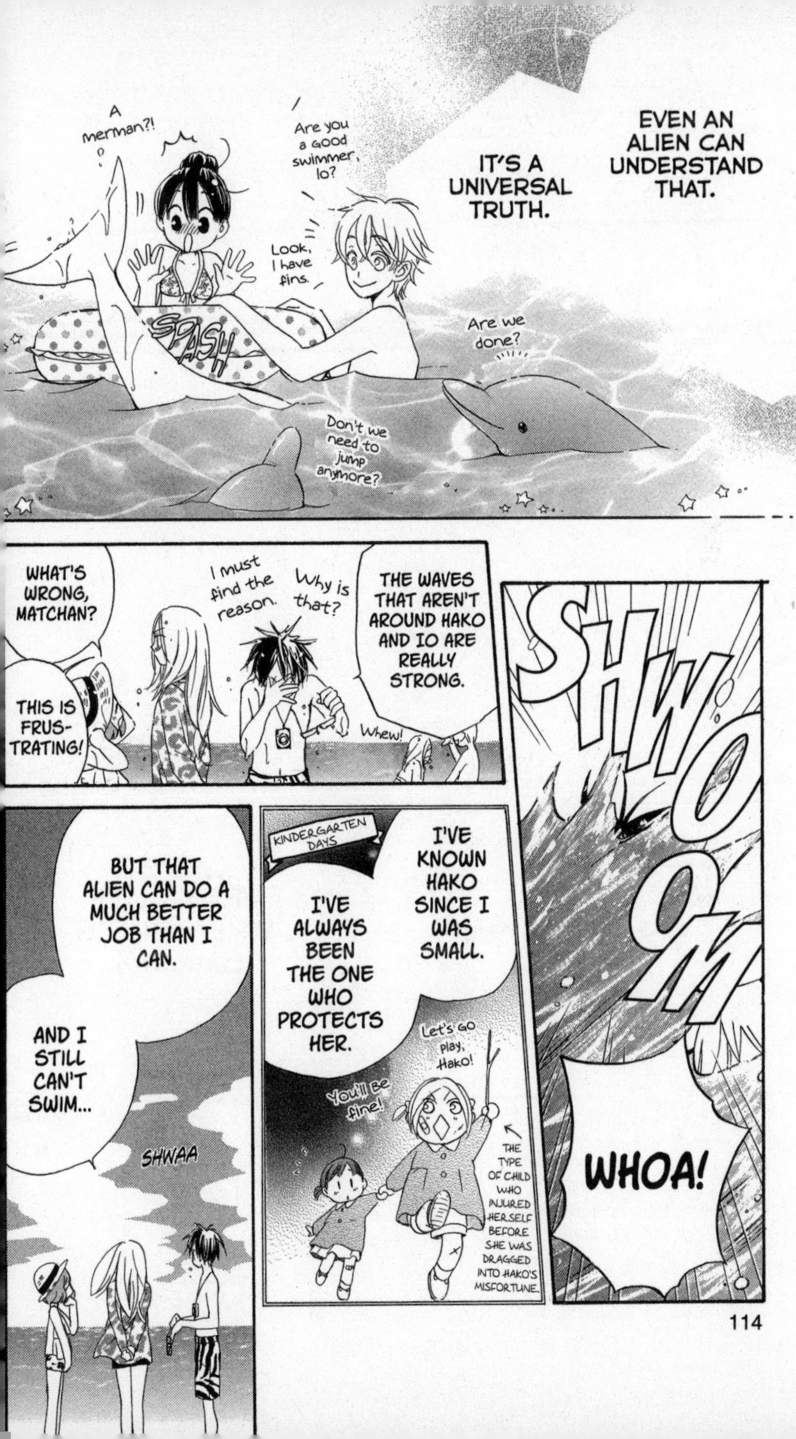
EVEN AN ALIEN CAN UNDERSTAND THAT.
IT'S A UNIVERSAL TRUTH.
Are you a good swimmer, Io?
A merman?!
Look, I have fins.
Are we done?
SPASH
Don't we need to jump anymore?
SHWOOM
WHOA!
THE WAVES THAT AREN'T AROUND HAKO AND IO ARE REALLY STRONG.
Why is that?
I must find the reason.
WHAT'S WRONG, MATCHAN?
THIS IS FRUS-TRATING!
Whew!
KINDERGARTEN DAYS
I'VE KNOWN HAKO SINCE I WAS SMALL.
I'VE ALWAYS BEEN THE ONE WHO PROTECTS HER.
Let's go play, Hako!
You'll be fine!
THE TYPE OF CHILD WHO INJURED HERSELF BEFORE SHE WAS DRAGGED INTO HAKO'S MISFORTUNE.
BUT THAT ALIEN CAN DO A MUCH BETTER JOB THAN I CAN.
AND I STILL CAN'T SWIM...
SHWAA

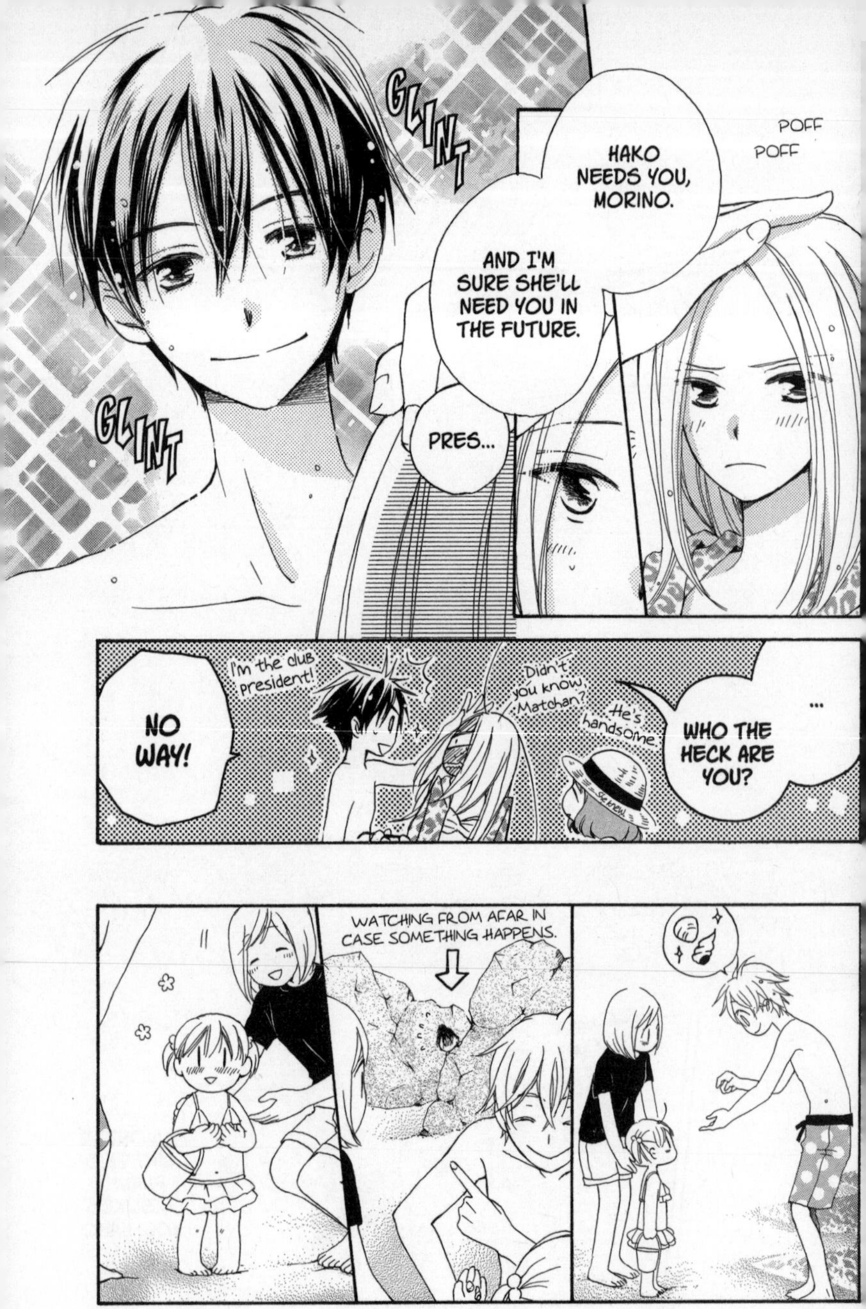
POFF
POFF
HAKO NEEDS YOU, MORINO.
AND I'M SURE SHE'LL NEED YOU IN THE FUTURE.
GLINT
PRES...
GLINT
...
WHO THE HECK ARE YOU?
He's handsome.
Didn't you know, Matchan?
I'm the club president!
NO WAY!
WATCHING FROM AFAR IN CASE SOMETHING HAPPENS.

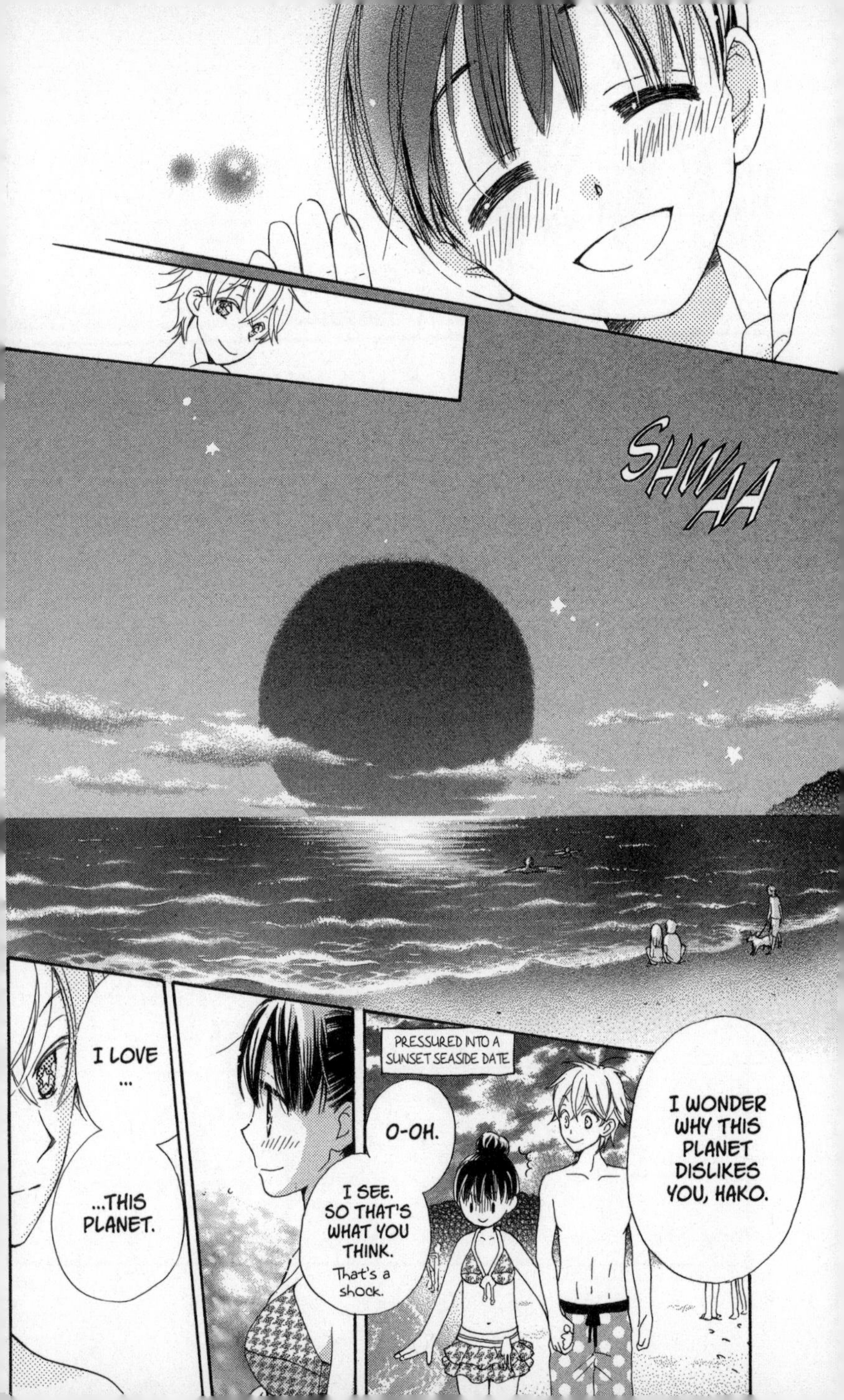
SHWAAA
PRESSURED INTO A SUNSET SEASIDE DATE
I WONDER WHY THIS PLANET DISLIKES YOU, HAKO.
O-OH.
I SEE. SO THAT'S WHAT YOU THINK. That's a shock.
I LOVE ...
...THIS PLANET.

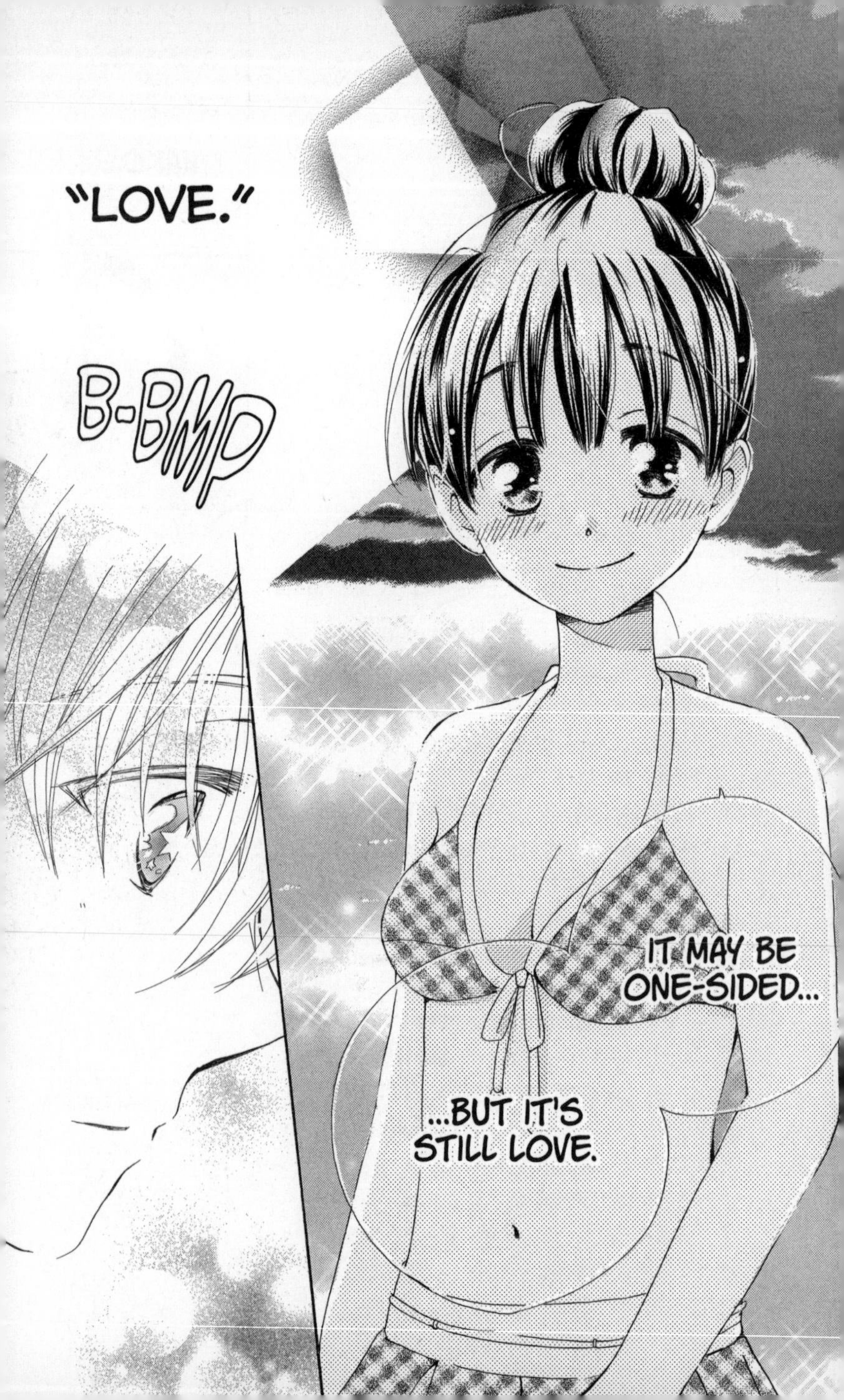
"LOVE."
B-BMP
IT MAY BE ONE-SIDED...
...BUT IT'S STILL LOVE.

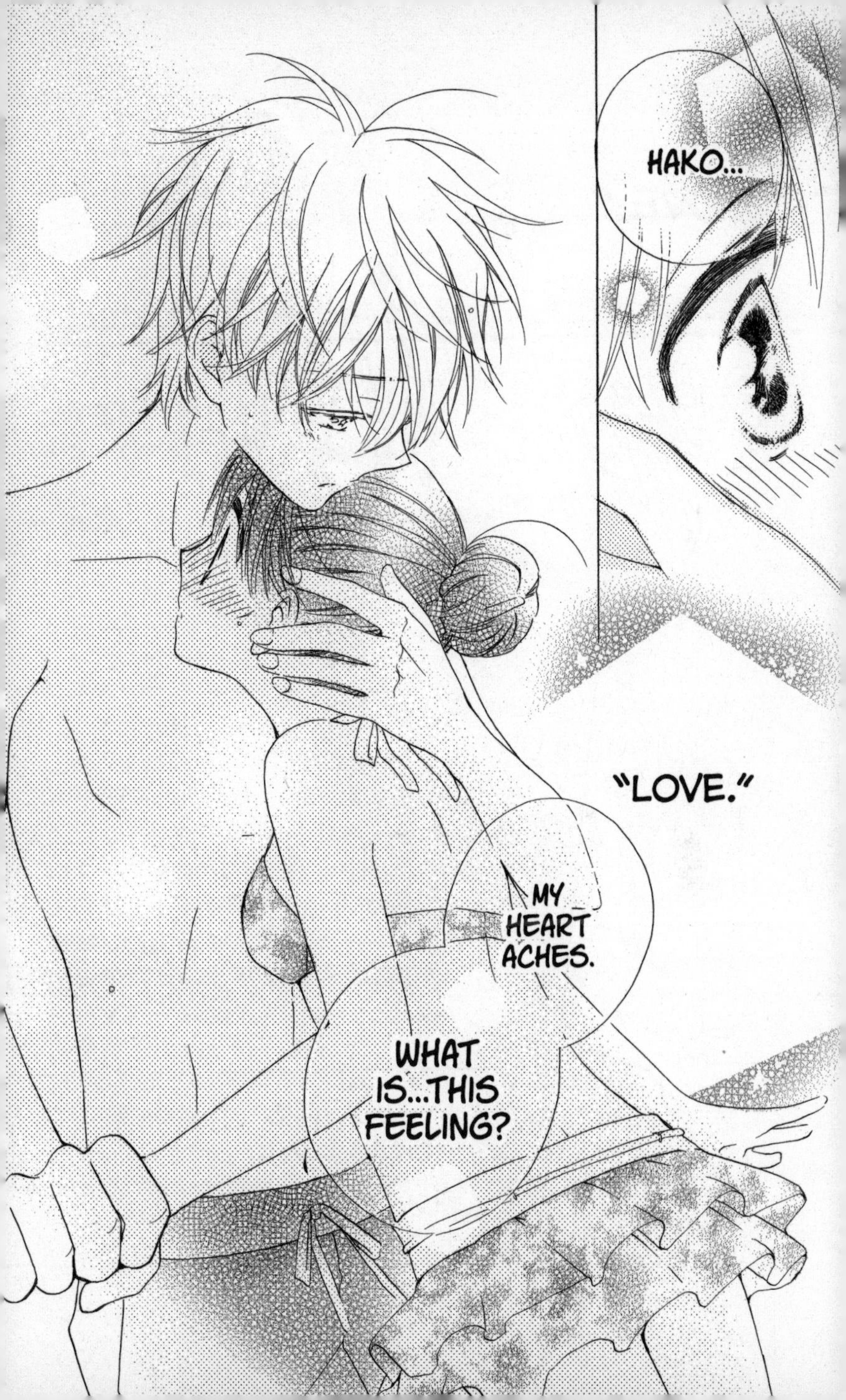
HAKO...
"LOVE."
MY HEART ACHES.
WHAT IS...THIS FEELING?

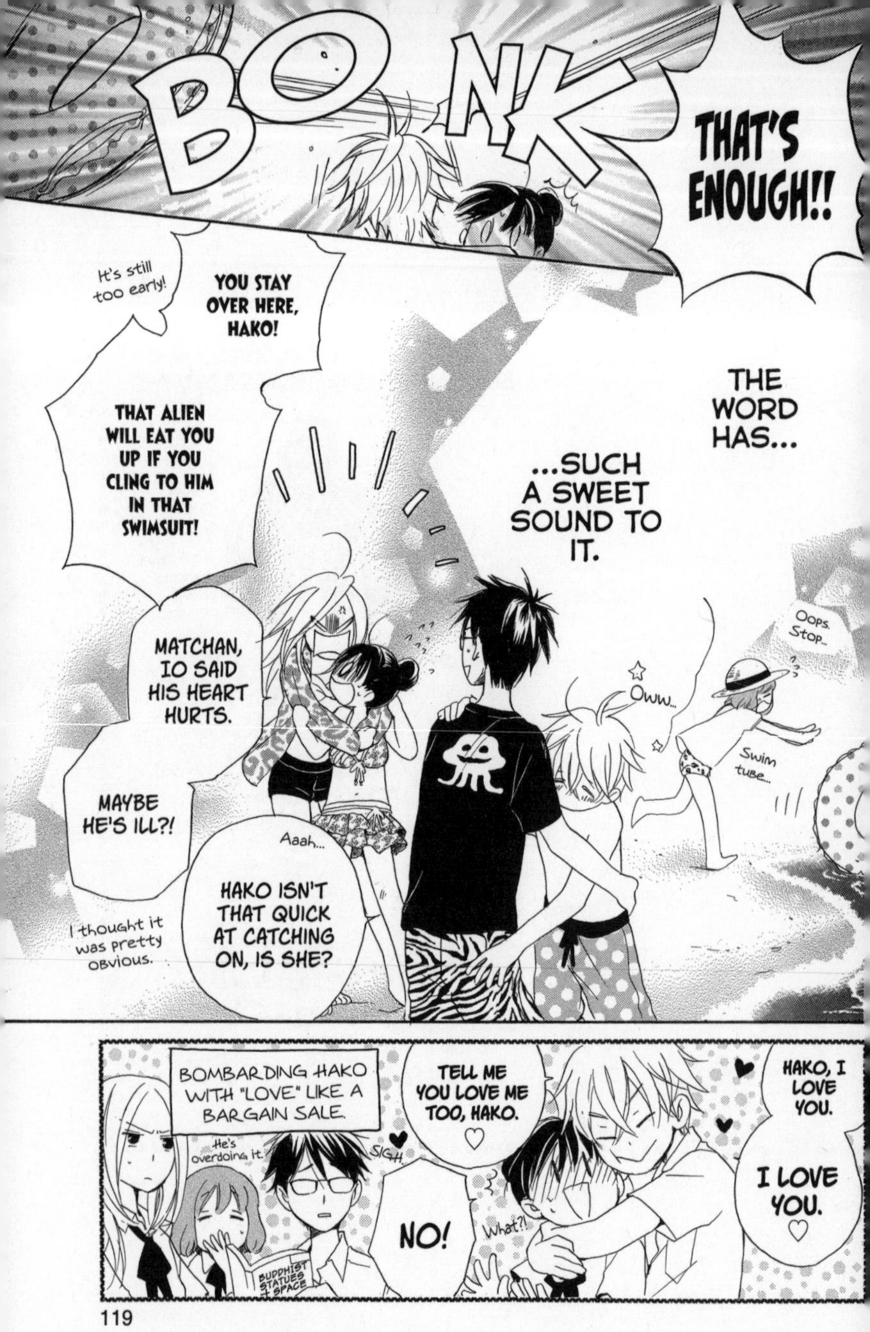

BONK
THAT'S ENOUGH!!
THE WORD HAS...
...SUCH A SWEET SOUND TO IT.
YOU STAY OVER HERE, HAKO!
It's still too early!
THAT ALIEN WILL EAT YOU UP IF YOU CLING TO HIM IN THAT SWIMSUIT!
Oops. Stop...
Swim tube...
Oww...
MATCHAN, IO SAID HIS HEART HURTS.
MAYBE HE'S ILL?!
Aaah...
HAKO ISN'T THAT QUICK AT CATCHING ON, IS SHE?
I thought it was pretty obvious.
HAKO, I LOVE YOU.
I LOVE YOU. ♡
TELL ME YOU LOVE ME TOO, HAKO. ♡
What?!
NO!
SIGH
BOMBARDING HAKO WITH "LOVE" LIKE A BARGAIN SALE.
He's overdoing it.
BUDDHIST STATUES + SPACE

HAKO IS A LITTLE CHUBBY, SO HER BELLYBUTTON STRETCHES SIDEWAYS.

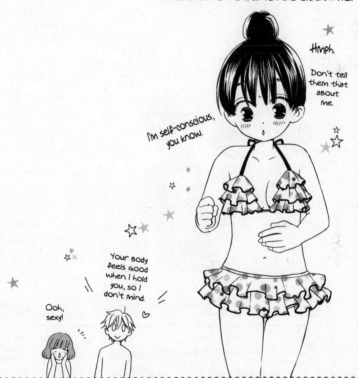

Hmph.

Don't tell them that about me

I'm self-conscious, you know.

Your body feels good when I hold you, so I don't mind.

Ooh, sexy!

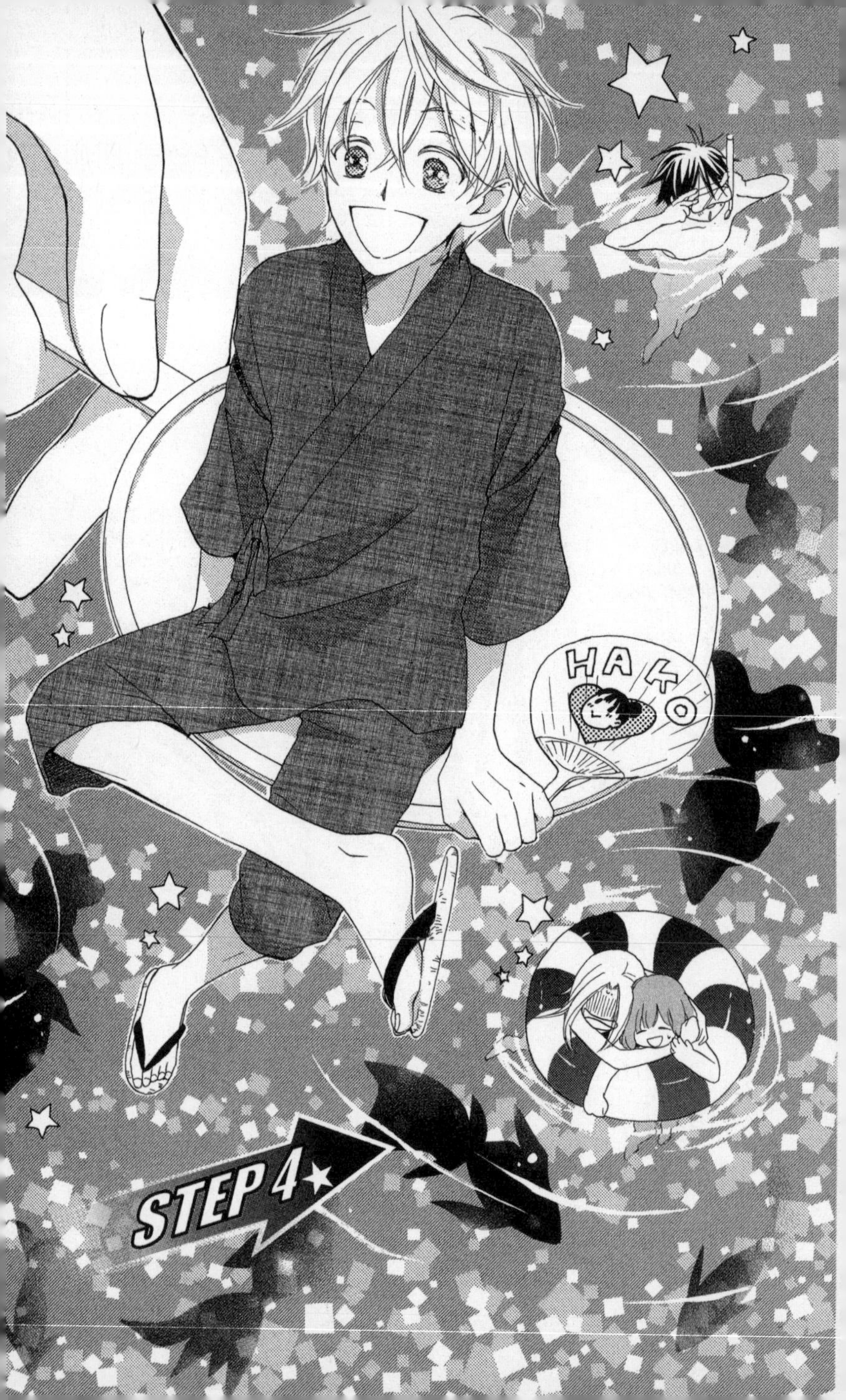
HAKO
STEP 4

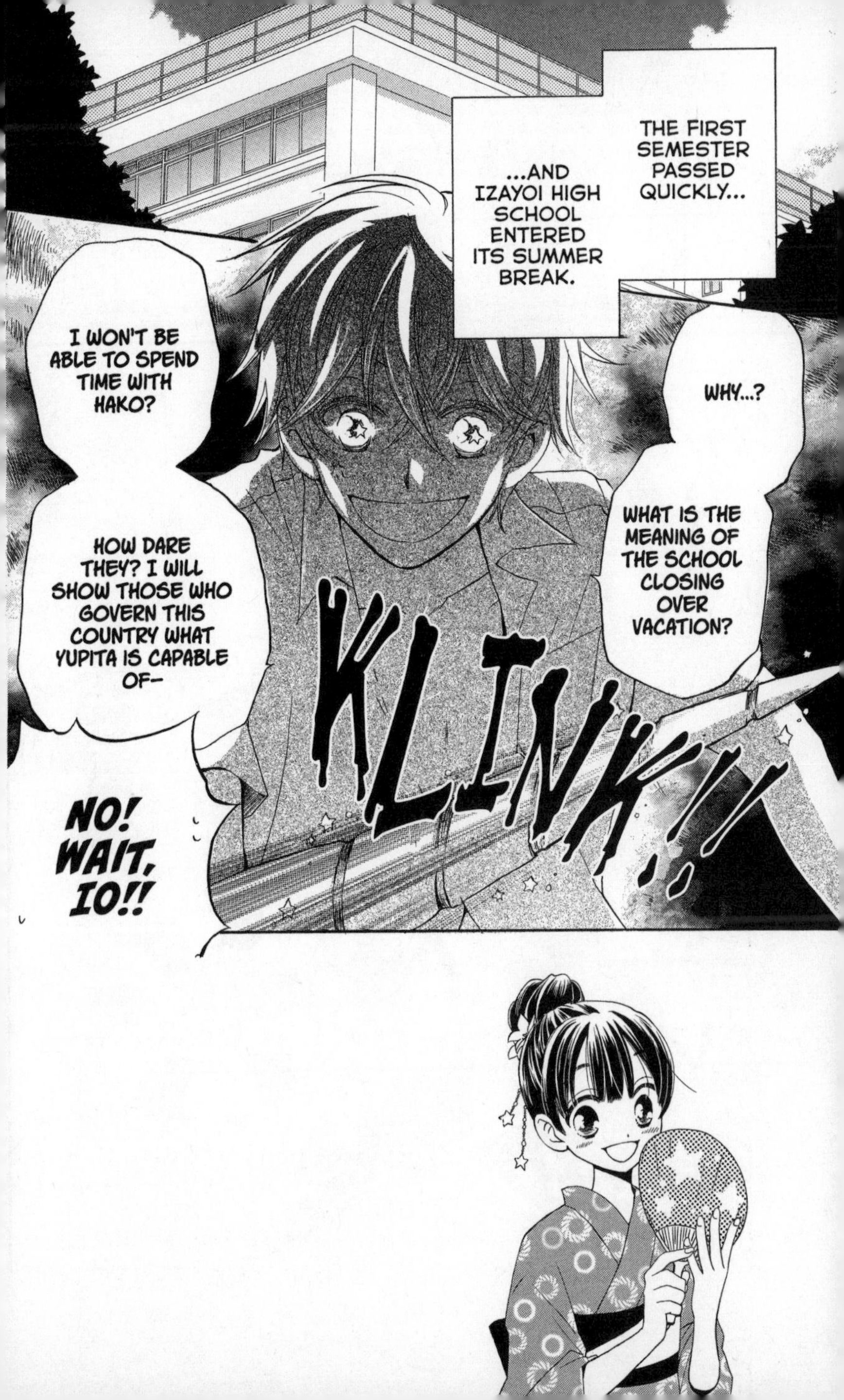
THE FIRST SEMESTER PASSED QUICKLY...
...AND IZAYOI HIGH SCHOOL ENTERED ITS SUMMER BREAK.
WHY...?
WHAT IS THE MEANING OF THE SCHOOL CLOSING OVER VACATION?
I WON'T BE ABLE TO SPEND TIME WITH HAKO?
HOW DARE THEY? I WILL SHOW THOSE WHO GOVERN THIS COUNTRY WHAT YUPITA IS CAPABLE OF-
KLINK!!
NO! WAIT, IO!!

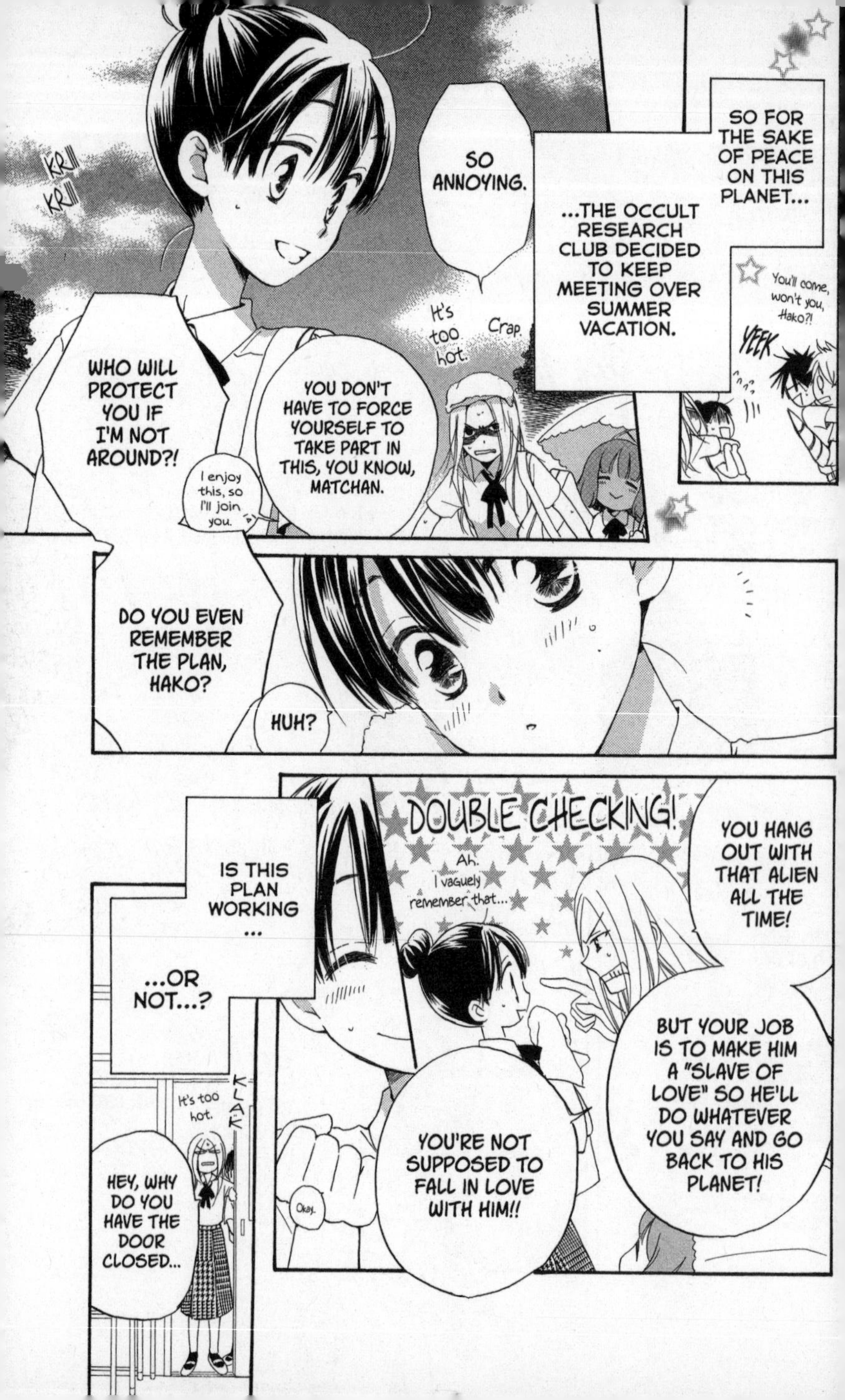
SO FOR THE SAKE OF PEACE ON THIS PLANET...
...THE OCCULT RESEARCH CLUB DECIDED TO KEEP MEETING OVER SUMMER VACATION.
You'll come, won't you, Hako?!
YEEK
SO ANNOYING.
It's too hot.
Crap.
YOU DON'T HAVE TO FORCE YOURSELF TO TAKE PART IN THIS, YOU KNOW, MATCHAN.
I enjoy this, so I'll join you.
WHO WILL PROTECT YOU IF I'M NOT AROUND?!
KRI KRI
DO YOU EVEN REMEMBER THE PLAN, HAKO?
HUH?
YOU HANG OUT WITH THAT ALIEN ALL THE TIME!
DOUBLE CHECKING!
BUT YOUR JOB IS TO MAKE HIM A "SLAVE OF LOVE" SO HE'LL DO WHATEVER YOU SAY AND GO BACK TO HIS PLANET!
Ah. I vaguely remember that...
YOU'RE NOT SUPPOSED TO FALL IN LOVE WITH HIM!!
Okay.
IS THIS PLAN WORKING...
...OR NOT...?
KLAK
It's too hot.
HEY, WHY DO YOU HAVE THE DOOR CLOSED...

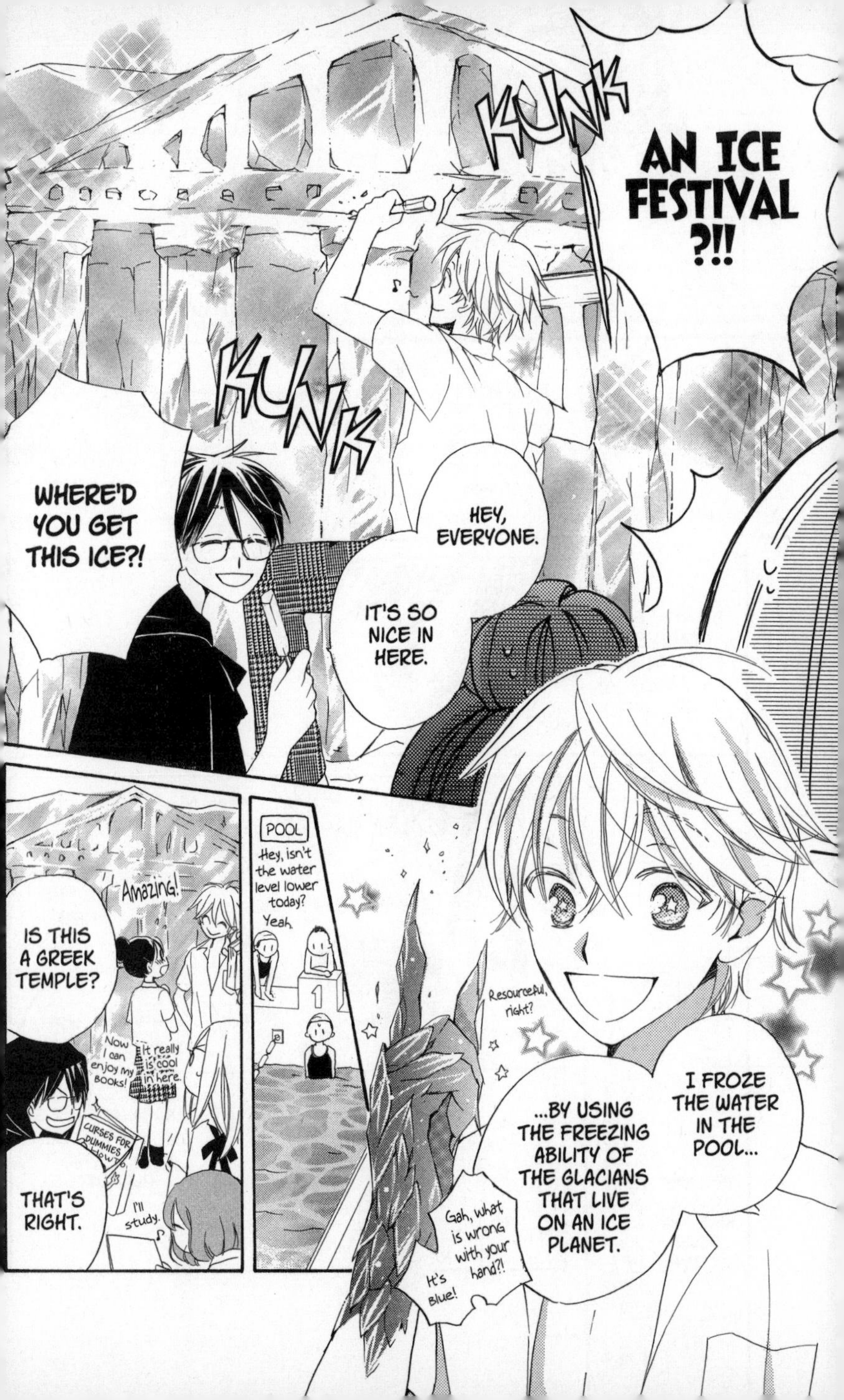
AN ICE FESTIVAL ?!!
KUNK
HEY, EVERYONE.
IT'S SO NICE IN HERE.
KUNK
WHERE'D YOU GET THIS ICE?!
I FROZE THE WATER IN THE POOL...
...BY USING THE FREEZING ABILITY OF THE GLACIANS THAT LIVE ON AN ICE PLANET.
Resourceful, right?
Gah, what is wrong with your hand?!
It's Blue!
POOL
Hey, isn't the water level lower today?
Yeah.
1
Amazing!
IS THIS A GREEK TEMPLE?
It really is cool in here.
Now I can enjoy my books!
CURSES FOR DUMMIES
THAT'S RIGHT.
I'll study.

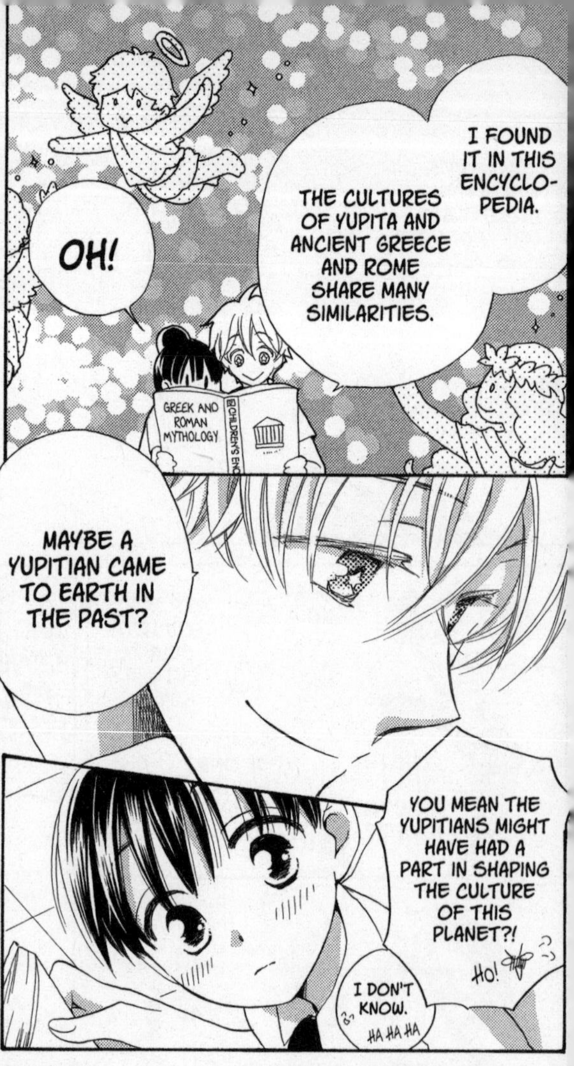

I FOUND IT IN THIS ENCYCLOPEDIA.
THE CULTURES OF YUPITA AND ANCIENT GREECE AND ROME SHARE MANY SIMILARITIES.
OH!
GREEK AND ROMAN MYTHOLOGY
MAYBE A YUPITIAN CAME TO EARTH IN THE PAST?
YOU MEAN THE YUPITIANS MIGHT HAVE HAD A PART IN SHAPING THE CULTURE OF THIS PLANET?!
HO!
I DON'T KNOW.
HA HA HA
HM?
Oh.
When did you get so close?
NOTHING.
I JUST THOUGHT YOU'D LOOK GOOD IN CLOTHES LIKE THESE.
You think so?

Dear Editor

I had to part with my editor with whom I've been working since *Faster Than A Kiss* volume 6. I feel so sad... She was a great comrade, and I could seriously debate otome game characters with her...

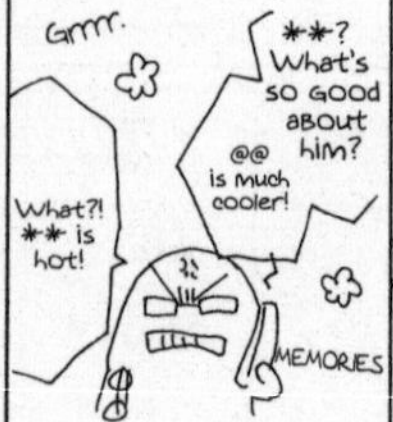

Grrr.
**? What's so good about him?
@@ is much cooler!
What?! ** is hot!
MEMORIES

I had so much fun working together with you! Thank you very much.

I hope I will be able to enjoy working with my new editor too.

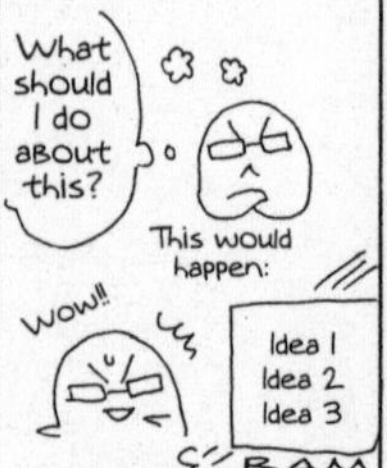

What should I do about this?
This would happen:
Wow!!
Idea 1
Idea 2
Idea 3
BAM

She is a very dependable editor who would quickly help me with ideas from many different points of view!

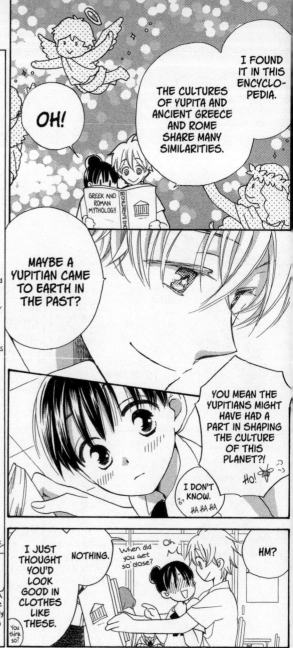

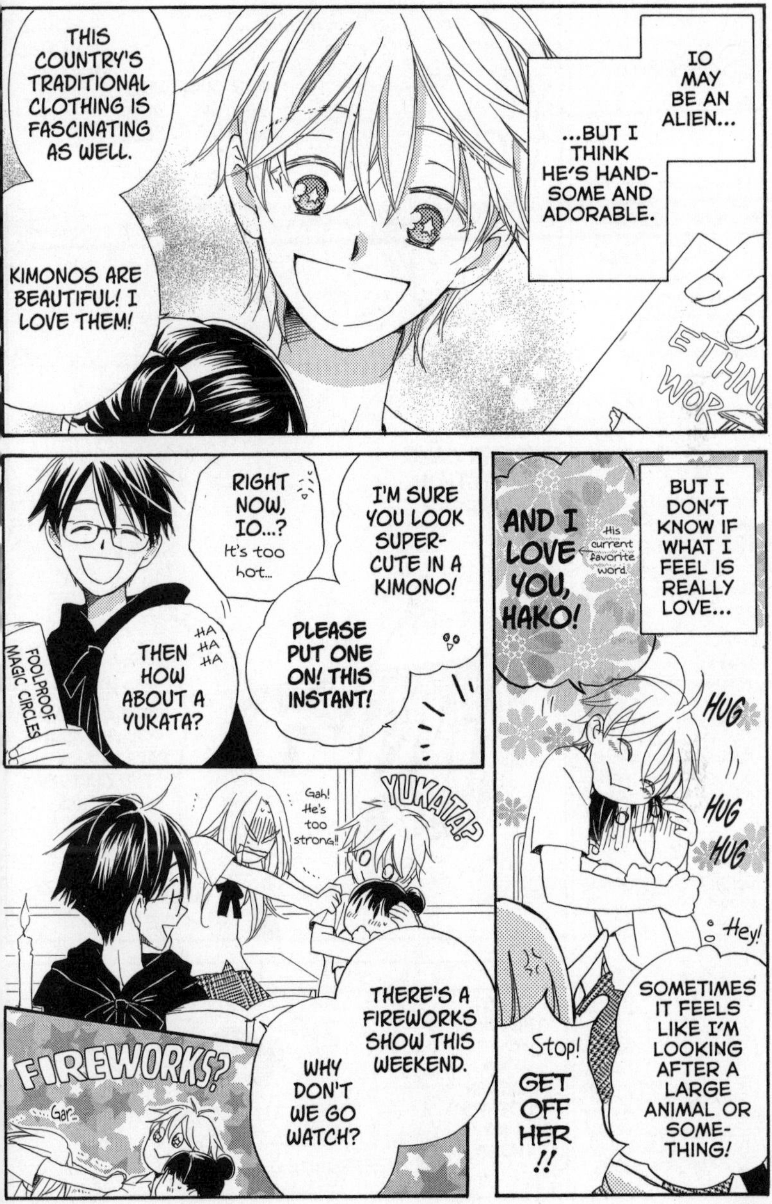
IO MAY BE AN ALIEN...
...BUT I THINK HE'S HANDSOME AND ADORABLE.
THIS COUNTRY'S TRADITIONAL CLOTHING IS FASCINATING AS WELL.
KIMONOS ARE BEAUTIFUL! I LOVE THEM!
BUT I DON'T KNOW IF WHAT I FEEL IS REALLY LOVE...
AND I LOVE YOU, HAKO!
His current favorite word.
HUG
HUG
HUG
Hey!
SOMETIMES IT FEELS LIKE I'M LOOKING AFTER A LARGE ANIMAL OR SOME-THING!
Stop!
GET OFF HER!!
I'M SURE YOU LOOK SUPER-CUTE IN A KIMONO!
PLEASE PUT ONE ON! THIS INSTANT!
RIGHT NOW, IO...?
It's too hot...
THEN HOW ABOUT A YUKATA?
HA HA HA
FOOLPROOF MAGIC CIRCLES
YUKATA?
Gah! He's too strong!!
THERE'S A FIREWORKS SHOW THIS WEEKEND.
WHY DON'T WE GO WATCH?
FIREWORKS?
Gar...

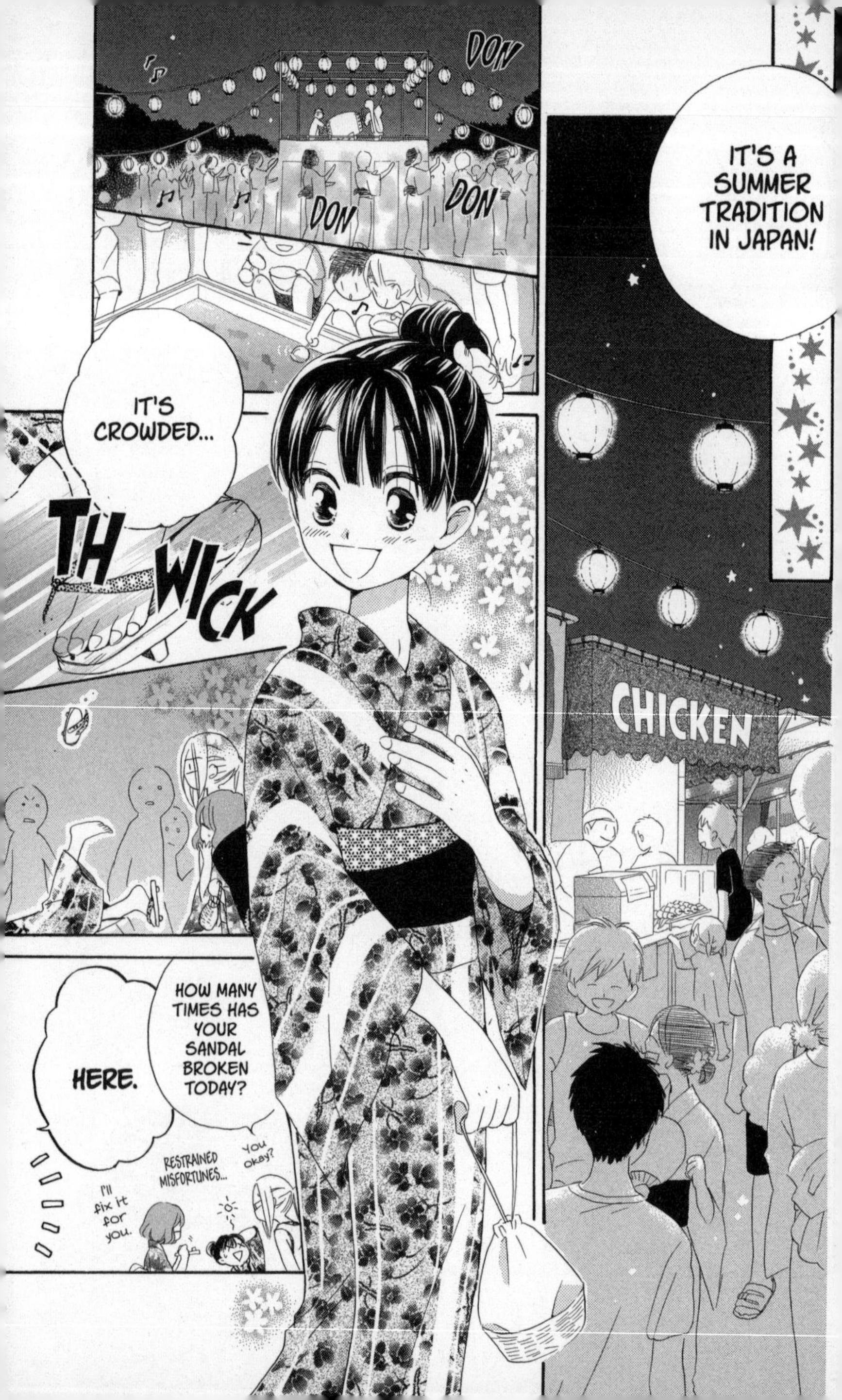

IT'S A SUMMER TRADITION IN JAPAN!
CHICKEN
DON
DON
DON
IT'S CROWDED...
THWICK
HOW MANY TIMES HAS YOUR SANDAL BROKEN TODAY?
HERE.
You okay?
RESTRAINED MISFORTUNES...
I'll fix it for you.

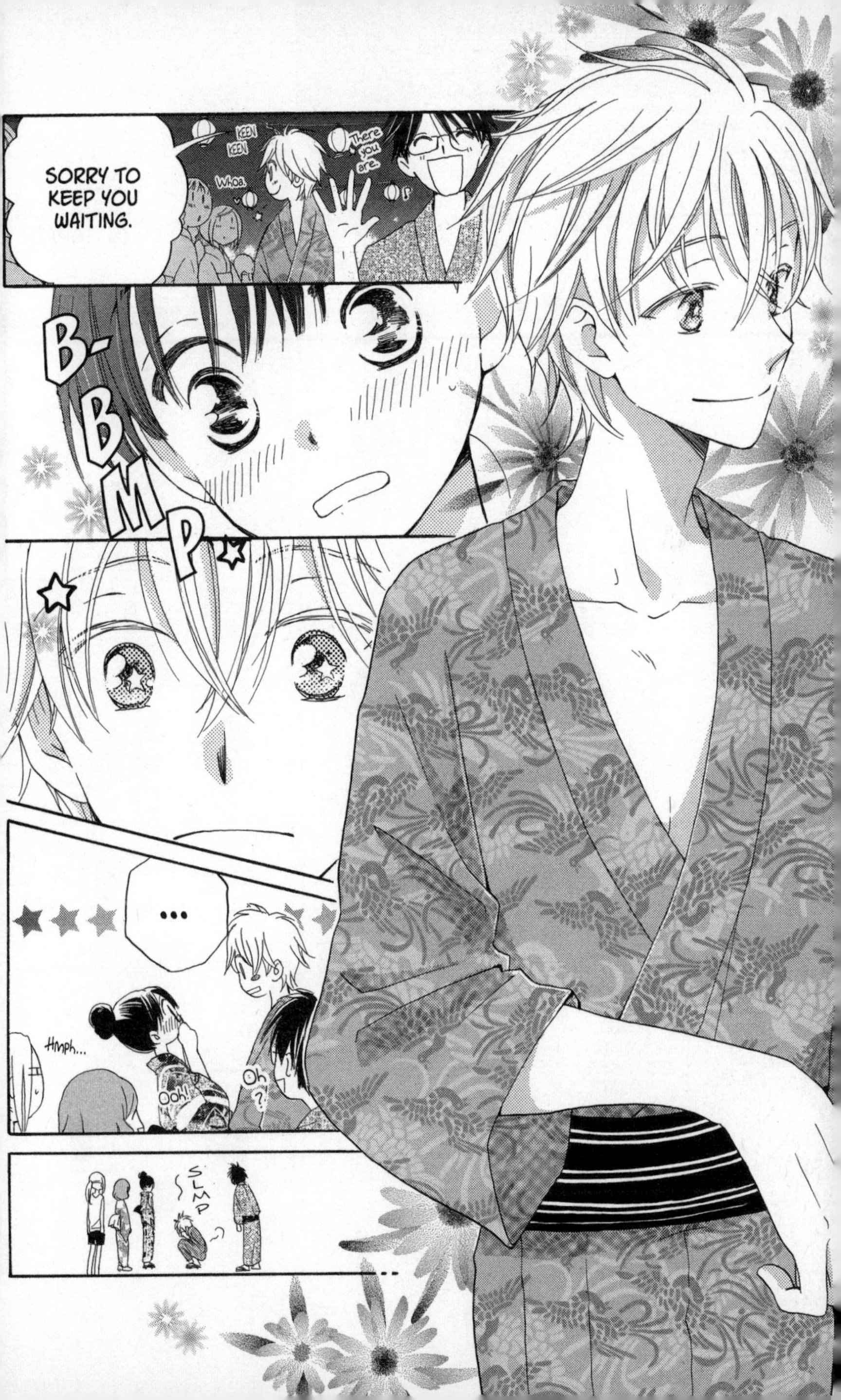
SORRY TO KEEP YOU WAITING.
KEEN KEEN
There you are.
Whoa.
B-BMP
...
Hmph...
Ooh!
Oh?
SLMP
...

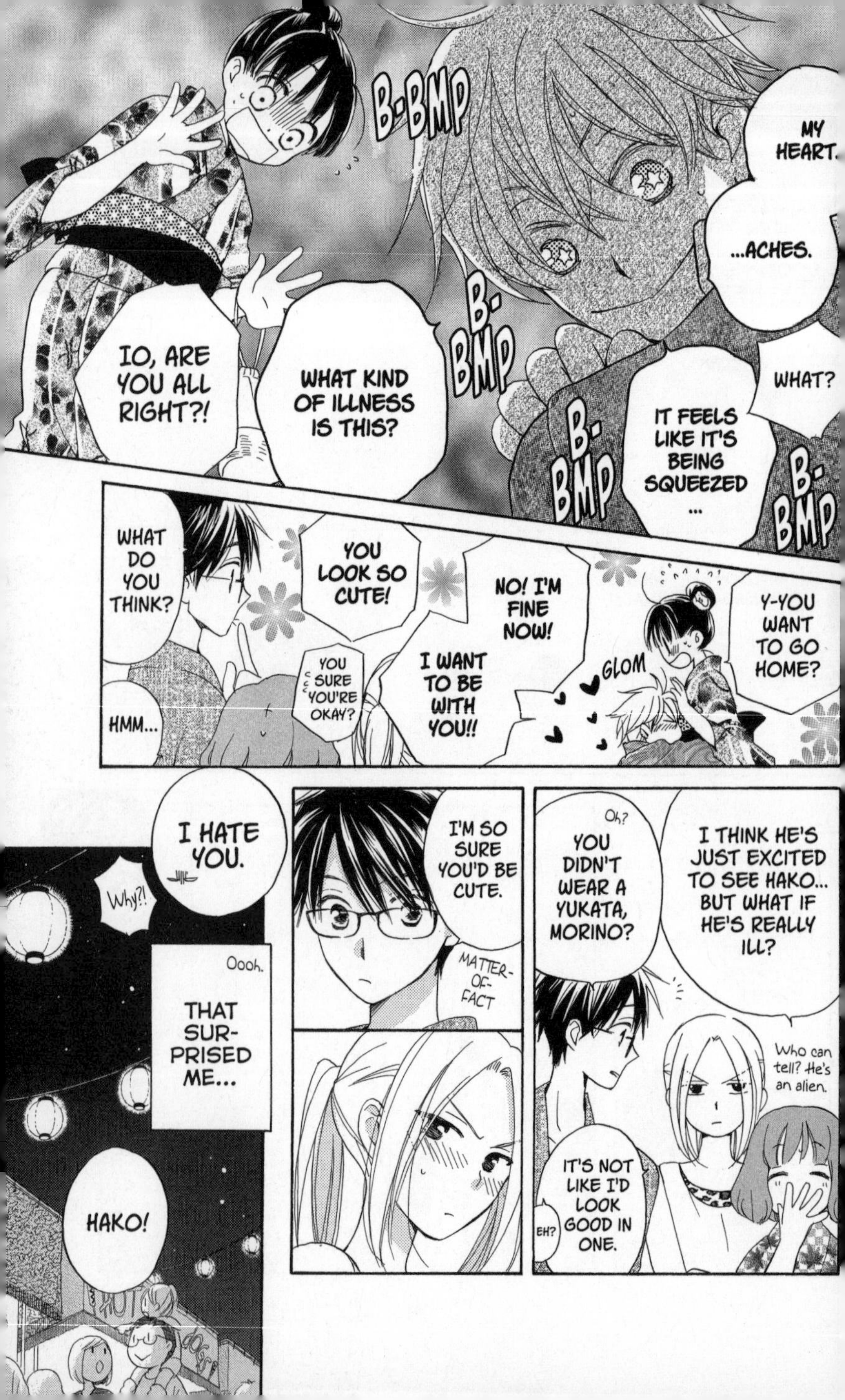
MY HEART.
...ACHES.
B-BMP
WHAT?
IT FEELS LIKE IT'S BEING SQUEEZED ...
B-BMP
B-BMP
B-BMP
WHAT KIND OF ILLNESS IS THIS?
IO, ARE YOU ALL RIGHT?!
Y-YOU WANT TO GO HOME?
GLOM
NO! I'M FINE NOW!
I WANT TO BE WITH YOU!!
YOU SURE YOU'RE OKAY?
YOU LOOK SO CUTE!
WHAT DO YOU THINK?
HMM...
I THINK HE'S JUST EXCITED TO SEE HAKO... BUT WHAT IF HE'S REALLY ILL?
Who can tell? He's an alien.
Oh?
YOU DIDN'T WEAR A YUKATA, MORINO?
IT'S NOT LIKE I'D LOOK GOOD IN ONE.
EH?
I'M SO SURE YOU'D BE CUTE.
MATTER-OF-FACT
I HATE YOU.
Why?!
Oooh.
THAT SUR-PRISED ME...
HAKO!

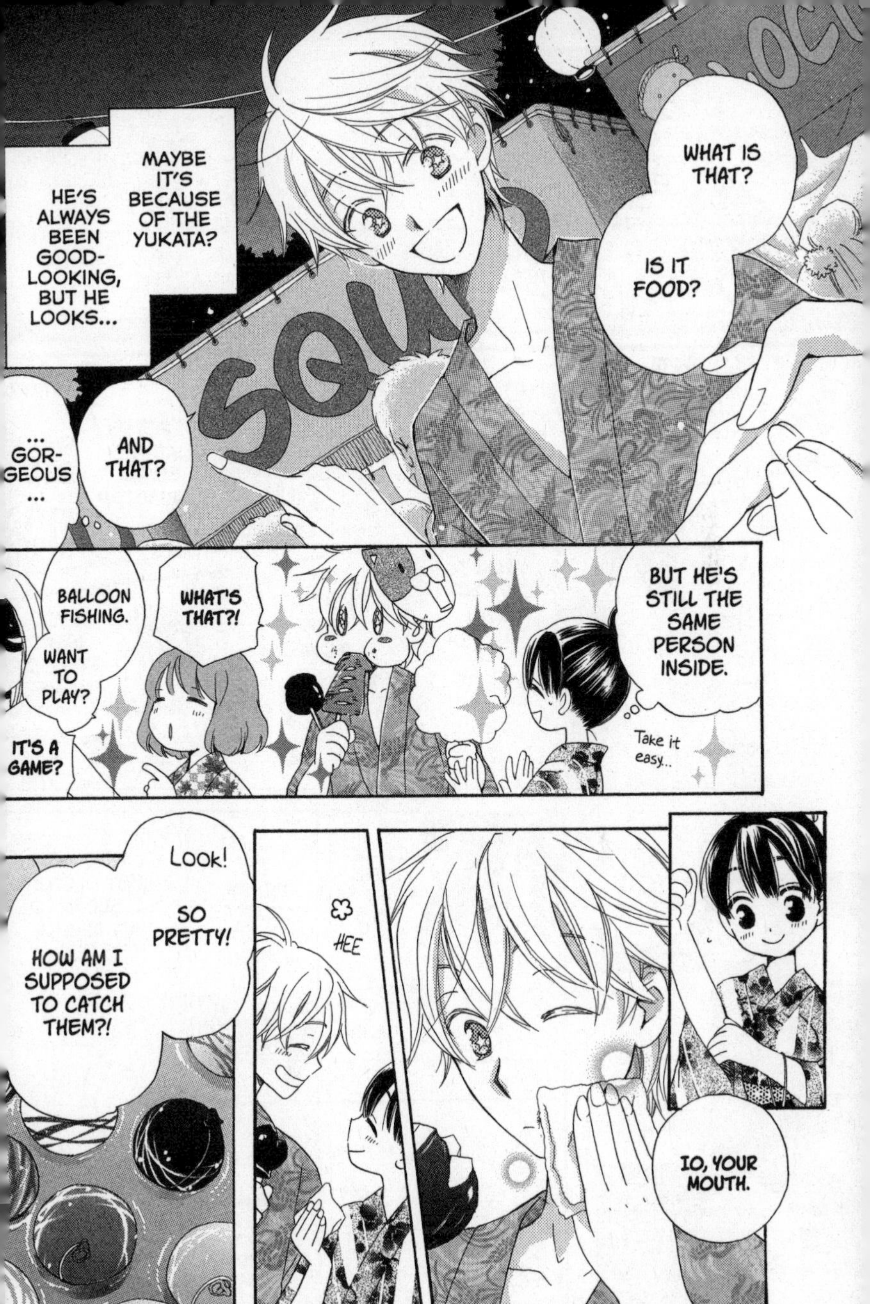
WHAT IS THAT?
IS IT FOOD?
MAYBE IT'S BECAUSE OF THE YUKATA?
HE'S ALWAYS BEEN GOOD-LOOKING, BUT HE LOOKS...
AND THAT?
...GORGEOUS...
BUT HE'S STILL THE SAME PERSON INSIDE.
Take it easy...
WHAT'S THAT?!
BALLOON FISHING.
WANT TO PLAY?
IT'S A GAME?
IO, YOUR MOUTH.
HEE
Look!
SO PRETTY!
HOW AM I SUPPOSED TO CATCH THEM?!

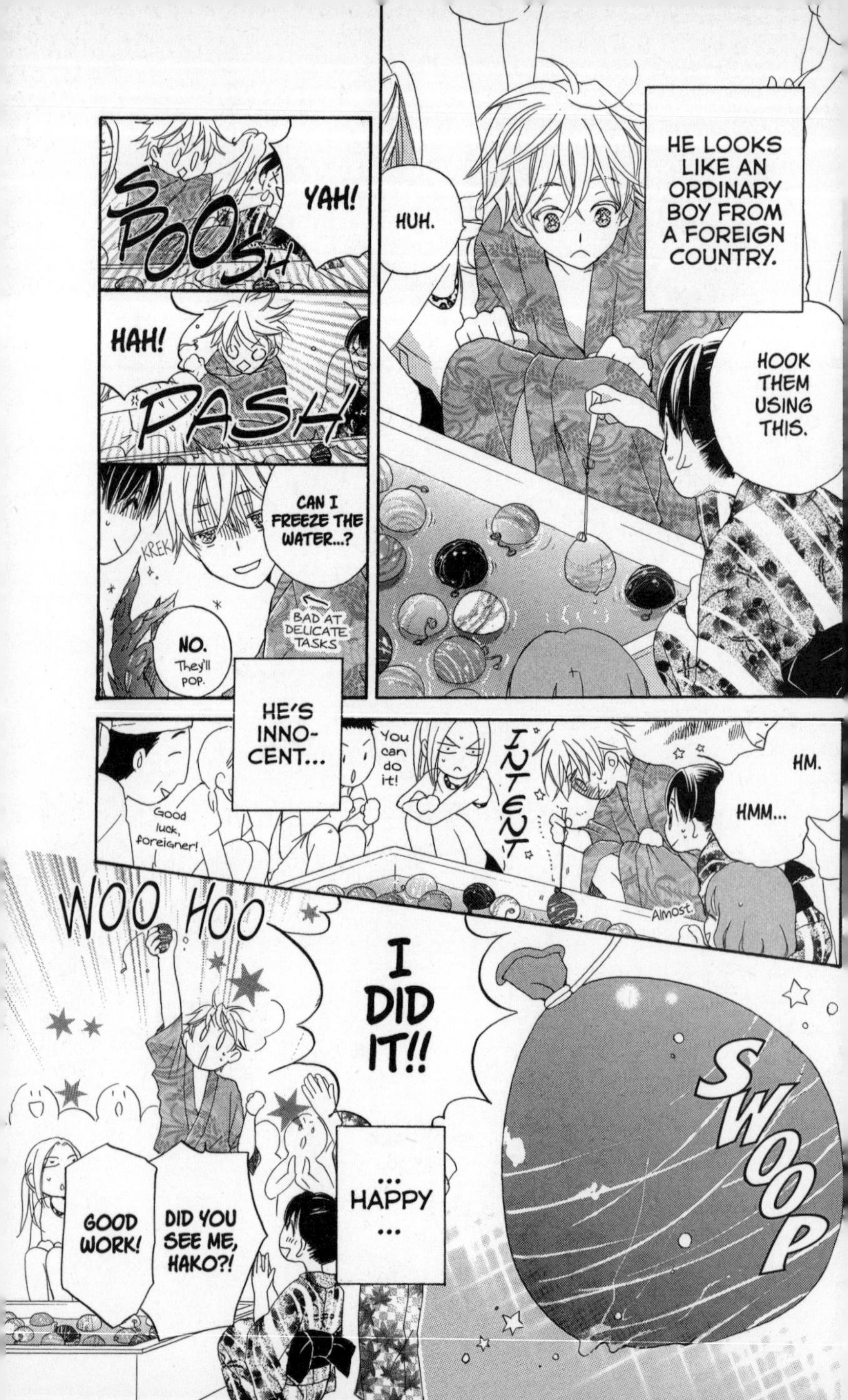

HE LOOKS LIKE AN ORDINARY BOY FROM A FOREIGN COUNTRY.
HOOK THEM USING THIS.
HUH.
SPOOSH
YAH!
HAH!
PASH
CAN I FREEZE THE WATER...?
KREK
BAD AT DELICATE TASKS
NO. They'll POP.
HM.
HMM...
Almost.
INTENT
You can do it!
HE'S INNO-CENT...
Good luck, foreigner!
SWOOP
I DID IT!!
WOO HOO
... HAPPY ...
DID YOU SEE ME, HAKO?!
GOOD WORK!

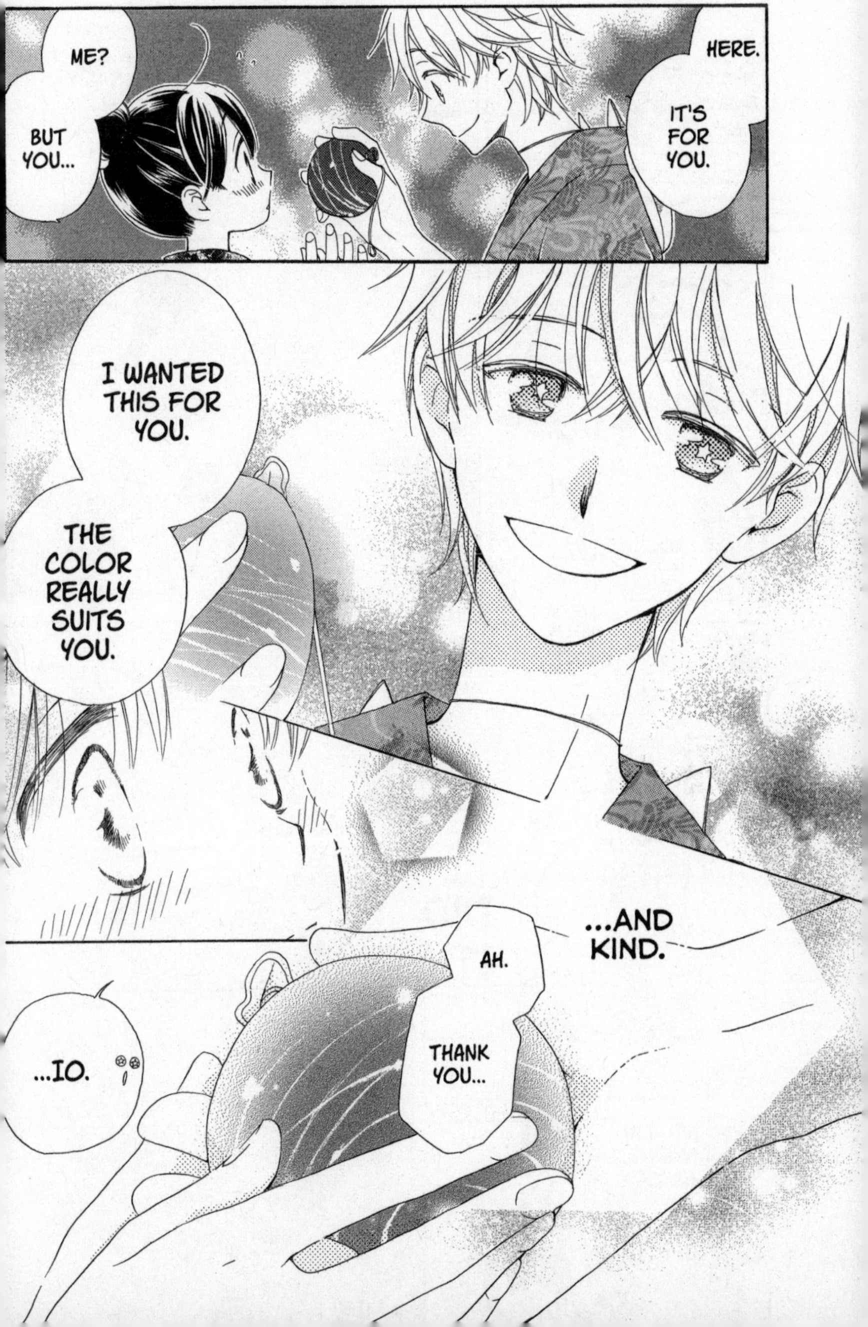
HERE.
IT'S FOR YOU.
ME?
BUT YOU...
I WANTED THIS FOR YOU.
THE COLOR REALLY SUITS YOU.
...AND KIND.
AH.
THANK YOU...
...IO.

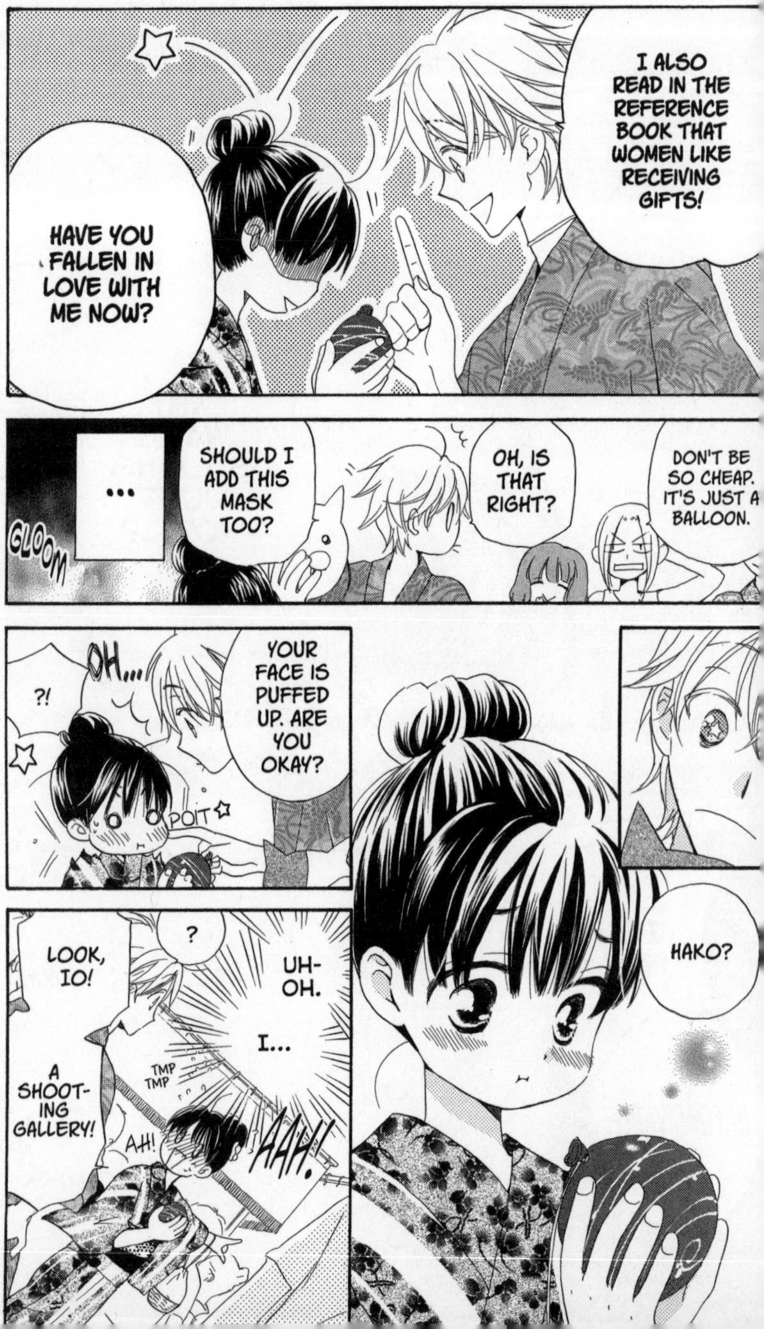

I ALSO READ IN THE REFERENCE BOOK THAT WOMEN LIKE RECEIVING GIFTS!
HAVE YOU FALLEN IN LOVE WITH ME NOW?
DON'T BE SO CHEAP. IT'S JUST A BALLOON.
OH, IS THAT RIGHT?
SHOULD I ADD THIS MASK TOO?
...
GLOOM
HAKO?
YOUR FACE IS PUFFED UP. ARE YOU OKAY?
OH...
?!
POIT
?
UH-OH.
I...
LOOK, IO!
A SHOOTING GALLERY!
TMP TMP
AH!
AAH!

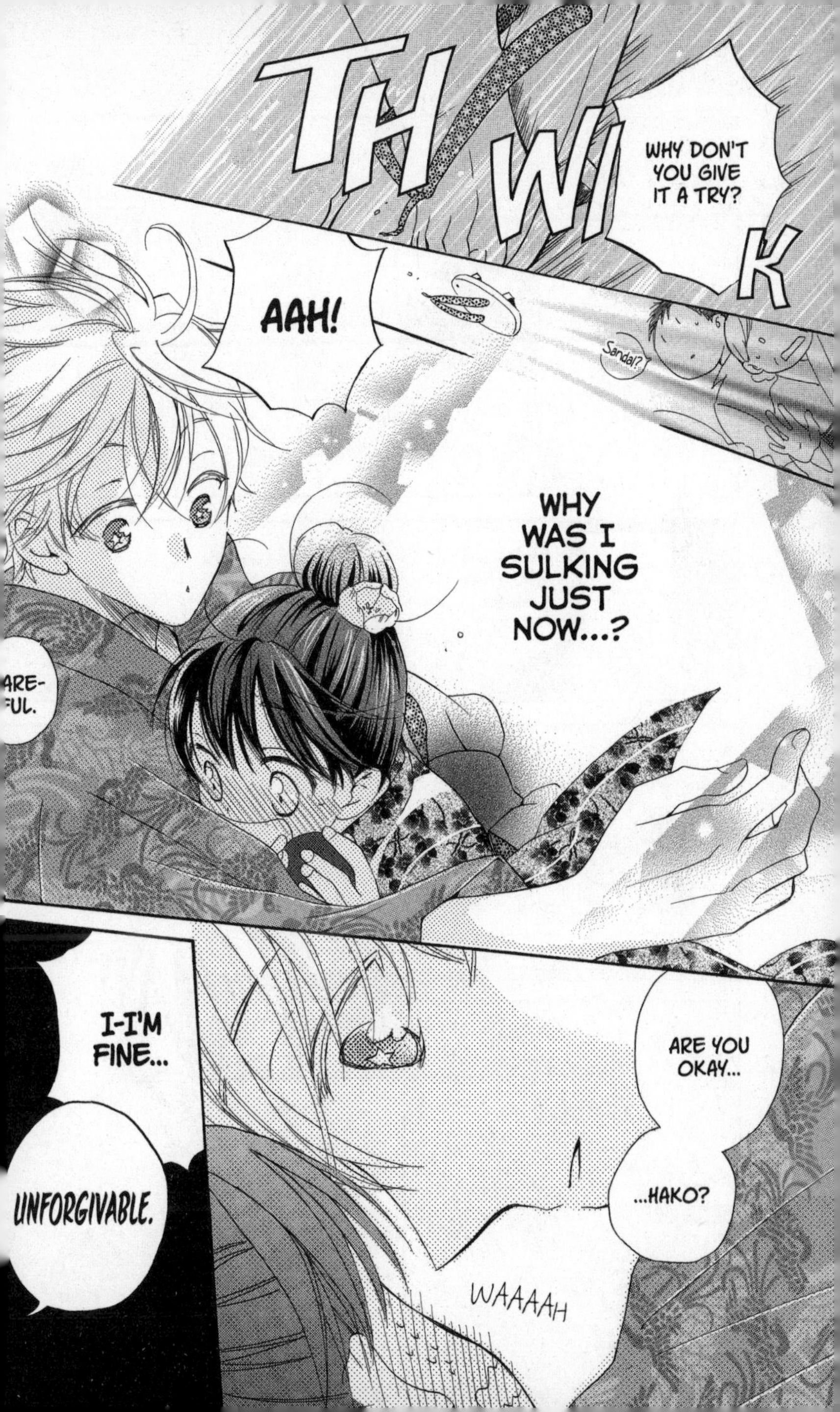
WHY DON'T YOU GIVE IT A TRY?
THWIK
Sandal?
AAH!
WHY WAS I SULKING JUST NOW...?
ARE- FUL.
ARE YOU OKAY...
...HAKO?
WAAAAH
I-I'M FINE...
UNFORGIVABLE.

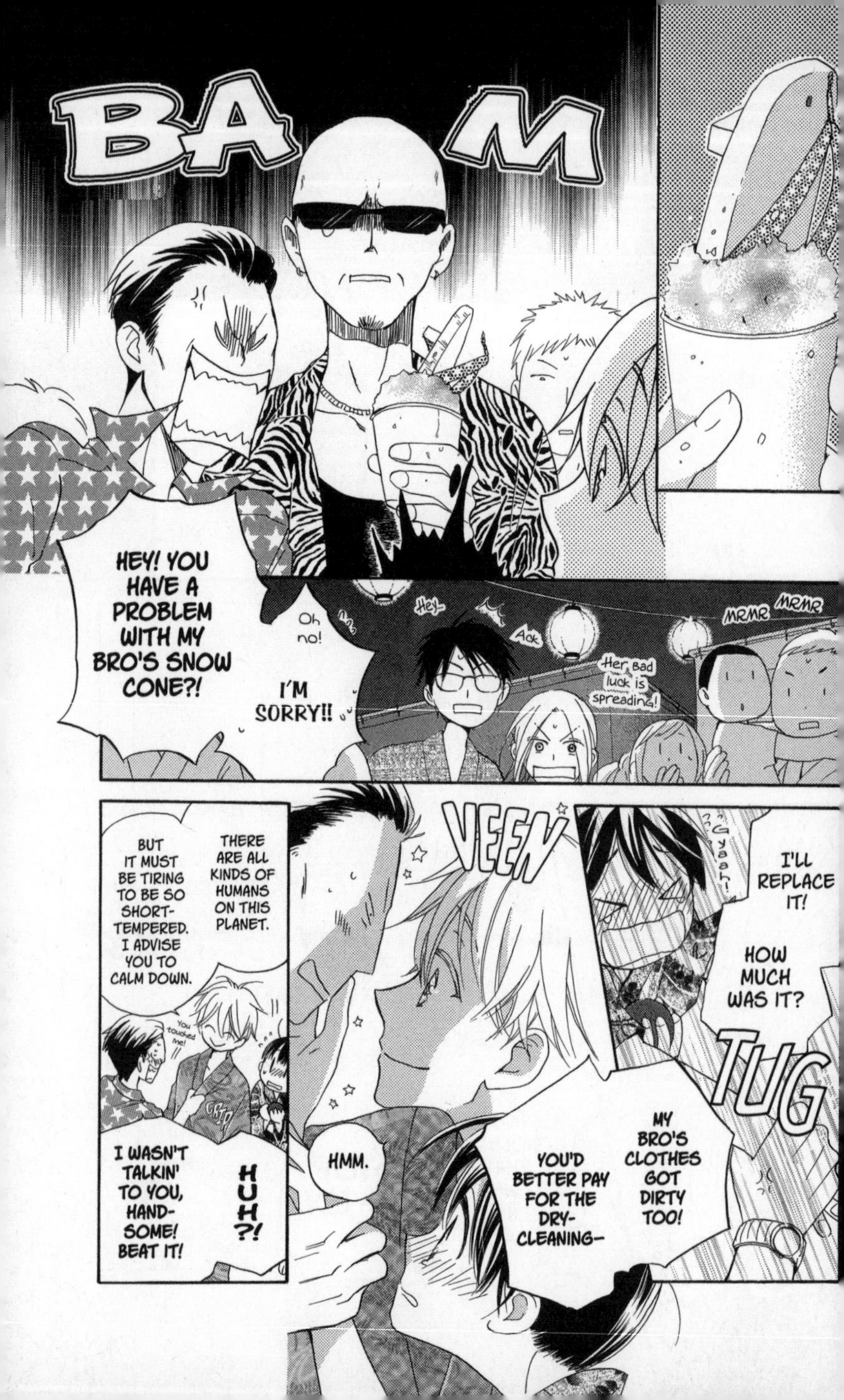
BAM
HEY! YOU HAVE A PROBLEM WITH MY BRO'S SNOW CONE?!
MRMR MRMR
Hey...
Ack
Her bad luck is spreading!
Oh no!
I'M SORRY!!
Gyaah!
I'LL REPLACE IT!
HOW MUCH WAS IT?
TUG
MY BRO'S CLOTHES GOT DIRTY TOO!
YOU'D BETTER PAY FOR THE DRY-CLEANING—
VEEN
HMM.
THERE ARE ALL KINDS OF HUMANS ON THIS PLANET.
BUT IT MUST BE TIRING TO BE SO SHORT-TEMPERED. I ADVISE YOU TO CALM DOWN.
You touched me!
I WASN'T TALKIN' TO YOU, HANDSOME! BEAT IT!
HUH?!

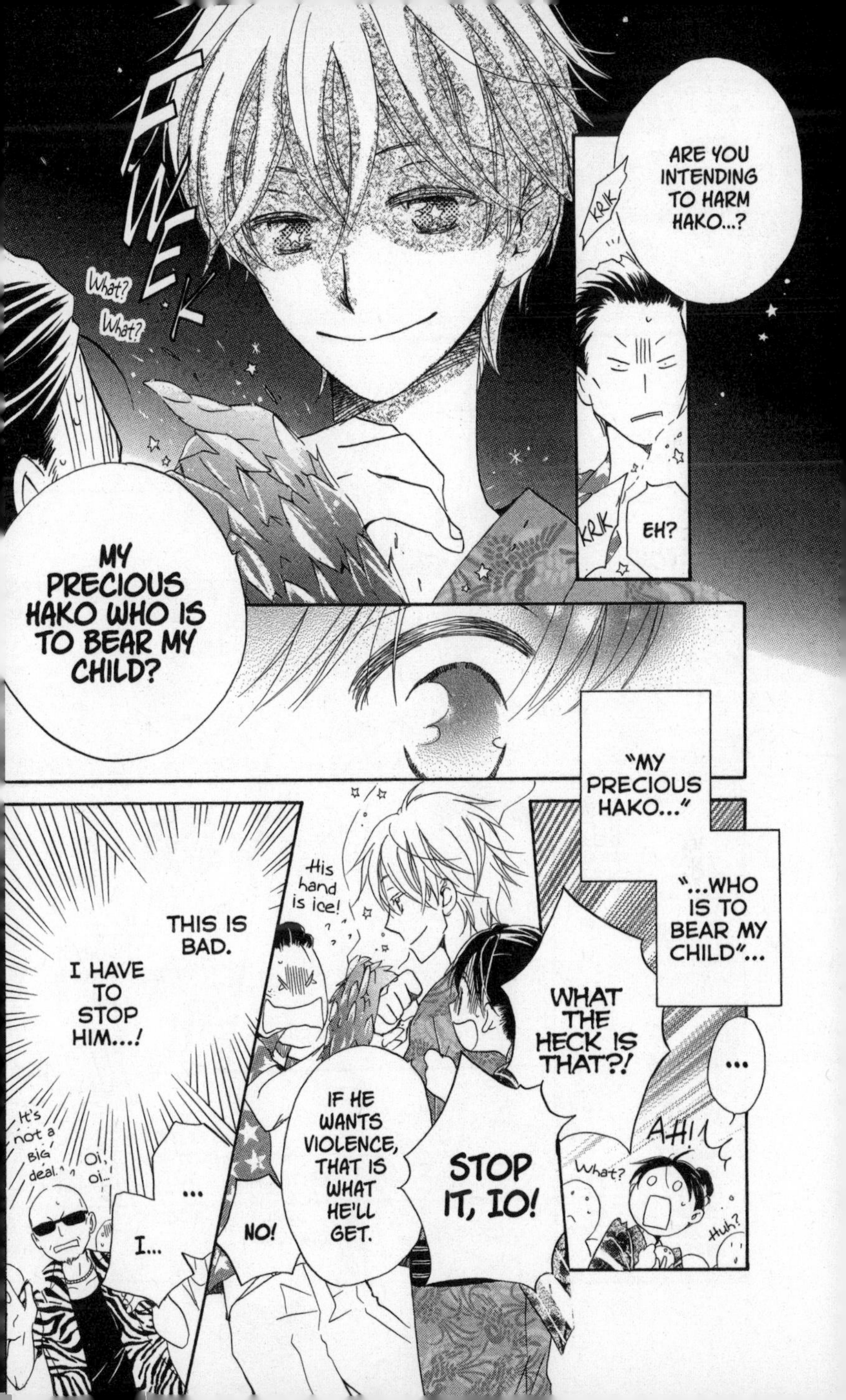
ARE YOU INTENDING TO HARM HAKO...?
KRIK
EH?
KRIK
What?
What?
MY PRECIOUS HAKO WHO IS TO BEAR MY CHILD?
"MY PRECIOUS HAKO..."
"...WHO IS TO BEAR MY CHILD"...
WHAT THE HECK IS THAT?!
...
AH!
What?
Huh?
STOP IT, IO!
IF HE WANTS VIOLENCE, THAT IS WHAT HE'LL GET.
NO!
His hand is ice!
THIS IS BAD.
I HAVE TO STOP HIM...!
...
I...
It's not a BIG deal.
Oi, oi...

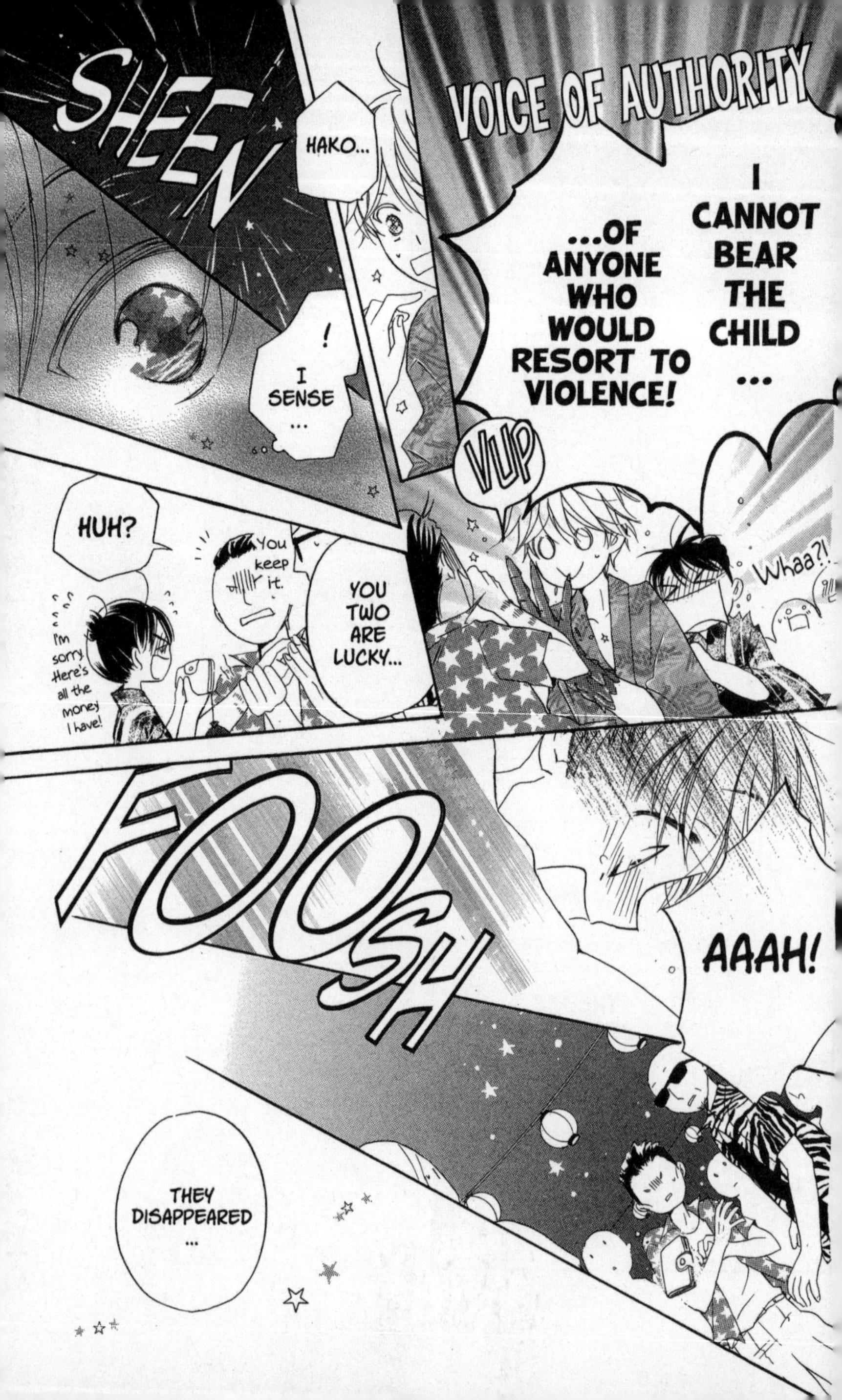
VOICE OF AUTHORITY
I CANNOT BEAR THE CHILD...
...OF ANYONE WHO WOULD RESORT TO VIOLENCE!
VUP
Whaa?!
HAKO...
SHEEN
! I SENSE...
YOU TWO ARE LUCKY...
You keep it.
HUH?
I'm sorry. Here's all the money I have!
AAAH!
FOOSH
THEY DISAPPEARED...

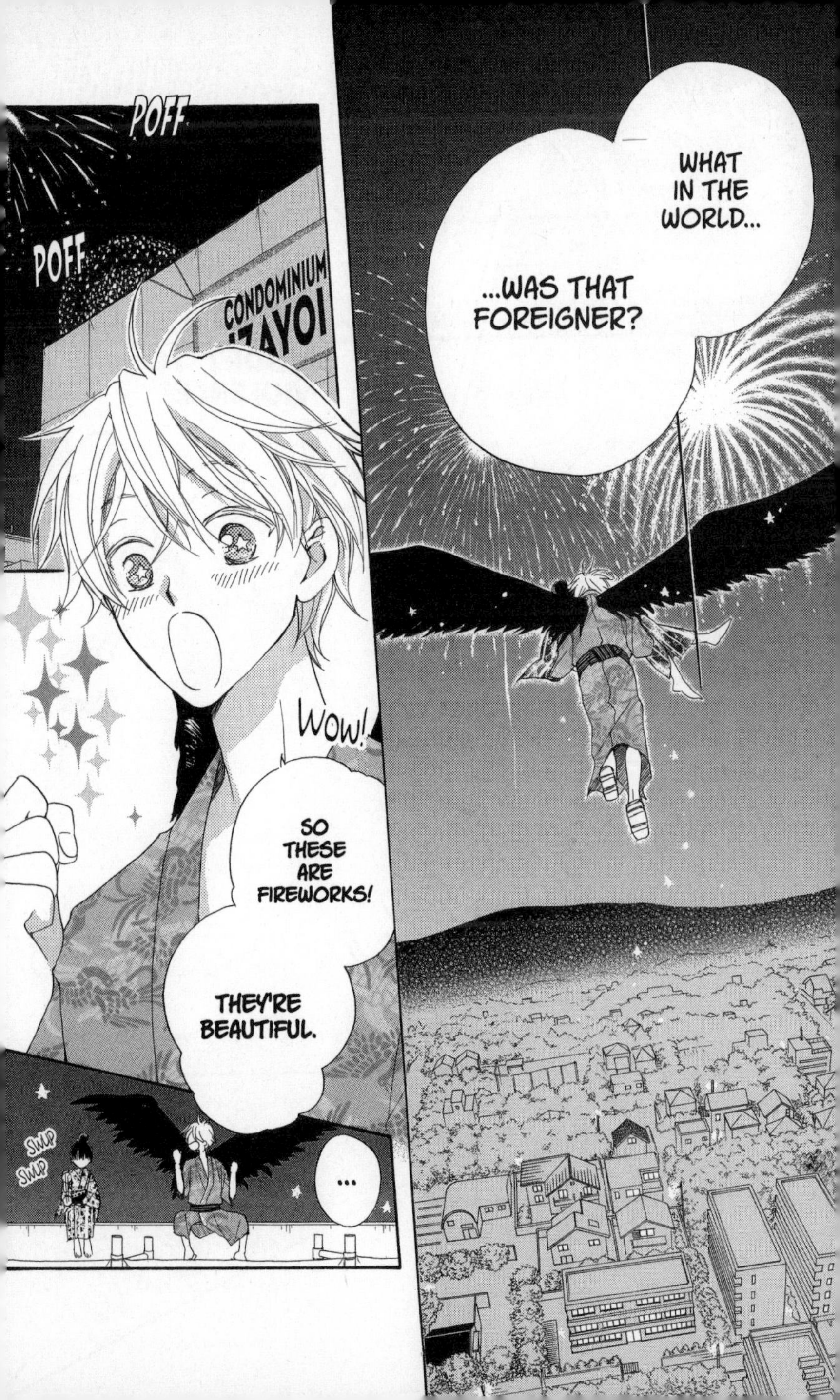
WHAT IN THE WORLD...
...WAS THAT FOREIGNER?
POFF
POFF
CONDOMINIUM IZAYOI
WOW!
SO THESE ARE FIREWORKS!
THEY'RE BEAUTIFUL.
...
SWP SWP

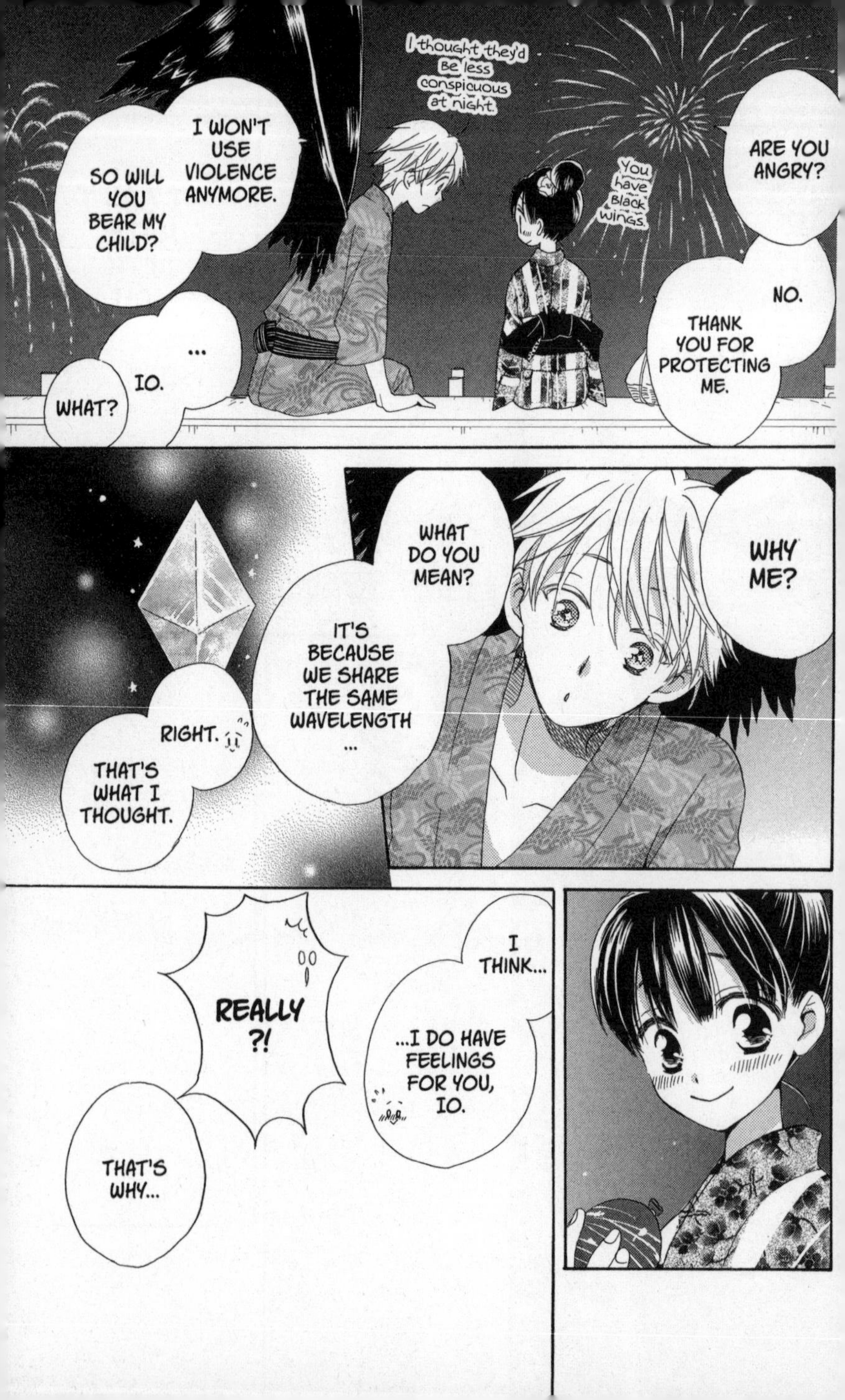
ARE YOU ANGRY?
You have Black wings.
I thought they'd be less conspicuous at night.
NO.
THANK YOU FOR PROTECTING ME.
I WON'T USE VIOLENCE ANYMORE.
SO WILL YOU BEAR MY CHILD?
...
IO.
WHAT?
WHY ME?
WHAT DO YOU MEAN?
IT'S BECAUSE WE SHARE THE SAME WAVELENGTH ...
RIGHT.
THAT'S WHAT I THOUGHT.
I THINK...
...I DO HAVE FEELINGS FOR YOU, IO.
REALLY ?!
THAT'S WHY...

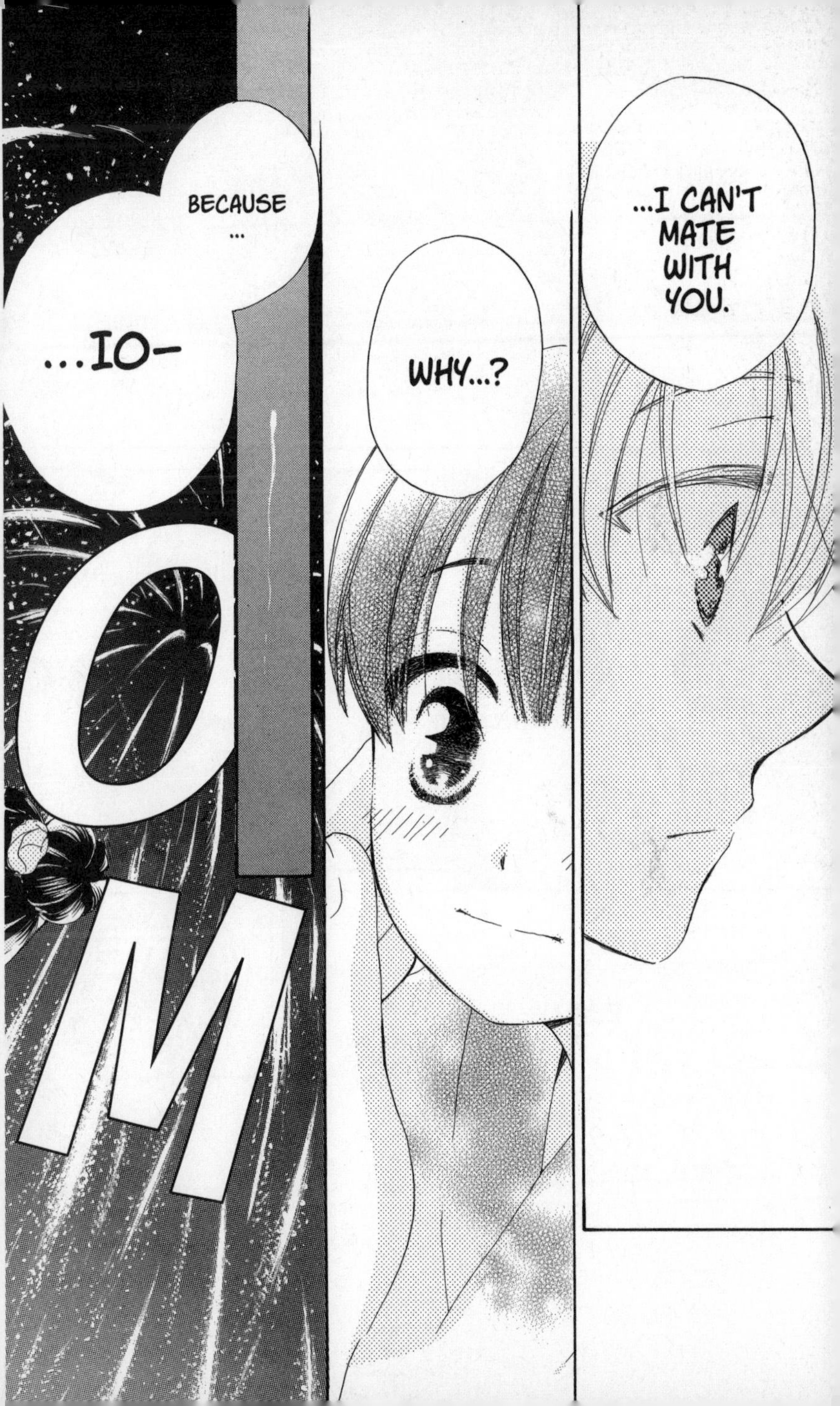
...I CAN'T MATE WITH YOU.
WHY...?
BECAUSE ...
...IO-
OM

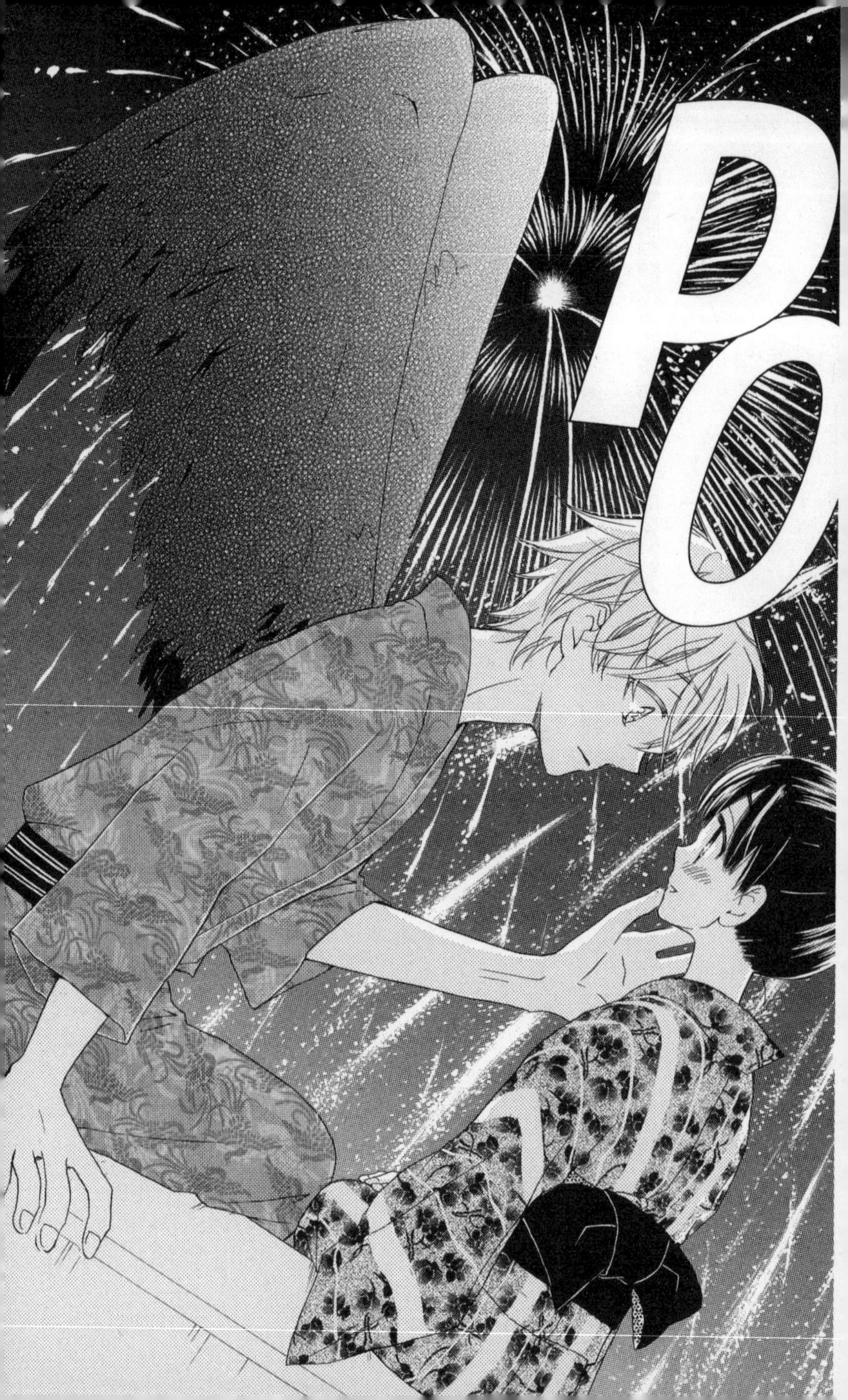
PO

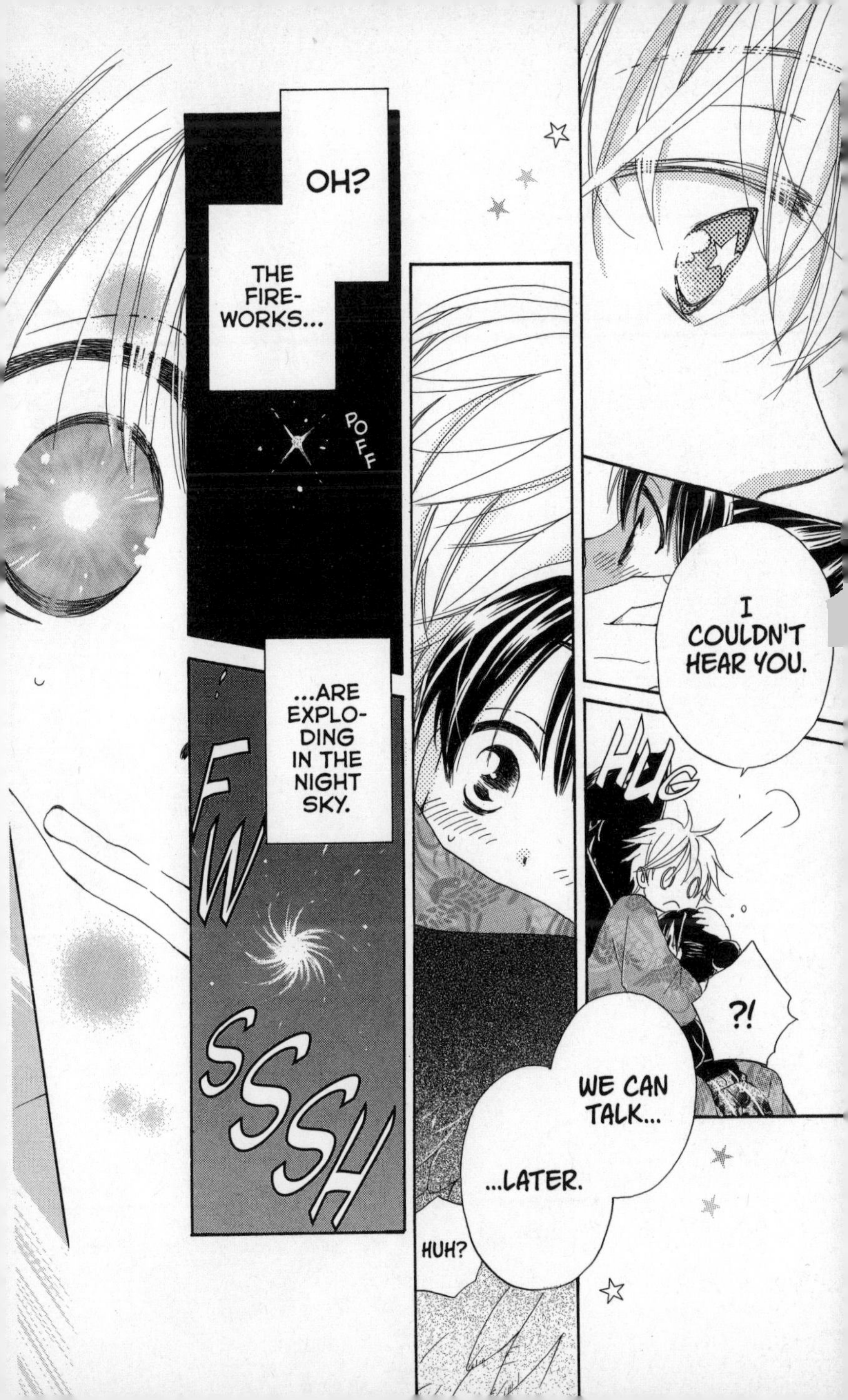
I COULDN'T HEAR YOU.
HUG
?!
WE CAN TALK...
...LATER.
HUH?
OH?
THE FIRE-WORKS...
POFF
...ARE EXPLODING IN THE NIGHT SKY.
FWSSSH

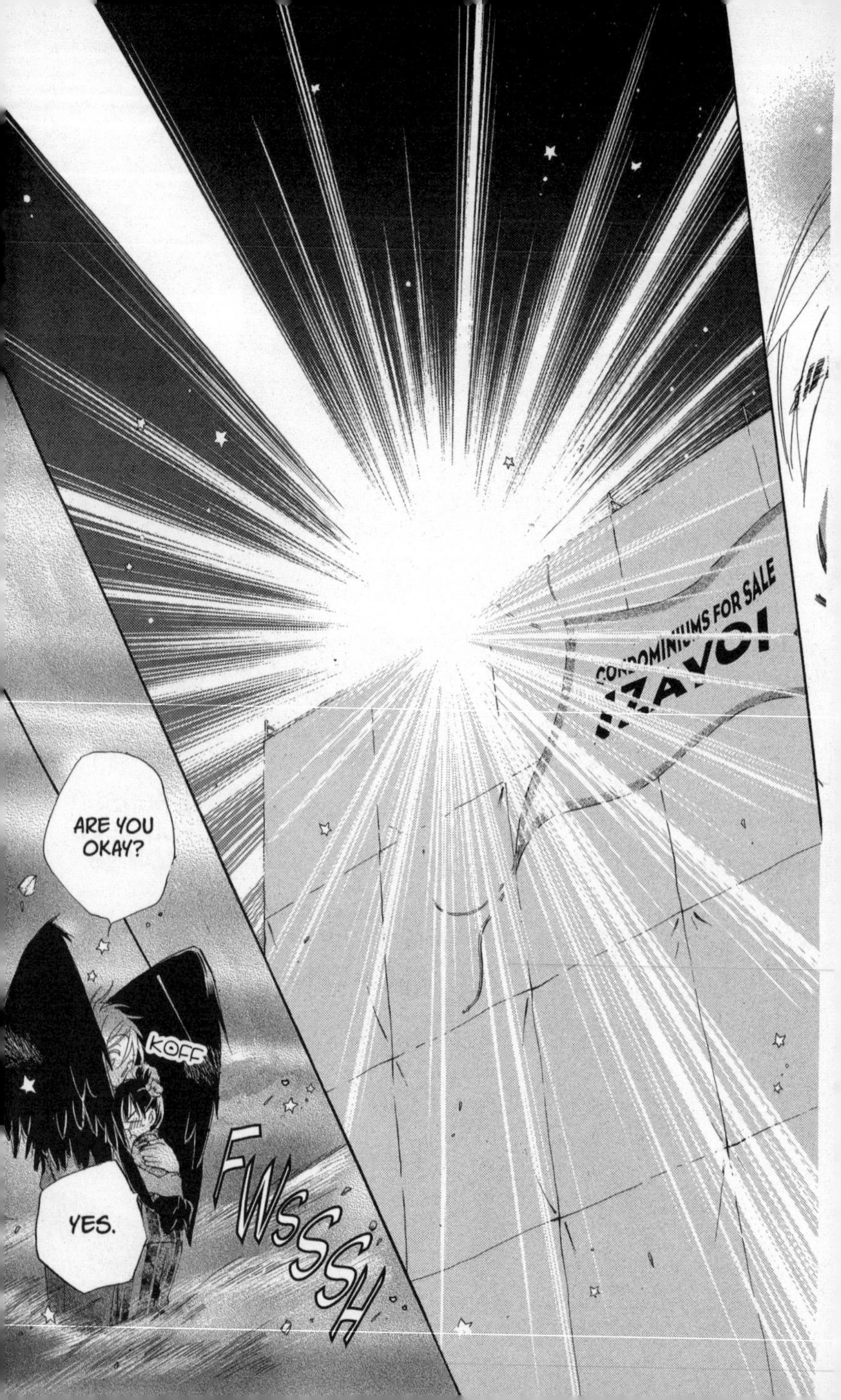
ARE YOU OKAY?
KOFF
FWSSSH
YES.

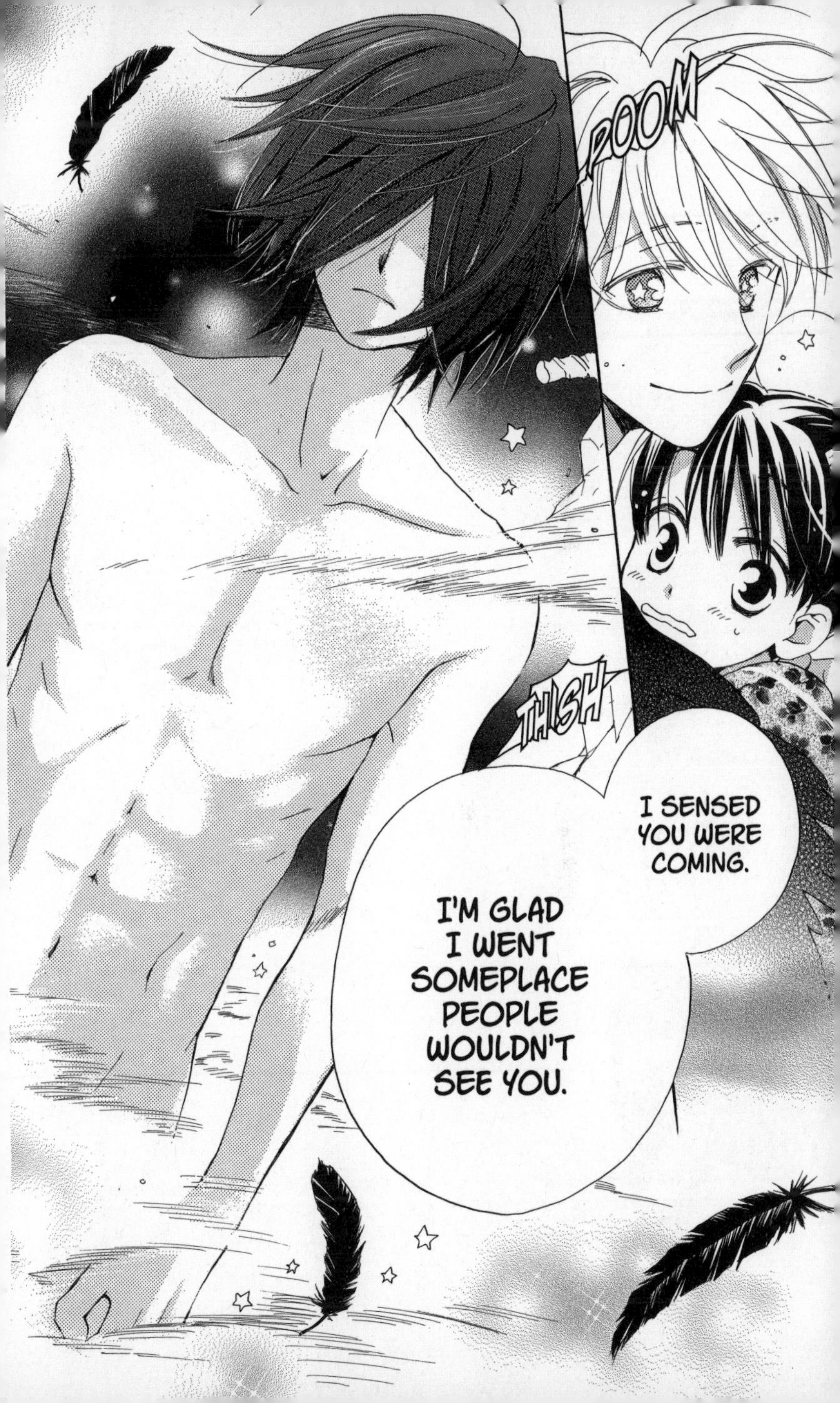
POOM
THISH
I SENSED YOU WERE COMING.
I'M GLAD I WENT SOMEPLACE PEOPLE WOULDN'T SEE YOU.

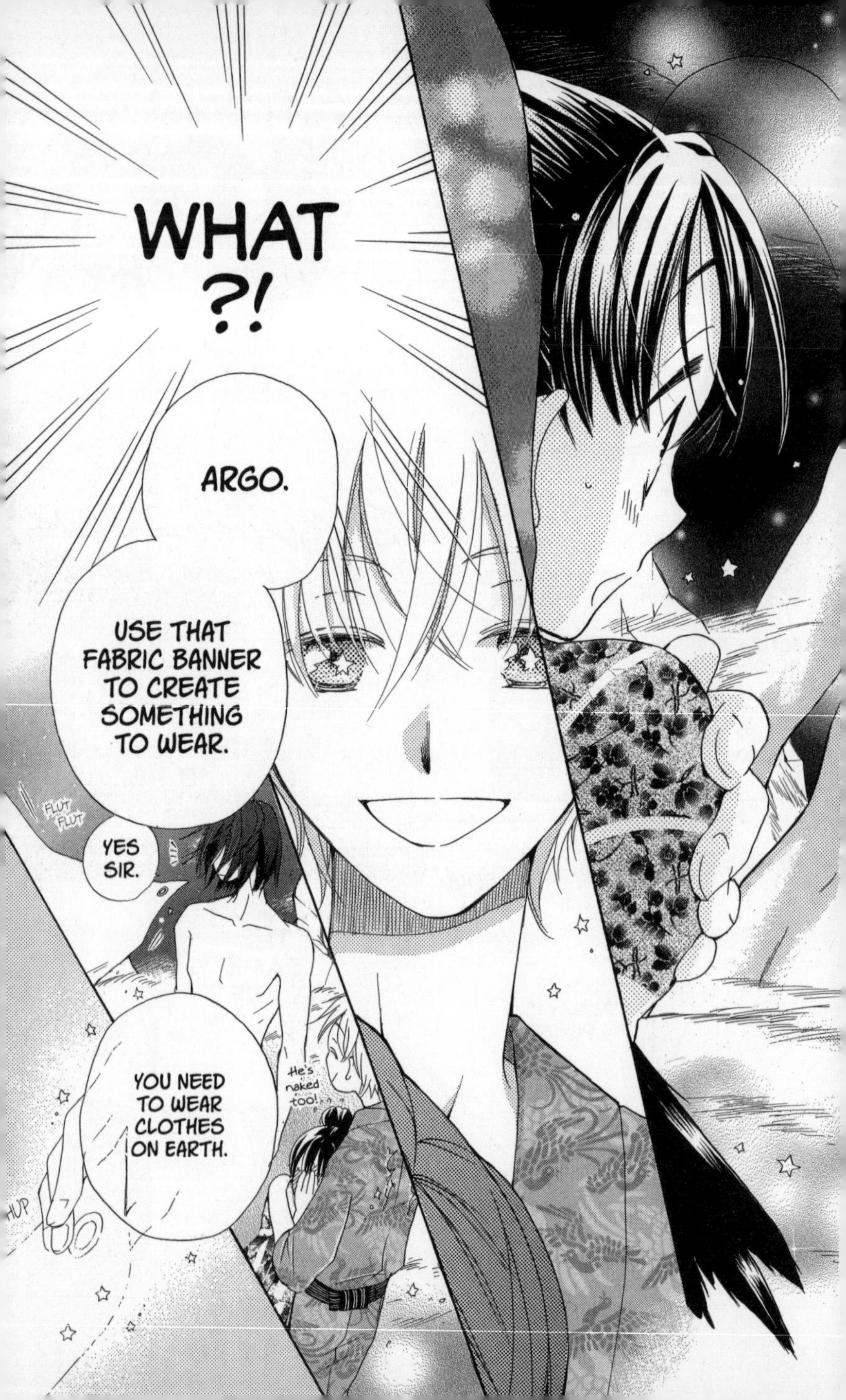
WHAT ?!
ARGO.
USE THAT FABRIC BANNER TO CREATE SOMETHING TO WEAR.
FLUT FLUT
YES SIR.
YOU NEED TO WEAR CLOTHES ON EARTH.
He's naked too!
HUP

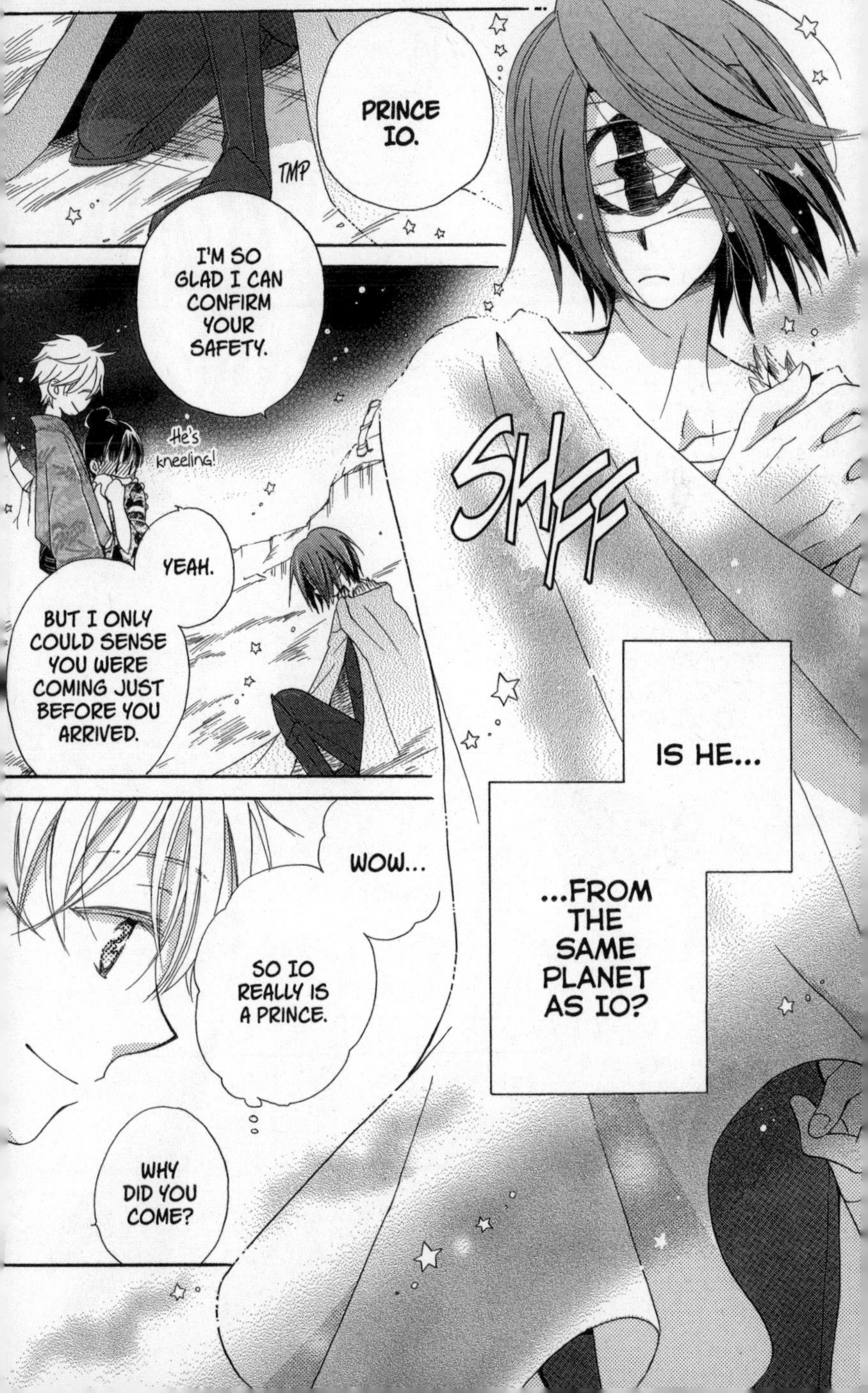
SHFF
IS HE...
...FROM THE SAME PLANET AS IO?
PRINCE IO.
TMP
I'M SO GLAD I CAN CONFIRM YOUR SAFETY.
He's kneeling!
YEAH.
BUT I ONLY COULD SENSE YOU WERE COMING JUST BEFORE YOU ARRIVED.
WOW...
SO IO REALLY IS A PRINCE.
WHY DID YOU COME?

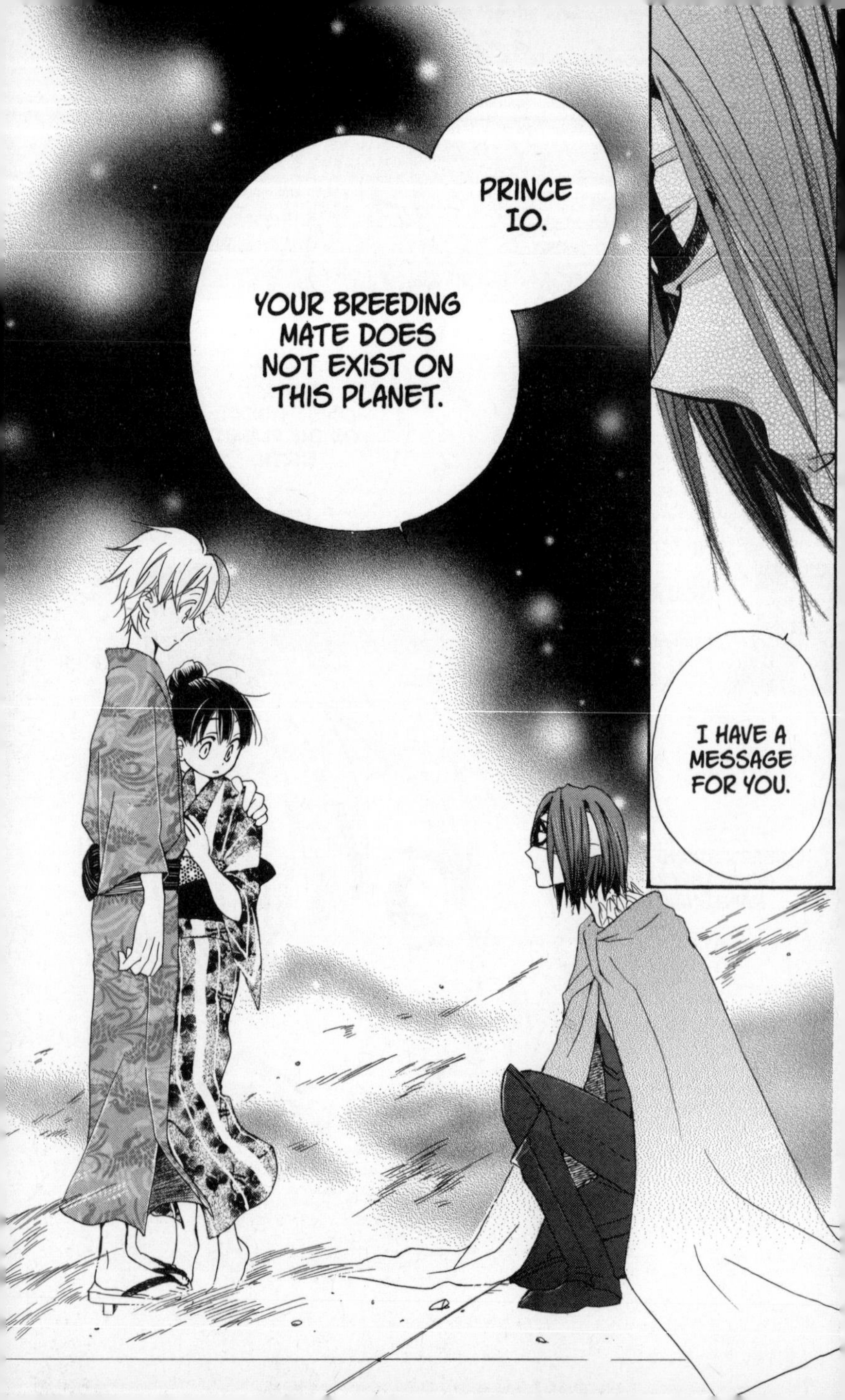
I HAVE A MESSAGE FOR YOU.
PRINCE IO.
YOUR BREEDING MATE DOES NOT EXIST ON THIS PLANET.

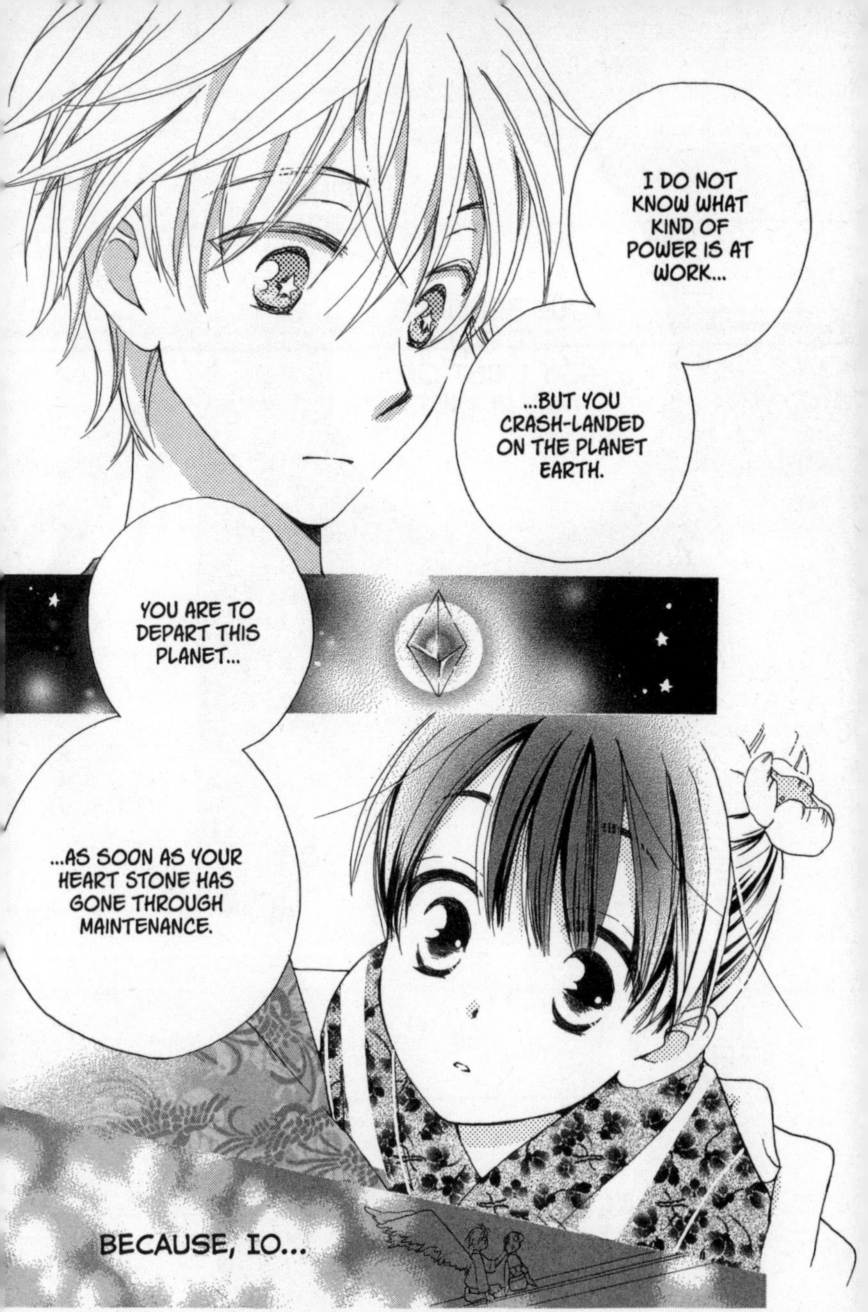
I DO NOT KNOW WHAT KIND OF POWER IS AT WORK...
...BUT YOU CRASH-LANDED ON THE PLANET EARTH.
YOU ARE TO DEPART THIS PLANET...
...AS SOON AS YOUR HEART STONE HAS GONE THROUGH MAINTENANCE.
BECAUSE, IO...

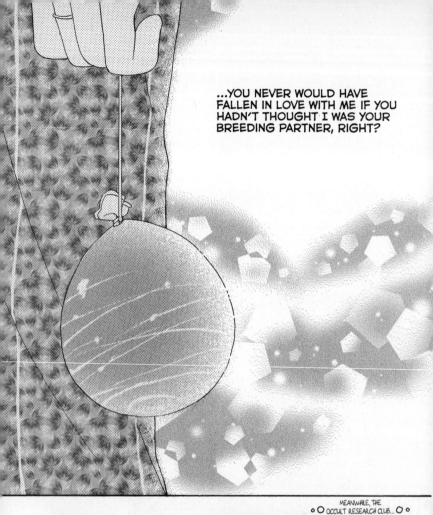

...YOU NEVER WOULD HAVE FALLEN IN LOVE WITH ME IF YOU HADN'T THOUGHT I WAS YOUR BREEDING PARTNER, RIGHT?

MEANWHILE, THE
○ ○ OCCULT RESEARCH CLUB... ○ ○

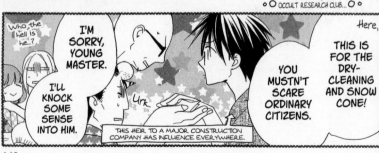

Who the hell is he...?

I'M SORRY, YOUNG MASTER.

I'LL KNOCK SOME SENSE INTO HIM.

Urk

YOU MUSTN'T SCARE ORDINARY CITIZENS.

Here, THIS IS FOR THE DRY-CLEANING AND SNOW CONE!

THIS HEIR TO A MAJOR CONSTRUCTION COMPANY HAS INFLUENCE EVERYWHERE.

Oh! The writing didn't come off.
CONDOMINIUMS

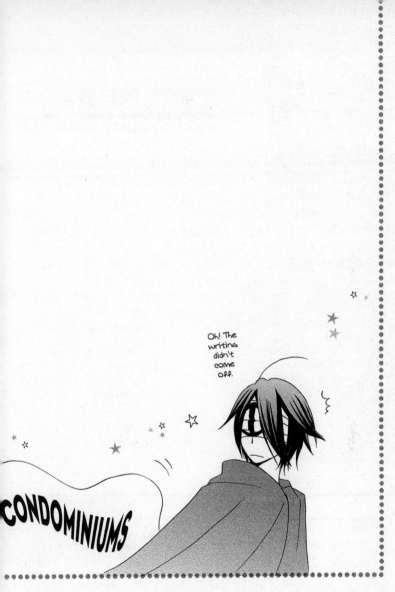

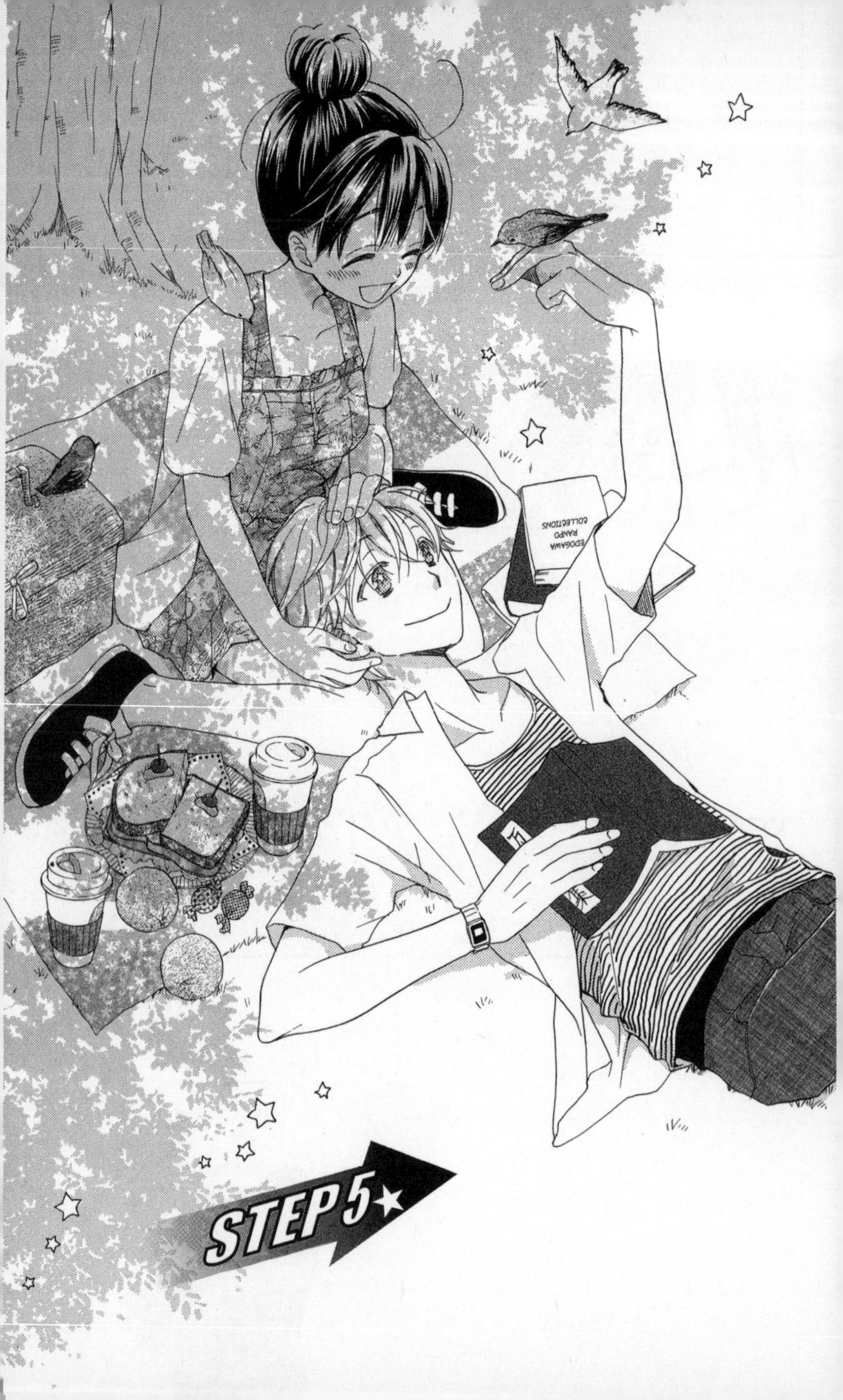
EDOGAWA RAMPO COLLECTIONS
STEP 5★

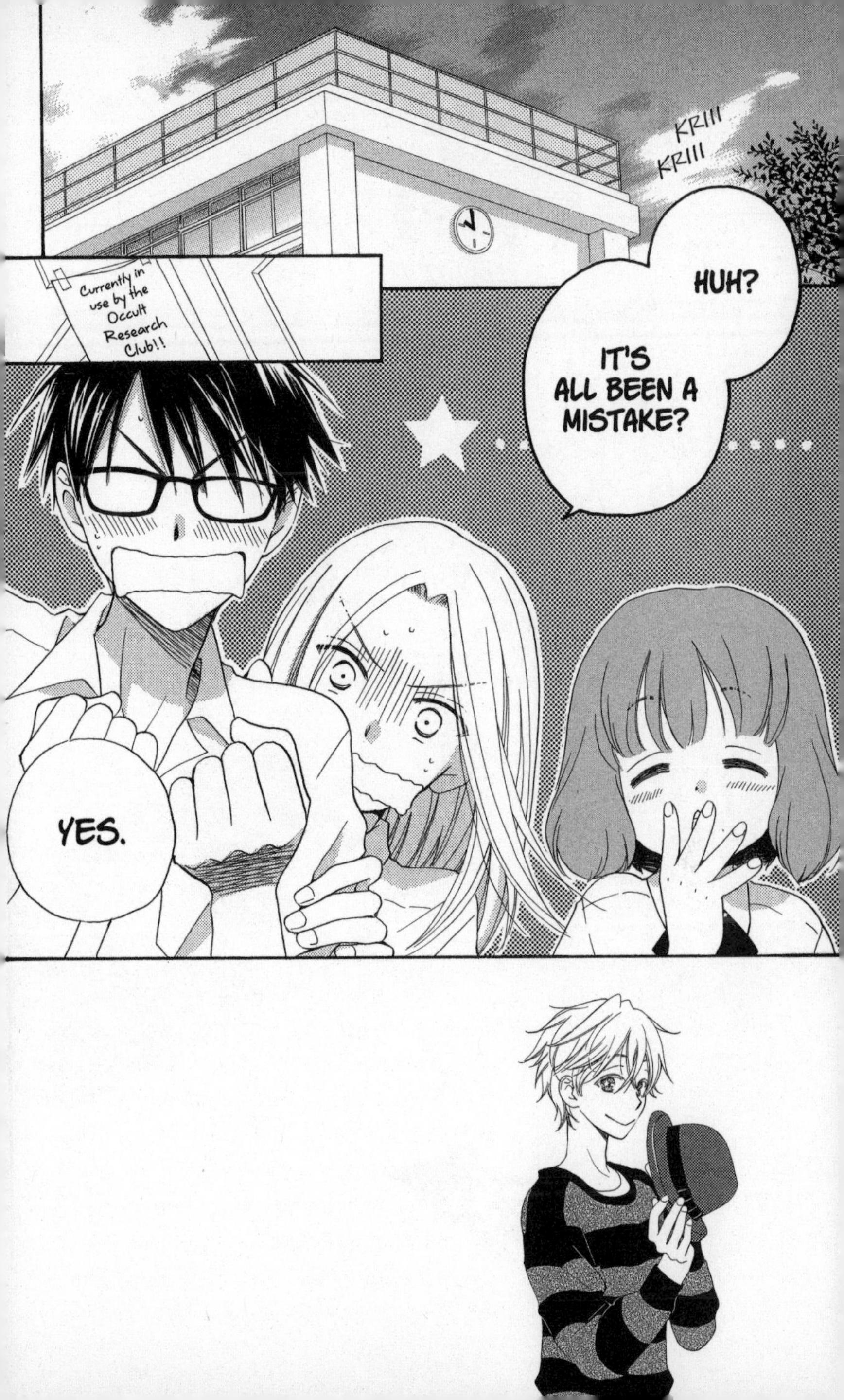
KRIII
KRIII
HUH?
IT'S ALL BEEN A MISTAKE?
Currently in use by the Occult Research Club!!
YES.

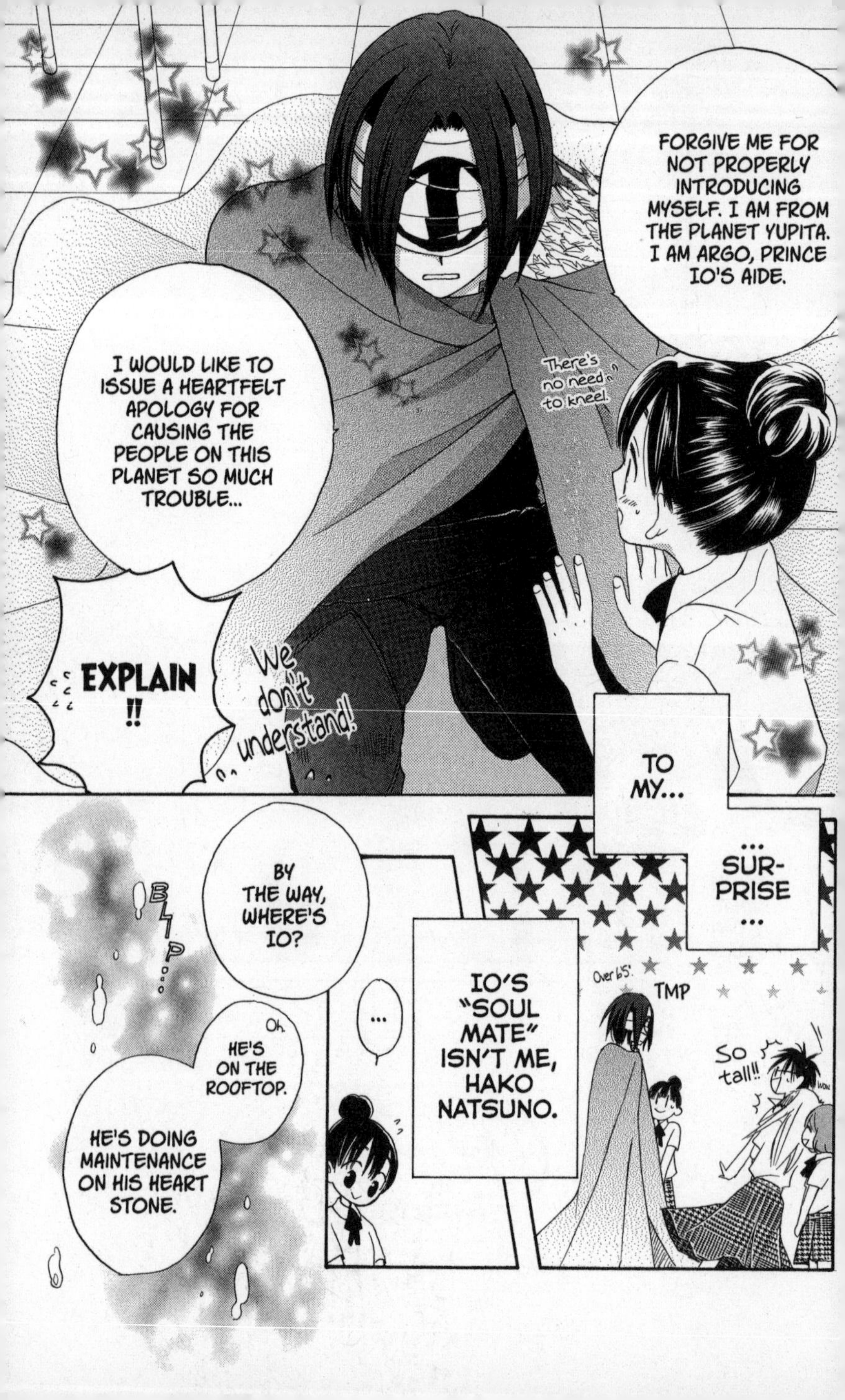
FORGIVE ME FOR NOT PROPERLY INTRODUCING MYSELF. I AM FROM THE PLANET YUPITA. I AM ARGO, PRINCE IO'S AIDE.
There's no need to kneel.
I WOULD LIKE TO ISSUE A HEARTFELT APOLOGY FOR CAUSING THE PEOPLE ON THIS PLANET SO MUCH TROUBLE...
EXPLAIN!!
We don't understand!
TO MY...
...SÜR-PRISE...
IO'S "SOUL MATE" ISN'T ME, HAKO NATSUNO.
Over 6'5".
TMP
So tall!!
BY THE WAY, WHERE'S IO?
...
Oh.
HE'S ON THE ROOFTOP.
HE'S DOING MAINTENANCE ON HIS HEART STONE.
BLIP

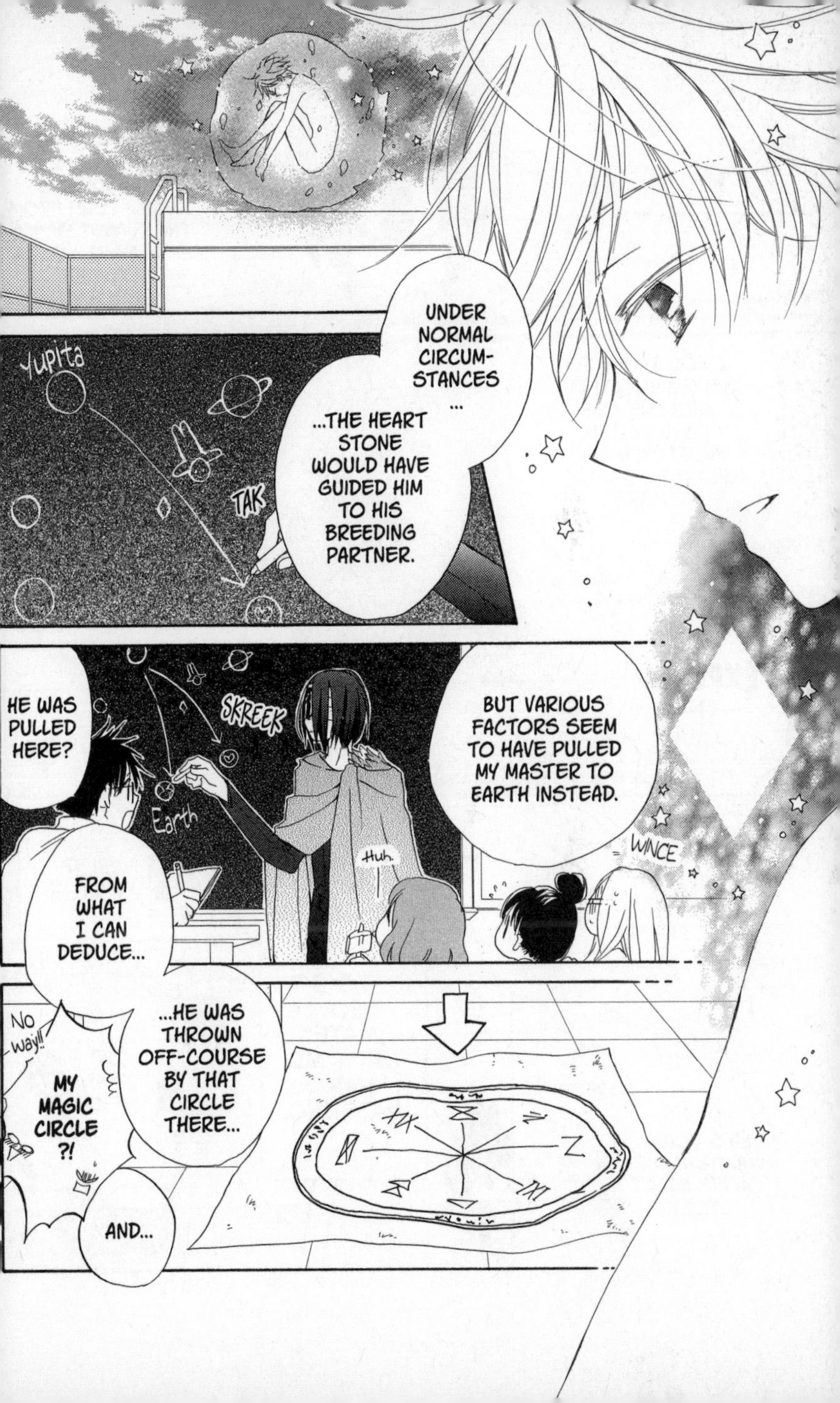
UNDER NORMAL CIRCUM-STANCES...
...THE HEART STONE WOULD HAVE GUIDED HIM TO HIS BREEDING PARTNER.
TAK
Yupita
BUT VARIOUS FACTORS SEEM TO HAVE PULLED MY MASTER TO EARTH INSTEAD.
WINCE
Huh.
SKREEK
Earth
HE WAS PULLED HERE?
FROM WHAT I CAN DEDUCE...
...HE WAS THROWN OFF-COURSE BY THAT CIRCLE THERE...
MY MAGIC CIRCLE?!
No way!!
AND...

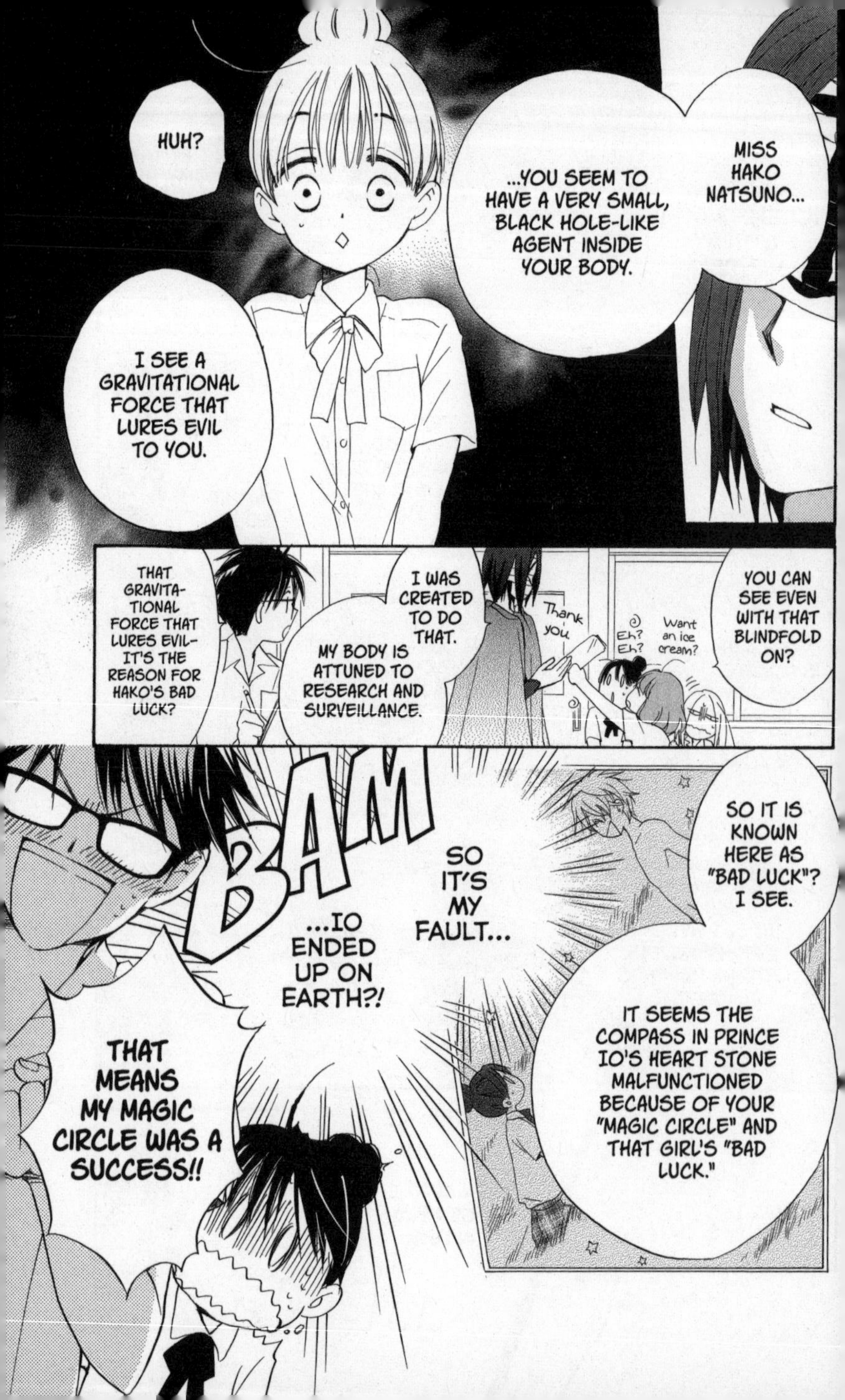
MISS HAKO NATSUNO...
...YOU SEEM TO HAVE A VERY SMALL, BLACK HOLE-LIKE AGENT INSIDE YOUR BODY.
HUH?
I SEE A GRAVITATIONAL FORCE THAT LURES EVIL TO YOU.
YOU CAN SEE EVEN WITH THAT BLINDFOLD ON?
Want an ice cream?
Eh? Eh?
Thank you.
I WAS CREATED TO DO THAT.
MY BODY IS ATTUNED TO RESEARCH AND SURVEILLANCE.
THAT GRAVITATIONAL FORCE THAT LURES EVIL–IT'S THE REASON FOR HAKO'S BAD LUCK?
SO IT IS KNOWN HERE AS "BAD LUCK"? I SEE.
IT SEEMS THE COMPASS IN PRINCE IO'S HEART STONE MALFUNCTIONED BECAUSE OF YOUR "MAGIC CIRCLE" AND THAT GIRL'S "BAD LUCK."
SO IT'S MY FAULT...
...IO ENDED UP ON EARTH?!
BAM
THAT MEANS MY MAGIC CIRCLE WAS A SUCCESS!!

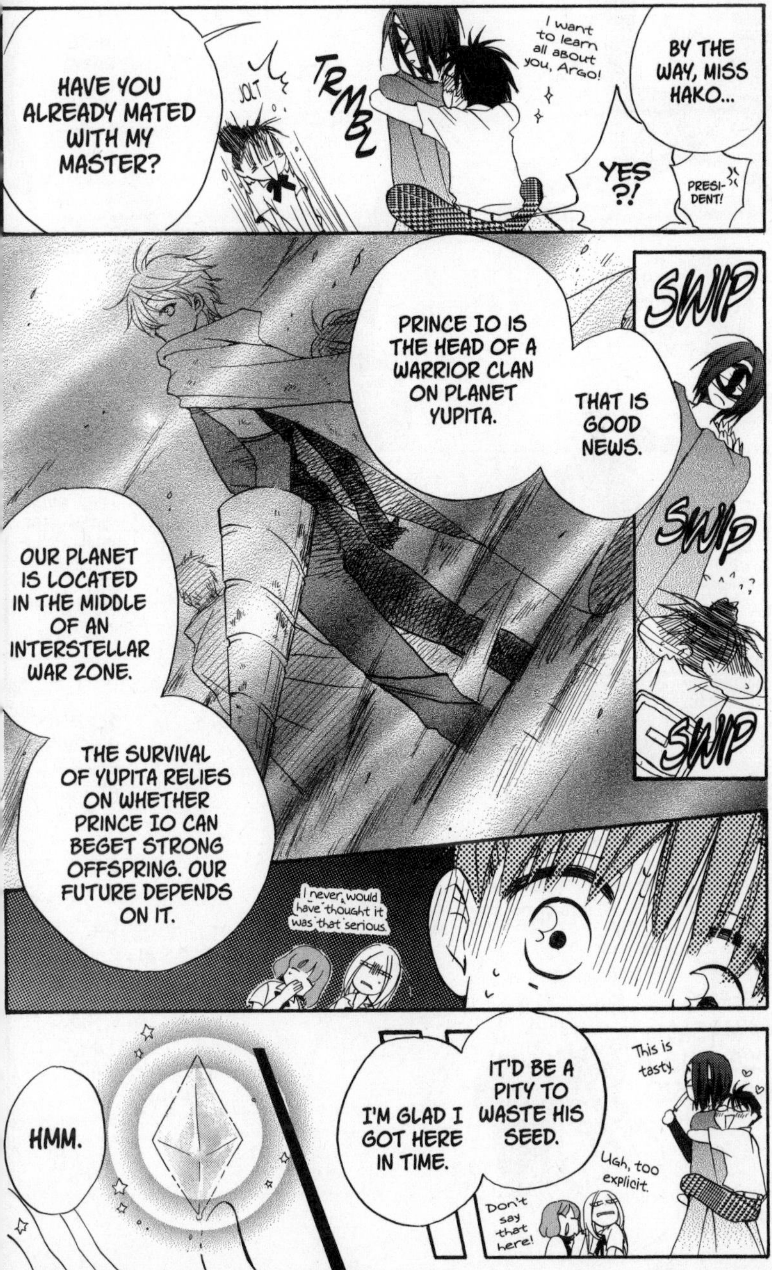
BY THE WAY, MISS HAKO...
PRESI-DENT!
YES?!
I want to learn all about you, Argo!
TRMBL
JOLT
HAVE YOU ALREADY MATED WITH MY MASTER?
SWIP
SWIP
SWIP
THAT IS GOOD NEWS.
PRINCE IO IS THE HEAD OF A WARRIOR CLAN ON PLANET YUPITA.
OUR PLANET IS LOCATED IN THE MIDDLE OF AN INTERSTELLAR WAR ZONE.
THE SURVIVAL OF YUPITA RELIES ON WHETHER PRINCE IO CAN BEGET STRONG OFFSPRING. OUR FUTURE DEPENDS ON IT.
I never would have thought it was that serious.
This is tasty.
IT'D BE A PITY TO WASTE HIS SEED.
I'M GLAD I GOT HERE IN TIME.
Ugh, too explicit.
Don't say that here!
HMM.

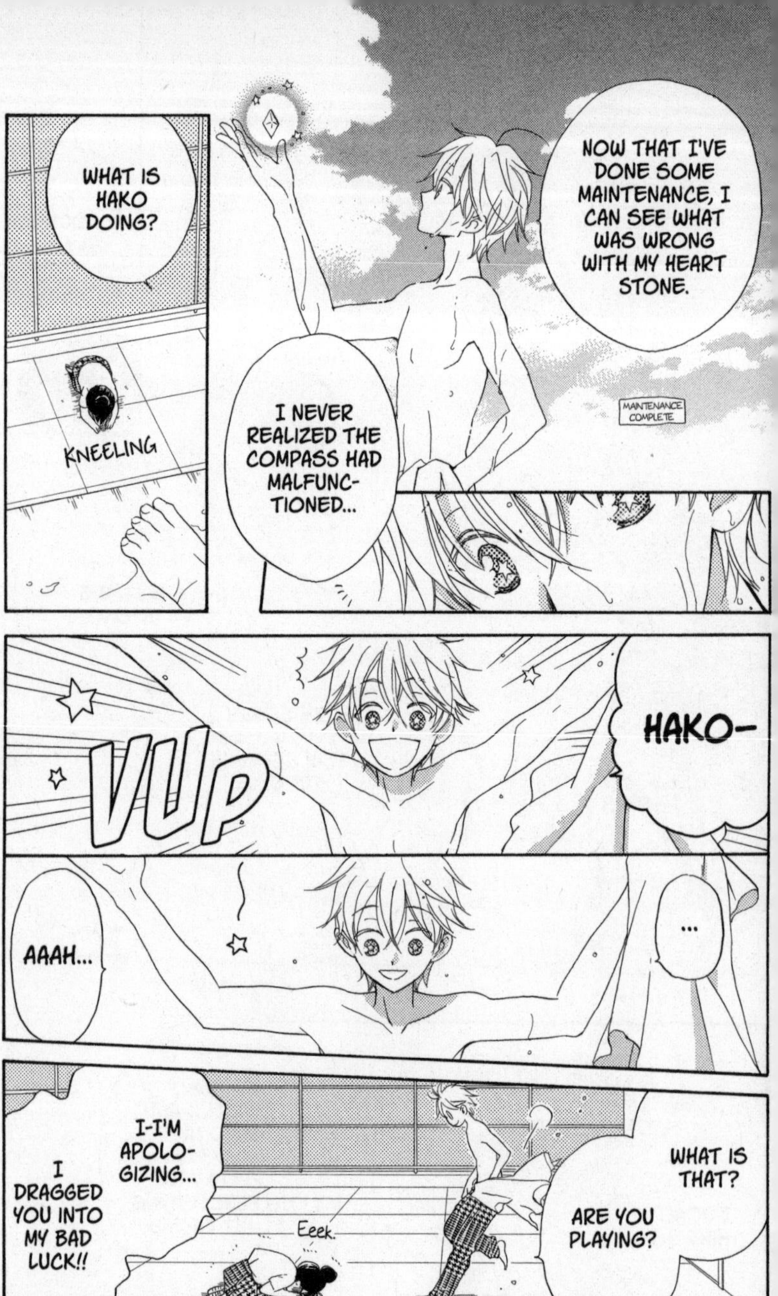
NOW THAT I'VE DONE SOME MAINTENANCE, I CAN SEE WHAT WAS WRONG WITH MY HEART STONE.
MAINTENANCE COMPLETE
I NEVER REALIZED THE COMPASS HAD MALFUNC-TIONED...
WHAT IS HAKO DOING?
KNEELING
HAKO-
VUP
...
AAAH...
WHAT IS THAT?
ARE YOU PLAYING?
Eeek.
I-I'M APOLO-GIZING...
I DRAGGED YOU INTO MY BAD LUCK!!

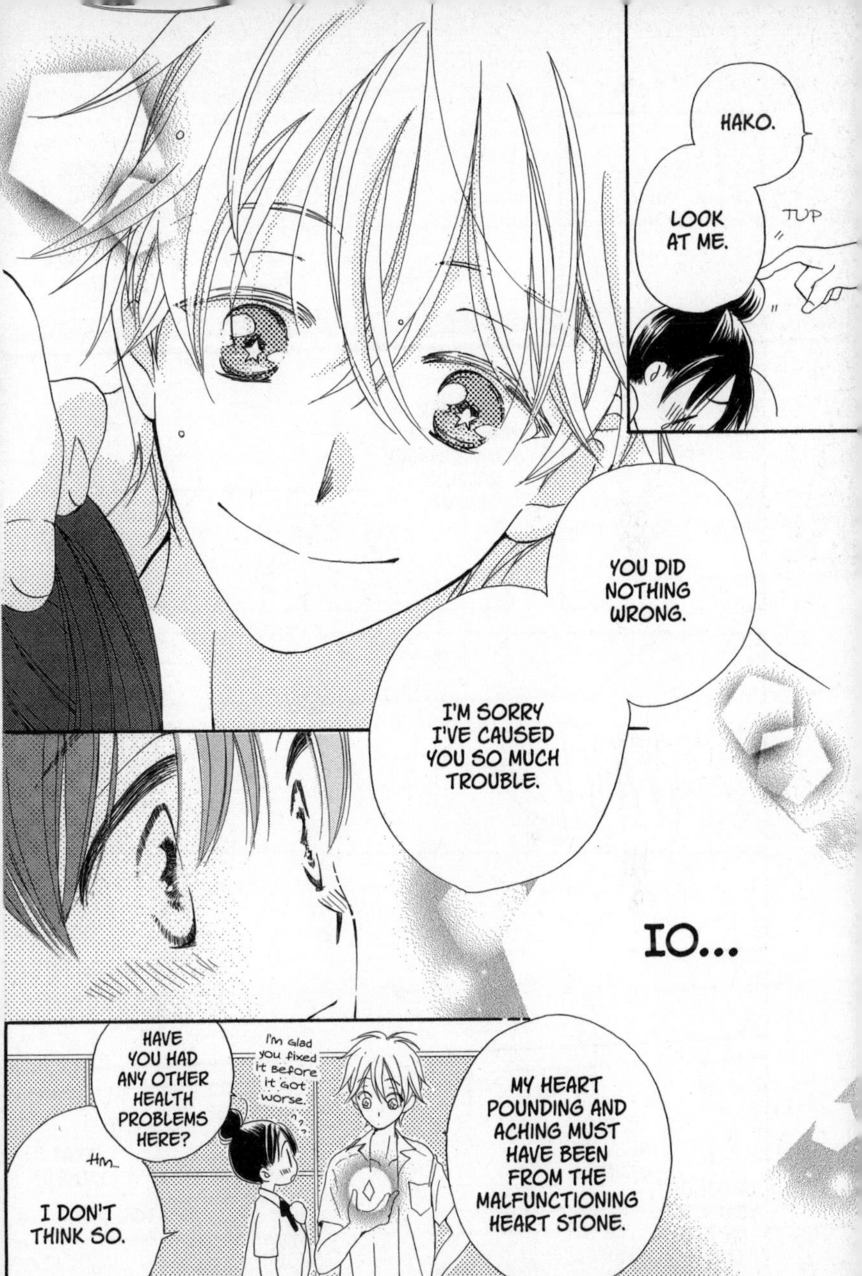
HAKO.
LOOK AT ME.
TUP
YOU DID NOTHING WRONG.
I'M SORRY I'VE CAUSED YOU SO MUCH TROUBLE.
IO...
MY HEART POUNDING AND ACHING MUST HAVE BEEN FROM THE MALFUNCTIONING HEART STONE.
I'm glad you fixed it before it got worse.
HAVE YOU HAD ANY OTHER HEALTH PROBLEMS HERE?
Hm...
I DON'T THINK SO.

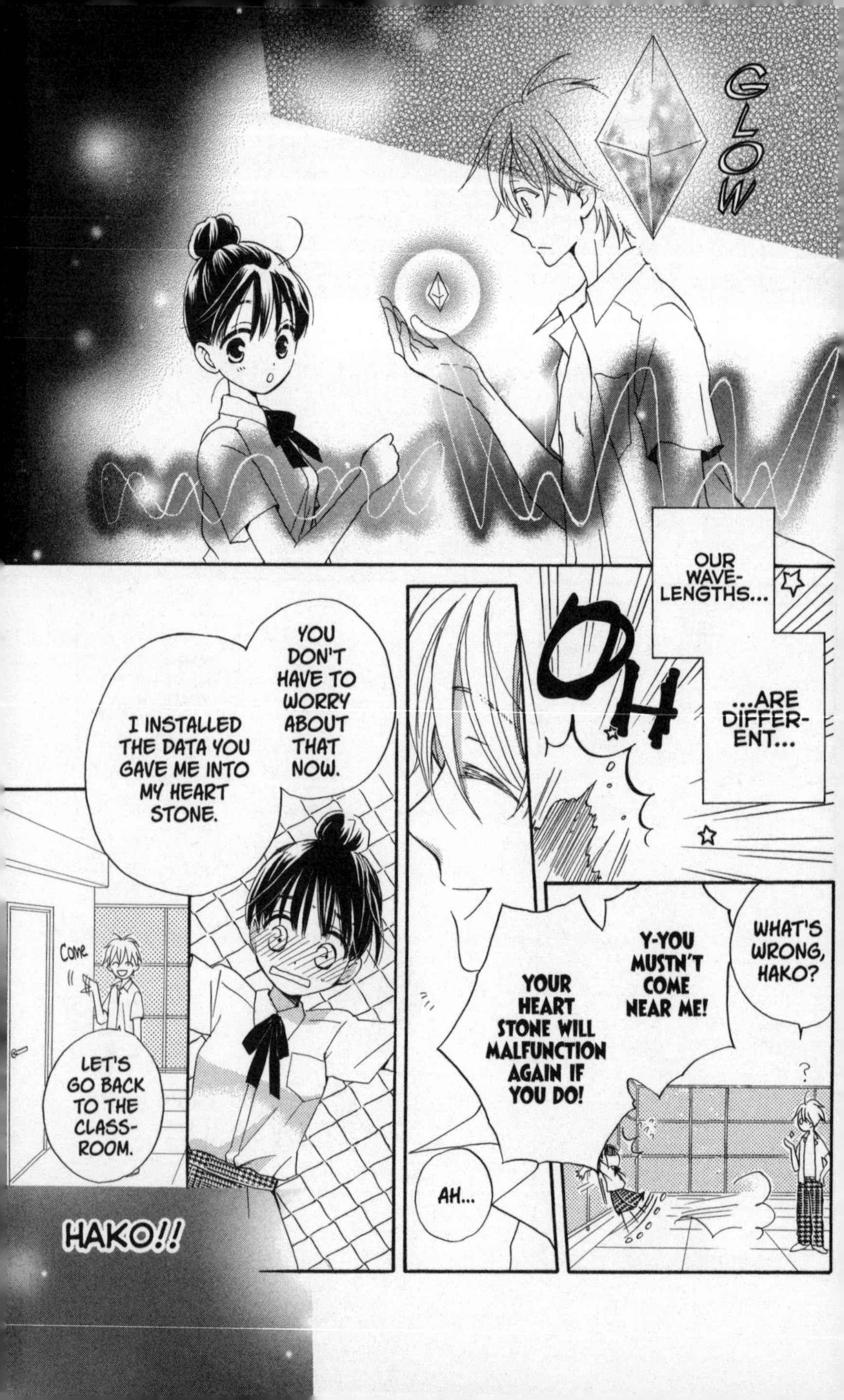
GLOW
OUR WAVE-LENGTHS...
...ARE DIFFER-ENT...
OH
WHAT'S WRONG, HAKO?
Y-YOU MUSTN'T COME NEAR ME!
YOUR HEART STONE WILL MALFUNCTION AGAIN IF YOU DO!
?
AH...
YOU DON'T HAVE TO WORRY ABOUT THAT NOW.
I INSTALLED THE DATA YOU GAVE ME INTO MY HEART STONE.
Come
LET'S GO BACK TO THE CLASS-ROOM.
HAKO!!

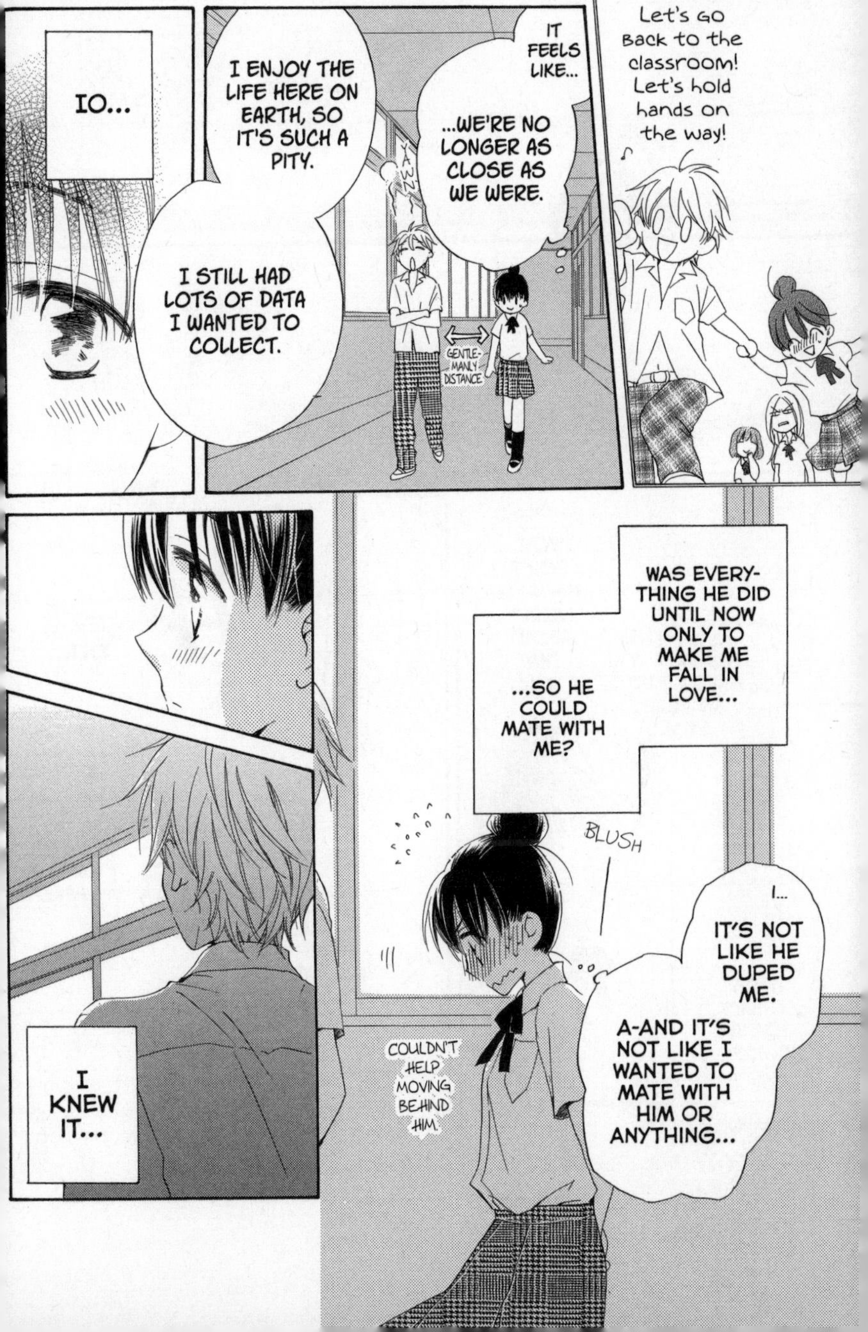
Let's go back to the classroom! Let's hold hands on the way!
IT FEELS LIKE...
...WE'RE NO LONGER AS CLOSE AS WE WERE.
YAWN
GENTLE-MANLY DISTANCE
I ENJOY THE LIFE HERE ON EARTH, SO IT'S SUCH A PITY.
I STILL HAD LOTS OF DATA I WANTED TO COLLECT.
IO...
WAS EVERY-THING HE DID UNTIL NOW ONLY TO MAKE ME FALL IN LOVE...
...SO HE COULD MATE WITH ME?
BLUSH
I...
IT'S NOT LIKE HE DUPED ME.
A-AND IT'S NOT LIKE I WANTED TO MATE WITH HIM OR ANYTHING...
COULDN'T HELP MOVING BEHIND HIM.
I KNEW IT...

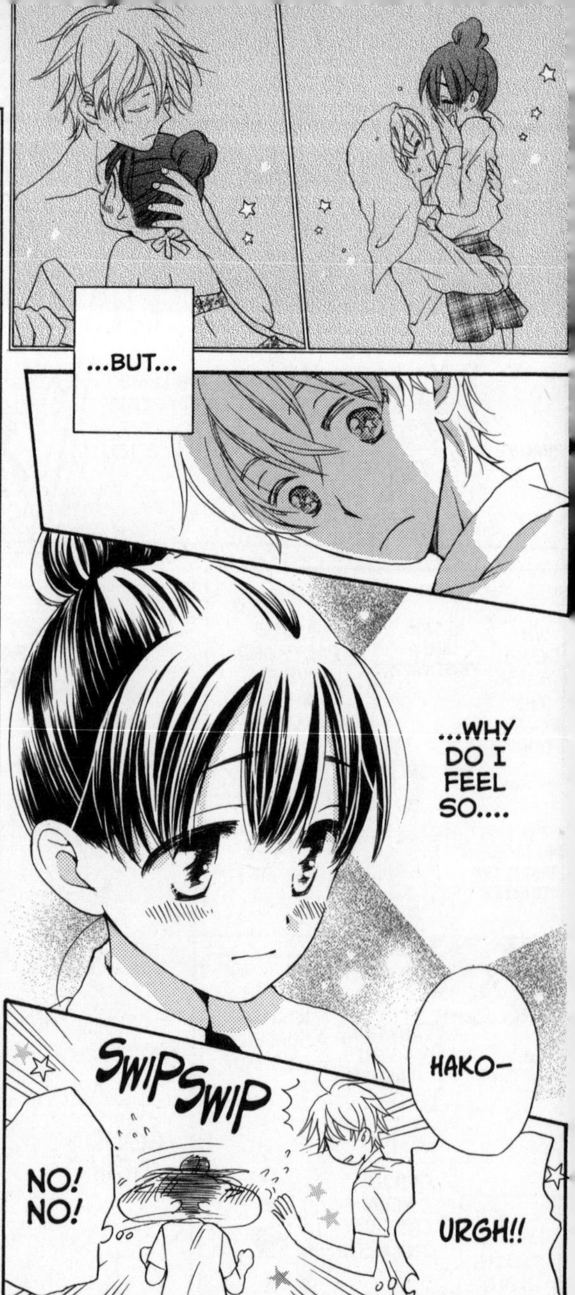
...BUT...
...WHY DO I FEEL SO....
HAKO-
URGH!!
SWIPSWIP
NO! NO!

THANK YOU

I would like to thank my editor for not hesitating when I decided to give this new manga genre a try!

Because I started drawing the artwork for this series in a different way than before, I've been able to keep the hard copies of my rough drafts. And so, I would like to send those rough drafts as a thank-you gift (I'll have to fold them) to those who bought the manga and sent letters to the editorial office in Japan.

田中メカ

Tanaka Meca

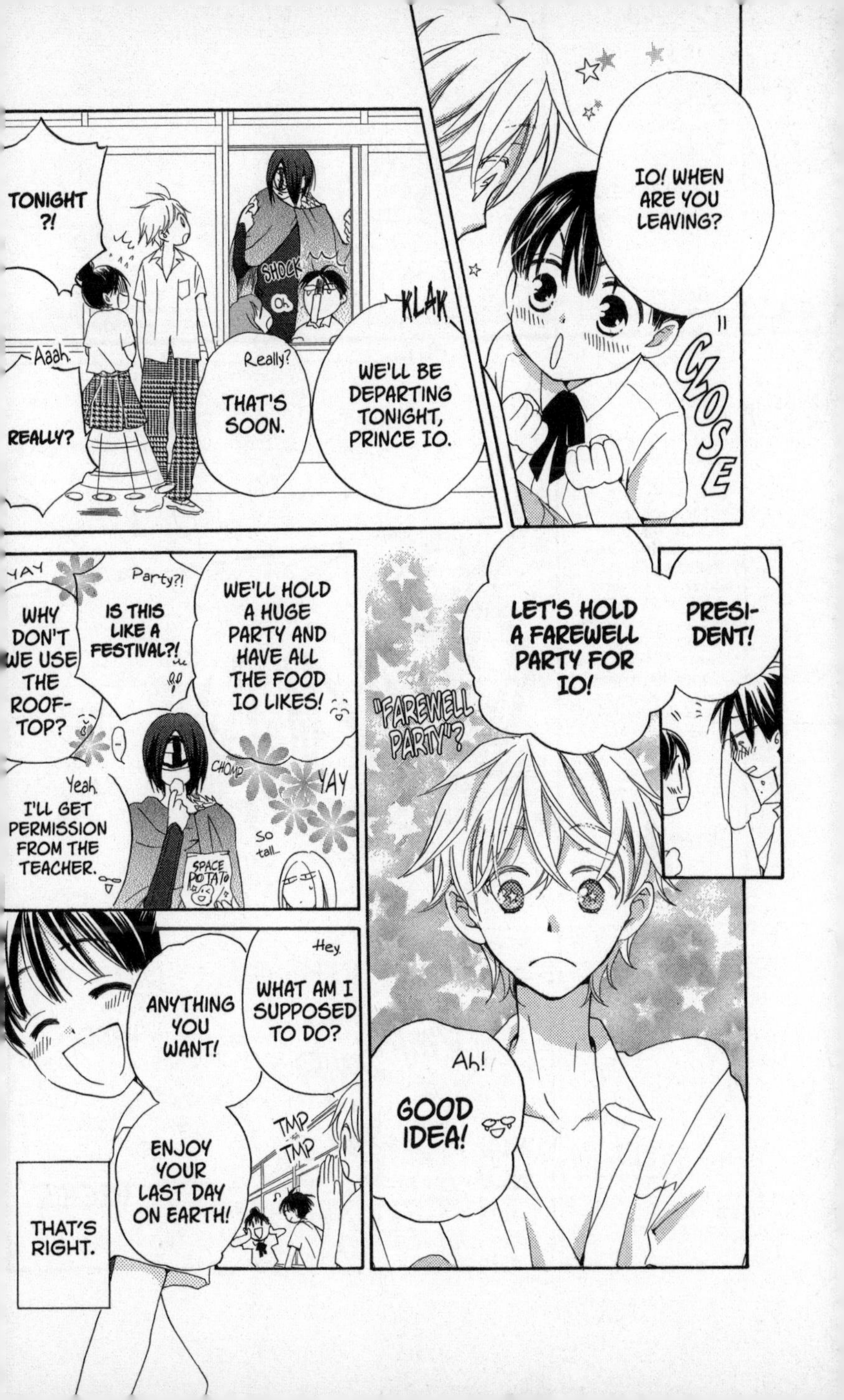
IO! WHEN ARE YOU LEAVING?
CLOSE
KLAK
WE'LL BE DEPARTING TONIGHT, PRINCE IO.
Really?
THAT'S SOON.
SHOCK
Oh.
TONIGHT?!
Aaah.
REALLY?
PRESI-DENT!
LET'S HOLD A FAREWELL PARTY FOR IO!
"FAREWELL PARTY"?
Ah!
GOOD IDEA!
WE'LL HOLD A HUGE PARTY AND HAVE ALL THE FOOD IO LIKES!
Party?!
IS THIS LIKE A FESTIVAL?!
YAY
WHY DON'T WE USE THE ROOF-TOP?
YAY
CHOMP
Yeah.
I'LL GET PERMISSION FROM THE TEACHER.
SPACE POTATO
So tall...
Hey.
WHAT AM I SUPPOSED TO DO?
ANYTHING YOU WANT!
TMP TMP
ENJOY YOUR LAST DAY ON EARTH!
THAT'S RIGHT.

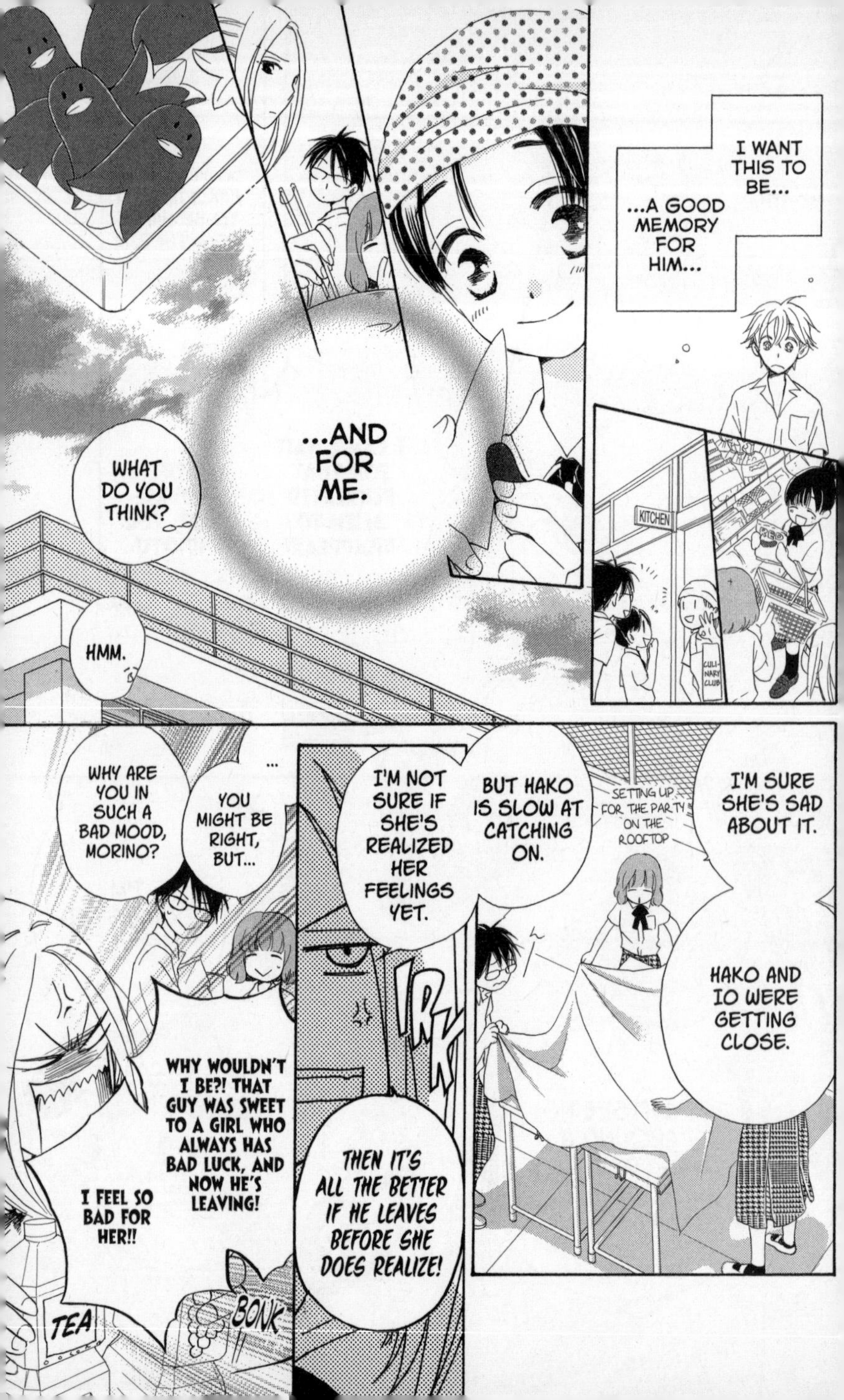
I WANT THIS TO BE...
...A GOOD MEMORY FOR HIM...
KITCHEN
CULINARY CLUB
...AND FOR ME.
WHAT DO YOU THINK?
HMM.
I'M SURE SHE'S SAD ABOUT IT.
HAKO AND IO WERE GETTING CLOSE.
SETTING UP FOR THE PARTY ON THE ROOFTOP
BUT HAKO IS SLOW AT CATCHING ON.
I'M NOT SURE IF SHE'S REALIZED HER FEELINGS YET.
IRK
THEN IT'S ALL THE BETTER IF HE LEAVES BEFORE SHE DOES REALIZE!
...
YOU MIGHT BE RIGHT, BUT...
WHY ARE YOU IN SUCH A BAD MOOD, MORINO?
WHY WOULDN'T I BE?! THAT GUY WAS SWEET TO A GIRL WHO ALWAYS HAS BAD LUCK, AND NOW HE'S LEAVING!
I FEEL SO BAD FOR HER!!
BONK
TEA

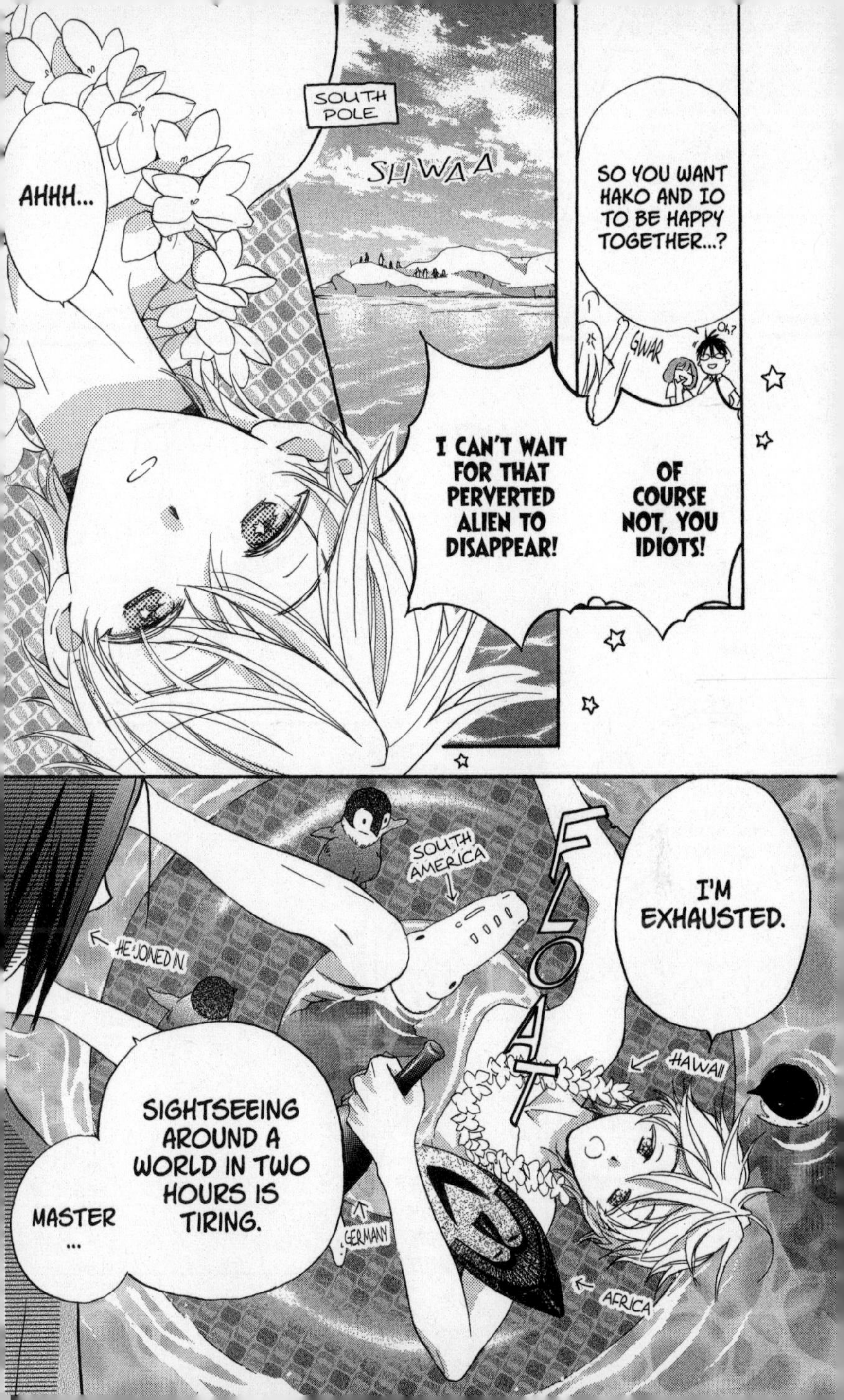

SO YOU WANT HAKO AND IO TO BE HAPPY TOGETHER...?
GWAR
Oh?
OF COURSE NOT, YOU IDIOTS!
I CAN'T WAIT FOR THAT PERVERTED ALIEN TO DISAPPEAR!
SOUTH POLE
SHWAA
AHHH...
I'M EXHAUSTED.
FLOAT
HAWAII
SOUTH AMERICA
AFRICA
GERMANY
SIGHTSEEING AROUND A WORLD IN TWO HOURS IS TIRING.
MASTER ...
HE JOINED IN

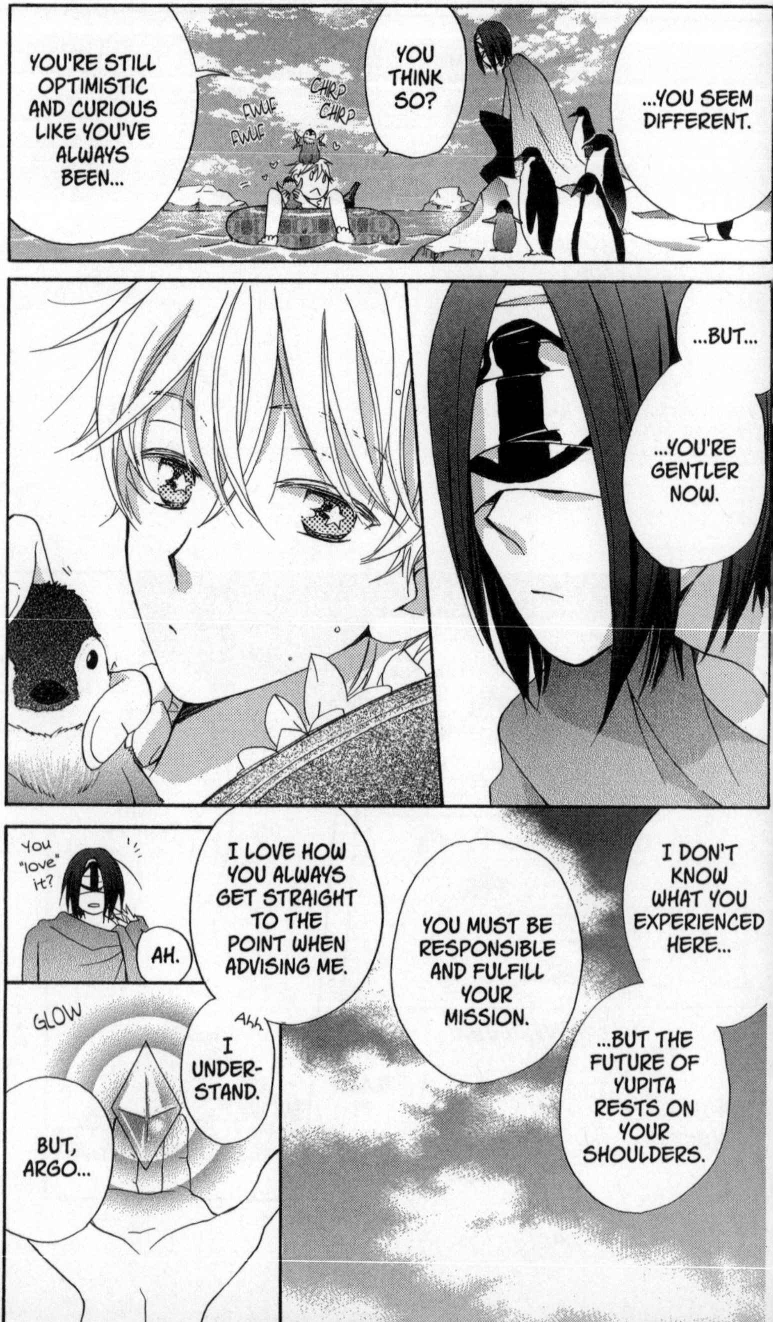
...YOU SEEM DIFFERENT.
YOU THINK SO?
CHIRP CHIRP
FWUF FWUF
YOU'RE STILL OPTIMISTIC AND CURIOUS LIKE YOU'VE ALWAYS BEEN...
...BUT...
...YOU'RE GENTLER NOW.
I DON'T KNOW WHAT YOU EXPERIENCED HERE...
...BUT THE FUTURE OF YUPITA RESTS ON YOUR SHOULDERS.
YOU MUST BE RESPONSIBLE AND FULFILL YOUR MISSION.
I LOVE HOW YOU ALWAYS GET STRAIGHT TO THE POINT WHEN ADVISING ME.
AH.
You "love" it?
GLOW
Ahh.
I UNDER-STAND.
BUT, ARGO...

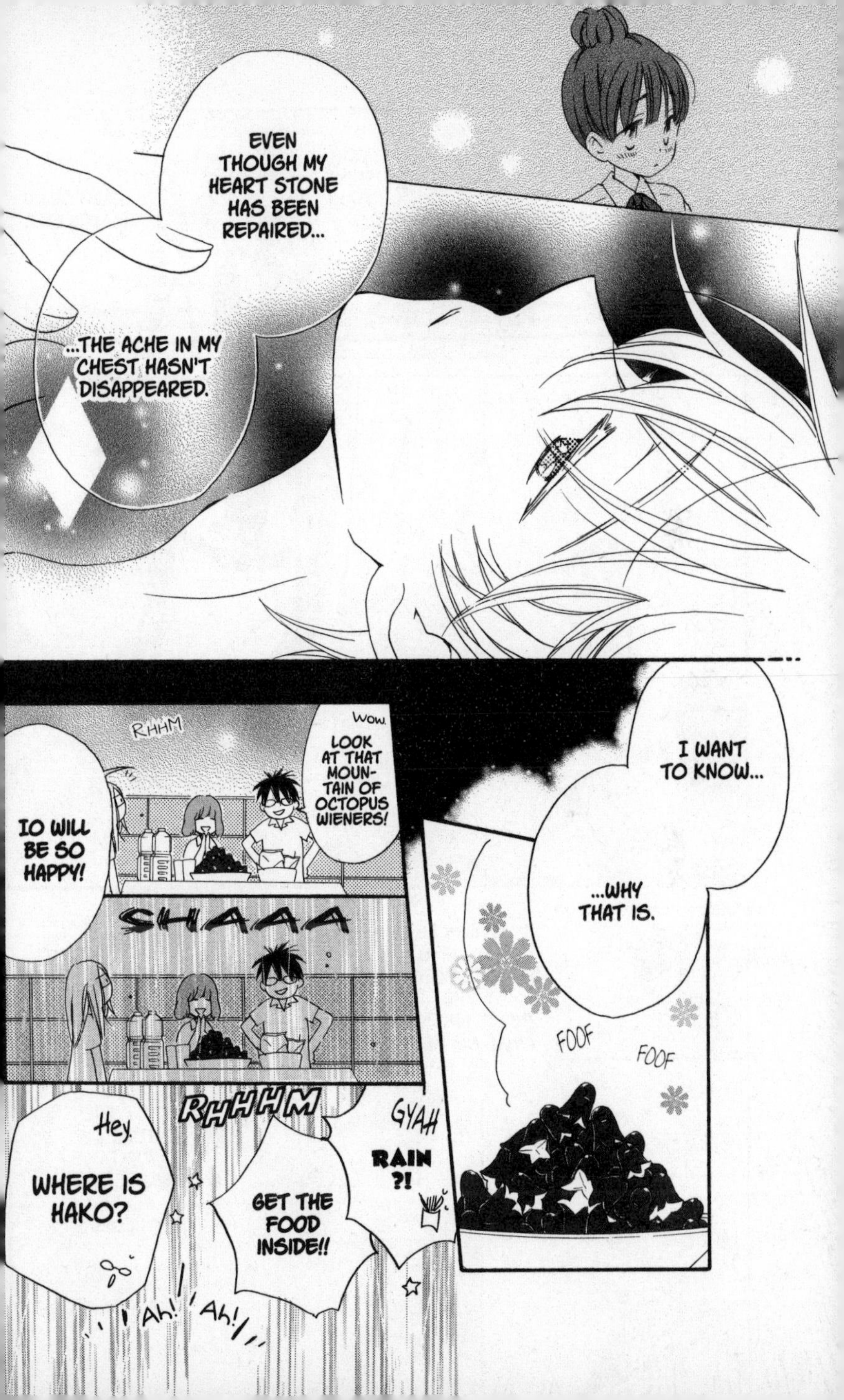
EVEN THOUGH MY HEART STONE HAS BEEN REPAIRED...
...THE ACHE IN MY CHEST HASN'T DISAPPEARED.
I WANT TO KNOW...
...WHY THAT IS.
FOOF
FOOF
Wow.
LOOK AT THAT MOUNTAIN OF OCTOPUS WIENERS!
RHHM
IO WILL BE SO HAPPY!
SHAAA
RHHHM
GYAH
RAIN?!
GET THE FOOD INSIDE!!
Hey.
WHERE IS HAKO?
Ah! Ah!

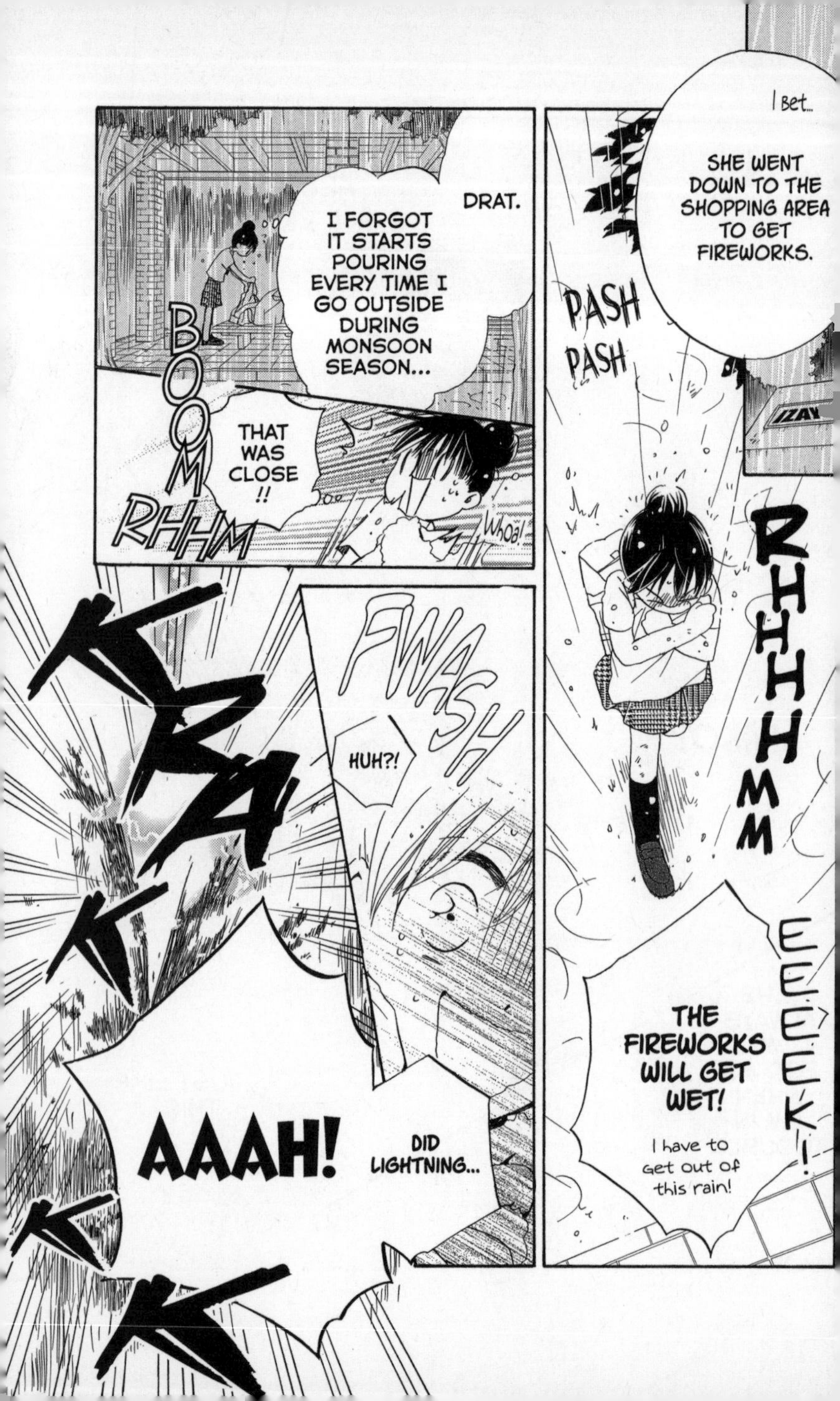
I Bet...
SHE WENT DOWN TO THE SHOPPING AREA TO GET FIREWORKS.
PASH
PASH
RHHHHMM
EEEEK!
THE FIREWORKS WILL GET WET!
I have to get out of this rain!
DRAT.
I FORGOT IT STARTS POURING EVERY TIME I GO OUTSIDE DURING MONSOON SEASON...
BOOM
THAT WAS CLOSE!!
RHHM
Whoa!
FWASH
HUH?!
KRAKK
AAAH!
DID LIGHTNING...

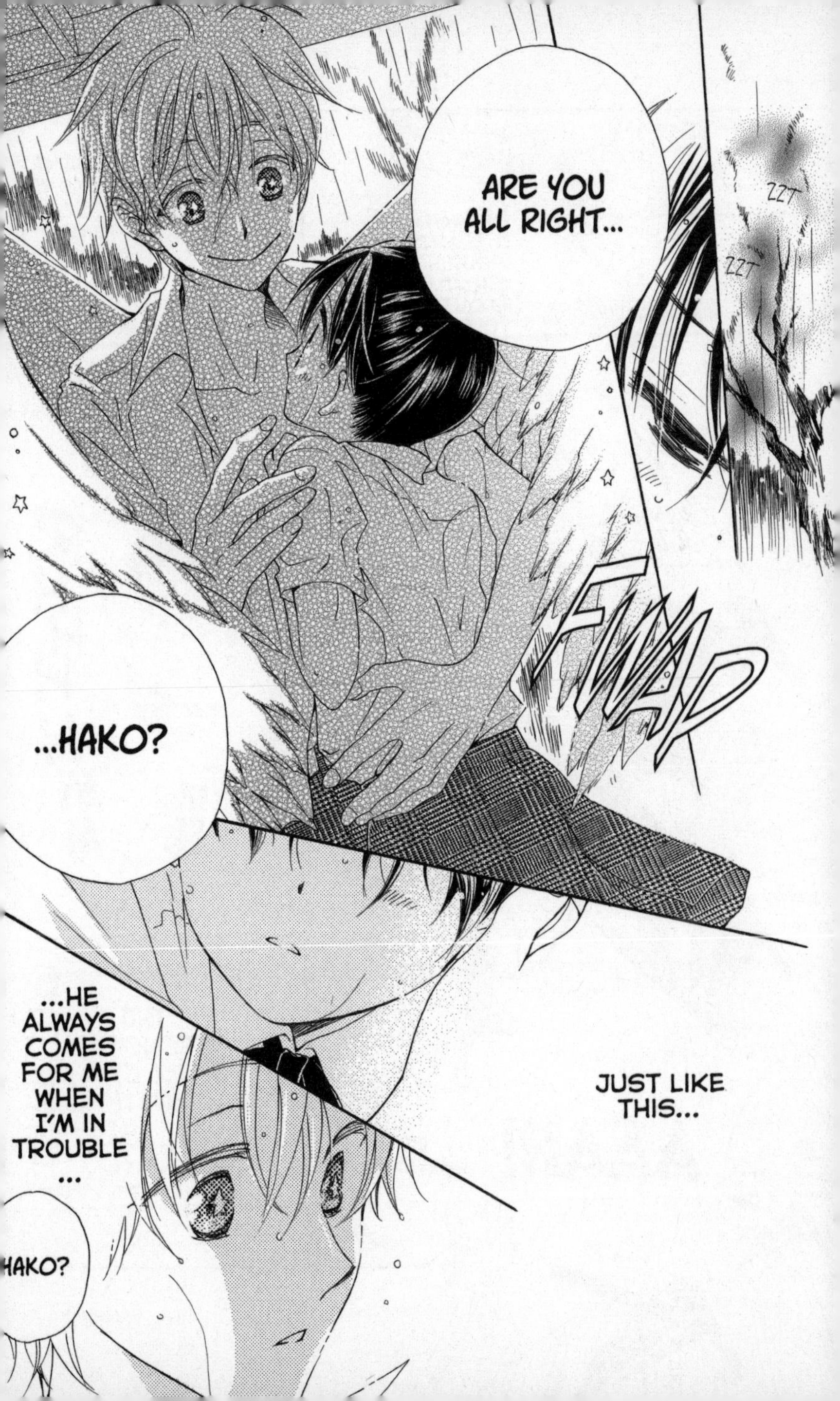
ARE YOU ALL RIGHT...
ZZT
ZZT
FWAP
...HAKO?
JUST LIKE THIS...
...HE ALWAYS COMES FOR ME WHEN I'M IN TROUBLE ...
HAKO?

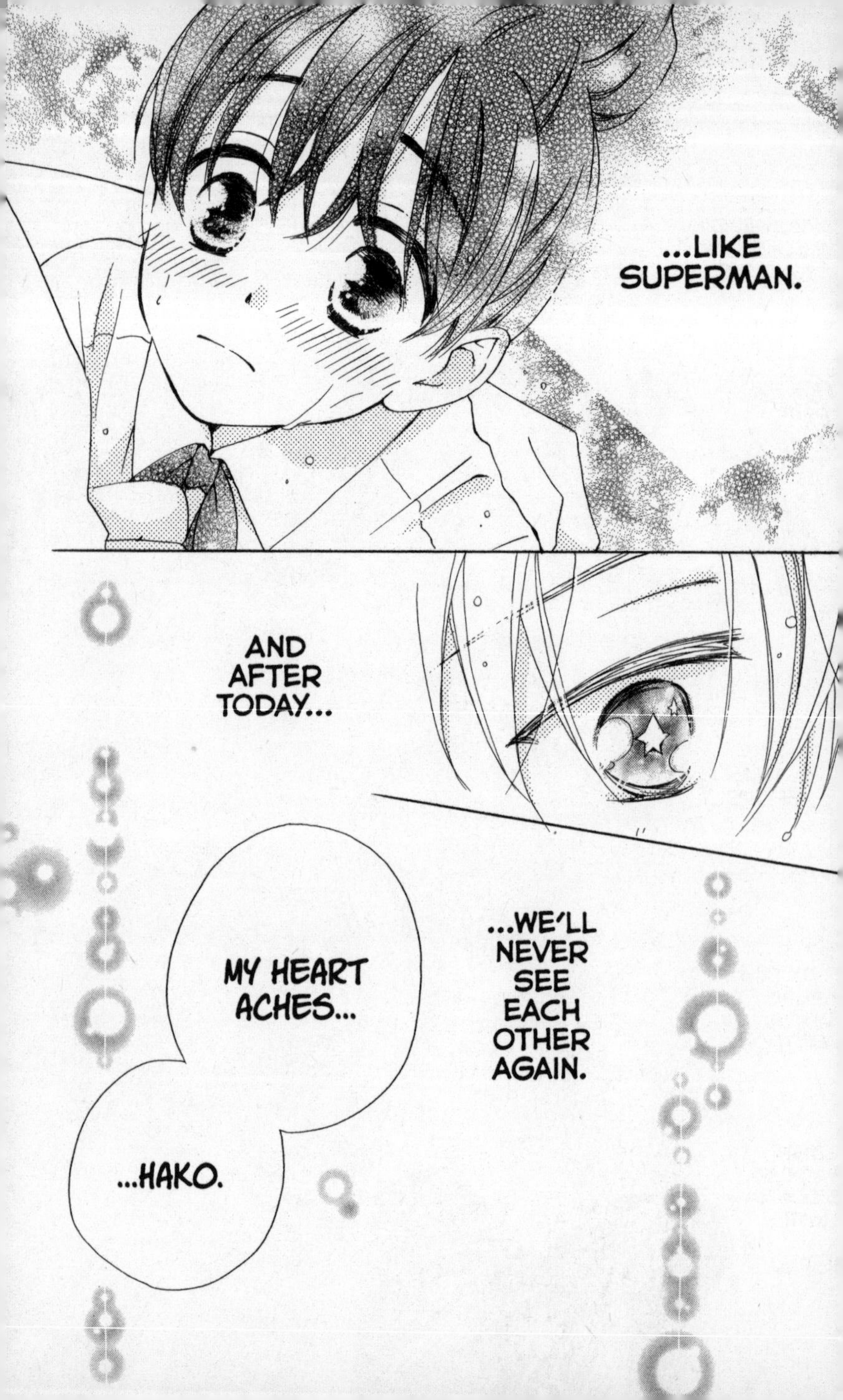
...LIKE SUPERMAN.
AND AFTER TODAY...
...WE'LL NEVER SEE EACH OTHER AGAIN.
MY HEART ACHES...
...HAKO.

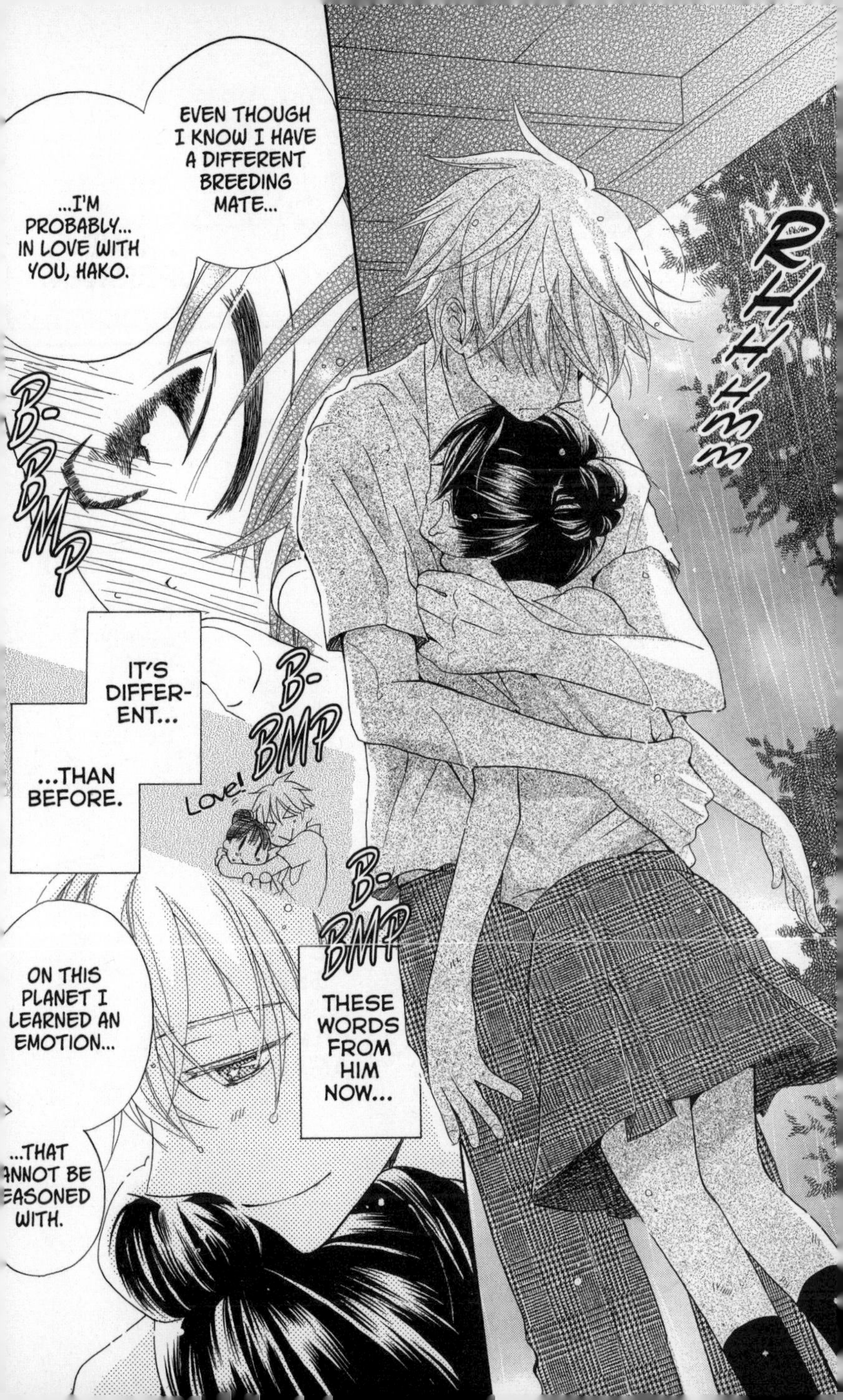
RHHHSSH
EVEN THOUGH I KNOW I HAVE A DIFFERENT BREEDING MATE...
...I'M PROBABLY... IN LOVE WITH YOU, HAKO.
B-BMP
IT'S DIFFER-ENT...
...THAN BEFORE.
B-BMP
Love!
B-BMP
THESE WORDS FROM HIM NOW...
ON THIS PLANET I LEARNED AN EMOTION...
...THAT ANNOT BE EASONED WITH.

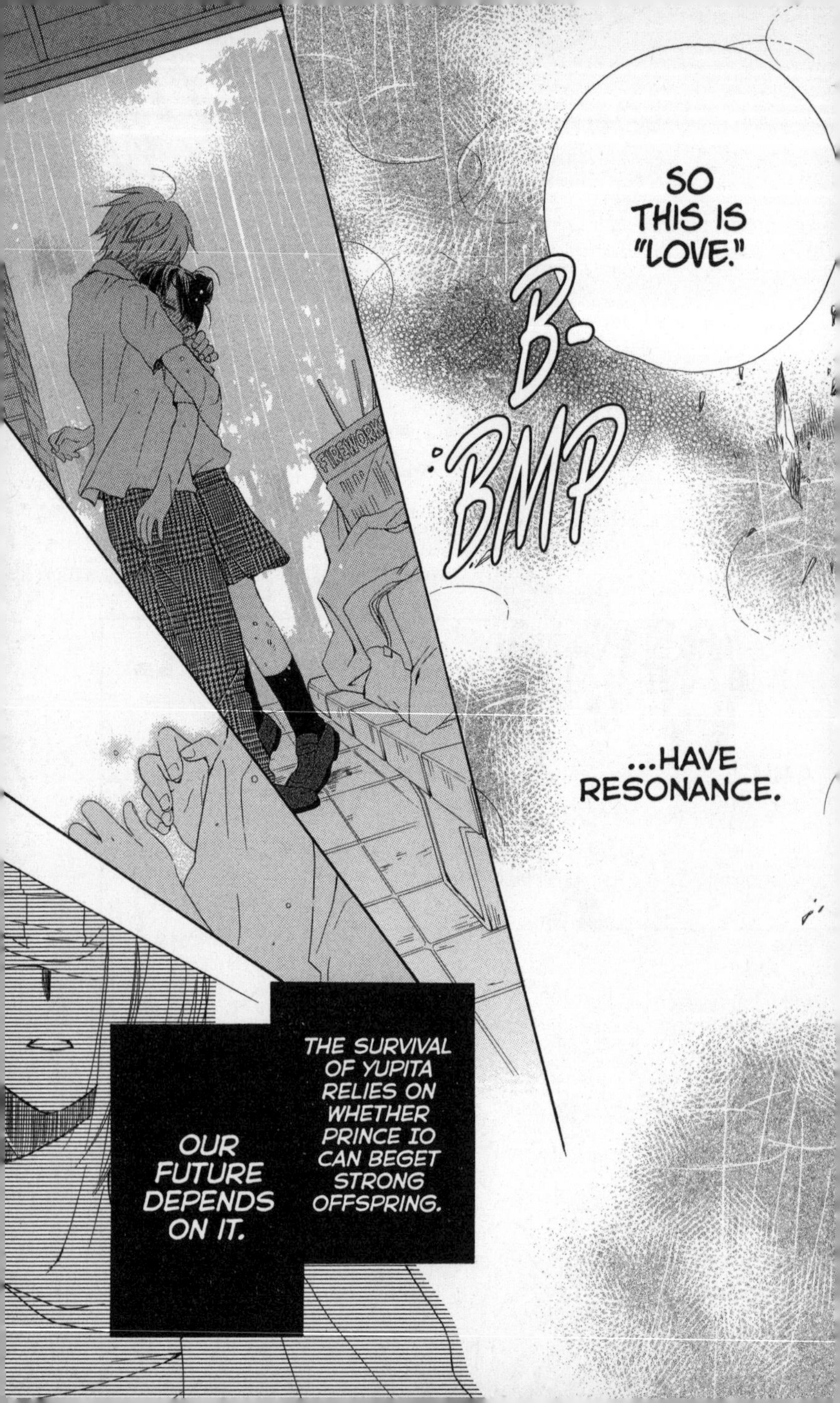
SO THIS IS "LOVE."
B-BMP
...HAVE RESONANCE.
THE SURVIVAL OF YUPITA RELIES ON WHETHER PRINCE IO CAN BEGET STRONG OFFSPRING.
OUR FUTURE DEPENDS ON IT.

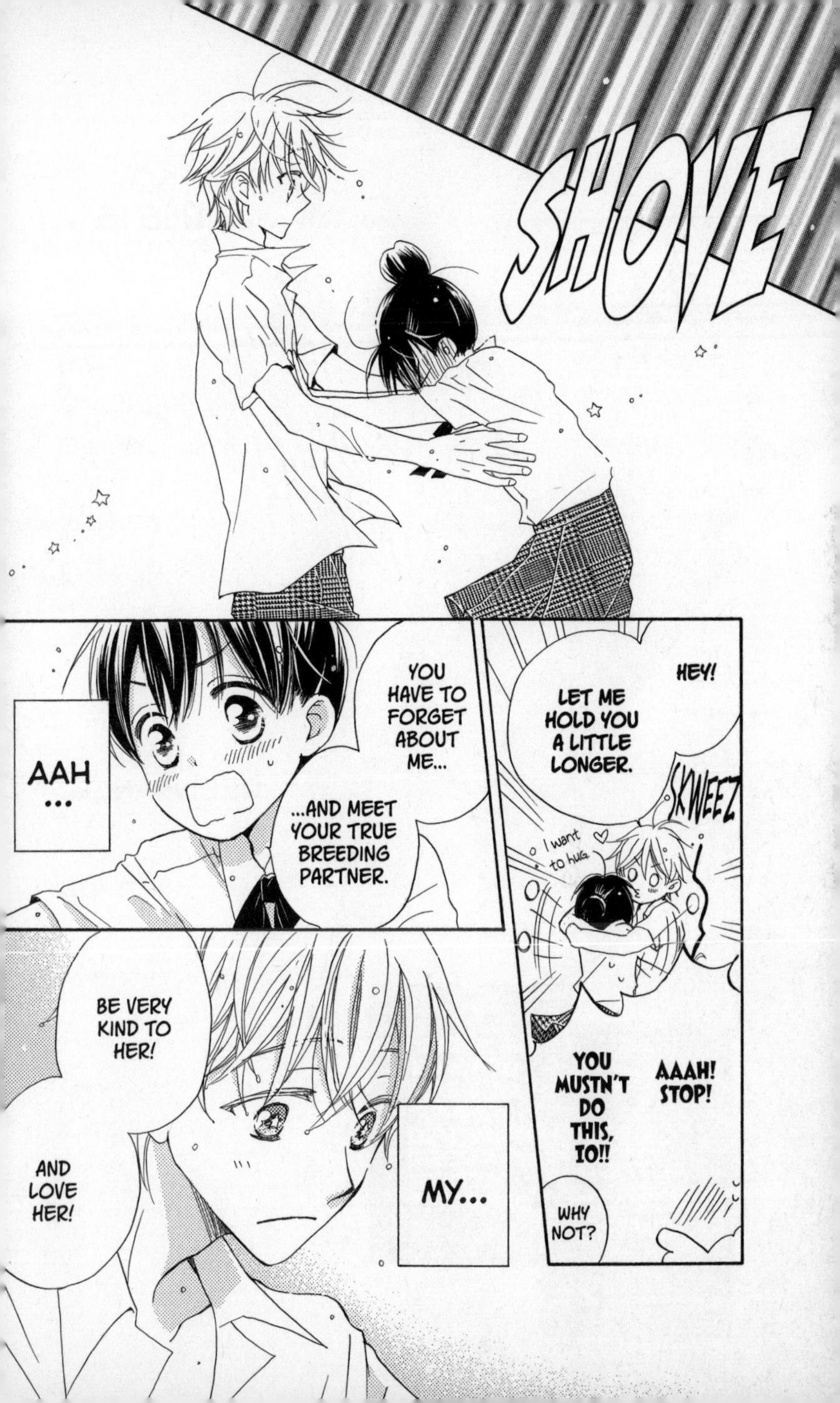
SHOVE
HEY!
LET ME HOLD YOU A LITTLE LONGER.
SKWEEZ
I want to hug.
AAAH! STOP!
YOU MUSTN'T DO THIS, IO!!
WHY NOT?
YOU HAVE TO FORGET ABOUT ME...
...AND MEET YOUR TRUE BREEDING PARTNER.
AAH ...
MY...
BE VERY KIND TO HER!
AND LOVE HER!

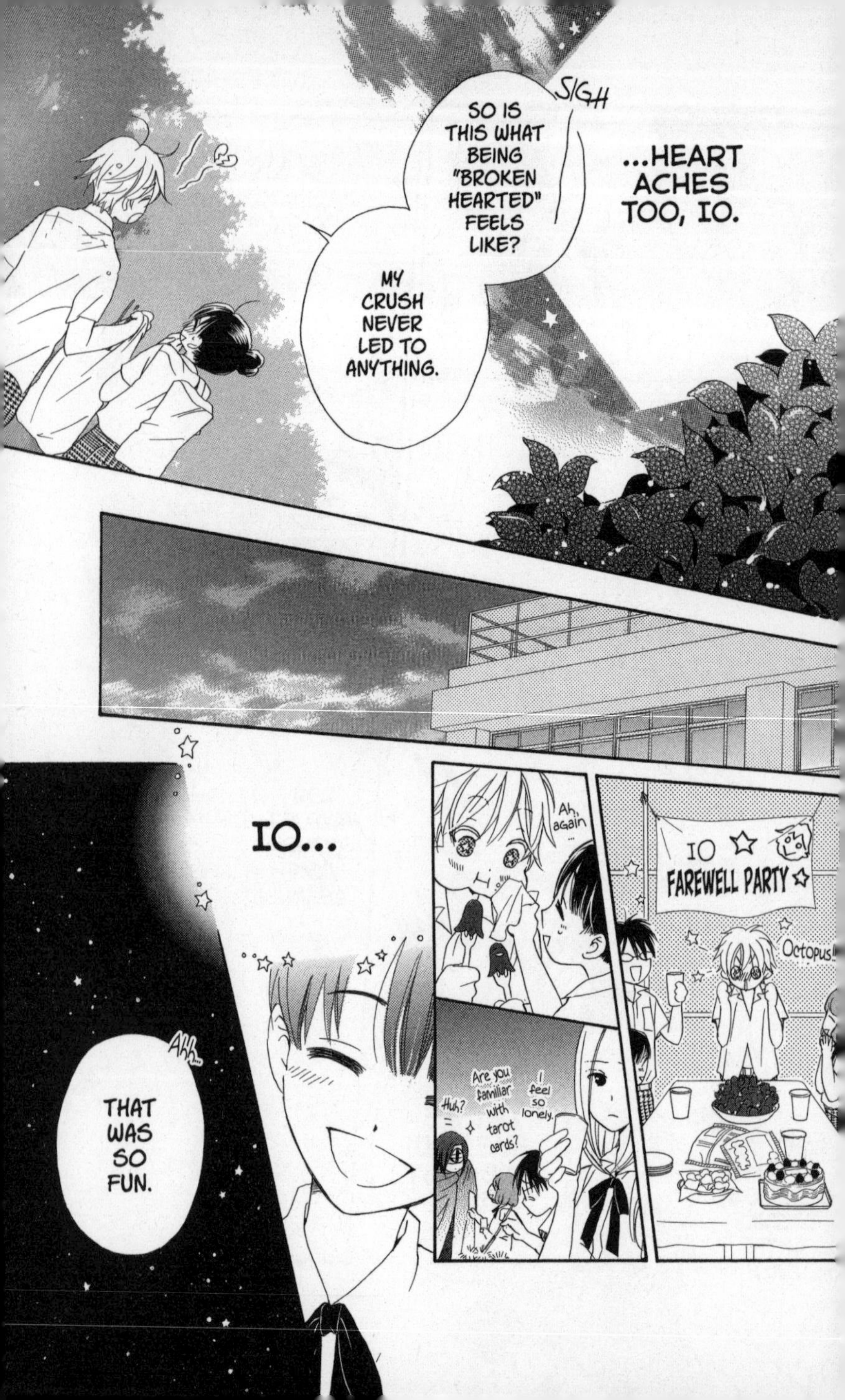
...HEART ACHES TOO, IO.
SIGH
SO IS THIS WHAT BEING "BROKEN HEARTED" FEELS LIKE?
MY CRUSH NEVER LED TO ANYTHING.
IO FAREWELL PARTY
Octopus!!
Ah, again...
I feel so lonely.
Are you familiar with tarot cards?
Huh?
IO...
Ahh...
THAT WAS SO FUN.

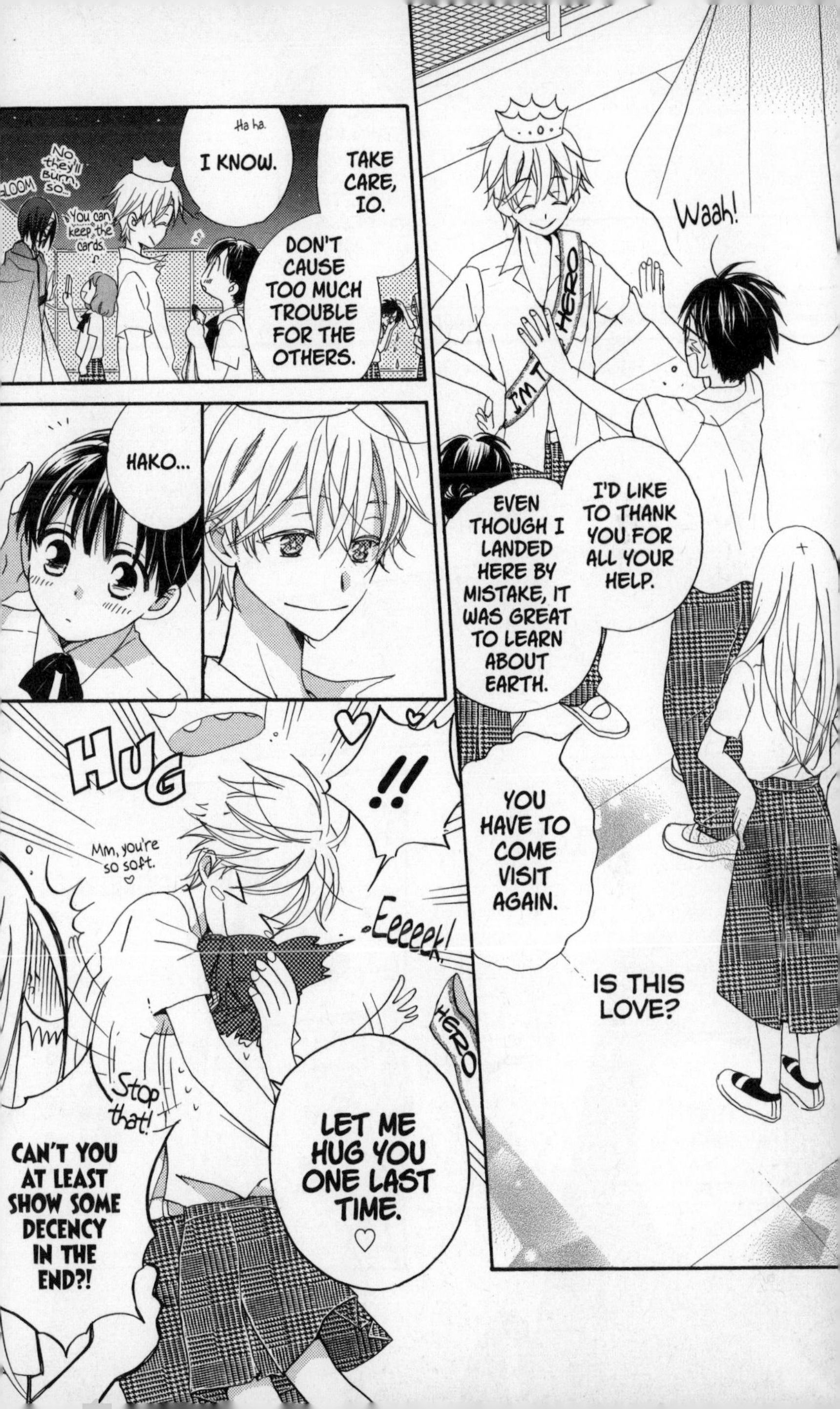
Waah!
I'D LIKE TO THANK YOU FOR ALL YOUR HELP.
EVEN THOUGH I LANDED HERE BY MISTAKE, IT WAS GREAT TO LEARN ABOUT EARTH.
YOU HAVE TO COME VISIT AGAIN.
IS THIS LOVE?
TAKE CARE, IO.
DON'T CAUSE TOO MUCH TROUBLE FOR THE OTHERS.
Ha ha.
I KNOW.
No they'll burn, so...
You can keep the cards.
HAKO...
HUG
!!
LET ME HUG YOU ONE LAST TIME.
Eeeeek!
Mm, you're so soft.
Stop that!
CAN'T YOU AT LEAST SHOW SOME DECENCY IN THE END?!

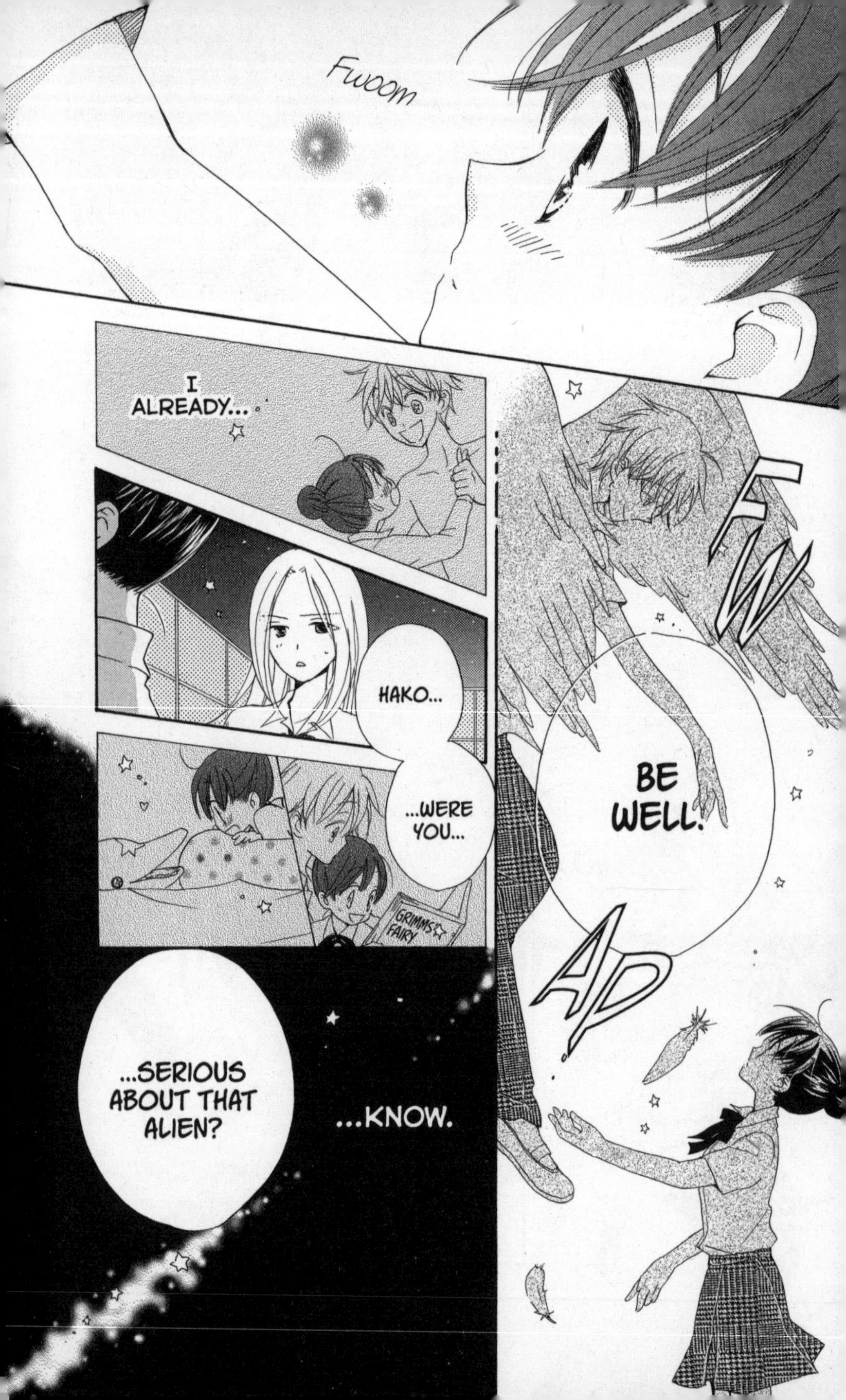
Fwoom
FW
BE WELL.
AP
I ALREADY...
HAKO...
...WERE YOU...
GRIMMS FAIRY
...SERIOUS ABOUT THAT ALIEN?
...KNOW.

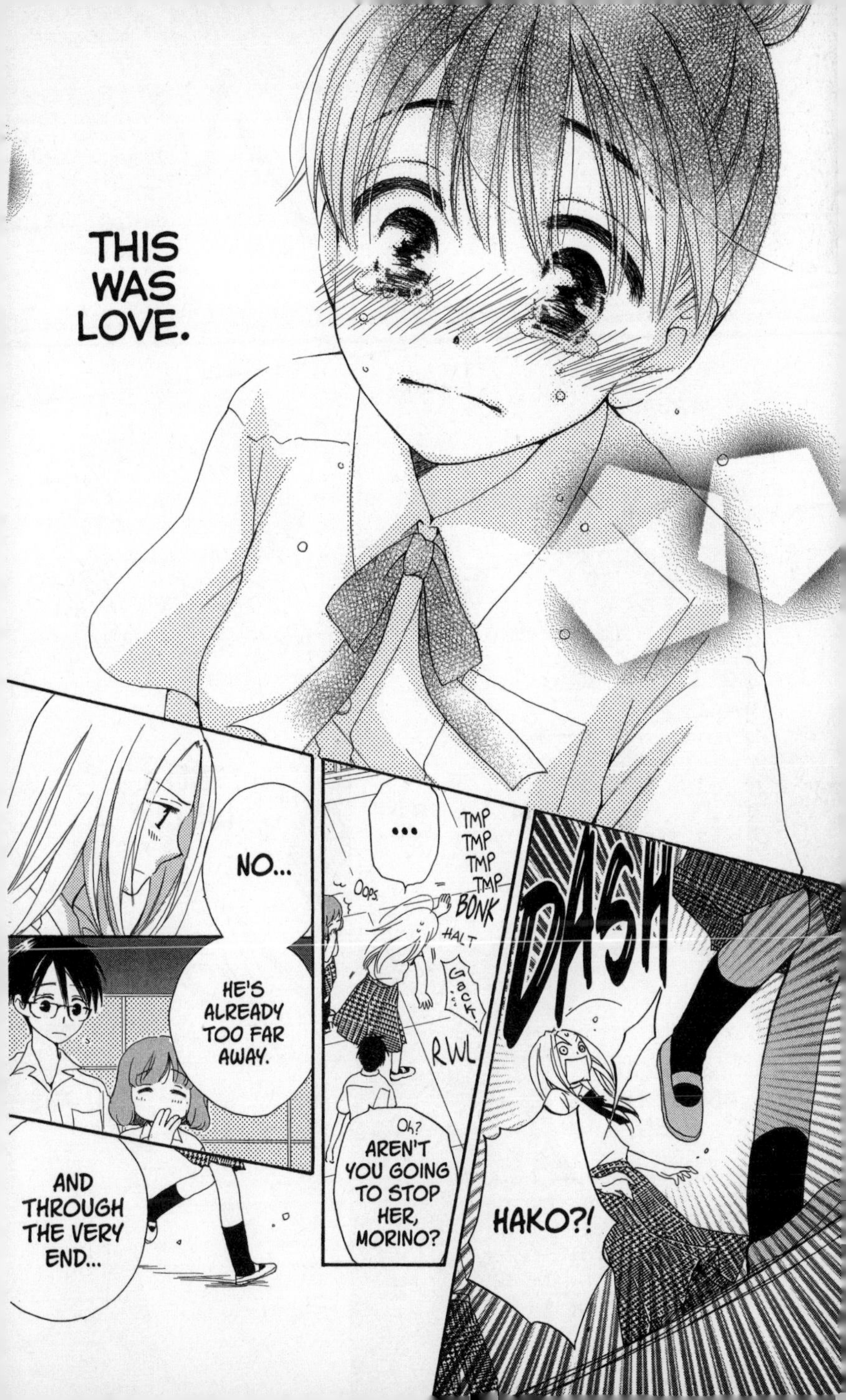
THIS WAS LOVE.
DASH
HAKO?!
...
TMP TMP TMP TMP
BONK
HALT
Gack
Oops.
RWL
Oh? AREN'T YOU GOING TO STOP HER, MORINO?
NO...
HE'S ALREADY TOO FAR AWAY.
AND THROUGH THE VERY END...

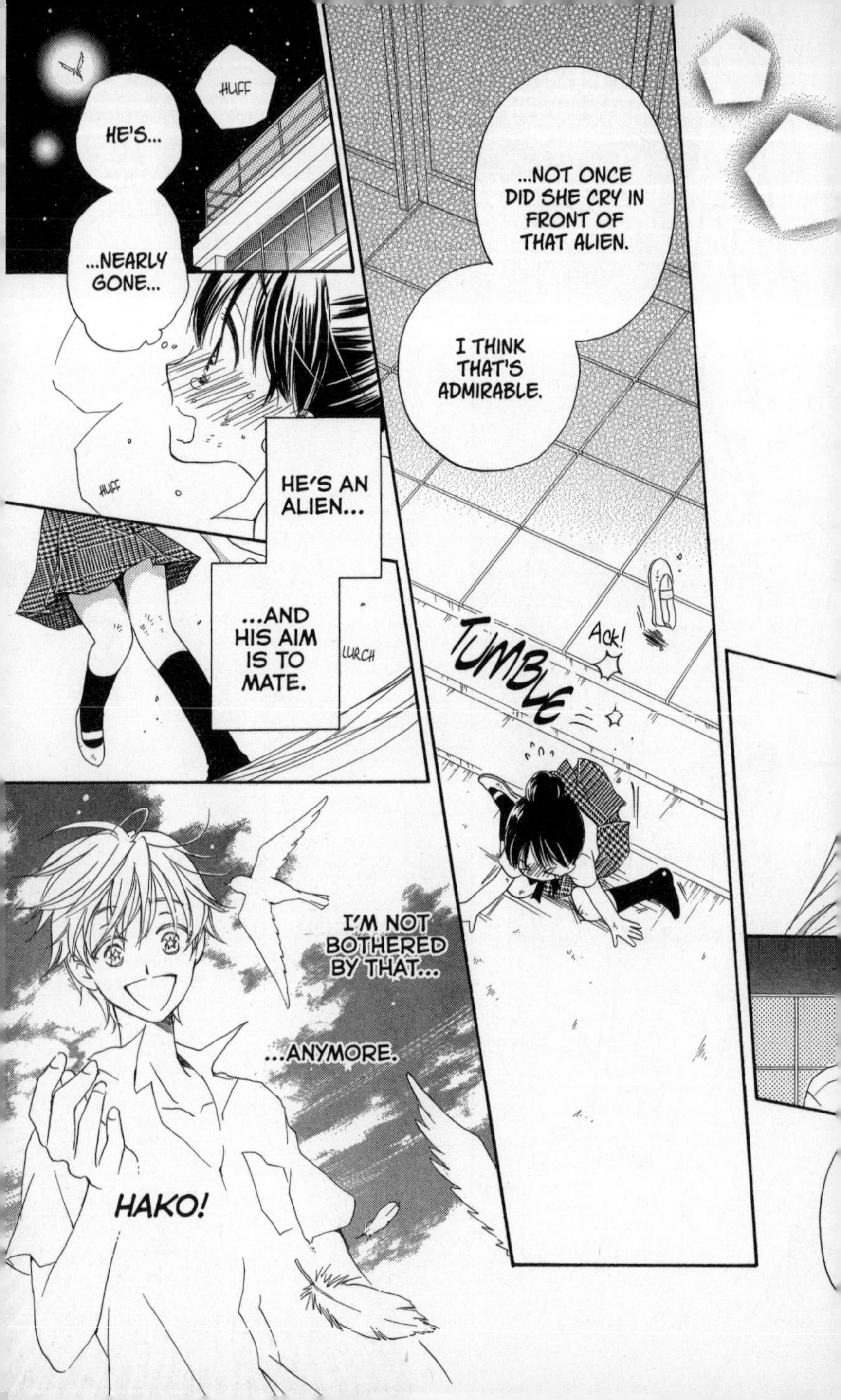
...NOT ONCE DID SHE CRY IN FRONT OF THAT ALIEN.
I THINK THAT'S ADMIRABLE.
ACK!
TUMBLE
HUFF
HE'S...
...NEARLY GONE...
HE'S AN ALIEN...
...AND HIS AIM IS TO MATE.
HUFF
LURCH
I'M NOT BOTHERED BY THAT...
...ANYMORE.
HAKO!

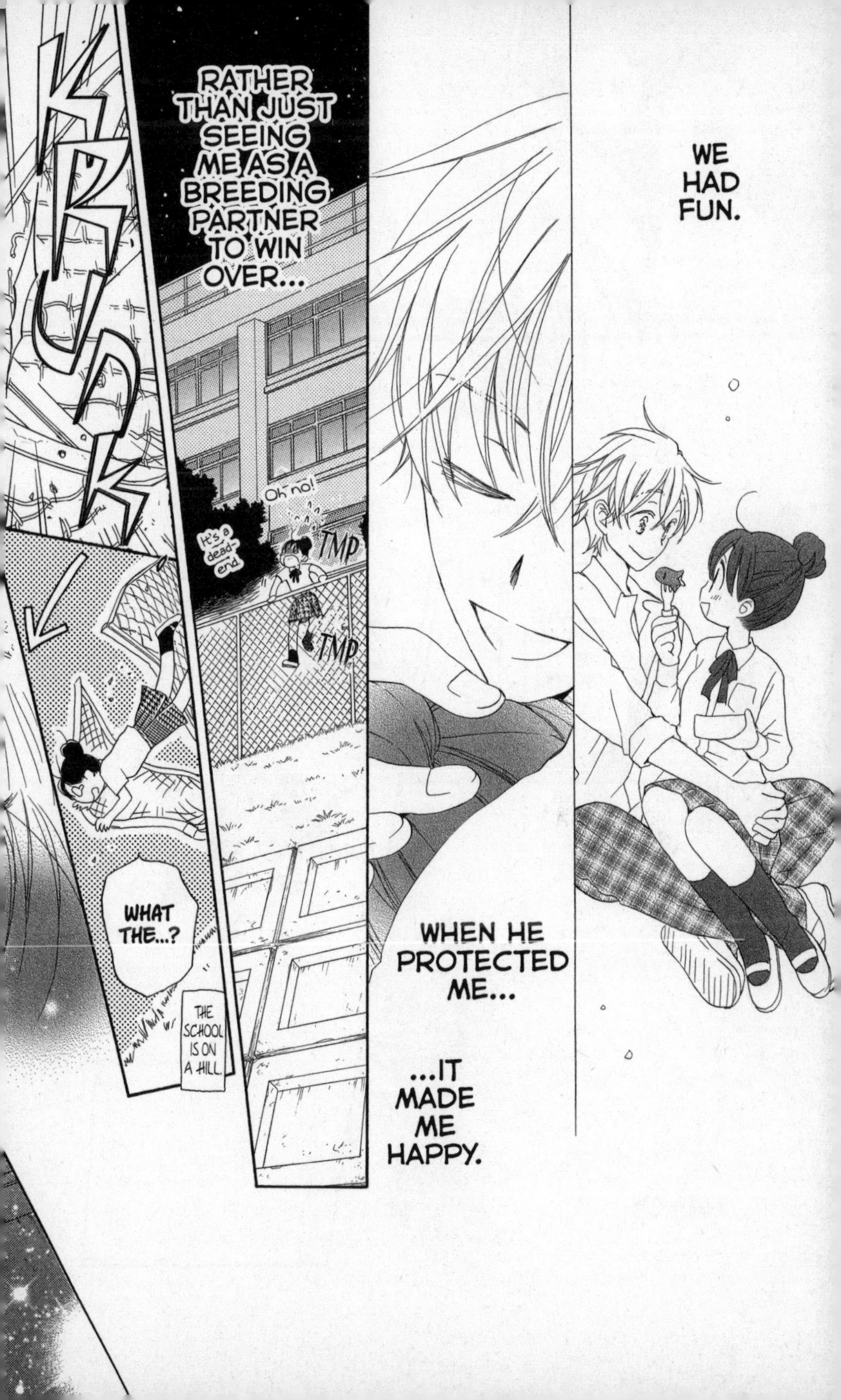
WE HAD FUN.
WHEN HE PROTECTED ME...
...IT MADE ME HAPPY.
RATHER THAN JUST SEEING ME AS A BREEDING PARTNER TO WIN OVER...
Oh no!
It's a dead-end
TMP
TMP
WHAT THE...?
THE SCHOOL IS ON A HILL.

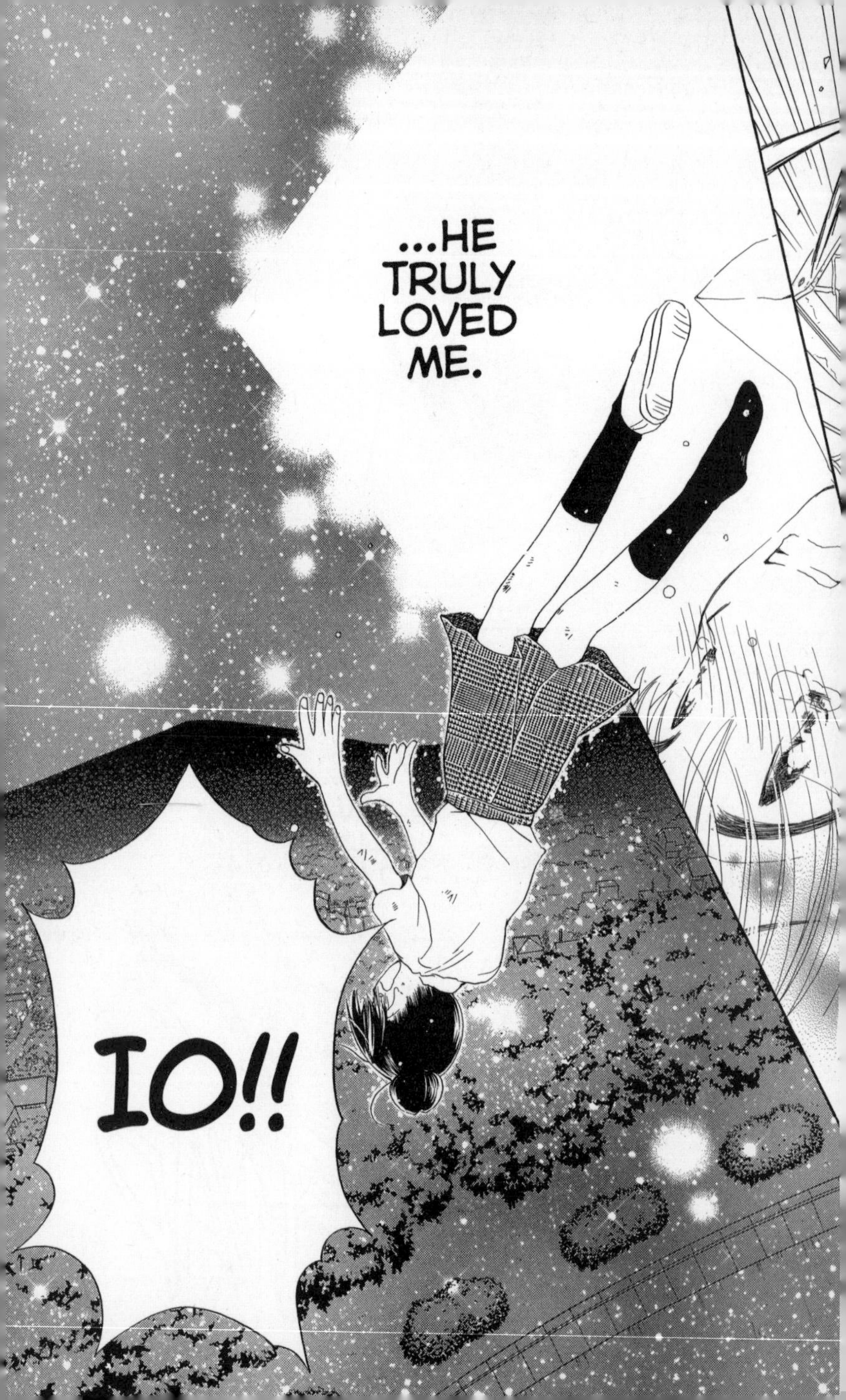
...HE TRULY LOVED ME.
IO!!

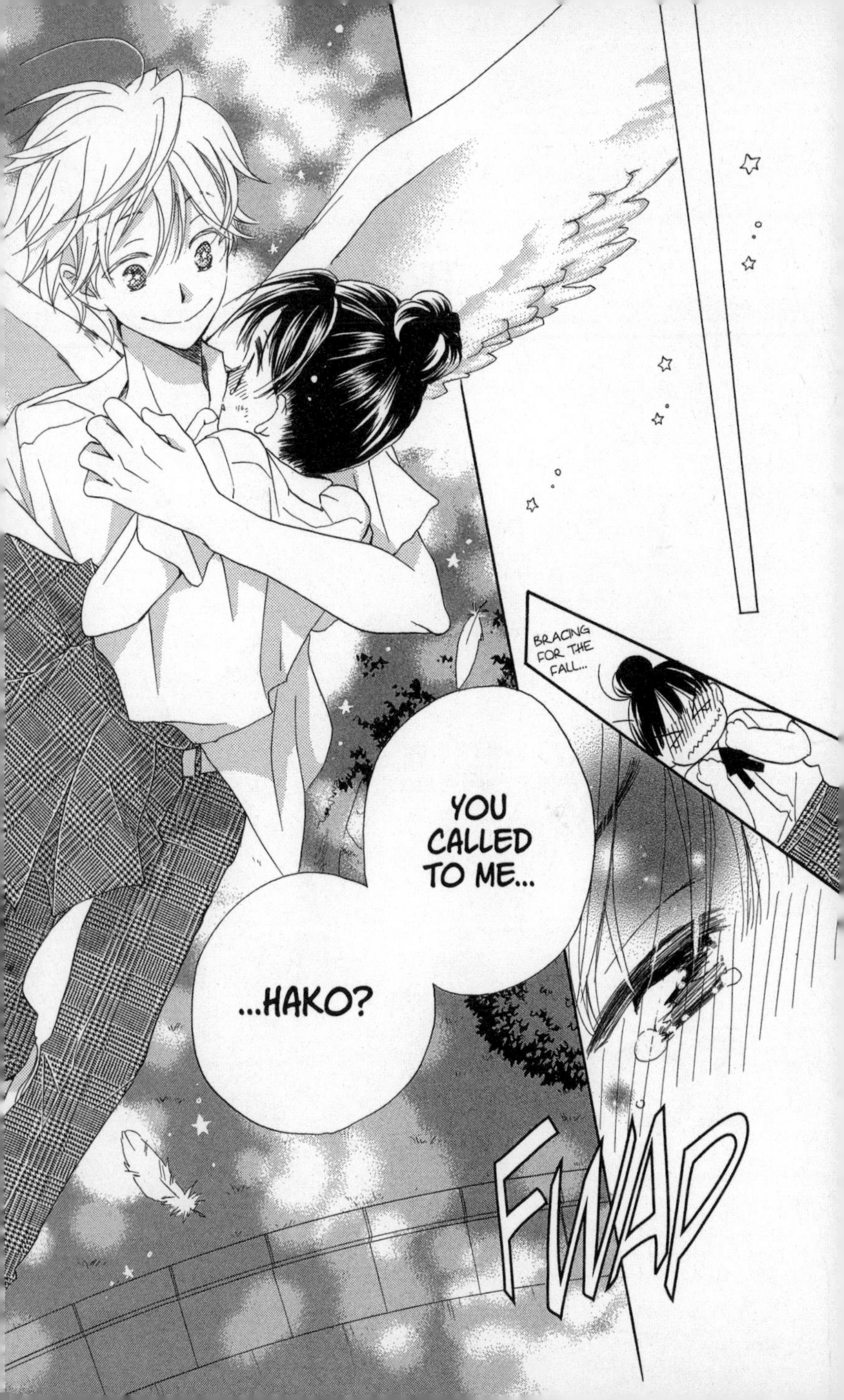
BRACING FOR THE FALL...
FWAP
YOU CALLED TO ME...
...HAKO?

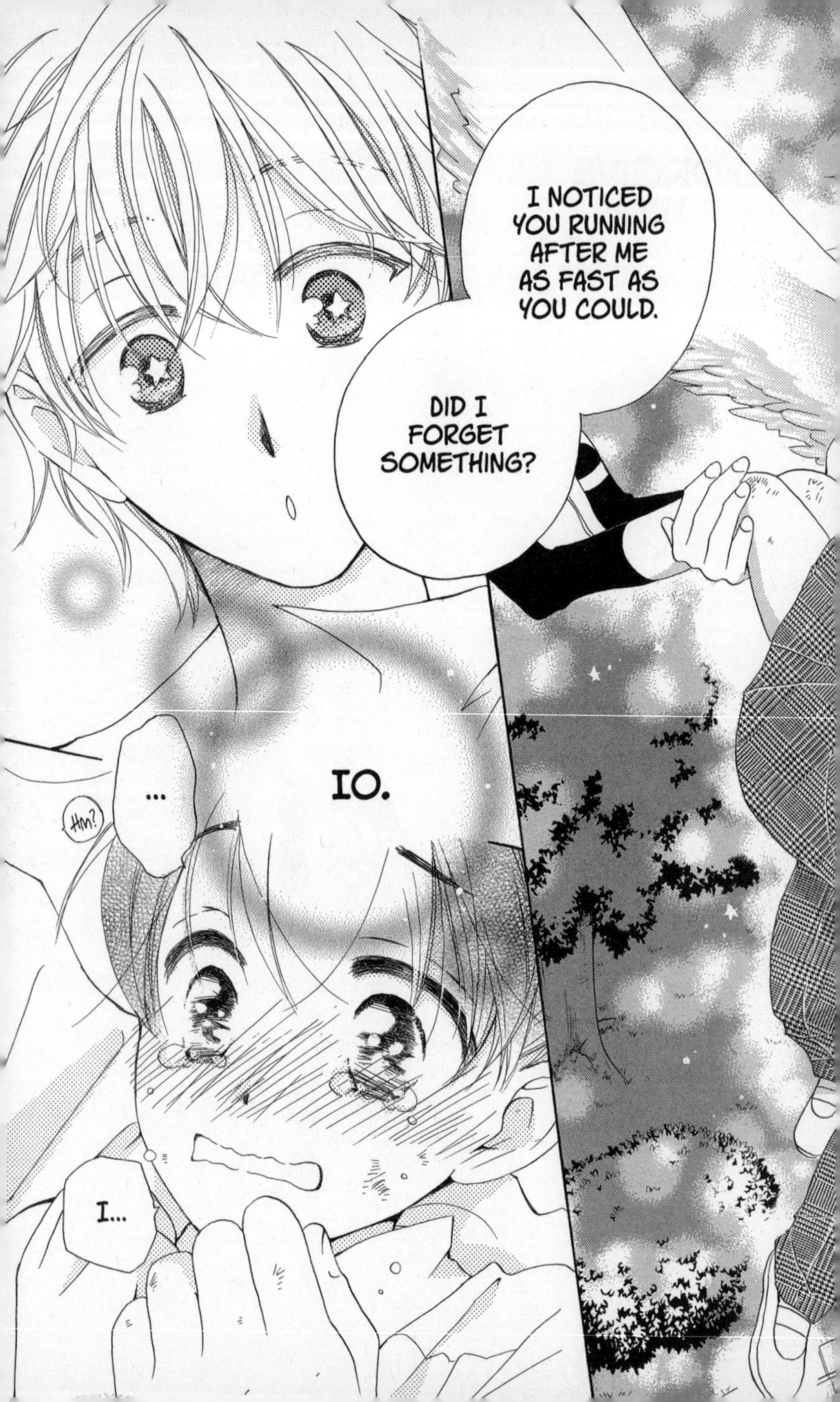
I NOTICED YOU RUNNING AFTER ME AS FAST AS YOU COULD.
DID I FORGET SOMETHING?
IO.
...
Hm?
I...

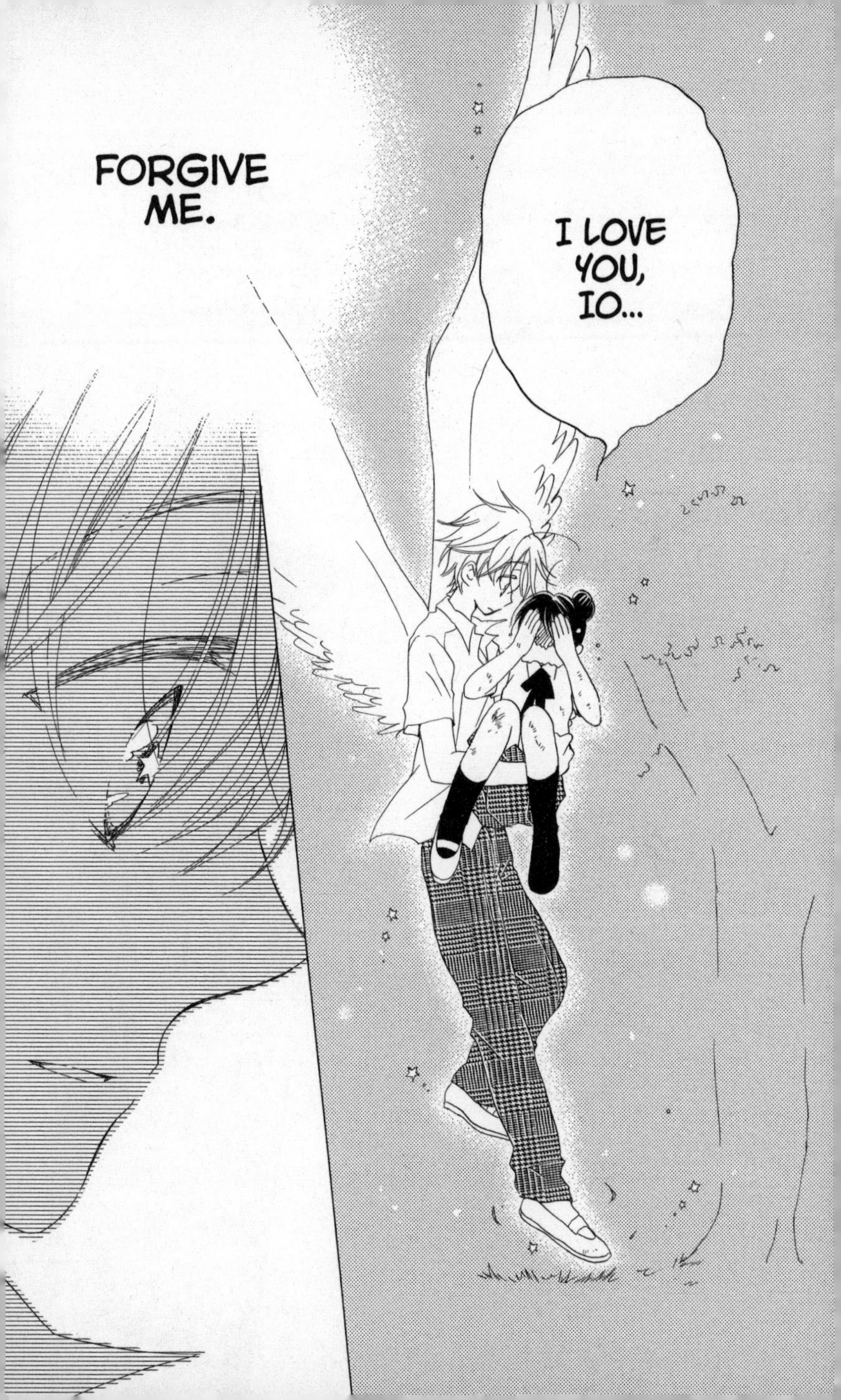
I LOVE YOU, IO...
FORGIVE ME.

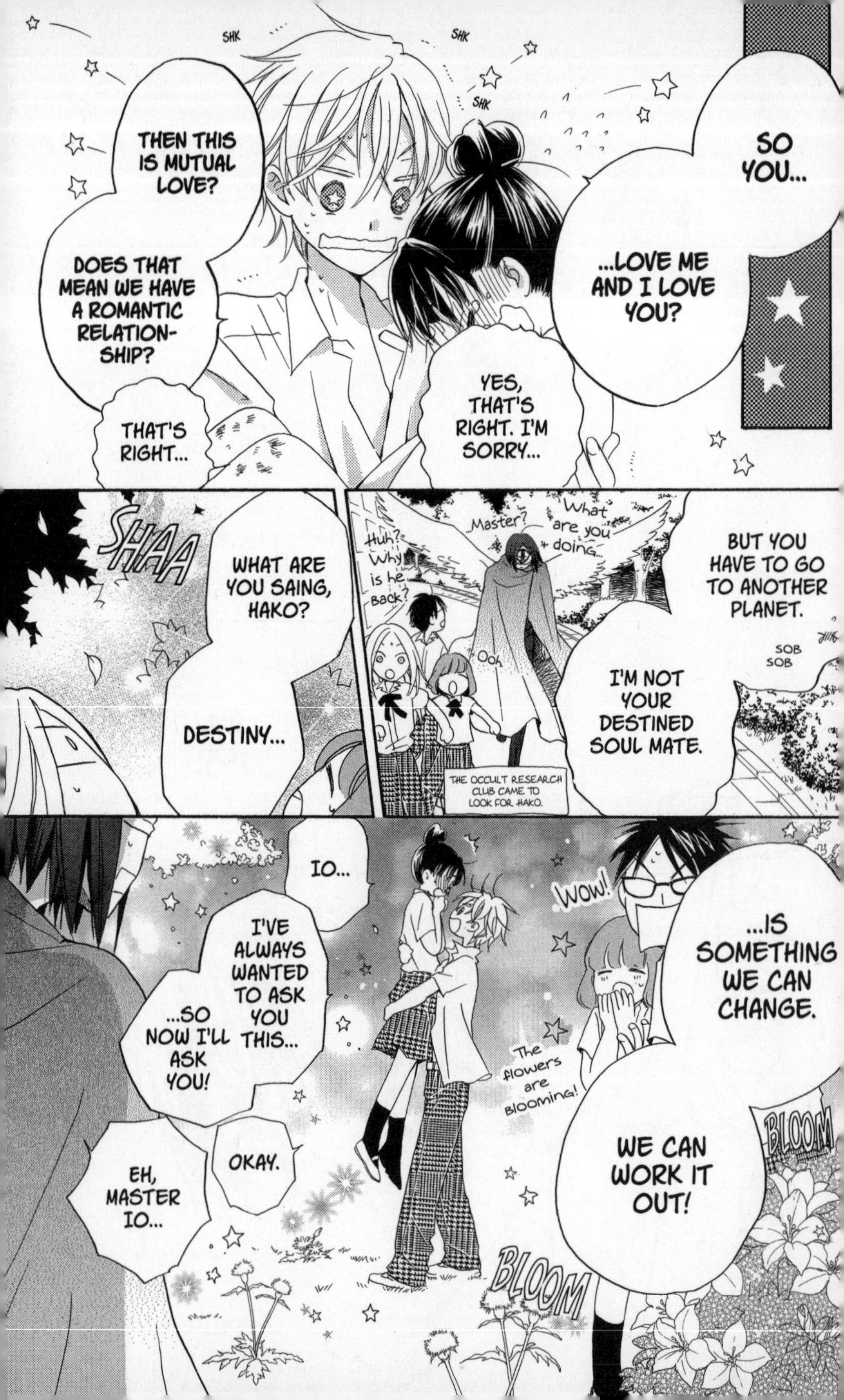
SHK
SHK
SHK
SO YOU...
...LOVE ME AND I LOVE YOU?
YES, THAT'S RIGHT. I'M SORRY...
THEN THIS IS MUTUAL LOVE?
DOES THAT MEAN WE HAVE A ROMANTIC RELATIONSHIP?
THAT'S RIGHT...
What are you doing...
Master?
Huh? Why is he back?
BUT YOU HAVE TO GO TO ANOTHER PLANET.
SOB SOB
I'M NOT YOUR DESTINED SOUL MATE.
Ooh
THE OCCULT RESEARCH CLUB CAME TO LOOK FOR HAKO.
SHAA
WHAT ARE YOU SAING, HAKO?
DESTINY...
...IS SOMETHING WE CAN CHANGE.
WOW!
WE CAN WORK IT OUT!
BLOOM
The flowers are blooming!
IO...
I'VE ALWAYS WANTED TO ASK YOU THIS...
...SO NOW I'LL ASK YOU!
OKAY.
EH, MASTER IO...
BLOOM

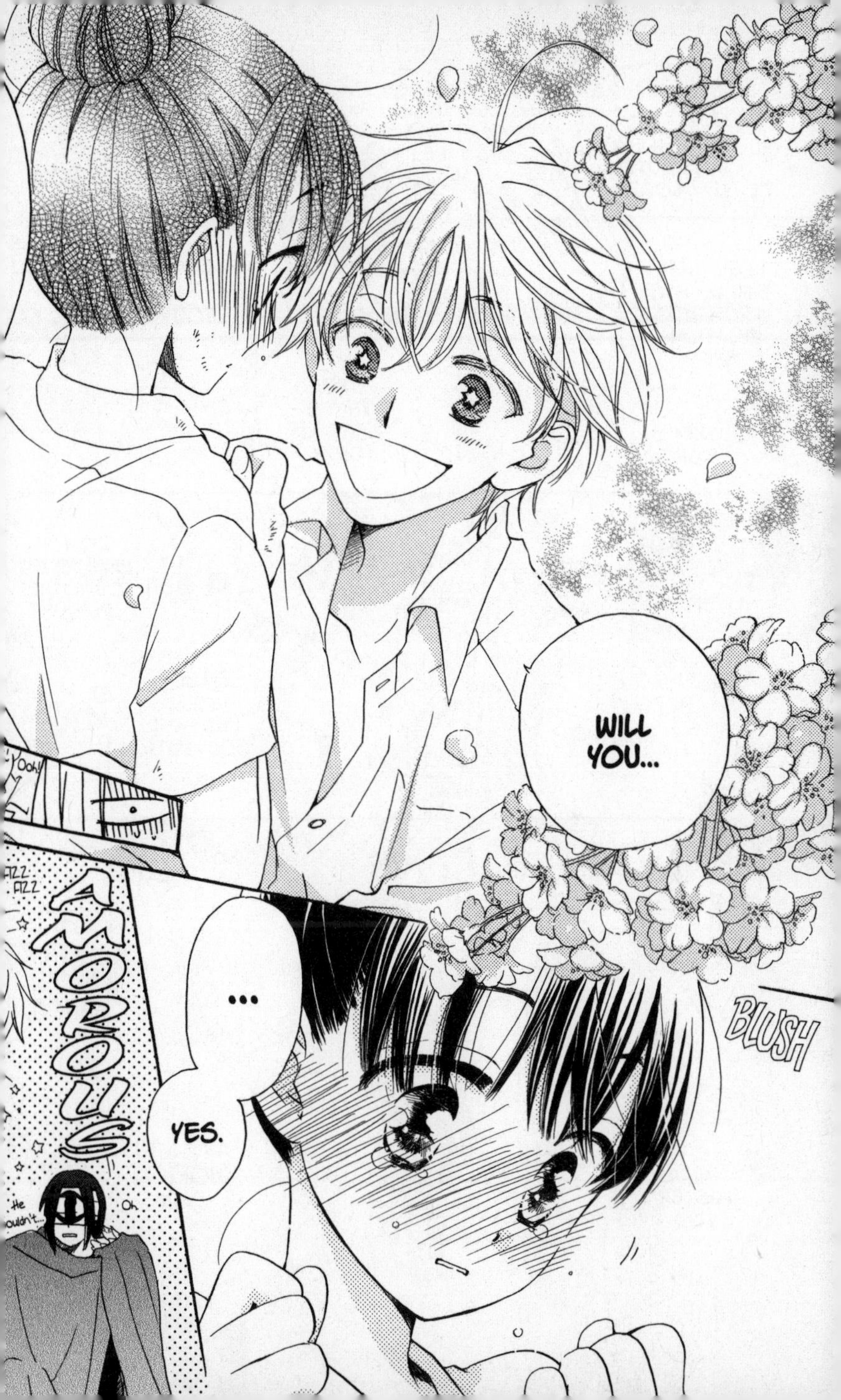
WILL YOU...
BLUSH
...
YES.
Ooh!
AMOROUS
Oh.

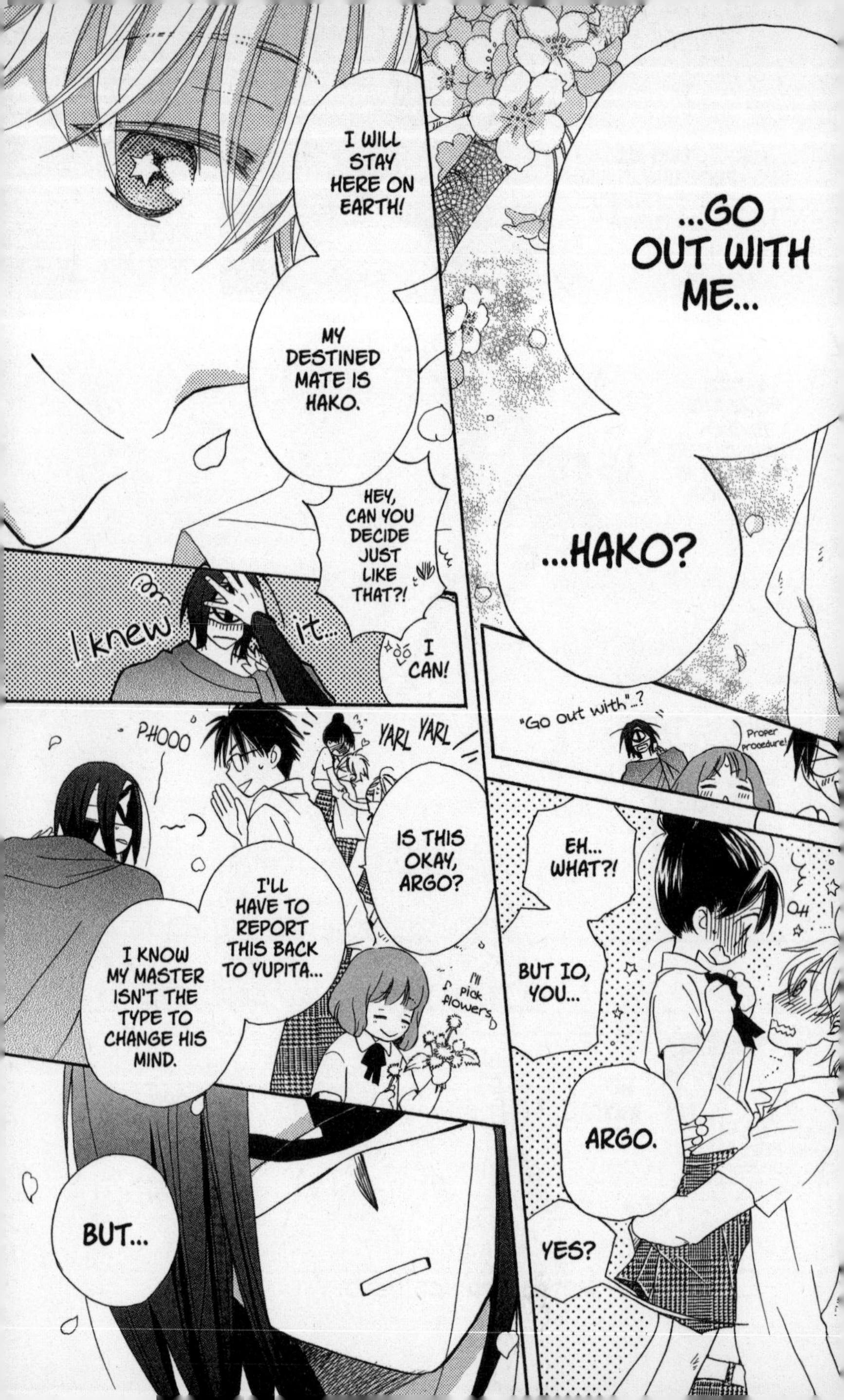
...GO OUT WITH ME...
...HAKO?
I WILL STAY HERE ON EARTH!
MY DESTINED MATE IS HAKO.
HEY, CAN YOU DECIDE JUST LIKE THAT?!
I CAN!
I knew it...
"Go out with"..?
Proper procedure!
EH... WHAT?!
BUT IO, YOU...
ARGO.
YES?
YARL YARL
PHOOO
IS THIS OKAY, ARGO?
I'LL HAVE TO REPORT THIS BACK TO YUPITA...
I KNOW MY MASTER ISN'T THE TYPE TO CHANGE HIS MIND.
I'll pick flowers
BUT...

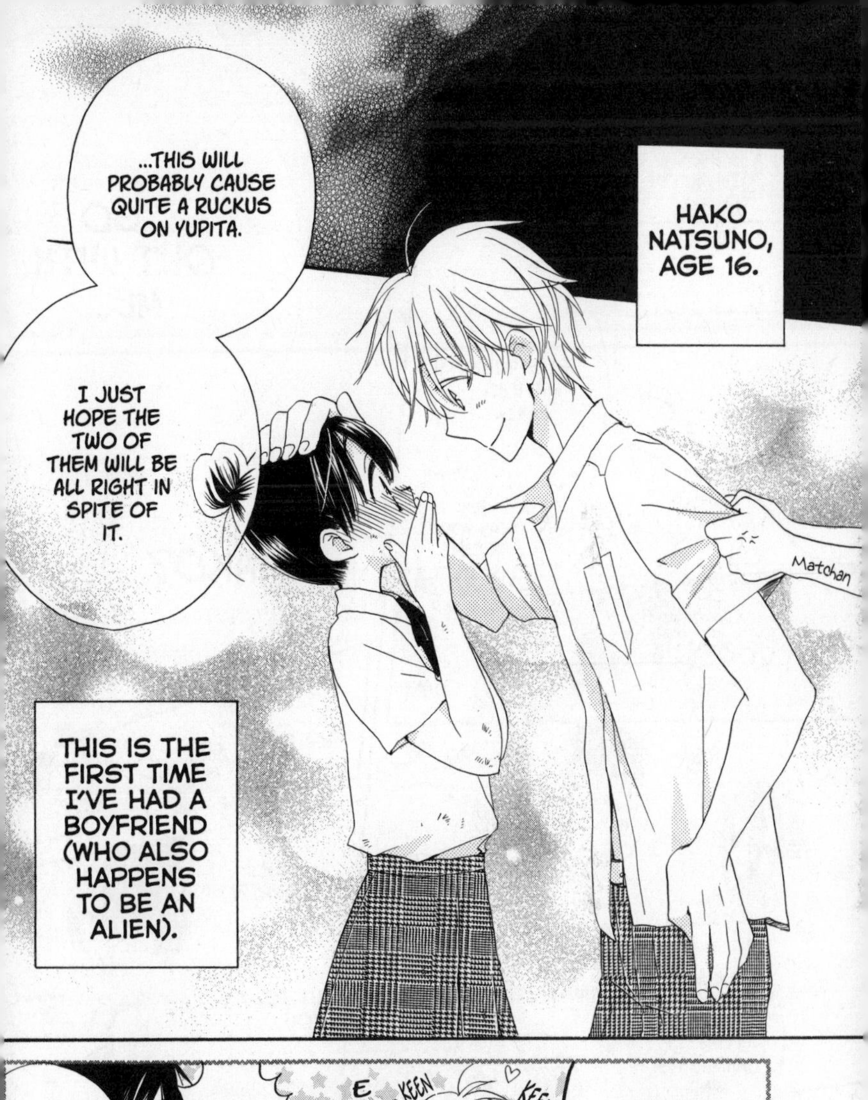
HAKO NATSUNO, AGE 16.
...THIS WILL PROBABLY CAUSE QUITE A RUCKUS ON YUPITA.
I JUST HOPE THE TWO OF THEM WILL BE ALL RIGHT IN SPITE OF IT.
Matchan
THIS IS THE FIRST TIME I'VE HAD A BOYFRIEND (WHO ALSO HAPPENS TO BE AN ALIEN).

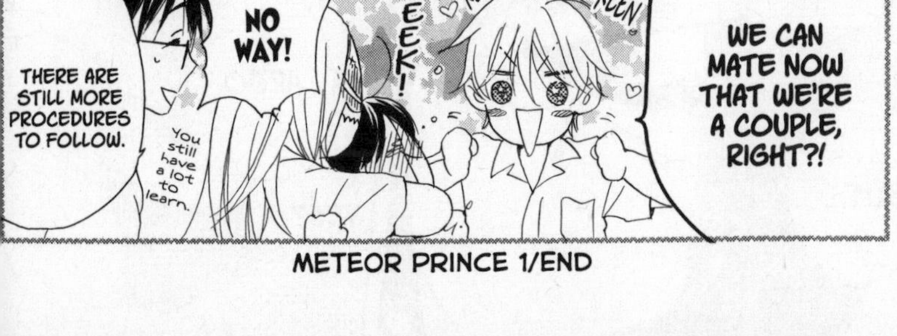
WE CAN MATE NOW THAT WE'RE A COUPLE, RIGHT?!
KEEN
KEEN
EEEEK!
NO WAY!
You still have a lot to learn.
THERE ARE STILL MORE PROCEDURES TO FOLLOW.

METEOR PRINCE 1/END

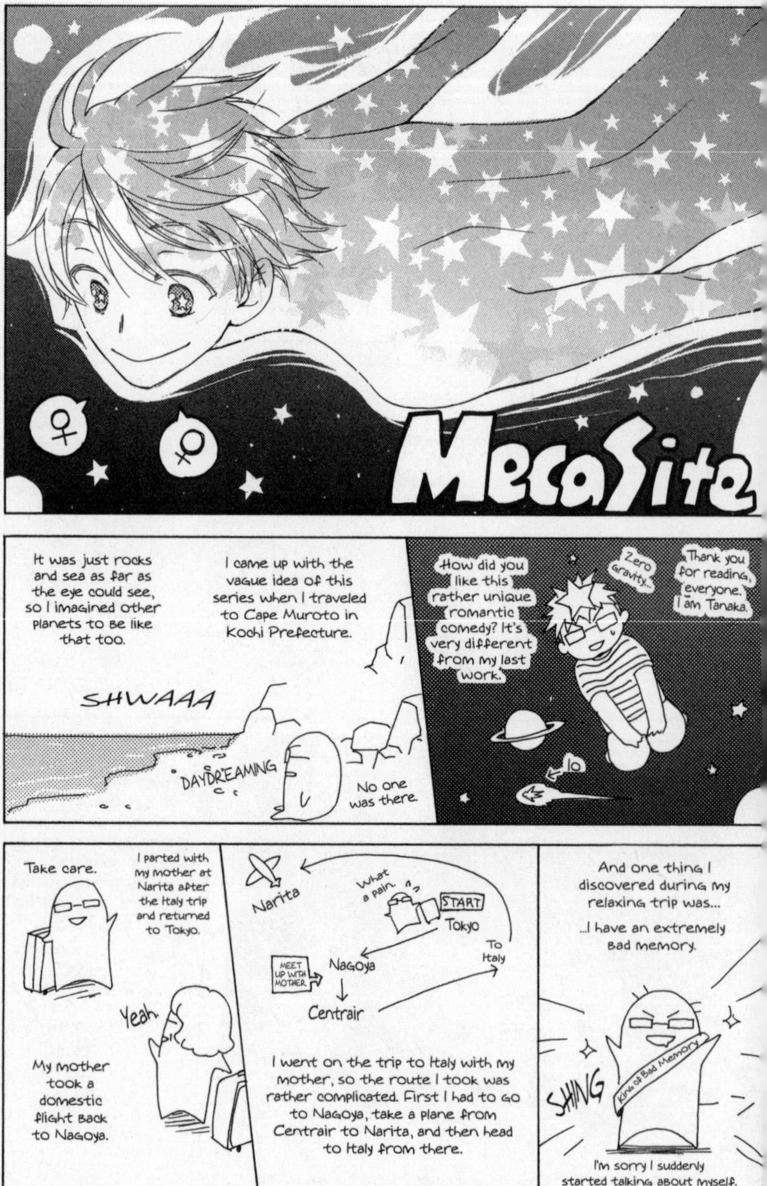
MecaSite
Thank you for reading, everyone. I am Tanaka.
Zero Gravity...
How did you like this rather unique romantic comedy? It's very different from my last work.
Io
I came up with the vague idea of this series when I traveled to Cape Muroto in Kochi Prefecture.
It was just rocks and sea as far as the eye could see, so I imagined other planets to be like that too.
SHWAAA
DAYDREAMING
No one was there.
And one thing I discovered during my relaxing trip was...
...I have an extremely bad memory.
SHING
King of Bad Memory
I'm sorry I suddenly started talking about myself.
Narita
What a pain.
START
Tokyo
To Italy
Nagoya
MEET UP WITH MOTHER
Centrair
I went on the trip to Italy with my mother, so the route I took was rather complicated. First I had to go to Nagoya, take a plane from Centrair to Narita, and then head to Italy from there.
I parted with my mother at Narita after the Italy trip and returned to Tokyo.
Take care.
Yeah.
My mother took a domestic flight back to Nagoya.

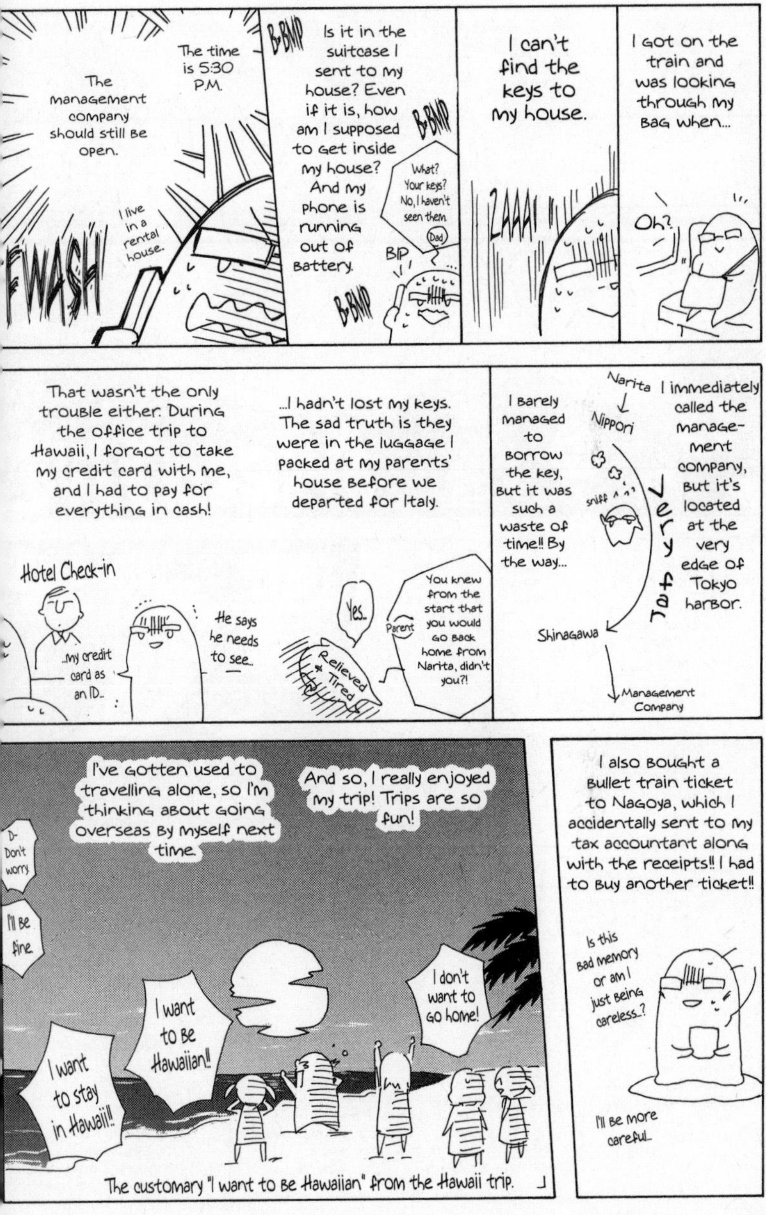
I got on the train and was looking through my bag when...
Oh?
I can't find the keys to my house.
ZAAA
Is it in the suitcase I sent to my house? Even if it is, how am I supposed to get inside my house? And my phone is running out of battery.
B-BMP
B-BMP
What? Your keys? No, I haven't seen them.
Dad
BIP
B-BMP
The time is 5:30 P.M.
The management company should still be open.
I live in a rental house.
FWASH
I immediately called the management company, but it's located at the very edge of Tokyo harbor.
Narita
Nippori
Very far
sniff
Shinagawa
Management Company
I barely managed to borrow the key, but it was such a waste of time!! By the way...
...I hadn't lost my keys. The sad truth is they were in the luggage I packed at my parents' house before we departed for Italy.
You knew from the start that you would go back home from Narita, didn't you?!
Parent
Yes...
Relieved + Tired
That wasn't the only trouble either. During the office trip to Hawaii, I forgot to take my credit card with me, and I had to pay for everything in cash!
Hotel Check-in
...my credit card as an ID...
He says he needs to see...
I also bought a bullet train ticket to Nagoya, which I accidentally sent to my tax accountant along with the receipts!! I had to buy another ticket!!
Is this bad memory or am I just being careless...?
I'll be more careful...
And so, I really enjoyed my trip! Trips are so fun!
I've gotten used to travelling alone, so I'm thinking about going overseas by myself next time.
D-Don't worry.
I'll be fine.
I don't want to go home!
I want to be Hawaiian!!
I want to stay in Hawaii!!
The customary "I want to be Hawaiian" from the Hawaii trip.

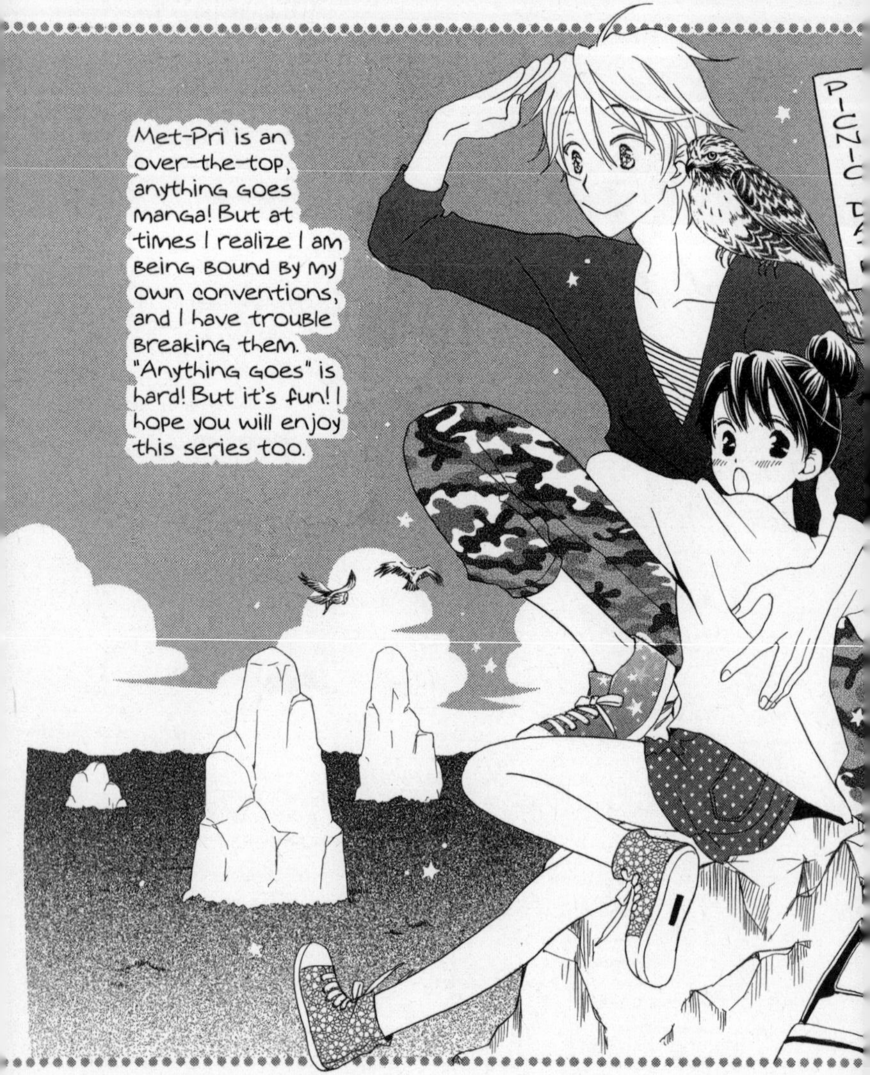
Met-Pri is an over-the-top, anything goes manga! But at times I realize I am being bound by my own conventions, and I have trouble breaking them. "Anything goes" is hard! But it's fun! I hope you will enjoy this series too.

THANKS!

Yamamoto-sama

Editor

Mother

Uchida-sama

Sano-sama

Hayashi-sama

Shino-sama

Karasawa-sama

Nakano-sama

Ogura-sama

Harumi-sama

Kono-sama

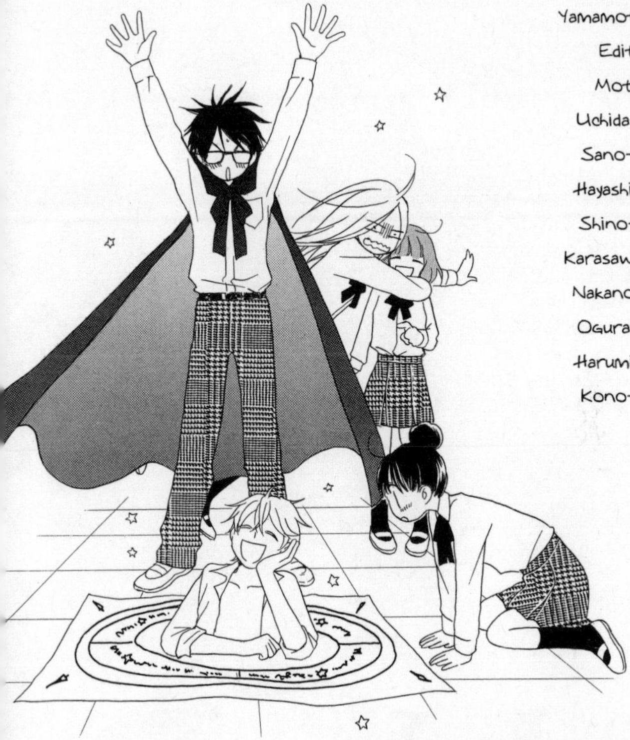

And to everyone who has supported me, and to you for picking up this manga volume. Thank you very much!

See you again!

田中×メカ

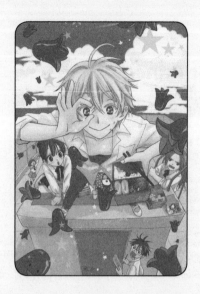

Space is an incredible place beyond anything we can imagine. It's something one ponders while falling asleep. I decided to create a "vast yet small love story" based on that. I don't think you'll see any scary-looking aliens in this, so just relax and enjoy it as if you were floating in zero gravity.

-Meca Tanaka

Meca Tanaka made her manga debut in 1998. Her previous works include *Omukae Desu, Tennen Pearl Pink* (Pearl Pink), and *Kiss Yori mo Hayaku* (Faster than a Kiss).

Meteor Prince
Volume 1
Shojo Beat Edition

STORY AND ART BY
Meca Tanaka

English Translation/Tetsuichiro Miyaki
Touch-up Art & Lettering/Deron Bennett
Design/Yukiko Whitley
Editor/Nancy Thistlethwaite

Printed in the U.S.A.

Published by VIZ Media, LLC
P.O. Box 77010
San Francisco, CA 94107

10 9 8 7 6 5 4 3 2 1
First printing, January 2015

www.viz.com

www.shojobeat.com

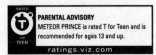

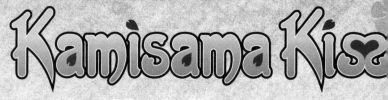

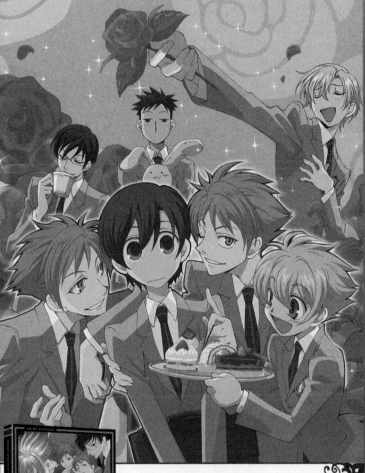

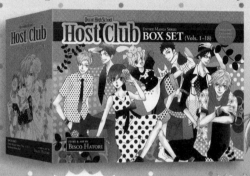

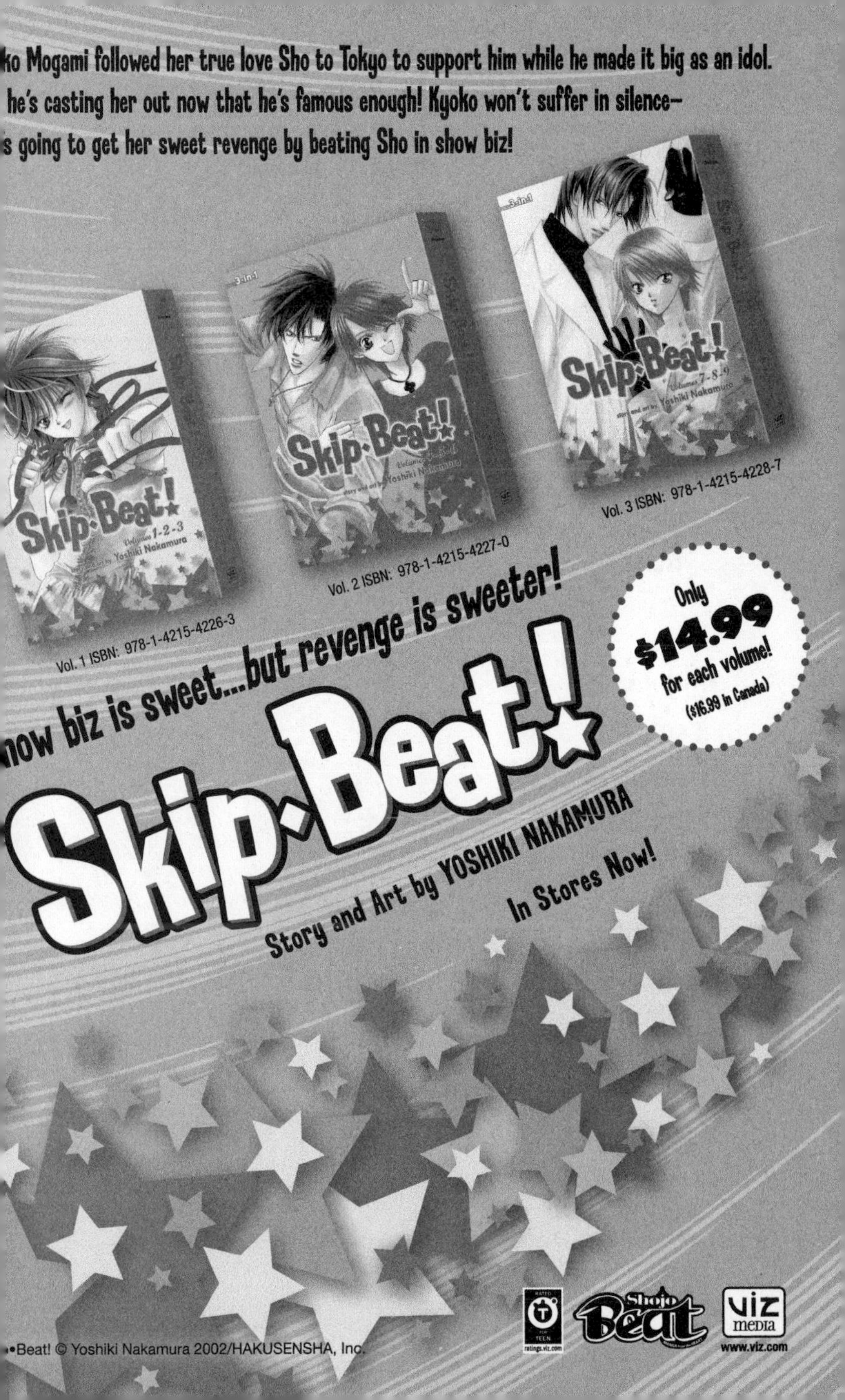
ko Mogami followed her true love Sho to Tokyo to support him while he made it big as an idol.
he's casting her out now that he's famous enough! Kyoko won't suffer in silence–
s going to get her sweet revenge by beating Sho in show biz!
Skip·Beat! Volumes 1-2-3 Yoshiki Nakamura
Vol. 1 ISBN: 978-1-4215-4226-3
Skip·Beat! Yoshiki Nakamura
Vol. 2 ISBN: 978-1-4215-4227-0
Skip·Beat! Volumes 7-8-9 Story and art by Yoshiki Nakamura
Vol. 3 ISBN: 978-1-4215-4228-7
now biz is sweet...but revenge is sweeter!
Only $14.99 for each volume! ($16.99 in Canada)
Skip·Beat!
Story and Art by YOSHIKI NAKAMURA
In Stores Now!
•Beat! © Yoshiki Nakamura 2002/HAKUSENSHA, Inc.
RATED T TEEN ratings.viz.com
Shojo Beat
viz media
www.viz.com

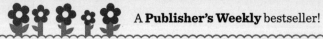
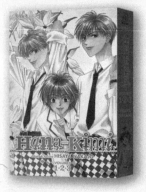
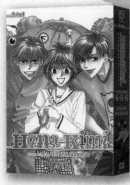
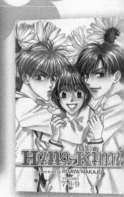

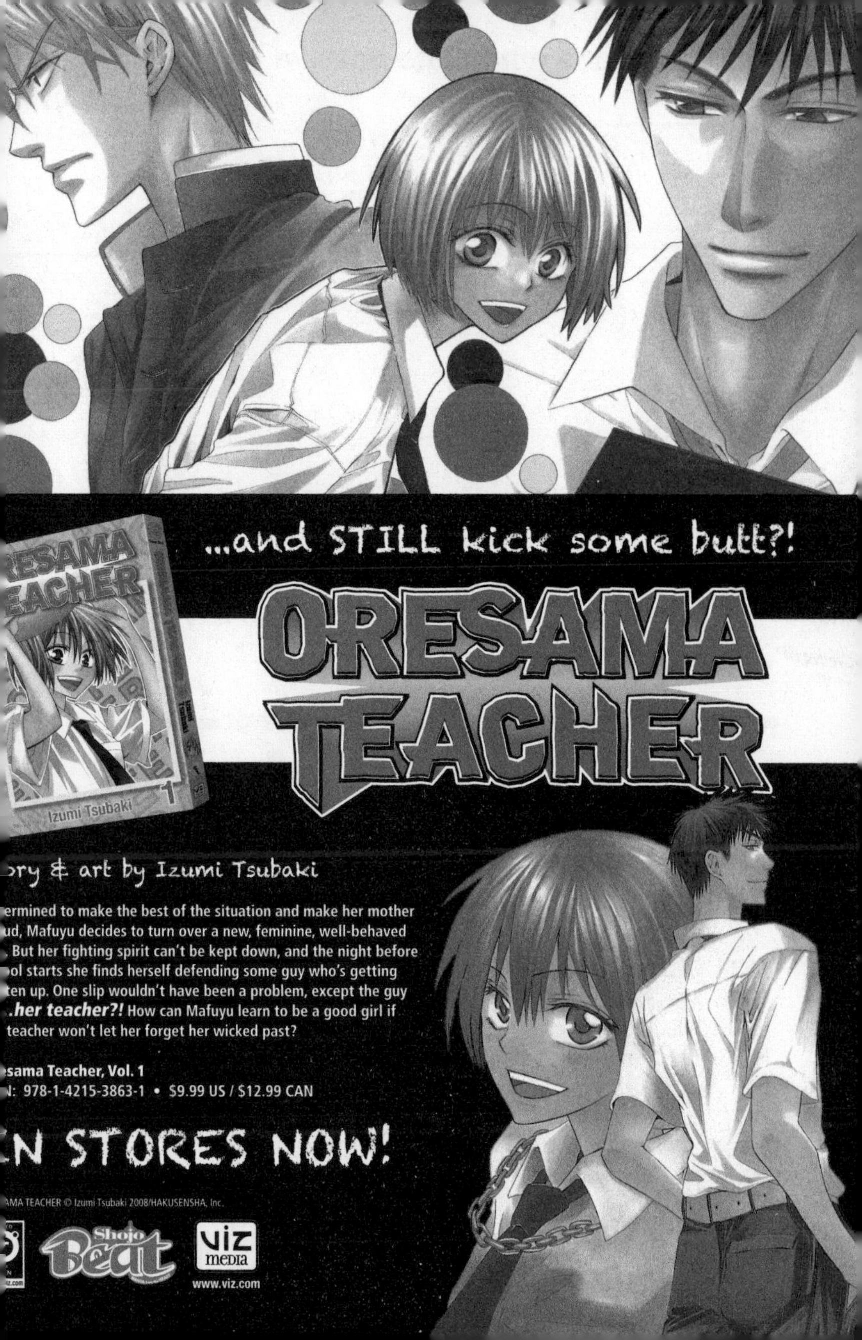
...and STILL kick some butt?!
ORESAMA TEACHER
ORESAMA TEACHER
Izumi Tsubaki
1
ory & art by Izumi Tsubaki
ermined to make the best of the situation and make her mother ud, Mafuyu decides to turn over a new, feminine, well-behaved . But her fighting spirit can't be kept down, and the night before ool starts she finds herself defending some guy who's getting ten up. One slip wouldn't have been a problem, except the guy *..her teacher?!* How can Mafuyu learn to be a good girl if teacher won't let her forget her wicked past?
esama Teacher, Vol. 1
N: 978-1-4215-3863-1 • $9.99 US / $12.99 CAN
N STORES NOW!
AMA TEACHER © Izumi Tsubaki 2008/HAKUSENSHA, Inc.
Shojo Beat
viz media
www.viz.com

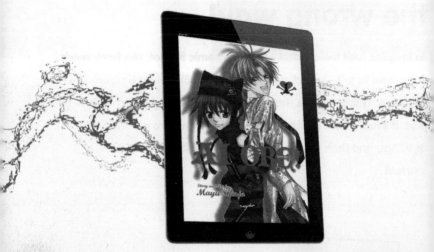
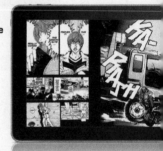
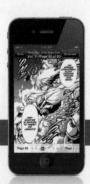

You may be rea
the wrong way

In keeping with the original Japanese co
from right to left—so action, sound effects, and word balloons are reversed. This preserves the orientation of the original artwork—plus, it's fun! Check out the diagram shown here to get the hang of things, and then turn to the other side of the book to get started!

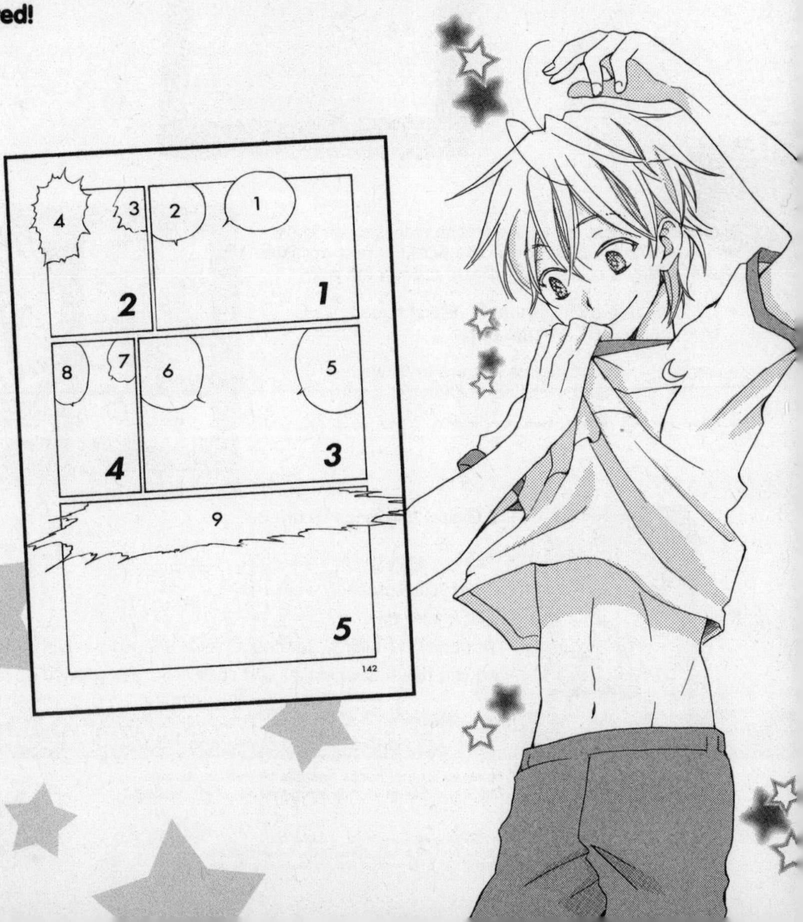
1
2
1
3
4
2
5
6
3
7
8
4
9
5
142